Strasbourg in Transition

1648–1789

FRANKLIN L. FORD

HARVARD UNIVERSITY PRESS

Cambridge, Massachusetts

1958

© 1958 by the President and Fellows of Harvard College

Distributed in Great Britain by Oxford University Press, London

Library of Congress Catalog Card Number: 58–7247

Printed in the United States of America

TO ELEANOR

PREFACE

A traveler approaching the city of Strasbourg is greeted today, as others have been for more than five centuries past, by a wonderful sight: the famous cathedral with its single tower, a gigantic blade of rose sandstone thrust into the sky, where it changes color with each passing cloud and each advancing hour of the day. You may glimpse it first from the top of the zig-zag descent called the "Staircase of Saverne," as you come out of the Vosges and start down to the rich Alsatian plain. If so, it will be only a dark sliver, fifteen miles off to the southeast. Alternatively, having passed Colmar and Sélestat on the way north from Belfort and Basel, you will see it through the orchards along the road ahead. You will still have a considerable ride into town; and if there is a broken sky, the cathedral will have time to show its full chromatic range, from pink through red to dull brown and even black, with buttresses and fretwork that seem like delicate ebony. From yet another quarter, if you are coming west out of Germany, you may catch sight of it from the high slopes of the Black Forest. In any case, you will come upon its full silhouette as you approach the Rhine.

This great building, so solid and yet so changeable in appearance when seen from different angles, is a dramatic reminder of much in Strasbourg's history. Swiss reformer of Calvin's time or imperial diplomat of Wallenstein's, bland tourist of the eighteenth century or breathless romantic of the nineteenth, French *revanchiste* of the Third Republic or German propagandist of the Third Reich, each viewed the town in a light determined by his period and his allegiances. It is not, however, sufficient to represent Strasbourg as merely a focus and symbol for varying outside interests. The city, which once might have served as the capital for an entire Middle Kingdom, has long been attentive to developments in France and Germany, as well as to events in the Rhineland from Switzerland to the Netherlands. By extension, we can do more than look *at* such a community. We can also look out *from* it.

Return for a moment more to the cathedral itself, this time to its high platform and the view it provides. On the east, the hurrying Rhine cuts violently through the landscape. Beyond are Kehl in Baden and the surrounding German villages, with the Black Forest for a backdrop. On the Alsatian side there is no mighty river, but the Ill does come meandering in through red-roofed hamlets against another, western, screen of mountains, the Vosges. Last but not least, the observer has below him the city itself, with its architectural record of successive dominations: the medieval quays and the steep-roofed German inner town, interrupted here and there by graceful palaces in French Baroque, all surrounded by the massive structures of Bismarck's and William II's Empire.

Considered thus, Strasbourg is a living document of wood and stone, and at closer range, of speech and manners. It is deeply and intricately a European city, the product of a culture not national, but continental. Part of my incentive for writing this book, in fact, came from the feeling that in trying to comprehend our widely shared and immensely rich civilization we are too often hampered by an over-emphasis on nationhood. The modern national state is an indispensable unit for diplomatic history and a useful frame for political analysis. For the history of religions or social forms or artistic production, however, that same nation-state is more often than not a cramped, distorting conception. Nowhere is this more apparent than in mixed communities which stand on or near the territorial frontiers of great nations.

The decision to limit this study essentially to the time span from the mid-seventeenth century to the French Revolution forces me to compress into a few pages the colorful background of the Middle Ages and the Reformation. Similarly, in this context I can justify only brief, concluding references to the French-German rivalry of the past century and a half, important as Strasbourg has been throughout this familiar struggle. Under other circumstances, the case for a longer survey might have been overpowering. However, having begun with certain questions in mind, questions about a border community, I have felt it better to concentrate on the period during which the introduction of new, French elements was most striking and their interweaving with older, German ones most marked.

Consider in bare outline what happened between 1648 and 1789. At the end of the Thirty Years' War, Strasbourg was still an imperial free city, a small republic within the Holy Roman Empire, German in speech, Lutheran in faith. Thus it remained until 1681, when annexation by Louis XIV made it part of an increasingly centralized Catholic kingdom. From that point on, we can observe and document a series of changes in local life — military, political, religious, economic, social, architectural, and literary — to mention only the more obvious areas in which paradox and varying degrees of adjustment are discernible.

I say "a series," but actually, as every student of history knows, changes occurring at so many levels simply mock our inability to describe or analyze more than one thing at a time. Allowing for all possible reminders of simultaneity and combination, it is still necessary to take up changes in an order suggested by the material and by the story it tells. With that in mind, I have begun with a survey of Strasbourg after the Peace of Westphalia, then turned to a discussion of the annexation of 1681, and thereafter to the changes that French rule brought about. As I hope to make clear in the Conclusion, the order of my chapters was not fixed by any arbitrary preconceptions, but instead, at least in a general way, by the timing of crucial changes under each heading. All the same, the crisscrossing of lines, the overlapping and interaction of processes must be repeatedly emphasized, until at last, by 1789, one reaches a point where he must consider the whole situation of the town under the glare of crisis.

Although one may insert a limited number of new facts and supply fresh illustrations from the sources, he cannot expect to add much to the purely narrative reconstruction of Strasbourg's history, already written by generations of French and German scholars. There remain, however, three contributions an American observer may reasonably hope to make. First, being an outsider, he is led to make fuller use of both German and French materials, in combination, than residents of either side of the Rhine have generally been inclined to attempt. Second, precisely because he has no advance commitment to either national "school," he should be able, is in fact obliged, to stand back and ask questions that are neither "French" nor "German" in their weighting. Third, he may be able to communicate further understanding of the life of early modern Europe by centering on a single, strategically located community and seeking to revive some impression of "how things looked from there."

During 1952–53 I had a Fulbright grant for post-doctoral research which enabled me to work in Strasbourg and in Paris. In 1955–56 I enjoyed an additional year in Germany, France, and Austria through a fellowship from the John Simon Guggenheim Memorial Foundation, as well as through the continuing support of Harvard University during my leave of absence. Further, I have had the benefit of financial aid extended by The Harvard Foundation for Advanced Study and Research in the final preparation of this manuscript, and a grant from The Ford Foundation has aided publication. For all of this subvention and encouragement I am sincerely grateful, as I am for the services rendered by the personnel of the libraries and archives in which I have been privileged to work: the Bibliothèque Nationale et Universitaire in Strasbourg, as well as the Archives Municipales and the Archives Départmentales there, the Bibliothèque Nationale in Paris, the Stadt- und Universitätsbibliothek in Frankfurt am Main, the Nassauische Landesbibliothek in Wiesbaden, the Badische Landesbibliothek in Karlsruhe, the Haus-, Hof- und Staatsarchiv in Vienna, and the Harry Elkins Widener Memorial Library and Houghton Library of Harvard University.

There are more individuals whose aid should be acknowledged than I can possibly enumerate here. One whom I must particularly thank, however, is M. Joseph Fuchs of the Archives Municipales at Strasbourg. M. Fuchs was as cordial as he was helpful, and the hours spent in his intelligent company are among my most pleasant memories. Here in America I am particularly indebted to Professors Crane Brinton and Henry Hatfield of Harvard for their many helpful suggestions, while to Miss Anna Maria Herbert and to Miss Ann Orlov is due a special expression of gratitude for their invaluable assistance in the final stages of checking and editing. The dedication of this volume expresses, as well as such things ever can, my awareness of all my wife has done and has meant along the way. Finally, I would add a word of appreciation to my sister, Frances M. Ford, who lived with us and helped us in Strasbourg — and who loves the old city too.

F. L. F.

Cambridge, Massachusetts
October, 1957

CONTENTS

MAPS AND ILLUSTRATIONS

the Alsatian-German roof. In the center of the row is a Gothic façade displaying the stair-stepped roof line of the fourteenth and fifteenth centuries. Finally, just to the right of that edifice is an example of "Rhenish Renaissance" — arches at the street level, plain windows on each of the three upper floors, and the heavy cornice described on page 200.

THE QUAI DE LA BRUCHE AND LA PETITE FRANCE. Photograph, Spehner, by permission of Editions "Tel," Paris.   29

For the remarkable etymology of the name of this famous site, see page 177. The actual "Petite France" is to the right.

THE BAIN-AUX-PLANTES. Photograph, Winter, by permission of Editions "Tel," Paris.   29

A typical Strasbourg canal scene, photographed in about 1870.

THE STRASBOURG CUSTOMHOUSE IN 1630 BY HOLLAR. From Emil von Borries, *Geschichte der Stadt Strassburg*, Strasbourg, 1909.   60

The great engraver, Wenzel Hollar, visited Alsace many years before his famous sojourn in London. This print, only one of a brochure he executed of Strasbourg, catches the activity of the cranes, the wine market, the Kaufhaus, *and the* Zollkeller. *In the background, the* Rabenbrück *or* Pont du Corbeau *crosses the Ill on the right, while on the left the cathedral towers over the entire scene.*

SEVENTEENTH-CENTURY AMMEISTERS. From Adolphe Seyboth, *Strasbourg historique et pittoresque*, Strasbourg, 1894.   61

These four representatives of famous patrician dynasties in Strasbourg all served both before and after the French annexation. Readers will doubtless be most interested in the portrait of Franziskus Reisseissen because he is encountered repeatedly as a chronicler in the present study. All four engravings are by Jean-Adam Seupel, mentioned on page 200.

PRINCE LOUIS-CONSTANTIN, CARDINAL DE ROHAN. From Adolphe Seyboth, *Strasbourg historique et pittoresque*, Strasbourg, 1894.   220

This engraving by Christophe Guérin, dated 1776, shows the Bishop of Strasbourg, third of his family to occupy the see and uncle of the better-known Louis-René-Edouard, his successor in 1779.

MARSHAL DE CONTADES. From Ernst Traumann, *Goethe, der Strassburger Student*, Leipzig, 1923.   220

Louis-Georges des Contades, shown in a steel engraving from a painting at Versailles, wears the ceremonial armor and holds the baton of his exalted rank. He served in Strasbourg as provincial commandant from 1763 to 1788.

BARONESS D'OBERKIRCH. From Ernst Traumann, *Goethe, der Strassburger Student*, Leipzig, 1923.

Henriette-Louise, Strasbourg's most important memoirist of the eighteenth century, is discussed at several places in the present volume, especially on pages 182 and 198.

BARON FREDERIC DE DIETRICH. From Ernst Traumann, *Goethe, der Strassburger Student*, Leipzig, 1923.

Dietrich, one of the last of Strasbourg's patricians of the old regime (his great-great-grandfather had been a contemporary of the Ammeisters shown opposite page 61), was also the first of the city's maires *under the constitutional monarchy, 1790–92.*

"LA BELLE STRASBOURGEOISE" BY LARGILLIERE. Photograph, courtesy of the Fogg Art Museum Library, Harvard University. Reproduced by permission of *Photographie Giraudon*, Paris. The painting is in the Meyer Sassoon Collection, London.

Nicolas de Largillière painted this portrait in 1703, during the Parisian artist's sojourn in Strasbourg. The identity of the subject is unknown, but her rich costume clearly marks her as a patrician lady. The huge bicorn of black velvet, the lace scarf and undersleeves, the "corsage" of gold brocade, and the black taffeta apron over a skirt of red silk are all characteristic of the heavy elegance discussed on pages 188–189.

A SCHWÖRTAG IN THE 1780's. From Adolphe Seyboth, *Strasbourg historique et pittoresque*, Strasbourg, 1894.

This conception by the nineteenth-century artist, Emile Schweitzer, is based on descriptive documents for 1786. On the high platform before the center portal of the cathedral, the Magistrat — Senators and members of the Secret Chambers — lead the Assemblymen of the Three Hundred, grouped below, as all take the annual inauguration oath to the Schwörbrief (see pages 4 and 236). The soldiers in tricorns, at the extreme left, are from the Régiment d'Alsace, *those in the high hats at the right, from the Swiss* Régiment d'Eptingen.

THE SACK OF THE HOTEL DE VILLE OF STRASBOURG ON JULY 21, 1789. From Robert Heitz, *L'Alsace vue par les artistes*, Paris, 1952, by permission of Horizons de France, Paris.

Jean-Martin Weis the Younger's contemporary engraving was based on a design by Jean Hans. For a verbal description of this tumultuous scene, see pages 245–246. In that description, the reader will find included a word picture by Arthur Young, who observed the episode from atop one of the wooden market stalls shown in the foreground of the Weis representation.

Strasbourg
in Transition
1648–1789

Oslo

Stockholm

Edinburgh

Copenhagen

Königsberg

Hamburg

Bremen

London · Amsterdam Utrecht · Osnabrück Berlin · Warsaw

Calais Brussels · Münster Dresden · Breslau

Rouen Cologne Cracow

Paris Reims Trier Mainz · Frankfurt Prague

Verdun Speyer Mannheim · Nürnberg Regensburg

Orléans Toul Nancy Karlsruhe Stuttgart

Tours Metz STRASBOURG Ulm · Munich Vienna · Budapest

Mulhouse · Freiburg Salzburg

Dijon Basel Zürich

Bordeaux Besançon Bern

Lyon Geneva Milan Trieste · Zagreb

Turin Venice

Toulouse Avignon Genoa

Marseille Florence

Barcelona Rome

Naples

Algiers Palermo

Tunis

Strasbourg in Europe

Eitan Schell.

CHAPTER ONE

The Imperial Free City

I

In 1648, having tried everything else, the powers made peace. Not all of them, to be sure — France and Spain were to fight on for eleven more years — but in the great, desolate arena of central Europe thirty years of slaughter finally ceased. Although the treaties of Westphalia represented a classic surrender to exhaustion, they were not, for that reason, any the less welcome. The various free cities of the Holy Roman Empire, even those not directly involved in hostilities, had had their own representatives on hand to follow the French-Imperial negotiations at Münster and the Swedish-Imperial ones at Osnabrück. So it was that Strasbourg learned of the final ceremonies at Münster in a dispatch from its chief plenipotentiary, Dr. Markus Otto.[1]

The courier from Münster either crossed the Rhine by ferry at Mainz, or used Strasbourg's own bridge (there was then no other between it and the sea), five hundred yards of wood, which swayed and creaked upon oaken piles and hollow boat hulls. In any event, on November 2 he came at last into the shelter of the town walls,[2] ramparts more than ever revered in 1648 by a city which for three decades had seen one rampaging army after another approach — and turn away. The messenger's long ride ended at the town hall or *Pfalz*, a few hundred feet from the soaring face of the cathedral.

Just how many Strasbourgers were alive to greet the word of peace from the north is subject to dispute. Estimates have varied from twenty thousand to more than thirty thousand; but the analyst who has made the most careful study of parish birth and death records puts the figure at about twenty-five thousand after the plague years of the 1620's, '30's, and '40's.[3] Even this population, the smallest the city has had since the fifteenth century, sufficed to make Strasbourg a big town by the standards of the day, comparable to Cologne, Nürnberg, and Hamburg, larger than Frankfurt or Mainz or Basel. It was a place whose irregular squares and narrow streets with their sharp-gabled, overhanging houses echoed all day to the sounds of an anxious, hurrying humanity. Yet the entire area enclosed by the fortifications amounted to only about five hundred acres.

Aside from its cathedral, Strasbourg was not architecturally remarkable. The town hall complex (the new Pfalz and the old, with the chancellery offices between them), the venerable treasury tower or *Pfenningthurn,* the warehouses, and several medieval churches, these as well as other buildings were there for any visitor to see; but none of them distinguished the town from numerous others in the Empire.[4] What did lend a certain personality was the system of waterways. "It is similar to Venice," Aeneas Sylvius (the future Pope Pius II) wrote after his visit in the 1430's, "in that it has so many canals, through which boats may be steered into almost all the streets; but it is much healthier and airier, because in Venice the water runs salty and stinking, but through Strasbourg, fresh and clear."[5]

II

To a literate townsman the year 1648, when the great war in Germany ended and France assumed control over most of Alsace, clearly stood for the opening of a new era, even though Strasbourg's own position was theoretically unchanged. (The city was specifically exempted from the territorial cessions at Münster.) Having read Caesar and some other Latin historians in the *Gymnasium,* the same townsman would know that his city's annals extended in one fashion or another back into the twilight of the last century B.C., when Celts and Swabians struggled for mastery of the Alsatian plain until the Romans came and conquered both.[6] He would probably know, too, that through the first four centuries of the Christian era his island in the Ill had been a major base for Roman armies and administration: "Argentoratum," where Julian defeated Chnodomar's Germans in 357 A.D.[7] The Eighth Legion, long stationed there, was withdrawn in 401, but what happened thereafter, during the invasions by Vandals, Alemans, and Huns, was a matter of surmise for the seventeenth-century Strasbourger. It still is for the twentieth-century historian.

Not until Carolingian times did an Alemannic village emerge with the name *Strazzeburc* or *Stratiburgum,* "fortress of the roads." Scene of the famous Strasbourg Oath of 842, assigned to Lothair's Middle Kingdom at Verdun the following year, wrenched out of the Lotharingian succession by Henry the Fowler in 925, it was formally annexed to the Holy Roman Empire by Otto the Great and almost immediately, like so many sister towns, turned over to the local bishop. For the next three hundred years its government was in the hands of the *Burggraf,* the *Schultheiss,* and other episcopal officers.[8]

This much of a backward glance is necessary for perspective on Strasbourg's later history; but to a burgher in 1648, to the chronicler, painter, and future Senator, Johann Jakob Walter,[9] for example, the past looked a good deal simpler. If Walter had been asked, "what are the great events of your history?" he would probably have replied without hesitation, from his patriotic catechism, "the defeat of the bishop, the adoption of the *Schwörbrief,* and the break with Roman Catholicism." Each of these did, in fact, help to explain some important characteristics of the local situation.

The town's status under the public law of the Empire, for example, stemmed directly from the successful revolt of the burghers in 1262, culminating in the victory over episcopal forces on the nearby hill of Hausbergen. The bishop remained lord of extensive lands in Lower Alsace; but the municipality, by throwing off his temporal power within its walls and winning its own charter from the emperor, left the company of ecclesiastical principalities like Mainz, Trier, and Cologne and entered the proud company of practically independent city republics, such as Nürnberg and Ulm, where it was

shortly joined by Frankfurt and Augsburg. Its economic importance
was already considerable. Into its market places and onto its quays
were beginning to crowd the merchants who would play a large
role in all its later history. This was also the town's first golden age
of culture. Here Gottfried von Strassburg produced his German *Tris-
tan,* and Albertus Magnus studied and preached in the Dominican
Cloister. Meister Eckhardt taught here in the early 1300's, as the
native Strasbourger, Johannes Tauler, was to do after him. And, in
the concluding years of the thirteenth century, Meister Erwin conceived the cathedral's façade, a creation which was later surmounted
by the tower designed by Johann Hultz and finished in 1439.

A second great event was the Schwörbrief or civic oath. In each of
the imperial free cities, acquisition of independent status was
followed by a long series of aristocratic coups, artisans' revolts, and
factional feuds, during which the internal distribution of power
was finally hammered out.[10] For Strasbourg this pulling and hauling lasted two hundred and twenty years; but once the essential
compromises were reached, they remained sacrosanct, at least in
outward form, for over three hundred more. The Schwörbrief of
1482 itself was a concise formula, a reminder of certain recognized
procedures, to which all municipal officers swore obedience every year
until the French Revolution. As such, it represented a hallowed
symbol of corporate continuity for officials and citizenry alike.

With increased political stability came another upsurge of power,
prosperity, and cultural productivity. For three-quarters of a century
after 1482 Strasbourg enjoyed an age of greatness comparable, save in
graphic art, to anything experienced by the most favored Renaissance
Italian republics. Although this upsurge ultimately became linked
with the Reformation and the European power system of the early
and mid-sixteenth century, its first manifestations were discernible
even before the religious revolution. For one thing, a major expansion in the city's commerce, wealth, and population occurred in
the later 1400's. For another, although Gutenberg left Strasbourg in
1444 and returned to Mainz before perfecting his movable type, his
legacy remained with talented and aggressive printer-publishers like

Schott and Gruninger, Knobloch and Schurer. The eloquent preaching of Geiler von Kaysersberg, the humanistic scholarship of Jakob Wimpheling, and the satires of the town secretary, Sebastian Brant, whose *Ship of Fools* Holbein later illustrated, all preceded the impact of Luther.

Nevertheless, it *was* the Reformation which changed the whole face of urban life in Strasbourg and thrust the town into a position of European prominence. Lutheranism had won the citizenry with remarkable speed and ease, and the official abolition of the Mass in 1529 merely formalized the existing situation in a now overwhelmingly Protestant community. By virtue of its location, Strasbourg was an outpost for the Reformation on the borderland of Catholic power, an asylum for French reformers, such as Farel, Roussel, and eventually Hotman, and a fair debating ground for Lutherans, Zwinglians, and Calvinists. By virtue of its wealth, its armaments, its alliances with Protestant states like Saxony and the abilities of its great patrician diplomat, Jakob Sturm, it was a bona fide power in the deliberations of the Empire throughout the reign of Charles V.[11]

In 1538 Johann Sturm founded the Scola Argentinensis, forerunner of the future University of Strasbourg, and opened with a theological faculty composed of Calvin, Bucer (the later adviser of England's Edward VI), Capito (Koepfell) of Haguenau, and Hedio of Ettlingen. The same era witnessed the scholarly writings of Sleidanus and Gebweiler, the savage but brilliant irony of the Franciscan, Thomas Murner, and, after mid-century, the more Rabelaisian humor of Johann Fischart.

Against this impressive backdrop of external splendor and internal freedom, the period from about 1560 to 1648 seems narrow and gloomy. Orthodox Lutheranism defeated all its rivals in local church politics and fastened a harsh intellectual censorship upon the town. Exhausting struggles with the Bishop of Strasbourg, still in possession of Saverne, Molsheim, and his other Alsatian fiefs, depleted the municipal treasury while disrupting commerce. When these regional skirmishes of the 1590's flared up again as part of the general conflict after 1618, a whole generation of Strasbourgers suffered from

famine, plague, and economic stagnation. The town managed to stay
out of the actual fighting in the Thirty Years' War, by dint of an
abject abandonment of its old Protestant alliances;[12] but the peace of
1648 could scarcely have been greeted with more relief inside the
faithful walls if the town had been an avowed belligerent. In less
than a century, Strasbourg had ceased to be a confident power. It
was left behind in a new age of national armies.

III

A free city, however, it remained, at least for the time being:
dess heyligen Reichs freye Statt Strassburg. As such, it had specific
obligations to the emperor, who in turn guaranteed its "immediacy,"
that is, he dealt directly with the municipal government, recognizing no assertion of authority over it on the part of any intermediate
prince or prelate. The town coined money, exercised high justice,
and operated its university, chartered in 1621, under various grants
of privilege from the Hapsburgs. During almost a century after the
death of Jakob Sturm in 1553, Strasbourg's place in the councils of
the Empire was uncertain, because of its continuing religious opposition to Vienna. In 1648, however, the settlement which fixed
the Reichstag at Regensburg also guaranteed permanent seats in that
body to the free cities.

The chief fiscal contribution of Strasbourg to the imperial treasury
bore a name which recalled the feudal obligations of an earlier era,
when each Holy Roman Emperor had crossed the Alps for his coronation. This payment was the *Römermonat* (Roman month) and was
calculated as a monetary commutation of what had once been an
actual provision of fighting men. There were also small levies upon
all the estates of the Empire to finance the supreme court at Speyer.
Here is how the inquisitive Martin Zeiller summarized Strasbourg's
dues, under the two headings, near the end of the Thirty Years' War:

Its regular monthly payment to the Empire is 900 florins, or 25
"mounted" and 150 "on foot." For the upkeep of the supreme court in
Speyer it gives annually, under the increased assessment, as I learned (for

in earlier years it was only 275 florins), 458 florins, 21 kroner, and 5 heller.[13]

The records in Vienna's Haus-, Hof- und Staatsarchiv[14] testify to the general accuracy of Zeiller's figures, though from 1521 on the number of infantry was actually listed not as 150 but 135, plus 273 florins in cash, making the total monetary value of each Römermonat just over 1,100 florins. This sum was not negligible, but neither was it a great burden in normal times.

Since the remote days of the thirteenth century, when Rudolf von Hapsburg had been the city's benefactor and its protector from the vengeance of the bishop, the personal relationship of successive emperors to Strasbourg had changed immensely. Around 1500 Maximilian I had been able to dramatize his patrimonial claims, granting the town judicial and minting privileges in return for money, armaments, and mercenaries. Such relations, however, were doomed by the Reformation. Ferdinand I in 1562 and Maximilian II in 1563 were, in fact, the last Holy Roman Emperors to enter Strasbourg as sovereigns, and subsequent addresses to Vienna reveal the municipal officers' coolness toward any claims on their allegiance. In 1639 they actually dismissed Professor Joachim Clutenius from the university and deprived him of his citizenship, on charges of having supplied military information to the imperial commanders at Breisach, up the Rhine.[15] The implications of such an attitude were discernible in 1648 and were to become even more apparent when Louis XIV's power closed about the city. The effort to play off the French monarch against the Hapsburg, turning a polite face toward one and then the other, but seeking to avoid close ties with either, involved walking a precarious tightrope, as even that agile acrobat, Jakob Sturm, had recognized in the days of Strasbourg's glory. Independent alliances with Swiss towns, such as Zürich and Bern, offered only uncertain insurance.

As a corporate personality in the German feudal structure, Strasbourg was not only a vassal of the emperor, but a landlord in its own right as well. It was in no sense the capital of Alsace, which was not a defined area capable of having a capital, despite a long series of

rather vaguely constituted provincial estates.[16] Nevertheless, the free
city did rule, through its bailiffs, a complex of rural communities.
Close to its walls lay Robertsau, Koenigshoffen, and Neudorf, a few
houses each, with Schiltigheim a little farther to the north. South
of town the bailiwick of Illkirch-Grafenstaden formed the most
considerable of the contiguous suburbs. Across the Rhine was the
bridgehead of Kehl, while scattered about on the Alsatian plain were
numerous other hamlets which owed allegiance to Strasbourg. One
cluster was wedged in among the fiefs of the Hanau-Lichtenberg
family, some twenty-five miles northwest of the city. Another larger
group centered in Wasselnheim (Wasselonne) and Marlenheim,
almost due west and about fifteen miles from the city's gates. Certain
individual villages, such as Dorlisheim, were completely surrounded
by lands of the bishop. Finally, the bailiwick of Barr, twenty miles
southwest of town, was especially important for its fine vineyards.
In 1648 these domains comprised some thirty settlements with a
total of between five and six thousand inhabitants.[17]

With its bailiwicks Strasbourg formed part of the bewildering
patchwork which was Alsace before, and even after, French annexation. In 1648, the House of Hapsburg had relinquished to that of
Bourbon its family holdings in this region; but it took time for the
French administration to define, let alone organize, what was ceded
by the Peace of Westphalia. Other parts of Alsace were equally
confusing. The Bishop of Strasbourg held some 115 villages grouped
in seven bailiwicks between the Vosges highlands and the Rhine
in Lower Alsace. To the north and west of Strasbourg lay the
holdings of the Hanau-Lichtenbergs, second only in extent to those
of the bishop. Then there were the Alsatian fiefs of the Elector
Palatine, the Prince of Zweibrücken, the Dukes of Lorraine and of
Württemberg, the Margrave of Baden, the Count of Veldenz, the
Bishops of Speyer and of Basel, plus a host of smaller territories held
by imperial knights, assorted barons, and a long list of ecclesiastical
foundations. In Upper Alsace the city of Mulhouse was a strange
political island, a detached member of the Swiss Confederation. Small

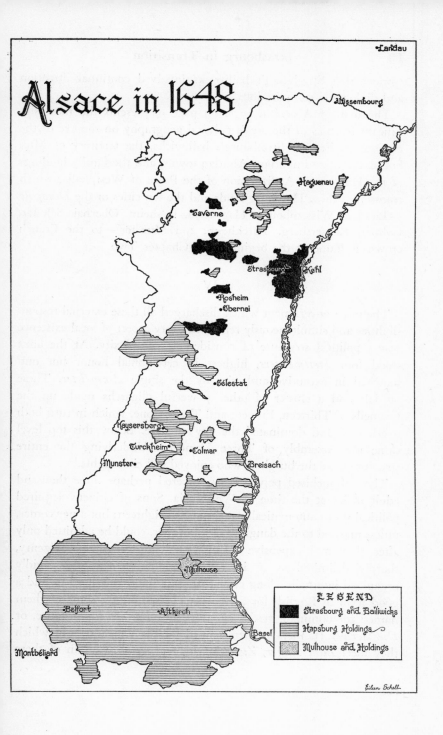

Alsace in 1648

•Landau

•Wissembourg

•Haguenau

•Saverne

Strasbourg• •Kehl

•Rosheim
•Obernai

•Sélestat

Kaysersberg•

Turckheim• •Colmar

Munster• Breisach•

Mulhouse

Belfort Altkirch

Basel•

Montbéliard

LEGEND
Strasbourg and Bailiwicks
Hapsburg Holdings
Mulhouse and Holdings

Eileen Schell

wonder that Strasbourg's bailiwicks involved continual litigation and diplomatic complications.

The map of Alsace in 1648, on page 9, presents the most significant features of the area's political geography on the eve of the cessions to France: Strasbourg's bailiwicks, the territory of Mulhouse, the more important Alsatian towns, and the family holdings of the Hapsburgs. A discussion of the Peace of Westphalia, which transferred these Hapsburg lands and the ten cities of the *Décapole* — Landau, Wissembourg, Haguenau, Rosheim, Obernai, Sélestat, Colmar, Kaysersberg, Turckheim, and Munster — to the French crown, is found at the beginning of Chapter Two.

IV

The town government which discharged all these external responsibilities and simultaneously regulated every aspect of local existence was a political structure of considerable complexity. At the apex stood four *Stettmeisters*, highest in ceremonial honor but outmatched in executive authority by the single *Ammeister*. These officials and a cluster of other powerful oligarchs made up the Councils of Thirteen, Fifteen, and Twenty-one, which in turn both overlapped and dominated the city's Senate. Below this top level came the Assembly of Three Hundred. Underlying the entire structure were the burghers who enjoyed full civic rights.[18]

The enfranchised population numbered perhaps three thousand adult males at the time of Westphalia. Sons of citizens acquired political status automatically at the age of eighteen; but a newcomer, unless married to the daughter of a burgher, could be admitted only after slow and expensive formalities. The recognized citizenry, sharply delimited as to its outer boundaries, was also rigidly organized internally along clear corporate lines. It is hard to find a good term in English for Strasbourg's corporations, some of them named for dominant trades or crafts, *Die Bäcker*, for instance, or *Die Gerwer* (tanners), others named for the winehouses in which they met: *Zum Anker*, *Zur Möhrin*, and so on. Certain of these corporations, to ignore the clubs of noblemen for a moment, were catch-alls for widely differing occupations. Hence, while *Zur Blume* contained only the local butchers, *Zum Spiegel* took in apothecaries, milliners and hatters, brandy distillers and combmakers, together with several other categories. All twenty of these groups included some doctors, lawyers, professors, and preachers not employed in crafts at all; and one man might, if he switched to a new occupation, actually maintain two affiliations (although he had to designate one of them as primary). These were, in short, not at all simple trade organizations. Nevertheless, since contemporaries referred to them as *Zünfte* (guilds), when they did not say simply *Stuben,* or lodges, it seems best to use what is for us the most familiar of available terms: guild.

It is important to have a convenient term, for the guilds appear constantly as the units of political representation within the city. The Assembly of Three Hundred directly represented these twenty corporations, each of which elected fifteen of its members as Assemblymen for life. The smaller and hence more effective Senate, the *Rat,* was also tied to the guilds. Its thirty members, half of them newly elected each year for a two-year term, included twenty commoners, one chosen by each of the guilds, and ten nobles, who were named by the outgoing Senate itself in relays of five per year.

It is characteristic of Strasbourg's system, as it was fashioned in the struggles of the later middle ages, that the highest official honors were reserved for the four Stettmeisters, all noblemen, but the Ammeister or real administrative chief was a commoner. The rotation of these officers was somewhat curious, yet it was typical of the regime. Each January, on inauguration day (*Schwörtag*), the five nobles just elected to the Senate chose two of their number to serve as Stettmeisters with the two others who were carried over from the year before. In any given year, each of the four incumbents served as "ruling Stettmeister" for three months. During this period the designated nobleman was the ceremonial representative of the free city, the bearer of its feudal insignia, the sponsor of all state documents, and the referee of voting in the Senate. The entire term of a Stettmeister was two years; however, for a year after his regular term, a Stettmeister still had some minor duties and retained his honorific prerogatives — hence an aggregate of six men bore this title at once.

The guildsman who was Ammeister served a solid year after his election by the twenty commoners in the Senate. He presided over the powerful Council of Thirteen, supervised day-to-day administration, received official dispatches and emissaries, and conducted his own summary court of petty claims. The rule that an ex-Ammeister could be reëlected after five years out of office resulted in the creation of a tight little circle of six prestigious commoners, all called Ammeisters, who, in effect, passed the active office around in order. Ordinarily, a new election was required only when the veteran who would otherwise have succeeded on a given Schwörtag had died since his last term.

Between these short-term officials, on the one hand, and the members of the Senate and of the Assembly of Three Hundred, on the other, there had existed since the early 1400's a combination of state councils strongly characteristic of German and Italian city republics. In Strasbourg they were called "the Secret Chambers," or sometimes "the Permanent Colleges" (since their members served for life). The Council of Thirteen, normally nine commoners and four nobles, dealt with defense and foreign relations, under the chairmanship of the ruling Ammeister. The Fifteen, which chose its own chairman semi-annually from among its ten commoner and five noble members, supervised internal administration. Neither body could include more than one representative of any guild, a rule, incidentally, which also applied to the rotating circle of Ammeisters. A concentration of power, however, was insured by the fact that almost no one was ever elected an Ammeister or Stettmeister unless he was already a member of one of the Secret Councils, or elected a Thirteener unless previously a Fifteener.

The Thirteen and Fifteen are easy enough to visualize, both in their makeup and in their functions. Far more bewildering is the Council of Twenty-one. From a logical point of view, there are two things wrong with its very name; first, it was not in itself really a council at all, and second, it generally had some thirty-two members. It included all the Thirteeners and all the Fifteeners, plus, as a rule, about four designated Twenty-oners, who had been recruited from the Senate and were awaiting advancement to the Fifteen, in the customary *cursus honorum*. The Twenty-one's actual size may mean that it was designed to balance the full Senate, but the origin of its name remains a mystery.[19] In any event, during the latter centuries of the free city's existence, the membership of the ⸳Twenty-one effectively dominated that of the Senate proper. Final authority came to rest with what was called the *Rat-und-XXI,* that is, the Senate and the Secret Chambers sitting together. This was the true governing elite, the famous *Magistrat* of Strasbourg — never more than fifty men at any one time, since some Thirteeners, Fifteeners, and Twenty-oners were also serving terms as Senators.

Out from the Senate-and-XXI, by delegation, radiated the more than eighty commissions which immediately controlled the departments of the city government: the masters of the treasury (*Pfenningthurnherren*), the three customhouse masters (*Pfundzollherren*), the four building inspectors (*Bauherren*), and the rest. Similarly, the whole judicial hierarchy was capped by the Council of Thirteen, acting in its capacity as an imperial supreme court of appeals. Below it, in the arrangement of the courts, stood the Senate and the Lesser Senate, composed of sixteen other commoners and six nobles who heard cases involving less than five hundred Strasbourg pounds. Then came a police court and a number of special tribunals for litigations relating to wardship, marriage, morals, resident non-citizens, etc. Finally, there was the modest but expeditious "Ammeister's audience" for minor affairs, accessible to all comers three mornings a week in the town hall.

In the two centuries that followed the promulgation of the Schwörbrief in 1482, the feature of Strasbourg's constitution which impressed outside observers most, whether or not they liked it, was unquestionably its apparent system of checks and balances, between guilds and assemblies, between assemblies and administrators, be-

tween nobles and commoners. In 1514 Erasmus of Rotterdam wrote
to Jakob Wimpheling after a visit to the town:

I saw a monarchy without tyranny, an aristocracy without factions, a
democracy without disorder, prosperity without luxury, happiness without
insolence. Can anyone imagine greater good fortune than harmony of
this order? O divine Plato, that thou shouldst not have had the joy of
beholding such a republic! [20]

In the 1570's Jean Bodin, starting from a political theory much
less friendly to divided powers, commented both sourly and in-
accurately in his *Six Books of the Republic*:

The people of Strasbourg, having killed all the nobility, ordained
that whosoever aspired to be Grand Burgomaster should prove that his
grandfather was a day laborer, an artisan, a butcher, or of some such
condition.[21]

And in 1600 the Duc de Rohan finished his account of Strasbourg's
government with a careful disavowal:

I have taken the trouble to describe this bizarre order of republic only
out of curiosity and caprice, and not to give approval to such a popular
state. What I liked best was the good time I was shown there, and all
that I want my memory to retain of it is the recollection of several
beautiful things I saw, things which would be as worthy of a great king
as such a population is unworthy of them.[22]

Lest we exaggerate the effects of French rule after 1681, however,
we need to recognize that Strasbourg in the seventeenth century
already had lost some of the political characteristics it had displayed
so prominently in the past. Even in Rohan's day a more acute
observer might have seen that it had ceased to be in any sense "a
popular state." The town government no longer represented a
circulating elite nor displayed the intricate balance of interest groups
described by earlier commentators. The Council of Three Hundred,
for example, was consulted less and less frequently, as a body at
least, since the Magistrat found it easier to control the guilds by
seeking their acquiescence piecemeal, in their twenty separate lodge-
halls. After 1626, an appointed *Oberherr,* always a Thirteener,

Fifteener, or Twenty-oner, presided over each guild to enforce
control from above. The once proud Senate declined in importance,
save as an adjunct to and a recruiting ground for the Secret Chambers, initially its own creations but now clearly dominant in all
plenary sessions.

Toward the end of its existence as an imperial free city, Strasbourg
was actually ruled by the Thirteen and the Fifteen. They, in turn,
relied heavily on a staff of agents and advisers, especially a handful
of legal counselors or *Advokaten*. The closed ring of Ammeisters
rotated through office every six years. The same few families supplied
practically all the Stettmeisters. More and more the Senate-and-XXI
seemed to be a debating society for brothers, cousins, and brothers-
in-law. Strengthened by relative isolation during the Thirty Years'
War, and by the dependable operation of family pride, the iron law
of oligarchy exerted itself with ever-increasing force.

V

The calcification of the government reflected the hardening of
social lines within the town's population and in turn affected the
relationships among various groups. The comprehensive Police
Ordinance of 1628, specifically the section devoted to authorized
clothing and adornment, provides a valuable insight into the Strasbourg of this period.[23] Not that sumptuary legislation ever reveals
how the men and women of past ages actually dressed — judging
from their frequent reissuance, always accompanied by unenforceable
threats, these laws must have been generally flouted. What they do
tell us is how the authorities of a given community visualized its
social hierarchy, and how groups were supposedly related to one
another in terms of public status, even if their members refused to
dress accordingly.

In the Strasbourg of 1628, the first category described in the
Police Ordinance was the humblest as well: "subordinate female
workers," including housemaids, cleaning women, barmaids, and
seamstresses. One step higher, in class two, were placed "subordinate

male workers": day laborers, porters, woodcutters, and the like.
Class three represented the normal placement for rank-and-file guild
members, that is, "common craftsmen and citizens," as well as the
lowest civil servants. The next two categories comprised two sub-
divisions each. Class four (lower) took in all who would otherwise
have been in class three, but who had been elected by their guilds to
the Assembly of Three Hundred, an honor which in all sections of
classes four and five elevated the new assemblyman to the grade
above his normal one. Also in the lower bracket of class four were
schoolteachers, notaries, midwives, skilled art-workers, and "music
teachers who do not play for dancing." Class four (upper) was for
the intermediate rank of city officials — chancellery clerks, customs
and tax collectors, secretaries of the various commissions — plus
lawyers lacking a doctor's degree and teachers in the Gymnasium.

In class five (lower) are the "merchants conducting large and
reputable businesses," as well as a generous category of "scholars who
have not stood examination for the licentiate or the doctorate, but
who have gone so far in their studies that they *could* do so." Class
five (upper) was reserved to members of old bourgeois families whose
ancestors had been in the Magistrat a century or more in the past,
the higher chancellery officials, and scholars holding the licenciate
or the doctorate, hence automatically all professors in the university.
Finally, at the pinnacle, in class six, came the Magistrat itself
(Thirteeners, Fifteeners, Twenty-oners, Senators), the city's legal
counselors, and members of the nobility.

The noblemen in class six, entitled to wear all the gold, jewelry,
and silk they wish, are the same individuals, it will be recalled, who
as town officers were guaranteed all the Stettmeisterships and one
third of the seats in the Senate-and-XXI. In the thirteenth century,
when they were emerging from the status of episcopal ministerials,
the original families of *Constoffler* had formed no fewer than
eighteen noble clubs. These aristocratic lodges had shrunk in number
through the stormy times after Hausbergen, until by the 1490's there
had remained only two, *Zum Hohensteg* and *Zum Mühlstein*.
Indeed, in the seventeenth century the former of these was ex-

clusively composed of members of the Empire's Immediate Nobility
holding lands in Lower Alsace but not enjoying full political rights
in Strasbourg. Hence *Zum Mühlstein* alone contained the true
Constoffler, the citizen-nobles, a loose cluster of families grouped
thus for electoral purposes. These families included a few who could
trace their titles all the way back to the episcopal regime. Many
more, however, had been ennobled at some time after 1262.

What complicates any discussion of Strasbourg's nobility in early
modern times is the peculiar relationship between the Constoffler
(who were also members of the Immediate Nobility of Lower
Alsace) and the urban patriciate, more broadly defined.[24] For the
town's ruling class included many powerful commoners, and in
terms of political influence there is little excuse to distinguish the
Constoffler from the technically non-noble elements within the
oligarchy. Nevertheless, since the constitution made specific concessions to the nobility, it is essential to recognize the line which
had survived from the Middle Ages. This, in effect, was what the
framers of the 1628 police ordinance were doing when they made
the highest sumptuary class primarily the functioning Magistrat,
but then singled out "nobles" as an overlapping group at the top level
of local society.

The compact body of citizens and their families, grouped in their
guilds and neatly arranged for us in the clothing schedule, did not
constitute the entire population of the free city. The government
recognized its responsibility to, even as it asserted its authority over,
a fluctuating but always substantial number of outsiders who had
been permitted to settle as protégés or *Schirmverwandten*. These
were unquestionably looked upon as second-class residents, who had
no voting rights, paid special fees, and were answerable to a single
court; but within these limits they enjoyed relative security.

Strasbourg was also constantly teeming with real transients: trad-
ers, pilgrims, students, tourists, and the city's own mercenary troops.
Finally, there was a daily invasion of peddlers through the Jews'
Gate and along the street still named the "Rue des Juifs." Anti-
Semitism had written some ugly pages in Strasbourg's medieval

history. In the seventeenth century the city accorded a tranquil, if contemptuous, toleration during daylight hours; but since 1387 no Jew had been knowingly permitted by the burghers to spend a night inside the walls. Though the *Judentor* swung open each weekday morning, two great horns were blown from the cathedral platform at sundown, warning the Jewish clothes dealers and money changers to return at once to their dwellings in neighboring hamlets.[25]

The population remaining in the city, once the Judentor was closed for the night, was all Christian and overwhelmingly Lutheran. In the early stages of the Reformation, Strasbourg had been noted for the wide diversity of Protestant sects represented by its residents and guests.[26] The broad humanity of Bucer and Hedio and Johann Sturm, however, was succeeded by the tight-lipped orthodoxy of Marbach and Pappus in the later decades of the sixteenth century; and the sweeping Church Ordinance of 1598 made the town almost as inhospitable a place for Calvinists, not to mention Catholics, as it long had been for Jews.

There remained some curious exceptions in the midst of this official unanimity. A local chapter house still belonged to the Order of Malta. The nuns in the urban convents of St. Magdalen and St. Margaret remained quietly in residence. In addition, there were always some Catholics among the resident non-citizens or Schirmverwandten. But Catholics were barred from all official positions; no public worship was permitted them; the sacraments of consecration and ordination were absolutely forbidden inside the walls; and a couple wishing to be married by a priest had to travel to a village belonging to the bishop. This was also the regular procedure for baptisms. About the best that can be said for Strasbourg's treatment of its Catholic minority is that the latter suffered less than did the Protestants of Alsatian towns, such as Haguenau and Kaysersberg, which had remained in the old faith.[27]

As for Calvinists, they too were denied all public worship, refused political rights, and theoretically obliged to accept Lutheran upbringing for the children of mixed marriages. In Strasbourg, where Calvin himself had helped to launch the teaching of Protestant theology, there were by 1648 probably no more than thirty families loyal to his confession. What protection they enjoyed was chiefly attributable to the powerful family of Hanau-Lichtenberg, which opened its lands to fellow members of the Reformed faith and interceded for them periodically with the Magistrat. It was to this family's nearby village of Wolfisheim, beginning in 1654, that Strasbourg's Calvinists marched solemnly each Sunday morning for their weekly services, previously conducted in various other outlying spots. The smaller sects such as the Photinians, Swiss Anabaptists, or Dutch Mennonites, received short shrift within the city, although they were tolerated in its rural bailiwicks.

The bulk of the local population acknowledged the authority of the Church Ordinance of 1598 and the religious organization it finalized.[28] Lutheran citizens were divided into seven parishes, including the central one of the cathedral. From these came the seven pastors and seven vicars who formed the professional nucleus of the Convocation, the *Kirchenkonvent*. Other members of this body included three lay wardens from each church, one chosen from the Thirteen or Fifteen, the second from the Assembly of Three Hundred, and the third from among the private citizens of the parish. In addition, the university's four professors of theology and the pastors of the city's nearest rural parishes were usually invited to attend, as were the parish schoolmasters on occasions when pending business concerned them.

The Kirchenkonvent was a seemingly representative assemblage of clergymen and laymen, but its democratic appearance was belied by the actual workings of ecclesiastical administration. In one case after another, it was the Convocation's President, together with the Magistrat members among the churchwardens, who decided upon the action to be taken before a particular matter ever came up for debate. And the power of the city government in religious matters did not end there. One of the most important of the many public commissions was that of the Cloister Masters (always one noble and three non-noble members of the Secret Chambers), which was charged with administering the church properties secularized during the Reformation and now devoted to charitable or educational uses.

Many pastors resented bitterly their subordination to secular authority, but, from the point of view of the community in general, the restraining influence exercised by the political leaders was all to the good. Such limited toleration as Catholics and Calvinists enjoyed was extended by the Magistrat, over the repeated protests of the Convocation, because some deference had to be shown to powerful neighbors. Strasbourg's own Lutheran merchants needed reciprocal favors, after all, when they traveled in the Rhenish bishoprics or in Switzerland. The two Thirteeners and two Fifteeners who constituted the Board of Censors condemned numerous books, including almost automatically anything imported from France with the word *amour, fille,* or *Madame* in its title; but they did not completely smother all non-religious publishing in Strasbourg, as the majority of clergymen seemed intent at times on having them do. Even in the frightful history of seventeenth-century Alsatian witchcraft trials, the city occupies a relatively small place — again, apparently, because Strasbourg's lawyers and town magistrates were less sure than were its preachers that they could tell a witch when they saw one.

VI

For seventeenth-century Europeans, education appeared first and foremost as an extension of religious training. Hence the elementary schools of Strasbourg, as Reuss says, were "branches of the sacristy" and generally not very impressive branches at that. Each parish had its school, where an underpaid master, who generally had to eke out his livelihood by working at other menial jobs, taught the three R's and the Lutheran catechism to such children as might be induced to attend for a few years. Inside the city walls not more than one-third of the eligible youngsters could be counted upon to follow even this thin intellectual diet, or could have been accommodated if they had, and in the rural parishes the fraction was much smaller. The only other primary training, aside from some home tutoring, was found in the miserable *Armenschul'* at the city workhouse.

The classical Gymnasium, which still conducted its classes where Johann Sturm had begun them in the former Dominican Cloister, offered little to justify its surviving reputation or the class-conscious pride of its graduates. After the economic retrenchment of 1634 it had only seven grades, in place of the original ten; but it still accepted beginners as young as six and hence turned out mere boys as certified men of culture. Its curriculum consisted of a deadly routine based on Latin texts, which few instructors seem to have connected in any way with the humanities, plus readings in Lutheran theology, a smattering of mathematics, and eventually some study of St. Paul's epistles in Greek.

The superior offshot of Sturm's *Scola,* renamed the Academy in 1566, and finally the University of Strasbourg under an imperial charter of 1621, was certainly more important than any other cultural institution in the city.[29] Like the Gymnasium, it was supervised by the Magistrat's commission of three Scholarchs, although the latter usually deferred to the wishes of the Convocation in making appointments in theology. Again like the Gymnasium, the university occupied rooms in the secularized Dominican Cloister, which also housed the academic library and sheltered a limited number of scholarship students. All classes, save for the German lectures in introductory anatomy, were conducted in Latin. Under a rector elected for a term of only six months, the four faculties, each with its dean, comprised a total of sixteen permanent professors, and even this small number was often further reduced by protracted vacancies. The six professors of philosophy, four of theology, four of law, and two of medicine usually waited a long time for their appointments. The thirteen senior ones enjoyed the income from prebends of the former chapter of St. Thomas — the church whose secularized assets constituted the basic endowment of the university — but there were few scholars who could afford to hold professorships unless they had private fortunes to begin with. It is not surprising that the urban patriciate filled most of the chairs of higher learning, as it did other places of local honor.

Arriving at a just evaluation of Strasbourg's cultural level in the mid-seventeenth century is by no means easy. At the very least, it demands a conscious choice between long-range historical and strictly contemporary standards of judgment. If one chooses the latter frame of reference, one can say that in the Europe of 1648 Strasbourg was a city which still represented a relatively important center of intellectual activity. Professors such as Bernegger and Clutenius enjoyed high reputations in the German scholarly world through the worst of the war years. The stiff Latin poetry of Samuel Gloner and the university's laureate, Johann Schneuber, may have long since lost whatever place they ever had in literary history; but the same charge cannot be made against *The Visions of Philander von Sittewald*, first published in Strasbourg by Mülbe in 1640. The creator of this outburst of erudite satire, Johann Michael Moscherosch, was a product of the local Gymnasium and university, the protégé of several professors, and, frequently, during the long wars, a resident within the walls of the city to which he devoted his *Imago reipublicae Argentinensis* in 1648.[30] Johann Carolus' pioneering venture in journalism, the weekly *Relation* — Germany's first known newspaper — was founded by 1609 at the latest, and at mid-century still reported news from distant points, especially Cologne, Vienna, Prague, Venice, and Rome.[31] And it was not uncommon for a young bourgeois patrician like Elias Brackenhoffer or an illustrator like J. J. Walter to journey through France, Italy, Switzerland, and the Empire in the best manner of the Grand Tour.[32]

Nevertheless, seen against the background of Strasbourg's brilliant, turbulent past, the years around 1648 can lay no claim to cultural greatness. Whatever its value in keeping open a few windows to the world, the university produced little that was either profound or original. The local publishers were for the most part only the timid heirs of a great tradition. The study of French among the upper classes never, before the eighteenth century, represented anything more than the cultivation of a useful foreign tongue. The assiduous private tutor, Daniel Martin, has left us precious sources for social history in his German-French conversational guides of in 1620's and '30's, but his wistful introductions also provide evidence of how conscious he was of a limited clientele.[33] With only a few exceptions, the citizens of Strasbourg emerged from the Thirty Years' War with their eyes fixed anxiously on narrow, immediate affairs. They seem, in the cultural and in the economic sphere, far less cosmopolitan than their medieval forebears.

VII

For contemporaries, no doubt, the sense of loss related more clearly to material things than to those of the spirit. Strasbourg's economic decline during the century, and particularly the half-century, preceding 1648 was all the more striking because its prosperity had for so long been a byword in western Germany. Since the high middle ages its merchant boatmen had held a crucial position in the north-south trade. Beginning in 1336, when Louis the Bavarian had authorized the first Strasbourg fair, that institution had grown into not one but two great meetings each year, one in June, the other at Christmas. Strasbourg was a ferry crossing as early as Roman times, perhaps even earlier, and the city had opened a new chapter in its commercial history when it completed its first Rhine bridge in 1388.[34] From then on, as a natural transit point for merchants traveling east or west, it had truly been the "crossroads city." It has remained that ever since; but in the seventeenth century, the long disruption of the Empire combined with the costs of military defense, year after year, to undermine the economic position of the little republic.[35]

There was cause to hope that things would improve, once the peace of Westphalia was signed. Placed as it was, Strasbourg could count on sharing in any general recovery of central and western European trade. Into the customhouse or *Zollkeller* beside the quays would flow increasing quantities of goods, there to pay the prescribed tolls before being either reloaded for transshipment or hauled to the nearby market house for sale under the supervision of city tax collectors. The local shippers still had their renowned fleet of river boats, some of them able to carry loads of up to forty tons out of the city and into the swift current of the Rhine. As Alsace itself recovered, the smaller barges of the local trade would once more, in growing numbers, come gliding into town along the Ill and be poled back out again, upstream, through Erstein and Benfeld, past Sélestat to Colmar.

The prospects for revival in shipping and commerce, however, could not make the economic outlook really bright, as long as the situation of local handicrafts remained depressed; and in 1648, depressed it assuredly was. There is no basis for even talking about industry, in the sense of relatively large-scale production, before the end of the seventeenth century. Most of the guilds had always produced under strict regulation and primarily for local consumption.[36] Nevertheless, even the carpenters, masons, bakers, tailors, shoemakers, and their colleagues in other trades benefited from the money brought into the city by its fairs and its commerce. The late sixteenth-century struggles with the bishop and even more the Thirty Years' War, with the protracted state of emergency it involved, had forced taxes higher and higher while the ability to pay had declined. Toward the end of this period the substantial Hieronymus Hatten, master weaver and dyer, recorded that his taxes now amounted to sixty per cent of his income.[37] With what he had left, Hatten elected to stay on in Strasbourg, but many of his fellow guildsmen did not; and even those who refused to emigrate suffered decimation in the plague years. The drapers' and weavers' guild had numbered 404 members in 1620 — by 1650 its membership stood at only 281.[38] *Zur Steltz,* as the artworkers and printers called their guild, received no fewer than 36 new master goldsmiths during the decade of the 1580's, bringing the total membership of the craft to perhaps 90. By contrast, in the 1670's just 15 were initiated.[39]

All Strasbourgers could see a decline in the condition of the city's finances. The two-century-old Strasbourg Bank had ceased to be a favorite depository for foreign funds — here the Dutch had taken over — and was no longer the best place for even the local citizen to invest.[40] Its resources had been strained to the limit by loans to the Magistrat for such sterile uses as the hiring of mercenaries and the buying off of potential invaders (in 1632, for example, the Swedes had demanded and received an "advance" of fifty thousand florins).[41] Whether or not the city government, in turn, could meet its obligations depended on a revival of regular income which no man could view as certain. The town had enough potential sources of money. Besides the direct property tax or *Stallgeld,* there were the excises on sales of wine and grain (*Umgeld*); fees from the customhouse, public market, and transit quays; fines and chancellery charges; taxes on resident non-citizens, as well as on Jews and certain other transients; rents from the public real estate; and dues from the rural bailiwicks.[42] But all of these depended directly or indirectly on the general level of trade and the prosperity of the town's population. Furthermore, the entire fiscal situation demanded not only the reduced costs of peaceful existence, but also, and more important in the long run, the subtle ingredient of public confidence. In 1648 this was a commodity in pitifully short supply.

VIII

This was Strasbourg, as it left the dark period which had been the first half of the seventeenth century and entered an era of new uncertainties. Behind, lay nearly four hundred years of virtual freedom from outside control, a record of independence longer than that of the Swiss city cantons. Behind, also, lay memories of medieval greatness and a record of both material and intellectual leadership in the Protestant cause it had made its own in the days of Bucer and Sturm. Here was a city German in speech and manners, Lutheran in faith, jealously watchful of its special position between the Holy Roman Emperor and the King of France, both of whom must be constantly propitiated but just as constantly evaded. It was a city whose rulers felt new pressures, new threats to its ancient pride.

As seen by an outsider, and indeed by some insiders, the situation of Strasbourg when the news arrived from Westphalia was not one to encourage a placid, self-satisfied conservatism. The leaders of the republic could scarcely afford to let the tendencies of the years before continue after 1648. The slough into which the cultural life of the community had sunk was apparent to sensitive contemporaries, and the economic crisis naturally impressed many more. Occasional voices were raised against the dead formalism of the official religion, as well as against the hauteur of the ruling group.

But who was to remedy these causes for concern? Reformers from the lower ranks of society? We know almost nothing about the thinking which went on in these strata, for most of the protests which have survived were necessarily written by critics within the literate classes. Occasionally a document will reflect some uproar among guildsmen or some attempt by members of the Assembly of Three Hundred to assert their rights. Sources such as these, however, fail to provide information about the attitudes of the mass of the population and certainly originate well below the level of real decisions and power. Hence we must return to a consideration of the Magistrat. What could or would the oligarchy do to steady a community whose own coinage had for thirty years featured the image of a storm-tossed ship?

Action to improve the economic situation, to promote trade along old lines, protect local crafts, cut city expenses, and increase income — in other words, traditional measures to restore sound finances — could be expected to constitute the town fathers' first preoccupation. By the mid-1650's they had, in fact, managed to balance the current budget, at the cost of certain land sales and of stringent economies which could be maintained only so long as the Rhineland was at peace.[43] However, there was not a chance for basic political reform or a change in the recruitment of the governing group. If the Schwörbrief contained some clauses which now had a mocking sound as they echoed across the cathedral square at the oathtaking ceremony each January, it was still a document which no critic dared attack openly, and which every holder of privilege held squarely in front of him, to exorcize dangerous spirits. Furthermore neither education nor religious organization could be improved so long as both, just as they stood, formed integral parts of the social and political *status quo*.

Strasbourg's rulers do not, as they should not, emerge from all this as peculiarly selfish or stupid men. On balance they look rather better than the even more restricted oligarchies of Frankfurt am Main or Nürnberg. The Strasbourg Magistrat, save for the inevitable minority of dissidents, simply reacted to new challenges in a manner dictated by its members' training, understanding of history, and conception of civic well-being.

Perhaps we should concede that the only real problem for Strasbourg was external, that given the power of Louis XIV's France, it would make little difference to the city, when the annexation crisis developed, whether its own regime happened to be more or less democratic. But this seems to me to be a false argument, whatever its apparent logic, because the local characteristics of the imperial epoch were carried over in remarkably large measure into the French period. Hence, if basic reforms had been carried out between 1648 and 1681, they would have continued to benefit the community, even in a changed political setting, at least until 1789. There is no denying, however, that internal problems fade in *immediate* significance when one turns to the diplomatic and military drama which was about to begin and which was to culminate in the triumphal coming of the Sun King.

CHAPTER TWO

Annexation

I

How Strasbourg passed under the control of the French crown is a story dramatic enough to have attracted countless historians, some romancers, and, it must be said, a certain number of romancers posing as historians. The resultant mixture of fact and legend, accusation and rebuttal has become, no doubt inevitably, one of the focal points for French-German hostility. The episode is still worth careful attention, however, because it involves far more than a local drama or a symbol for rival patriotisms. It is an incident of more than routine interest which helps to clarify the portentous changes taking place in seventeenth-century Europe, when a series of small polities like Strasbourg were swallowed up by territorial states. It offers a demonstration of military and diplomatic techniques characteristic of Louis XIV's era. It provides, also, an opportunity to observe certain classic problems of human existence — power versus legality, action versus delay, prudence versus defiance — which emerge in Strasbourg's crisis as clearly as in the events recounted by Thucydides or Guicciardini or Churchill. Finally, it sets the stage for the special relationship of a city to a kingdom with which the remainder of this book deals.

The story begins with the rights and territories in Alsace acquired by France at the conclusion of the Thirty Years' War. (See page 9.) The tortuous record of the preceding negotiations is not directly connected with Strasbourg's peculiar situation, but what is directly connected is the change which took place in the free city's political environment once the imperial cessions had been made in 1648.

he Cathedral of Strasbourg

Kammerzell House

The Quai Saint-Nicolas

The Quai de la Bruche and La Petite France

The Bain-aux-Plantes

SCENES

OF

STRASBOURG

Under Articles 73 and 74 of the Treaty of Münster, Emperor Ferdinand III surrendered to ten-year-old Louis XIV all of the following: (1) the city of Breisach on the right bank of the Rhine; (2) the Landgraviates (*Landgrafschaften*) of Upper and Lower Alsace; (3) the Sundgau, a compact Hapsburg domain in the extreme southern end of the region; and (4) the governorship or *Landvogtei* of the Ten Cities, the *Décapole* as the French called this group of communes. On the other hand, in Article 87 the King of France explicitly pledged himself to respect the freedom and existing relations to the emperor of the city of Strasbourg, the Alsatian lands of the Bishops of Strasbourg, Basel, and Speyer, the Immediate Nobility of Lower Alsace, a series of religious establishments, and even the Ten Cities themselves.[1]

All this, as complicated as anything touching Alsatian geography was bound to be, was made infinitely more confusing by the soon notorious "Ita tamen" clause which concluded Article 87. It stipulated that the French crown's renunciations just listed were to be understood "in such a way, however, that through this reciprocal declaration [the King of France] shall suffer no diminution of the sovereign rights accorded him above." This was one of the several fishhooks hidden in the smooth verbiage of the treaty. The apparently explicit exceptions to French royal sovereignty in the first portion of the article could not possibly be reconciled with an unlimited reassertion of that sovereignty. French diplomacy subsequently chose to infer that the "Ita tamen" clause practically nullified the restrictions preceding it. In reply, imperial spokesmen insisted that it simply assured the Bourbons the status and rights previously enjoyed in Alsace by the Hapsburg family.

Where the matter became particularly bewildering was in connection with the Ten Cities of the Décapole. The French read Article 74 to mean that these had been ceded outright to Louis XIV. The imperials interpreted the cession of the *Landvogtei* in terms of German usage, giving the royal governor the right to the towns' carefully limited oath of "customary loyalty and good faith" and assuring him nominal dues, as well as the income from a substantial

domain appertaining to the Landvogt himself, as a feudal lord.[2] The
Décapole, however, had Vienna's support in claiming that Article
87 left them still "immediate," still subject in last resort to the
emperor or to the imperial supreme court at Speyer, and answerable
to the governor appointed by Louis XIV only insofar as they had
been subject to the emperor's Landvogt at Haguenau before 1648.

Side by side with the Décapole issue stood the question of the
two Landgraviates transferred from Ferdinand to Louis. What was
an Alsatian *Landgraf*? In Upper Alsace there was no great problem
since the Hapsburgs had held the title *and* most of the land, the
latter as a family possession. Both title and land now passed to
Louis XIV. In Lower Alsace, however, which is to say in the northern
half of the future province, where most of the lands were directly
controlled by the Bishop of Strasbourg, the Count of Hanau-Lichtenberg or the city of Strasbourg, only two small villages came with the
Landgrafschaft.

The underlying conflict was somewhat simpler than all these
details might suggest. The cessions had been made by one man, but he
represented quite a different person depending on your point of view.
To Vienna, he was in this context only Ferdinand von Hapsburg,
ceding family lands; to Paris, he was Emperor Ferdinand III, trans-
ferring sovereign rights. For the first years after Westphalia, however, both sides were satisfied to let the confusion remain until some
future settlement, when each believed it might profit from the
original vagueness. It was not a situation that could long survive the
clear preponderance of either party.[3]

While Strasbourg was apparently secure behind the guarantees its
agents had won at Münster, it was actually involved in the newly
created situation, if not in the tangle of legal theories. French armies
were now established in Alsace, on the lands of a king for whom
the Rhine was a frontier of supreme importance. How long he would
permit an independent power, however weak, to command the best
and hence the most dangerous river crossing, no man could say. Nor
could anyone be sure how long he would deny himself the advantages

of making "Landgraviate" a full-blown territorial concept, whatever objections a German feudal lawyer might raise. If ever the crown began to treat Alsace as a compact royal province, there could be little doubt as to what would appear its natural capital!

II

At the very least, it was obvious that a new stage had been reached in the previously irregular intercourse between Strasbourg and the kingdom of France. The free city's first direct encounter with the monarchy itself took place in 1444, when the future Louis XI, then still Dauphin, led an army of mercenaries into Alsace on what was little more than a foraging expedition to get them out of France. Friendlier relations began only with the Reformation, when Francis I showed himself especially eager to achieve close ties with the town, as with other Protestant powers, in his struggle against Emperor Charles V. In return, Settmeister Jakob Sturm had been consistently polite, sometimes even encouraging, but always cautious, so that at this time the French connection served Strasbourg as a makeweight in German diplomacy, but never became the commitment King Francis sought. The second half of the sixteenth century, from Henry II's threatening expedition over the Vosges through the intrigues and alarums of the French religious wars, had been a tense period for the city. In the 1570's, particularly, fear of Catholic spies and the armies of Guise repeatedly brought the Magistrat to the brink of panic.[4]

It was Henry IV, long aided by loans from the Bank of Strasbourg and consistently friendly even after his personal abandonment of Protestantism in 1593, who restored the old cordiality. In fact, no French king before or after him ever enjoyed such popularity in the town. Through his gifted agent, Jacques Bongars, Henry made Strasbourg his diplomatic base in the Rhineland, repaying this convenience by supporting the burghers in their disputes with the Carthusian Order and with the Hapsburg bishop during the 1590's.[5]

Strasbourg joined Henry's Protestant Union; but his death in 1610 and, even more, the city's withdrawal from the Union early in the Thirty Years' War left Richelieu with the task of having to build a new relationship. In 1624, the cardinal sent two emissaries to sound out the Magistrat; but not until the emperor's Edict of Restitution five years lated did the recalcitrant Protestants of Strasbourg clearly turn toward France once more. 1630 found Josias Glaser, Secretary of the Fifteen, conferring over a loan with Père Joseph in Paris and with Richelieu and Louis XIII at Monceaux, where the king greeted him by mumbling, "Well, Mr. German, come here, come here." [6]

It is useful to note the points of contact between seventeenth-century Strasbourg and the French court. Ever since the Reformation, as already mentioned, there was travel back and forth by special missions. In addition, Louis XIII converted his occasional observers in the town into accredited "residents," beginning in 1631 with the half-French, half-German Protestant, Melchior de l'Isle. It was no accident that this man, like Bongars before him in the 1590's and Gravel after him in the 1650's, was a central figure in French dealings with the Holy Roman Empire as a whole; for the king's resident in Strasbourg not only dealt with the local Magistrat but also collected information from and distributed money to French hirelings throughout southwestern Germany.

As for representation in the other direction, the free city regularized its agency in Paris, where Resident J. Beck was established by 1647. Another important source of intelligence concerning French affairs was the convenient observation post of Metz. Most important of a whole series of correspondents there was one Jean de Flavigny, a member of the Metz town government, who sent over 250 newsletters to designated Thirteeners in Strasbourg between 1597 and 1626; and even his less prolific successors were valuable observers for their employers on the Rhine.[7] Through its agents, its correspondents, and its merchants the city thus entered the new era of proximity well-informed about, though not altogether at ease with, its powerful neighbor to the west.

III

The quarter-century immediately following 1648 was a time not so much of obvious external danger as of tense and often depressing conditions within Strasbourg's walls. The 1650's seemed, outwardly, to be a time of economic improvement, but the next decade brought a variety of new or renewed difficulties. On the one hand, the recently elected Emperor Leopold I began in 1659 to press, unsuccessfully, for a binding oath of allegiance from the defiant Magistrat. On the other hand, French troops in Alsace tended more and more to forage wherever they chose, even in Strasbourg's rural holdings, so that by 1671 the Thirteen felt impelled to send Syndic Frid and Secretary Güntzer, a figure destined to loom large in the ensuing chronicle of events, to lodge a formal protest in Paris. In 1666 the plague swept in again and ravaged the city for three years. At the same time a variety of shortages, for which contemporaries blamed Louis XIV's war in Spanish Flanders, struck urban consumers and inflated the city's military provisioning costs.

Something else characterizes this period, something difficult for the historian to describe precisely but impossible to overlook in the accounts of chroniclers like J. J. Walter and Franziskus Resseissen.[8] This is a general atmosphere of malaise, of strained and often ugly human relations, punctuated by savage personal crimes and by equally savage executions. The increasingly numerous acts of official corruption detected almost every year — the Undersecretary of the Treasury Tower was beheaded in 1667, for example, just a few days before the *Rheinlohner,* or superintendent of the bridge and dikes, was caught padding his payrolls[9] — help to explain why both disgust and foreboding are expressed so strongly in the pages of Ammeister Reisseissen.

Meanwhile the great powers, France and the Empire, while leaving Strasbourg largely to its own devices, were engaged in a series of disputes concerning Alsace in general. During the first decade after Westphalia, the French government was too distracted by civil conflicts and the continuing war against Spain to permit itself any great concern over Alsatian affairs. Yet it was in just these years that Charles Colbert (later Colbert de Croissy), named intendant in 1655, had his staff at Breisach prepare the massive study of the region which was to be basic for royal calculations over the following four decades.[10] As the Pyrenees settlement with Spain approached, French diplomacy turned toward Germany with renewed interest. The attempt to prevent Leopold's election as Holy Roman Emperor miscarried at Frankfurt in 1657–1658, but in the latter year Gravel succeeded in forming the Confederation of the Rhine under French patronage. Simultaneously, the crown began applying pressure to secure the full submission of the Décapole towns, which continued to send their judicial appeals to Speyer and by 1663 were demanding support from the Imperial Diet in Regensburg.

In 1658, Johann Frischmann, a German-born Lutheran scholar and pamphleteer who had graduated from Strasbourg's university, began his long period as royal resident there. One of his first tasks was a vigorous, albeit unsuccessful, effort to draw the city into the Confederation of the Rhine with Mainz, Trier, Cologne, and the Elector Palatine.[11] He also entertained the Duc Mazarin, governor general of Alsace, when the latter made a resplendent state visit to Strasbourg in 1661.[12] On the whole, however, the royal ministers were still moving warily, still following Croissy's policy recommendations, which called for a gradual *prise de possession* in Alsace pending "an exact investigation of all the king's rights." [13]

As for the emperor, he made his futile effort to secure a formal oath of fealty from Strasbourg in 1659–1660; and his representatives at Regensburg lent their support to Colmar, Haguenau, and the other cities of the Décapole when they brought their complaints against French encroachments before the Diet.[14] Otherwise, Leopold was too deeply involved in combating Turkish raiders and Hungarian rebels to intervene at all consistently in the affairs of Alsace.

Yet Strasbourg felt threatened, encircled, and suspended in a situation of only temporarily inactive peril. The official reaction was first to sponsor meetings of the Estates of Lower Alsace within the walls in 1650 and 1652–1653. Then, when these proved ineffectual (as well as irritating to France), the Magistrat turned toward Switzerland, seeking initially to join the French-Swiss treaty system and then, in 1667, to secure actual admission to the Helvetic Confederation, as Mulhouse had done a century and a half earlier. Both efforts failed. The Catholic cantons wanted no change in the Swiss balance; and even Protestant cities such as Zürich, Basel, and Bern recoiled before an extension of federal responsibilities to include so exposed a center as Strasbourg, lying eighty-five miles north of Basel, on flat terrain, and surrounded by French troop units.[15] Thus formal diplomacy got nowhere. The populace of the free city could do little to express its sentiments save break the windows of the French resident's home three times in the space of a few months.[16]

IV

Viewed from this distance, the crescendo which ended with Strasbourg's capitulation may be seen to have extended over fully nine years and to have included at least three stages of sharply declining duration. The first was the long military crisis of Louis XIV's Dutch War, lasting from 1672 until the Peace of Nymwegen early in 1679. The second comprised the ensuing two and a half years, when French power was focused squarely on the seizure of additional territory in the upper Rhineland by application of the expedient of "reunions." The third stage brought the decisive events of September 1681.

Louis XIV's decision to invade Holland and the other United Provinces was the act of a young monarch filled with confidence in his own abilities, commanding the most powerful military machine Europe had yet seen, and prepared to risk much in the belief there was much to be won. Gone was the cautious France of Mazarin's last years. At the king's bidding, the great struggle for Europe had begun. From here on, even so famous a free city as Strasbourg could scarcely be more than a pawn. Hence, in November 1672, before the newly formed alliance between the emperor and the Elector of

Brandenburg could undertake any operations across the Rhine in support of the Dutch, the Duc de Condé calmly resolved to cut the Strasbourg crossing. On the 13th of that month he dispatched some three hundred French sappers, with fireboats, from his upstream base at Breisach. They struck without warning during the night and by dawn had burned out a half-dozen spans of the cherished bridge.[17]

This was the first shock of direct military violence the city had experienced in three generations; and the response, though energetic, was understandably confused. The Magistrat ordered the reconstruction of the bridge, which was again open to traffic by the following February 20, and simultaneously protested to Louis XIV. The French king replied politely that he intended no injury to the city itself and would see to later restitution, but for the time being he must insist that the bridge sections be broken anew. The Magistrat, after sending an urgent deputation to Paris in March, decided it must yield. It ordered that seven or eight spans be knocked out secretly during the night of May 5, 1673, and then suppressed a riot by indignant citizens in town the next day.

Not until almost a year and a half later, after the Empire's formal declaration of war on France and the arrival of a big imperial army before the bridge on the Baden side, did the city fathers dare to reconnect the shattered links. In the five days beginning September 27, 1674, the timbers were hammered back into place, and a long column of Austrians, South Germans, and Croats poured across into Alsace (though only small parties were permitted within the city gates at any one time). A fortnight later, the Great Elector led his Brandenburgers across, an impressive column of eighteen thousand blue-clad troops whose appearance delighted the always impressionable Walter,[18] but who were to go back into Germany after three months in Alsace having done nothing, the less emotional Reisseissen noted sourly, but "create more poor people."[19] The French army awaiting this expedition was commanded by Turenne. Though the "incomparable marshal" had less than a year to live, he began that year with a brilliant campaign of forced winter marches, oblique attacks, and general deception which landed his disorganized enemies back in Baden by mid-January 1675, and secured his own reputation as the general whom Louis XIV would never quite manage to replace.

Meanwhile, besides permitting military use of its bridge — a dangerous decision, as it now seemed — Strasbourg took certain steps of its own. It imposed a stern internal discipline, beheading Dr. Georg Obrecht in 1672 for having circulated charges that members of the government, including Ammeister Dietrich, had sold out to the French, and the next year fining one Botzheim heavily for a milder offense of the same order.[20] It applied again, in vain, for admission to the Swiss Confederation.[21] It sought to strengthen its military organization by completing the division of the entire city into militia districts, which had previously existed only in neighborhoods adjacent to the walls.[22] Furthermore, beginning with two companies from Zürich and Bern in April 1673, and continuing with two more in May 1675, it built up a small, but well-trained and well-equipped Swiss mercenary force to bolster its existing garrison.[23]

As the long war dragged on, with imperial armies alternately advancing and retreating across the bridge, while the French used ferries and the bridge at Breisach, municipal difficulties increased. The populace was each year paying property taxes of three or three and a half times the normal Stallgeld rate.[24] City Advocate Gottfried Stoesser came back from Vienna late in 1676 with promises of monetary aid; but the emperor's subsidies proved to be a most undependable resource. No matter what was tried, the expenses of mercenary troops seemed to soak up every florin the town could lay hands on. Yet the decisive step, the acceptance of an imperial garrison financed by the Reich, was postponed month after month. This was partly because no direct French action seemed as yet to demand so drastic a move, partly because the old fear of subjection to Vienna remained acute. Furthermore, influential voices in the Council of Thirteen still insisted that the best hope of escaping French retaliation lay in formal neutrality.[25] Hence although the king's resident, Frischmann, had fled when the imperials crossed the bridge in 1674, a replacement named Frémond d'Ablancourt was permitted to present his credentials the following January and was succeeded in 1676 by Louis Verjus, later that year by one Dupré, and in 1678 by the uncommonly arrogant Simon de La Loubère. Technically speaking, relations remained normal.

The logic of events, however, could not long tolerate so unreal a situation. By the summer of 1678, hostilities moved back to center once again on the Upper Rhine; and on July 27 a French army under Créquy, which had moved north through Baden until it was just across the river from Strasbourg, suddenly attacked Kehl, the city's eastern bridgehead, occupied the little fort on that side and burned the town, before abandoning it to the Duke of Lorraine's approaching army. The Magistrat could not possibly hesitate any longer. On August 14 a formal treaty was concluded with the emperor, providing for the occupation of the city by an imperial garrison and for a subsidy of five thousand *Reichstaler* per month from Vienna. Even before this agreement was signed, units detached from the Duke of Lorraine's forces had begun to file into town — 1,800 men on August 4, 1,600 more on August 9, and in late September another 2,300 with high officers, including Count von Mansfeld, Count von Arco, and the Saxon cavalry general, Berlepsch. By the end of the year, Strasbourg had within its walls 5,700 imperials, 3,800 mercenaries (including the 600 Swiss), and some 4,500 citizens in the militia.[26] The proponents of neutrality were overwhelmed.

V

Scarcely had these decisive military steps been taken when the Treaty of Nymwegen revolutionized the whole situation. The signing of the peace in February 1679 undercut the position of the pro-imperial "war party" in Strasbourg; and though Count von Arco and his staff were reluctant to evacuate so strategic a locality, the Magistrat insisted that it would be satisfied only with the complete withdrawal of the voracious and disorderly troops, especially the Hungarian cavalry.[27] Local impatience might have failed to secure the desired result, had not the French-Imperial treaty itself stipulated that both armies must evacuate strong points occupied during the war. Even so, it was not until August 1679 that the last imperials marched back across the bridge to rejoin the Duke of Lorraine at his headquarters in Swabia. During that same summer the town government discharged all but a fraction of the mercenary force.[28] Two companies of the Swiss infantry went home in May, and the other two departed on September 1. The disappearance of the big garrison was a relief to most of the citizens and a boon to the municipal treasury, but the obvious result was a return to military impotence.

At this point it is important to distinguish between the changes which by 1679 had come about in France's power position in the east and the additional changes which were shortly to result from Louis XIV's new moves in that quarter. Regardless of what the French might do after Nymwegen, they had now achieved a grip on the region between the "old kingdom" and the Rhine which could not fail to affect the status of Strasbourg. For one thing, in 1670, technically a year of peace, the royal army suddenly occupied the Duchy of Lorraine and thus took control of an area which had previously been open to the passage of French troops but which had nevertheless tended to make Alsace and Paris seem farther apart. Secondly, the year 1673 witnessed the final solution of the Décapole question, with Louis XIV himself crossing the Vosges to supervise the demolition of Colmar's and Haguenau's fortifications and to receive in person the Ten Cities' long withheld oaths of unqualified allegiance. And now, at Nymwegen, Louis obtained all of the formerly Spanish-controlled province of Franche-Comté southwest of Alsace, as well as the city of Freiburg im Breisgau on the right bank of the Rhine. Never before had access to the great valley been so easy for France nor defense of it so difficult for the Empire.[29]

Hardly had the various peace instruments been signed when the monarchy of the Sun King adopted new methods in its drive for aggrandizement, without noticeable loss of momentum. The famous *chambres des réunions,* established at Metz, Besançon, and Breisach, began the systematic scrutiny of all legal records which might conceivably give the king a claim, however remote, to territories previously outside his jurisdiction but allegedly attached to lands he had acquired in 1648 and 1679. Not surprisingly, since these chambers were royal tribunals, Louis' title was found to be superior to those of the current possessors in cases affecting no fewer than six hundred communities and amounting to a total area actually exceeding that of the original cessions at Münster. On March 22, 1680, the Sovereign Council at Breisach issued a decree assigning the king unlimited sovereignty over all of Upper and Lower Alsace. On August 9, it followed this with a judgment requiring all Alsatian landholders and communities, lay and ecclesiastical alike, to pay formal homage to their ruler.

What was happening was clear enough. The royal administration and judiciary had at last started to hammer Alsace into a province. They could not wholly unify its bewildering legal geography; but they could make it far more compact than the jumble of rights, half-rights, and territorial enclaves which the king had acquired in 1648. This process had been visible from the time the Ten Cities were subjugated in 1673 and was pushed another step when Jacques de La Grange arrived in Breisach later the same year, to begin a quarter-century as Intendant of Police, Justice, and Finances for Alsace. The work of this ruthless, avaricious, but unquestionably able administrator was now going forward with strong support from the royal advisers, especially from one who at times made even La Grange seem mild by comparison: Michel Le Tellier, Marquis de Louvois. The terrible war minister found the Rhine frontier a matter of importance from his official point of view. More than that, he seems to have developed almost as strong a geographical obsession with Alsace in general, and eventually Strasbourg in particular, as Colbert felt for the Low Countries.

Month by month, the position of the free city grew more precarious. In September 1680, on the strength of the Sovereign Council's August 9 ruling, French officials took over control of Strasbourg's remaining rural bailiwicks: Illkirch-Graffenstaden, Wasselonne-

Marlenheim, and Barr.[30] One after another, the ecclesiastical lords and communities exempted from Louis' sovereignty by Article 87 of the Treaty of Münster bowed to the demand that they now recognize his sovereignty. Then, in May 1681, the *Reichsritterschaft,* the supposedly "immediate" imperial nobility of Lower Alsace capitulated and at their spring assembly swore fealty to the king through the agency of La Grange, who had come to Niedernai with a force of dragoons expressly for this purpose.[31] Strasbourg was now the only political entity in Alsace still clinging to its independence of Louis XIV and asserting its shadowy allegiance to the emperor. Still there came no explicit French demand for its submission. The former resident, Frischmann, resumed his old post upon La Loubère's departure in the summer of 1679 and in 1680 was succeeded after death by his son, who also bore the name Johann Frischmann. Apparently the free city continued to enjoy full diplomatic recognition.

Nevertheless, the sparring was almost over. The sequence of events as seen from within the town walls can be followed by reading the minutes of the Thirteen, at least down to February 18, 1681, old style (the volume covering the remainder of that crucial year has since disappeared). We can in effect sit in on the long meetings, three or four or sometimes even five per week, where the Thirteeners and their legal advisers, the *Advokaten* Frantz, Binder, and Stoesser, debated the pressing issues. Here it is another temporizing message from the emperor which is read and discussed with transparent exasperation; there, a harsh demand from Louvois, that the re-fortification of Kehl be abandoned, for example, or that restitution for war damages be paid to the pro-French Baron de Wangen. These are men still sending one agent after another to Vienna, Regensburg, and other German centers to seek support, still maintaining counsel to represent their interests before the French law court at Breisach, still seeking to find the polite phrases which will mollify Paris without yielding on essentials. But they are also men who are becoming adjusted, as their less informed fellow-citizens outside are not, to the facts of French military power and its relentless advance. A few of them, only a few, may have welcomed that advance, though the documents give no evidence of such sentiments. Most of them were simply accepting with reluctance the idea that, barring a miracle, the old political system of the town, which is presumably what an oligarch means when he says "freedom," could not long survive.

Only one other aspect of this uneasy interval demands attention here, and it is significant that it requires scarcely more than an aside. This is the matter of imperial aid to Strasbourg. The emperor had his own resident, Neveu, in the city; and in May 1681 a special emissary arrived from Vienna, a Baron von Mercy who was to do all in his power to prevent capitulation to France. In addition, Leopold's ministers received the successive counselors sent by the Thirteen, while his delegation at the Diet, led by Dr. Johann von Stratmann, maintained contact with the city's agents in Regensburg.[32] Finally, his ambassador to France, Baron von Mansfeld, who stopped in Strasbourg en route to Paris in August 1680,[33] sought to keep the imperial court informed of the monarchy's intentions and capabilities.[34] The emperor and the Diet were not indifferent to the situation. Strasbourg was voted a special *Römermonat* for its defense costs, to be paid by the various estates of the Empire, while Vienna seemed consistently sympathetic to the appeals of Binder, Stoesser, and the city's other spokesmen.

The campaign for real assistance from the German side, however, was never able to overcome a formidable set of obstacles. One persistent difficulty was that funds pledged either by Regensburg or by Vienna seldom became funds paid. So far as I have been able to discover, the special *Römermonat,* for example, was actually sent to Strasbourg's Pfenningthurn by only a handful of the more sympathetic free cities, such as Nürnberg and Bremen,[35] and by none of the princes at all, while the various subsidies promised by the emperor during the Dutch War were still 22,500 local pounds (*Pfund*) in arrears when discontinued in 1679.[36] Secondly, the emperor again had to face the Turks, who were about to launch their last great offensive up the Danube. Hence those German princes

who had decided to accept French patronage, above all the powerful Elector of Brandenburg, Louis XIV's ally within weeks after
Nymwegen, found it easy to prevent any sustained, general action
in the west.[37] Thirdly, there was the unbridgeable gap between the
imperial generals' desire to put a garrison of their own back into
Strasbourg and the Magistrat's demand that funds be sent so that
mercenaries could be hired by the city itself.[38] While France was
moving quietly, skillfully, and purposefully toward its goal, the
Empire reacted noisily, clumsily, and, in the long run, ineffectually.

In his sermon on January 13, 1681, Dr. Sebastian Schmidt, President of the Church Convocation in Strasbourg, concluded:

> The year which has just ended has been one of uncertain and troubled
> peace, and everyone who has thought at all seriously about things spent
> every day of that year suspended between fear and hope. Not only have
> those who wish us no good begun already to rejoice over our ruin, which
> they consider certain, but even those who have heretofore felt some
> affection for us have almost despaired of our maintenance and preserva-
> tion.[39]

VI

The expedition against Strasbourg is a classic example of the
logistic planning for which Louvois has remained famous. Exactly
when the definite resolution to launch it was taken cannot be fixed
with complete precision. As late as the summer of 1678 the war
minister was still cautioning Marshal Créquy against any rash action with respect to the town, though at the same time forbidding
him to reconstruct its bridge forts, then momentarily in French
hands, so as not to make a siege more difficult "when the time comes
that His Majesty may decide to attack Strasbourg."[40] Three years
later, writing to La Grange, Louvois reminds the intendant at
Breisach that this is an undertaking "which you have known about
since your visit to St-Germain last winter."[41] Since La Grange had
had home leave the preceding March, this would place the final
decision sometime very early in 1681.

Selections from the archives of the Depôt de la Guerre in Paris, published by Coste, by Legrelle, and most fully by Maurer, supply all the documentation needed to follow the main steps in the careful military preparation. On July 29, 1681, Louvois sent instructions to the Lieutenant-general of Artillery, La Frezelière, to start assembling draft horses in Burgundy and to prepare a nationwide inventory of munitions. As in all these orders, the minister kept the ultimate objective completely secret, in this instance telling La Frezelière that "His Majesty might order you into Dauphiné," i.e., southward, in the latter part of September.[42] On August 8, the officer commanding the artillery stables in Alsace was warned to be sure all his equipment was ready for use at a moment's notice.[43] The above-mentioned directive to Intendant La Grange, dated August 14, was the first flat announcement to any official below ministerial rank that the king was now preparing "to subject Strasbourg to obedience between now and the end of the year." An accompanying schedule of bread rations to be stockpiled in Alsace was based on a prospective force of almost thirty-three thousand men.[44] Eight days later, the minister arranged with treasury officials to have thirty thousand *louis d'or* "or good Spanish *pistoles*," for troop pay, packed in six crates and marked as firearms.[45] These were later sent to Besançon and thence smuggled into Alsace.

On August 25, from Fontainebleau where the court was then in residence, Louvois wrote to the king's chief military engineer, Vauban, ordering him to set off for Lyon. Vauban was to let it be understood that he was going to Dauphiné, for a campaign in Italy, but was actually to follow a planned route through small towns, arranging to be in Belfort, eighty-five miles from Strasbourg, not later than October 1 or 2, "so that you can easily get to the place you know about within two days."[46] Then comes the most bizarre touch of all, a letter to La Grange, also dated August 25, concerning the delivery of final operational orders for study and distribution by the royal commandant in Alsace, Baron Joseph de Montclar. These papers, the war minister writes, will arrive at Lure, in Franche-Comté, on the 10th of September. La Grange is to have two of his men, with blue and yellow ribbons on their hats, waiting that day in the cabaret nearest the abbey. Two messengers from the capital will arrive, also wearing blue and yellow hatbands. The intendant's agents are to have ready for presentation a sealed note addressed to "Sieur Mesière," and reading: "I beg you to place in the hands of those who give you this letter the box entrusted to you by M. de Louvois." [47] La Grange, who was waiting with Montclar at Belfort, later reported that these secret documents had been delivered without mishap.[48]

Finally, in mid-September, the veil of secrecy was lifted, so far as the French troop commanders were concerned. A round of orders went out to garrisons in Alsace, Franche-Comté, Burgundy, Champagne, even Flanders; and dozens of selected regiments began to move toward their rendezvous with Montclar. The answer to any idle inquiries along the way was to be a vague reference to routine reinforcement of the southeastern frontier. On September 19, Count von Mansfeld wrote from Fontainebleau to Vienna that troops were definitely on the move, but that he understood their target was Italy. On the 24th, he wrote again of rumors concerning "einem mysteriosen dissegno"; yet he still had no inkling of any plan touching Strasbourg.[49] The very next day Louvois himself slipped away from the court, saying he was off to visit installations in the west, but in fact he rode swiftly toward Alsace.

Louis XIV, of course, moved with more measured dignity.[50] First, he let it be noised about that the court would soon be moving from Fontainebleau to Chambord. The Duc d'Aignan was actually sent on ahead, with various actors, dancers, and musicians, to prepare the usual diversions at that château. Then, without warning, on September 26, the king personally announced to his astonished retinue and to guests, including the luckless Mansfeld, that he intended to depart in four days, not southward to Chambord but eastward to Strasbourg, there to "accept the homage due him." On the 29th, in keeping with the now highly developed techniques of French diplomacy, an official circular went off to the royal ambassadors and ministers accredited to courts all over Europe, setting forth precisely why Louis felt constrained to enforce his "absolute

sovereignty . . . over the whole extent of Upper and Lower Alsace"
and over "the city of Strasbourg which is the capital thereof." [51]
The king's entourage traveled from Fontainebleau to Provins on the
following day, then pushed on majestically across Champagne.

VII

It was about two o'clock on the morning of Sunday, September 28,
when the autumn darkness enveloping Strasbourg suddenly erupted
into wild ringing from the cathedral's alarm bell, the *Mordglock*.
The cause was soon common knowledge: French troops had just assaulted the *Zollschanze,* the little fort about one mile southeast of
the nearest city walls at the entry onto the bridge, and had scattered
the outpost's tiny garrison. While it was still night the other bridge
forts — the half-demolished one at Kehl across the Rhine and the
Rheinschanze on what was then a midstream island — were swiftly
occupied by assailants whose approach had not even been suspected
until they struck.

At dawn the city herald went out to ask for an explanation from
the French commander, who proved to be a Colonel d'Asfeld, sent
by Montclar with three regiments of dragoons to seal off the main
target on the river side. Asfeld had orders to say simply that the
burghers should apply to his superiors for further enlightenment.
As soon as this news came back, the Council of Thirteen composed
and sent off written appeals to Vienna, Frankfurt, and Regensburg,
appeals which were promptly intercepted by French cavalry patrolling both banks of the Rhine.

By afternoon preliminary consultations were over, so that the
Secretary of the Senate, Christoph Güntzer, could be sent to Montclar's field headquarters in Illkirch, a few miles south of town. He
was courteously received by the general but told that the approach of
an imperial army had occasioned this forestalling action by the
French and that, in any event, the city should ponder its duty to the
king. Montclar also announced that the Marquis de Louvois would
be arriving shortly and would expect a delegation of the Magistrat

to wait upon him at Illkirch the next morning at seven. As Güntzer rode home he had ample opportunity to observe the masses of French troops, artillery, and supply wagons crushing into the immediate vicinity of Strasbourg. That night, to observers on the cathedral tower, the whole plain seemed dotted with watchfires, as far as the eye could see.

Monday morning, the 29th, the required delegation, composed of Stettmeister Zedlitz, Ammeister Reisseissen, and again Güntzer, rode out to Illkirch, where they found Louvois awaiting them as predicted. Characteristically, the Marquis wasted few words. He opened with perfunctory references to a threatened assault by forces of the Empire, then got down to business: Strasbourg was the capital of a province ceded to the king in 1648; His Majesty had had enough of its stubborn refusal to recognize his sovereignty while it lent aid and comfort to his enemies; the Magistrat had now only to submit or have their city leveled to the ground, with no quarter given. If the emissaries doubted that such action was possible, let them look around the countryside. Louvois dismissed them with instructions to deliver an answer by evening, though he later agreed to allow a postponement until the following morning because of Strasbourg's involved constitutional provisions for making a decision of such moment.

The Thirteen had in fact decided that in this instance they must go to the people, or at least to the three hundred Assemblymen, meeting separately in their twenty different guildhalls. During the rest of that morning of the 29th special prayer services were held, speeches were delivered from the ramparts (by the special imperial envoy, Mercy, among others) and a second, frankly despairing letter from the Magistrat was dispatched, this time successfully, to the emperor.[52] While all this was going on, someone in the inner counsels (probably Advocate Frantz) drew up a memorandum to serve as a basis for the impending discussion and vote by the Assemblymen. No other surviving document better summarizes the situation or conveys so well the agonized atmosphere in which this, the last genuinely free decision of the republic, was made. It is a memorandum of superficial precision, with its numbered rubrics and subheadings; but its language and its repetitions are indicative of the haste and strong emotion which must have attended its composition.[53]

After bringing members of the Three Hundred up to date on the military position and the negotiations conducted thus far, the paper sets forth three alternatives open to the municipality. It might resist to the limit. For this choice one could argue that French armies had sometimes treated freely surrendered cities even worse than bravely defended ones; that capitulation would presumably mean the loss of political independence, religious self-determination, and stored material resources; that to become a border fortress of France would either make the city an accomplice in future crimes against "our dear fatherland, the Holy Roman Empire," or else, if it were too weakly held by its new rulers, the victim of attacks by the same dear fatherland. Furthermore, the emperor, the Empire, the local citizenry itself, as well as all Protestants everywhere would view surrender as betrayal; that God sometimes employed a small David to humble a proud Goliath; that maybe, just maybe, the French were bluffing and would retire before a show of firmness.

Second, the Assemblymen could vote to yield. The military strength of France was great and imminent. Strasbourg had on hand, for the defense of fourteen different bastions and the intervening ramparts, only five hundred trained mercenaries, of whom many were ill, plus a militia shrunken by the absence of numerous citizens at the Frankfurt fair. There was no real hope of relief from outside. If the walls were successfully stormed, the populace would be at the mercy of furious French regulars, whose reputation offered little promise that anyone would be spared, "even unto babes in the womb." And of course, timely surrender might yet save some of the town's liberties if decent terms could be arranged.

Finally, and somewhat half-heartedly, the tract offers a third possible course: limited resistance, without intent to fight to the finish, but with hope of better terms after an initial clash. However, the writer points out, this might also result in no terms at all, in treatment simply as rebels and felons. With more French regiments arriving all the time, the odds would get worse for the burghers with every new onset. In any case, Louvois was not apt to be more generous after bloodshed than before.

"And now," concludes the memorandum, in effect, "it is up to you to decide." There seems to have been some early inclination toward the third alternative, a token defense. As the afternoon and evening wore on, however, and as debate slowly brought out the full extent of the physical danger faced by the isolated city, the Assemblymen swung toward less heroic expedients. The final tally showed only one member of the Three Hundred, a seventy-year-old tailor, still in favor of resistance.

Thus the matter came back to the Thirteen, who had now to draft the best set of terms they felt Louvois could be induced to accept. This time we know it was Frantz who had the task of composition, working all night in the Council's chamber at the Pfalz, amid a city grown suddenly quiet after the tumult of the day. From his house the French resident wrote to Louvois: "It is midnight, and there is not a sound in the streets. All the burghers must be on the ramparts." [54]

The document signed the next morning, Tuesday, the 30th, in a house at Illkirch unquestionably surprised the townsmen, who had expected much more trouble over details.[55] Louvois simply read the draft prepared by Frantz, scrawled "Granted" in the margin beside some of the ten articles and beside others noted modifications on which the crown would insist. The city recognized His Most Christian Majesty as its sovereign lord and protector. The king confirmed the municipality's privileges and customs, promised to permit the free observance of Lutheran worship, and pledged himself to maintain the town government in its existing form. Strasbourg was to continue to collect all its own revenues, was to build barracks to relieve the citizens of billeting garrison troops, and was to be exempt from personal taxation by the crown. A general amnesty was to be extended to local inhabitants and to the imperial representatives. All this was accorded as drafted by Frantz. Louvois, on his side, imposed the insertion of several clauses which, though few in number, clearly revealed the primary concerns of the royal government. The cathedral must be returned to the bishop and reconsecrated for Catholic worship. Legal judgments by city courts in matters involving more than two thousand French livres could henceforth be appealed to the Sovereign Council of Alsace. All armaments, including privately owned firearms, were to be surrendered to the officers of His Majesty. And finally, the king's forces were to enter Strasbourg at four o'clock that same afternoon.

Back into town rode the emissaries, bearing the news that after all much had been salvaged from the catastrophe. Louvois dispatched a jubilant announcement, with a copy of the capitulation, to meet Louis XIV, then sent off other couriers post haste to turn back the unneeded regiments still moving up from distant bases.

Promptly at the appointed hour the Butchers' Gate in the south wall of the city swung open to admit the first French garrison of Strasbourg, some 5,500 men from Montclar's forces. As the infantry battalions filed in they turned sharply right or left, taking up positions around the whole perimeter of fortifications. The three squadrons of cavalry, however, clattered directly through the streets to bivouac in the Barfüsserplatz, today the Place Kléber. The crowds of onlookers appear to have been neither jubilant nor overtly hostile, but primarily curious. Most of the citizens must have been comforted by the thought that at least these troops were entering with lances at rest and sabers sheathed. A note of comedy, not untouched by pathos, was supplied by the city's old troop commander, who galloped about shouting directions in German at the French officers, until Louvois suggested, through an interpreter, that he take the rest of the day off, lest some Gascon or Picard become irritated and run him through.

VIII

Louis XIV was at Vitry-le-François when Louvois' message reached him on October 2, and he decided to remain there until the ladies and non-military gentlemen of the court could join what would now become a triumphal procession. He ratified the capitulation at once, however, and returned it to Louvois, with words of high praise for the minister, for Montclar and for Asfeld.[56] By October 6, the rest of the court arrived: the Queen, the Dauphin and the Dauphine, the Duc and Duchesse d'Orléans, Bishop Bossuet, Mesdames de Montespan and de Maintenon (the reigning mistress and her future successor), as well as the Princesse de Conti, daughter of the king by still another mistress, La Vallière. As always, there was present a journalistically inclined courtier, in this case the Avignonese Abbé Esprit Fléchier, Almoner to the Dauphin, whose letters to Madame Des Houlières, back in Paris, give a good account of the party's glittering progress into Alsace.[57] By October 14 the king had reached Sélestat, thirty miles south of Strasbourg, and on the next day he received a deputation from the Magistrat of the newly occupied city. Louis was properly paternal toward the kneeling burghers, but informed them that he would delay his own entry until the bishop could arrive and prepare the cathedral for the proper ceremonies. Thereafter, the court made a leisurely tour of Upper Alsace and even crossed the Rhine to inspect Breisach and Freiburg, before at last starting northward toward Strasbourg.

Meanwhile, on the 20th, François-Egon de Furstemberg, Bishop of Strasbourg, always a faithful protégé of the French monarch and now at last returned in triumph to his see after years as guest and agent of the Archbishop of Cologne, made his entry between two companies of cuirassiers. The next day he proceeded to reconsecrate the great temple "so long defiled by Lutheran rites." Finally, on the 23rd, came the great day: the king himself, in a procession of carefully arranged splendor, amid the booming of over 250 cannon, rode into the city, and took up residence in the princely mansion of Baden-Durlach. Next day monarch and court were formally welcomed at the main portal of the cathedral by the bishop, then attended the *Te Deum* sung within. The remainder of Louis' visit was devoted to reviewing troops and receiving congratulatory visits from prelates such as the Archbishop of Reims, Cardinal Bouillon, the

Bishops of Beauvais and Basel, as well as from German dignitaries: the Elector Palatine, representatives of the three archbishop-electors and even a delegation from the supreme court at Speyer.

Long before the king departed for Saverne on October 27, carefully composed messages of pride and rejoicing flooded in from all over France. The fact that Casale in Italy had also been occupied on September 30 made it easy to portray Louis as an ambidextrous Caesar, who did not even have to come and see in order to conquer. J. Joly sent a long poem from Paris, suggesting that His Majesty would shortly, in the very heart of Germany, prove himself the reincarnation of both Clovis and Charlemagne.[58] And as though Roman and Frankish metaphors were not enough, the presidial tribunal of Meaux turned to the Bible, writing ecstatically: "Sire, the submission of the city of Strasbourg to Your Majesty's authority is an event more glorious for France than was the taking of the city of Jericho for the Hebrews of old!"[59] Yet the medal which was struck to commemorate this achievement maintained a properly non-aggressive tone in the legend it bore: "Clausa Germanis Gallia." France did indeed seem closed to the Germans. Germany, on the other hand, had never stood so wide open to the French.

IX

Much was written in the nineteenth century, beginning with a famous article by Scherer in Raumer's *Historisches Taschenbuch* of 1843, "Strasbourg's Betrayal," to show that the Magistrat was not compelled to yield but had sold out in advance to French bribery. It was pointed out by various angry scholars that later in 1681 Louis XIV ordered his goldsmith to prepare two chains for presentation to a pair of unnamed Strasbourgers; that Christoph Güntzer, after having played an active part in the surrender negotiation, was almost immediately given a special appointment as royal syndic; and that French diplomats at Frankfurt that autumn, awaiting the opening of the conference on *réunions,* spoke openly to the Emperor's Dr. Stratmann and other Germans about the capitulation's having been amicably arranged. Numerous contemporaries accepted the treason theory without question.[60]

This explanation of the event, however, finds almost no support among the writers of our own century. The presentation of gold chains by a Bourbon monarch, for example, was about as significant as a modern government's bestowal of a few decorations or orders, to celebrate a state visit. Anyone who believes that the Council of Thirteen was riddled with treason should note that not a single voting member of that body, as constituted in 1681, received any additional offices or emoluments after the capitulation. It is true that Stettmeister Zedlitz and one or two others had reputations for being "pro-French"; but the "imperialists" were always numerous enough to more than outmatch them, while neutralists like Dietrich and Reisseissen formed a majority, save for the imperialists' brief triumph in 1678. In the closing months of the Dutch War, La Loubère, the French resident, informed Paris that so far as he could see, not a single Senator had been won over to France.[61] The city fathers simply kept hoping that, by constantly reasserting the rights of a neutral, they could avoid occupation by the French *or* the imperials.

There remain the figure of Güntzer and the claims of French diplomats after the event. As for the opportunistic Secretary of the Senate, he was indeed one of the Strasbourgers who gained political advancement by virtue of the capitulation; but it should be remembered that he was used in the negotiations almost solely because he knew French. In 1681 he was still a relatively minor official with little chance to influence policy decisions by the Thirteen. Nor is the evidence of remarks passed at the Frankfurt Conference that autumn any more impressive. Of course the French envoys in Germany hinted at a sell-out of Strasbourg.[62] It was in the king's immediate interest that potential indignation against him be confused and diverted by such suspicions. Here is how Louvois outlined the policy in a letter to the royal mission at Frankfurt:

. . . It would do no harm, it seems to me, if you would talk in whatever manner you feel would be most apt to excite suspicion on the part of deputies who are in Frankfurt that the attack on this stronghold had been previously agreed upon with the city's Magistrat, which desired a pretext to induce the common people to submit to His Majesty.[63]

No, the Magistrat's memorandum to the Three Hundred before the voting on September 29, the farewell message dispatched to the emperor that same day, the memoirs of Ammeisters Reisseissen and Wencker, the accounts written by Frantz soon after the event and by his fellow Advocate, Stoesser, some years later, all tell the same story of yielding to overwhelming force. Especially when read in combination, they all ring true.[64] Louis XIV and Louvois did not corrupt the Strasbourg government, because they did not need to. They simply terrified it into submission, incidentally terrifying much of the rest of Germany at the same time. They did not bother to upset the internal arrangements unduly, instead they granted a liberal set of terms, because Strasbourg was from their point of view primarily a strategic military position. The cathedral must return to its bishop, to be sure, and the Magistrat must bow to its new suzerain. Otherwise, at least for the moment, let these touchy burghers keep their strange constitution, their barbarous language, and even their misguided religion! The main thing was that henceforth French troops would be patrolling the ramparts and French guns commanding the bridge.

CHAPTER THREE

Fortress of France

I

Three men who figure prominently in the annals of seventeenth-century Europe, a tactician, an administrator, and an engineer, did most to establish French military power under Louis XIV. Thus, to appreciate the strategic importance of Strasbourg, one need only observe that the city's destiny was touched at critical points by all three. It was Turenne whose maneuvers saved Alsace for the armies of the king in 1674–5. It was Louvois whose meticulous preparations culminated in the thunderbolt of 1681. Neither the field commander nor the minister, however, left as significant an imprint on the community as did Marshal Sébastien Le Prestre de Vauban. What Turenne had kept accessible and what Louvois had seized was entrusted to Vauban to make secure.

Even before Strasbourg was taken on September 30, he had arrived in Belfort as directed, and he quickly covered the remaining eighty-five miles upon receipt of Louvois' summons. Hence, the royal battalions were scarcely settled in their new billets when practiced eyes and a powerful mind were brought to bear on the problem of future defense. While the local Magistrat, under the direction of the military governor, Chamilly, began the construction of permanent barracks for the garrison, Vauban was busy inspecting the walls and tramping over the ground between the city and its Rhine bridge. The skill and experience which went into this project emerge clearly from the report prepared by the marshal himself after his initial survey. The manuscript, now at the Bibliothèque Nationale in Paris,[1] begins with notes on the distances separating Strasbourg from a number of French, German, and Swiss towns, then goes on to analyze in detail the present state of its defenses, including topography, hydrography, and available construction materials. Criticisms of the existing fortifications follow in quick succession. The gap where the Ill flows out of the city is a vulnerable point, where French troops could most easily have stormed the place if an attack had been necessary to secure its capitulation. The moats are too shallow and the walls too weak in numerous sectors. The protective glacis is not wide enough and is too steeply banked.

Nevertheless, Vauban's memorandum continues, the old works, taken as a whole, are the product of much care and foresight, providing an excellent basis for improvements. Subject to the king's approval, weak points in the walls are to be strengthened and the moats dredged. The glacis embankment can easily be deepened and given a slant better calculated to deflect enemy cannon fire. The walled salients should be extended at various points. On the north and west, two small bastions, the Fort de Pierre and the Fort Blanc should be built into the parapets by the Stone and White Tower Gates. But most important, a whole new citadel should be erected to the southeast, between the town and the bridge, completely dominating both. Across the Rhine, the Kehl fort is to be expanded, as is the blockhouse on the midstream island. On another small island a new emplacement will make any hostile crossing still more difficult.

Once all this work was completed — and it went forward at a rate which both amazed and exhausted the townspeople — Strasbourg was converted into a gigantic porcupine.[2] The city, though it had never been taken by storm, could have been in 1681, by such an army as Louvois had assembled.[3] When Vauban had finished, it was again virtually impregnable to direct attack. The citadel, connected to the town by a walled esplanade, obviously offered the crown a special advantage by placing the burghers themselves permanently at the mercy of royal commanders. Vauban, however, scoffed at any danger of local revolt. For him, as always, the end in view was a star-shaped complex of strongpoints and angling façades which no enemy could assault without instantly coming under a raking fire from other parapets.

Louis XIV came back to Alsace in June 1683 and devoted one full day to inspecting the new fortifications. In the morning he avoided the city itself, reining up outside the Butchers' Gate, on his way to the citadel and Kehl, just long enough to give the waiting representatives of the town government a curt assurance that "he was happy to accord them these proofs of his affection." Only at the end of the day did he ride into town for a brief tour of the walls, then galloped off with his party to spend the night in the Capuchin monastery at Molsheim.[4] The king, who was then in his most devout period, clearly showed his disapproval of his Lutheran subjects; but he had reason to be delighted with the state of his most recently acquired fortress. Strasbourg might still be lost as a result of distant battles and general peace settlements, but it was not going to be taken from Louis as he had taken it in 1681.

II

For more than a generation after it was annexed by France, the "royal free city," as it now styled itself, was to occupy an important place in European diplomacy, recognized as a crucial issue in negotiations among all the great powers of the age. Its full significance in this setting, however, could not emerge immediately after 1681, because of the conflicting interests and motivations then operative on the continent and across the Channel.

The emperor himself learned the news of Strasbourg's capitulation a week after it was signed, when the Magistrat's farewell letter of September 29, followed shortly by a circumstantial report from the imperial resident, caught up with him at the Hungarian Diet in Sopron.[5] Leopold was already facing an uproar in that assembly; word had just reached him that the Turks were advancing into Styria; Casale in Italy had been lost to the Hapsburgs on the same day as Strasbourg. Comments by imperial officials covered a wide range. Bishop Count Kollonitsch, chief of Vienna's delegation to Sopron remarked, in the hearing of the Dutch envoy, "Let the Lutheran fools dance to the piper!" [6] Much more general was the reaction of anger at Strasbourg's alleged treason, mixed with incipient panic. France, it was felt, might now attack Ulm and the rest of Swabia. What if the Dauphin were put forward as heir to the imperial throne?

A paralyzing wave of fear and uncertainty dominated other German centers in the autumn of 1681. At Frankfurt, where the long-delayed conference on French territorial *réunions* still had not opened, the assembled German delegates privately traded opinions as to whether Worms or Trier would be the next city to fall. Cologne was full of rumors that a French army was on its way.[7] The court of Hesse-Darmstadt sent out anguished appeals for support in defending its territory, while even its sister capital of Kassel, where less proximity to French power made for more truculence, temporarily adopted a cautious tone.[8] Once it was apparent that Louis XIV intended no further action for the time being, official circles in the Empire subsided into a more or less sullen relief which offered little hope for early counter-measures against France.

That the Empire should be thus immobilized was not the result of sheer chance. Beginning with the royal circular issued at Fontainebleau while Strasbourg was already surrounded, the elaborate mechanism of French diplomacy had gone smoothly into action. The customary mixture was applied: soothing assurances, thinly veiled threats, and quite open appeals to the cupidity of rulers and selected ministers. Sebbeville at Vienna, Delahaye at Munich, Rousseau at Dresden, Bidal at Hamburg, Foucher at Mainz, not to mention a number of touring envoys, such as Bourgeauville, d'Arcy, and Schomberg, all performed their tasks with admirable synchronization.[9] The most formidable German prince, Frederick William of Brandenburg, was indeed upset by the news from Strasbourg, which reached Berlin on October 9, 1681, but only, as he told his councilors, because "this could throw all Germany into the arms of the emperor." The French minister at his court, Rébenac, reported: "They may make a lot of noise here, but it will come to nothing." Within a few days the Great Elector was again cheerfully discussing the possibility of French support for his claims to Swedish Pomerania.[10] Louis XIV could thus count on good will or inaction from no fewer than five of the eight electors: Brandenburg, Mainz, Trier, Cologne, and the Palatine of the Rhine.

Spokesmen for the king were equally effective in neutralizing any immediate danger of interference by powers outside the Empire.[11] D'Avaux at The Hague could boast of good relations with the republican party, while in Switzerland Gravel encountered no seriously hostile reaction to the circular of September 29. In Stockholm, it is true, officials were still angry and belligerent over the French occupation of the Swedish king's own Duchy of Zweibrücken, as well as over Louis XIV's treaty with Brandenburg; but the defensive agreement concluded between the Swedes and the Dutch Stadholder on the very day Strasbourg fell was only a small cloud on the Sun King's horizon. As for England, Charles II was in the pay of France, and no Englishman wanted to die for the Upper Rhine.

By 1684 the French grip on Alsace seemed secure. Article 4 of the Truce of Regensburg, concluded that year, specifically stated that "His Most Christian Majesty remains in the free and peaceful possession of the city of Strasbourg, the fortress of Kehl, and the other forts situated on the Rhine between the said city and the said fortress," together with all territories annexed by reunions up to August 1, 1681.[12] Thus France found itself confirmed in de facto possession of the whole fortified belt it had created on the left bank of the Rhine, as well as its three bridgeheads on the right bank, Breisach-Freiburg south of Strasbourg, Kehl directly to the east, and the shore installations opposite the island Fort Louis some twenty miles to the north.

Nevertheless, this position on the imperial frontier was not quite so safe as it appeared. The trouble, from Versailles' point of view, was that it could be lost if some future war were to undermine the French position in Europe as a whole. Furthermore, it is often taken for granted that in the late seventeenth century the French viewed

German power as negligible, an object for their unqualified contempt. Actually, the potential strength of the Empire, if it were ever to be mobilized, was a source of genuine concern for the royal ministers. While they were happy to feed on German disunity, their nervously defensive tone, even in 1681–1684, was never altogether fraudulent. The emperor and his allies had managed to turn back the Turks in 1683, and the long Hapsburg offensive down the Danube was underway. Hence, any signs of resurgent German confidence and resentment against France were to be taken with the utmost seriousness.

We know from numerous monographs that Strasbourg's fall and the subsequent humiliation of the Regensburg concessions touched off a storm of anti-French indignation among the literate classes of the Empire. The output of hostile pamphlet literature reached a new high.[13] Admittedly, such expressions could influence French-subsidized princes and ministers only if and when patriotism began to look profitable. Not that the wrath of publicists was necessarily an expression of public opinion in any present-day sense of the term; but the views of a wide variety of German-speaking individuals might under certain circumstances awaken significant echoes in the chancelleries. Louis XIV's own sister-in-law, Duchess Elizabeth Charlotte of Orléans, born a princess of the Palatinate, wrote to her brother after the royal tour of Alsace in 1681:

> I wished with all my heart that it might have been possible for me to embrace you at Strasbourg. I believe we should have had a good cry together [*miteinander geheüllet haben*]. When I was driven by the Oxen Inn, it occurred to me how I had last seen His Grace the Elector [their father] there. Tears came upon me so violently that I could not hold them back.[14]

It is clear from other remarks of the Duchess that she was not overcome simply by familial nostalgia. Another reaction, similarly private but equally genuine, showed that not all German Catholics viewed with equanimity the humbling of Protestant Strasbourg. Prior Hieronymus Ziegler of the nearby Benedictine monastery of Gengenbach in Baden listened to the rumble of cannon saluting

The Strasbourg Customhouse in 1630 by Hollar

Franziskus Reisseissen
1631–1710

Johann Leonhard Froereissen
1629–1690

Jakob Wencker
1633–1715

Daniel Richshoffer
1640–1695

SEVENTEENTH-CENTURY AMMEISTERS

Louis XIV's triumphal entry after the capitulation and then inscribed in the chronicle of his community: "Foolish is he who thinks the King of France a slave to his pledged word!" [15]

The translation into action of sentiments such as these had to await a more general recognition that German princes and cities were themselves facing apparently endless demands from Versailles. As early as June 1682 the Dutch agent at Vienna managed to bring a number of medium and small west-German states into an agreement with the emperor, the so-called "Laxenburg alliance" for the defense of the Rhine frontier.[16] This abortive effort could not overcome the objections of Brandenburg and other pro-French parties, or the distractions of the Turkish invasion; but it pointed the way to a new form of arrangement between Vienna and the most exposed of the ten *Kreise* or imperial districts. It foreshadowed the appearance in 1686 of the League of Augsburg, linking the emperor, the King of Spain for the Burgundian Circle, the King of Sweden for his German holdings, the Franconian and Upper-Rhenish Circles as a whole, the Elector Palatine, and the Elector of Bavaria, together with several less important estates of the Reich. This was a loose alliance at best, but it comprised several principalities long accustomed to bow before Louis XIV. Furthermore, with the Turks in full retreat, it marked the end of post-1681 apathy and the beginning of more than twenty-five years of vicissitudes for France, which were repeatedly to bring the Empire within a hair's breadth of recovering Strasbourg.

III

The first diplomatic negotiations in which a possible French surrender of Strasbourg occupied a central place were those culminating in the Ryswick settlement of 1697. The War of the League of Augsburg — or the War of the Palatinate, as German usage has it — began in the summer of 1688 with what Louvois had mistakenly assured Louis XIV would be a brief thrust toward Heidelberg to cow the Empire. The king was at the time seeking to enforce the claims of his sister-in-law to at least a share in the Palatinate succession. He was also attempting to overcome both German and Papal resistance to the naming of one of his most dependable protégés as Archbishop-elector of Cologne. Appropriately enough, it was Guillaume-Egon de Furstemberg, brother of the deceased François-Egon and his successor as Bishop of Strasbourg, whom Louis hoped to place in the even more powerful chair to the north.[17]

This time, however, the Empire did not crumple. It fought back, led in the field by an unusually able commander, Margrave Ludwig Wilhelm of Baden, "Türkenlouis," as he was called in honor of his victories against Ottoman armies. Worse still, William of Orange established himself and his Stuart wife on the throne of England, whence the Sun King's most tireless foe was able to direct both Dutch and English power against France. As early as 1691 the vast commitments involved in simultaneous warfare against the Empire and the Maritime Powers, not to mention Sweden, Spain, and Savoy, forced Louis to recognize the exhausted state of his long-triumphant nation. He had to negotiate, and he had to offer enough to make negotiation attractive to his enemies. From then on, while French armies went on fighting pitched battles at a cost which they could not indefinitely sustain, the chancelleries buzzed with projects and secret communications.[18]

Much of the preliminary, as well as the final, negotiating centered on Strasbourg, as was inevitable, given the importance attached to it by both French and German leaders. In August 1696, Elector Frederick III of Brandenburg, who had followed the line adopted by his father after 1684 in repudiating the French alliance, advised the emperor that Strasbourg must be recovered, "no matter what equivalent might be offered in its stead." [19] A few months later, during the summer of 1696, the Margrave of Baden wrote to Vienna:

For Germany this city would serve as nothing but a permanent insurance of peace. For France, however, it is an open gateway for war, though which [that nation], whenever it chooses, can break loose its power into the open country.[20]

The question of equivalents was critical, since the French were desperately pressing other offers which might serve to distract imperial attention. Pomponne had drafted a memorandum for Louis XIV in 1693, stating that alternative concessions would doubtless satisfy Vienna and remarking: "If there is one essential advantage, it is that of keeping Strasbourg; all the rest is of infinitely less importance." [21] This view was supported by the military judgment of Vauban. On September 13, 1696, he wrote to the poet, Racine:

> To surrender a Rhine crossing and location of Strasbourg's size and strength, worth more than all the rest of Alsace, would mean relinquishing to the Germans the finest and most secure arsenal in Europe.[22]

Three days later, in a memorandum to Michel Le Pelletier, Director-general of Fortifications, the marshal spelled out his views more fully:

> Strasbourg is the more considerable in its present state because I perceive no power in Europe capable of surrounding it, with the Kehl fortress. . . . The excellence of its fortifications make it practically invincible, assuming defense by a garrison of ten to twelve thousand men, well-supplied and commanded by people of common intelligence.

And then follows a particularly telling argument for the ear of Louis XIV:

> With Strasbourg the King can call himself sovereign in Alsace, but without it he would always be weak, at best considered no more than a great nobleman of the region.[23]

Yet, when the formal peace congress opened on May 9, 1697, in the Dutch castle of Nieuwberg near Ryswick, the French delegates knew that Strasbourg's fate was still in the balance. Facing them were English, Dutch, Spanish, and imperial negotiators (Savoy and Sweden having by this time retired from the hostilities). Furthermore, around the emperor's own mission, Kaunitz, Seilern, and the younger Stratmann, were grouped other German representatives of individual Kreise and principalities. Leopold's instructions to his spokesmen required them to press for Strasbourg, Freiburg, Haguenau, Wissembourg, Landau, and all lands taken by French reunions, as well as for the unconditional reëstablishment of the House of Lorraine in its hereditary duchy.

It is indicative of the situation after almost nine years of war that France felt compelled to go a long way toward meeting these demands. Nevertheless, the sweeping French project delivered to the Swedish mediator on July 20 retained two characteristics of Louis XIV's diplomacy in its palmier days. First, the Empire was simply offered a choice: *either* Strasbourg *or* Freiburg, Breisach, and all other French emplacements east of the Rhine. Second, Vienna was to reply by August 31. Failing that, the king would consider himself released from even this qualified offer.

The ensuing six weeks have turned out to be one of the most angrily debated periods in the history of the Holy Roman Empire. There was disagreement at the time, between those who, like Leopold's Bohemian Court Chancellor, Count Kinsky, insisted on holding out for all the envisaged concessions, and a group including Ludwig of Baden, who favored taking Strasbourg while it was available. There has been disagreement ever since, between German historians who blame the emperor for allegedly having sacrificed the Reich to Hapsburg family interests and other German scholars who maintain that Vienna was at worst taking a reasonable chance in rejecting the whole idea of a choice imposed by France.

The most recent and most thorough study of the imperial side, that by Srbik, makes out a good case for Emperor Leopold.[24] A narrow Hapsburg policy would actually have dictated not intransigence but prompt acceptance of Freiburg and Breisach, since these had belonged to one of the family's own domains, the Breisgau. Instead, the emperor appears to have taken a firm position during July and August 1697, partly because he felt it was his duty to the Empire to do so; partly because Kinsky was urging him to avoid any hasty, yielding peace which might prejudice Vienna's future claims to the Spanish succession; and partly because a marriage between Louis XIV's niece, Mademoiselle de Chartres, and Leopold's son, Joseph — at the time considered quite possible — held out hope of a much more favorable settlement than France had yet offered.

Whatever the decisive reason or reasons, Vienna let the specified period expire without accepting either of the proffered choices; and promptly on September 1, Callières announced for France that Strasbourg could no longer be considered a subject for negotiation. Louis XIV, having assured himself of an imminent peace with his other enemies, would now concede to the emperor only the alternative set of terms proposed in July. This time the Allies were given until September 20 to accept or reject the draft treaty. Up to a week before the new deadline, the imperials were still talking of continuing the war, necessarily assuming that England, Holland, and Spain would agree to maintain the military pressure. Instead, all three signed with France on the 20th, as demanded by Louis. The English, Dutch, and Spanish stipulated only that Vienna be given until November 1 to adhere to the peace, if it so desired. Finally, on October 30, Kaunitz and his colleagues signed for Emperor Leopold, terminating all hostilities.

The Germans actually gained a good deal. Philippsburg was restored as an imperial fortress; Freiburg and Breisach came back to the emperor; Kehl was accepted by the Empire as a whole, then in 1699 assigned by the Diet to the House of Baden-Baden, whose margrave would hereafter face Strasbourg directly across the Rhine bridge. The Duchy of Zweibrücken and the Archbishopric of Trier were evacuated by French troops, as were the towns in the Palatinate formerly occupied under reunion judgments. Lorraine was restored to its duke, subject to less extensive rights of military passage than France had enjoyed before 1670. But one great prize was not won. Strasbourg, despite all the announced determination to recover it, was still subject to the king at Versailles. In fact, Article 16 of the Treaty of Ryswick provided for its *de jure* cession to Louis XIV, thereby legalizing the state of affairs which had in fact existed since 1681.[25]

As in so many other instances, it is hard to estimate the degree of disappointment which this settlement produced within the Reich. About all one can say with confidence is that reactions were extremely mixed. Numerous complaints arose at once from tireless pamphleteers, and the western Circles or districts expressed through various spokesmen their renewed feeling of insecurity. On the other hand, Catholic opinion in Germany was still, even at this date, by no means unanimously hostile to the pious works of Louis XIV. Leopold himself had accepted without protest the last-minute addition of the "Ryswick clause," specifying that Catholicism must be maintained in all areas retroceded by France, though this clearly violated the settlement of 1648. There would always be echoes of Bishop Kollonitsch's preference for letting Lutherans "dance to the piper." In 1698, for example, the Magistrat of Frankfurt am Main discovered and confiscated two printings of a satirical half-German and half-Latin poem, written or at least put in definitive form by a Dominican friar in Mainz and entitled "The Empire's Final Farewell to Strasbourg." Although ostensibly addressed to the lost city, with an appended reply from the latter, the doggerel verses were actually an attack on the Protestant or semi-Protestant free cities still within the Empire. There was praise only for the emperor and for Cologne (the latter scarcely a standard-bearer against France), while Augsburg, Regensburg, Nürnberg, Frankfurt, Ulm, Worms, Speyer, and Hamburg all received unflattering treatment in turn. Strasbourg was in this case not being mourned, only used as a pretext.[26]

The international issue, however, was far from settled. In 1707 the former Strasbourg law professor and *Advokat* for the city's Council of Thirteen, Dr. Friedrich Schrag, who had accepted a post as imperial assessor at Wetzlar after emigrating in 1698, published two aggressive treatises: *Libertas Argentoratensis stylo Ryswicensi non expuncta* and *Nullitas iniquitasque reunionis Alsatiae*. By the time these legal briefs appeared, a new and greater war was in progress, which offered the Empire a second big chance to recover Strasbourg.

IV

There is no need here to recount the complicated diplomatic maneuvering which preceded the War of the Spanish Succession, nor to follow in detail the farflung military operations it involved. It is enough, for present purposes, to observe that beginning in 1702 the revival of the Grand Alliance against France inevitably raised once again the question of Alsace in general and Strasbourg in particular. This time, German demands were put forward not only by the emperor in Vienna but also by a recognized grouping of princes and cities especially interested in the creation of a secure "Reich barrier" on the Rhine. At Nördlingen, on March 20, 1702, a defensive instrument was signed by representatives of the Franconian, Swabian, Upper-Rhenish, and Electoral-Rhenish Circles, and adhered to by the emperor himself, on behalf of the Austrian Circle, to which southern Alsace had formerly belonged. Thus one-half of the Empire's ten *Kreise* joined together as a negotiating unit in opposition to France; and the Margrave of Baden accepted his final military assignment, that of building an army out of units from over two hundred participating estates.[27] This "Association of the Five Circles" maintained its own representation at all the major conferences of the ensuing decade.[28]

As in the 1690's, so again in the bloody years of Blenheim, Turin, Ramillies, and Oudenarde, nationwide misery drove Louis XIV toward costly renunciations, to secure the peace France needed. While Versailles moved dejectedly in the direction of concessions, the Allies raised their sights correspondingly. By the spring of 1709, both Vienna and Berlin (the latter because of its Swiss claims based on Neuchâtel and the Orange patrimony) were savoring the possibility of acquiring even Franche-Comté, lost by Spain at Nymwegen thirty years before.[29] Simultaneously, the Five Circles, from their April assembly in Frankfurt, advised the Dutch Pensionary, Heinsius, that they would press for the total retrocession of Alsace.[30] The Maritime Powers, through Marlborough and Heinsius, presumably would support at least a return to the boundaries of 1648.

Right here, however, even before the start of serious bargaining, it is possible to perceive ultimately fatal weaknesses in the imperial position with regard to Alsace. The Allies were not at any time

unequivocally committed to a clear program of cessions to be imposed upon France; and aside from the successive general conferences, which he could not avoid, Louis XIV made skillful use of
separate negotiations with London and Amsterdam. Equally serious,
there were some officials even in Vienna who did not share the Five
Circles' preoccupation with the Rhineland. Bohemian Court Chancellor Wratislaw, for example, discreetly informed the Austrian
delegation at The Hague early in 1709 that Hapsburg *Hauspolitik*
should not be encumbered with "extensive demands on behalf of
the Empire." [31] Specifically, Emperor Joseph's representatives were
told not to recognize even Alsace and the Sundgau as equivalents
for Sicily. This did not mean that Strasbourg should not be accepted, and gladly; but it did mean that recovery of the city stood
lower than several other items on the Hapsburg priority list, now
that the Spanish domains were up for division.

One further obstacle to German diplomatic success should be
borne in mind: the continuing French military grip on Alsace. The
imperials took Landau in 1702, lost it in 1703, retook it in 1704,
finally lost it again in 1713. In 1705 Louis XIV's forces seemed to
have no secure base left in the province save Strasbourg itself; but
the next year Marshal Villars succeeded in driving the polyglot
army of the Five Circles back across the Rhine, actually pursuing it
into Swabia in 1707. As always, there remained the possibility that
losses elsewhere would compel France to surrender Alsace. Nevertheless, the protracted discussions in Holland lacked reality as long
as they were unsupported by local military victories for the Reich.

The various peace projects of 1709–1714, spelled out in countless
diplomatic histories, reveal the stages by which Strasbourg again
slipped through the fingers of the Empire.[32] The forty-point ultima-
tum, the famous "Preliminaries of The Hague," delivered to Colbert
de Torcy by Heinsius on May 27, 1709, stipulated the return of
Strasbourg and French evacuation of all positions on the right bank
of the Rhine. Torcy himself informs us in his memoirs that he had
been empowered by Louis XIV to accept these points, if absolutely
necessary,[33] though he snatched in vain at a suggestion, first made,

then withdrawn, by one of the Dutch spokesmen, Van der Dussen, that the free city might perhaps be neutralized with a Swiss garrison. German delegates were at this point too confident of their bargaining position to entertain any such proposals. Even Wratislaw in Vienna expected Strasbourg's gates to be opened to an imperial occupation force within a month to six weeks.[34] The French negotiators returned to Versailles resigned to this portion of the terms.

As things turned out, however, peace was still distant. On June 2, less than a week after they were presented, the Preliminaries of The Hague were rejected by Louis XIV, specifically because they would have required him to assist in expelling his own grandson, Philip V, from Spain. Yet the king could not turn his back on diplomacy. After Malplaquet that September, Marshal Villars advised the court that "the nation itself is exposed to the risks of a single battle." [35] So in March 1710, France went back to the conference table, this time at another Dutch town, Gertruydenberg. Even before this meeting, in a declaration of January 2, Louis again offered both Strasbourg and Landau to the Empire, and again the multiple German interests combined to reject the offer. Vienna now assumed recovery of Strasbourg to be a safe minimum, which could be taken for granted without jeopardizing more extensive aspirations. Once more, however, peace negotiations collapsed over the Allies' demand that the French king help liquidate the Spanish succession he had himself sponsored.

During the two years which remained before the decisive conference opened at Utrecht, French armies hung on grimly while Versailles concentrated on dividing the Allies, promising England huge colonial cessions, playing on Dutch war-weariness and invoking the threat of a new Madrid-Vienna axis when the Hapsburg pretender to the Spanish throne became Emperor Charles VI on the death of his brother, Joseph I, in 1711. At the same time, Louis XIV's diplomats were becoming more and more resistant to "senseless German demands" for Strasbourg and the rest of Alsace. Yet, in the face of French refusal to do more than restore the pre-war boundaries, those of Ryswick, both the Austrians and the delegates of the Five Circles

arrived at Utrecht in February 1712 with a demand not only for
Alsace, Lorraine, and Franche-Comté, but also for the Three
Bishoprics: Metz, Toul, and Verdun. Such terms could have been
imposed only with an Allied army before Paris, whereas the
imperials were barely maintaining a foothold on the Upper Rhine.
As one Dutch observer remarked, "a sluggard dies with his
dreams." [36]

The hopelessness of German claims was revealed, as it had been
in 1697, when the other Allies refused to prolong the war. Queen
Anne's speech from the throne on June 17, 1712, made clear that the
British, with the Whig ministry banished from power, considered
the French offers a reasonable basis for peace. The Dutch kept up
token support for at least the retrocession of Strasbourg until the
following January, then quietly dropped it, and on April 11, 1713,
all the Empire's allies made peace with France. By that time, the
Germans dejectedly abandoned everything save their demand for
Landau; Strasbourg was recognized as no longer within reach. At
last even Landau, retaken by the French that summer, was passed
over in the treaty signed by Villars for Louis XIV and by Prince
Eugene for Emperor Charles VI at Rastatt on March 6, 1714, and
confirmed by the Empire at Swiss Baden the following September.
When the smoke cleared, the French monarch had given up only
some positions on the Rhine's right bank occupied during the war.
He still held everything he had possessed in the east before the
conflict began.

The diplomatic settlement of the War of the Spanish Succession,
at least as between France and the Germanies, seems so similar
to that of the preceding War of the League of Augsburg that one
might be tempted to dismiss 1709–1714 as merely a study in repetition. One difference should, however, be noted, for it was to be
extremely important for the situation of Strasbourg during the
eighteenth century. At Ryswick Emperor Leopold I had sincerely
endeavored to recover the lost city. At The Hague, Gertruydenberg,
and Utrecht his sons, Joseph I and then Charles VI, claimed Alsace

almost automatically; but this time with the intention of letting nothing distract them from the acquisitions they coveted in Italy. Since the former Spanish Netherlands also came with the final settlement, the Treaty of Rastatt looked much more like a triumph to Vienna than it did to numerous German princes.

However, Hapsburg egoism cannot even here be made the sole reason for Strasbourg's remaining in French hands. Throughout the twenty-five years of struggle which had begun in 1688, Louis XIV's other enemies, notably the English and the Dutch, had never been brought to consider retrocession of Alsace as a war aim of their own. On the other side of the coin, the vaulting ambitions of the Germans, especially of the Five Circles after 1702 and of Prussia after 1707, had unquestionably done much to prejudice chances for creating a solid "Rhine barrier." Strasbourg entered the eighteenth century still a fortress of France, still coveted by patriots within the Empire, but an object of indifference so far as the Maritime Powers were concerned and no longer a focus of attention even for Vienna, where the Hapsburgs were now creating, in the south and east, an Austrian, as opposed to a Holy Roman, Empire. The struggle for the Upper Rhine had exercised the seventeenth century, but it was not to recover its old importance until the nineteenth.

V

A case which demonstrates this indifference is the role played by Alsace in the War of the Austrian Succession, when Maria Theresa was struggling, with British support, to maintain her Hapsburg patrimony against Prussia and "Charles VII," the Bavarian claimant supported by France for the imperial throne. Here, in the 1740's, three decades after Utrecht and Rastatt, is to be found the only occasion in the years separating Louis XIV from Napoleon on which Strasbourg figured at all prominently in the calculations of European dynasts.[37] The episode, though not insignificant, seems a far cry from the great struggles at either end of the century.

The chief problem of historical interest has always centered about Frederick the Great's part in canceling what some German scholars have insisted was another excellent chance to reunite Strasbourg with the Empire. The Prussian king invaded Silesia in 1740 and then accepted the rich province as the price of peace with Vienna two years later, only to reënter the war with an invasion of Bohemia in August 1744. At that juncture, Hungarian *Panduren* of the queen's forces were actually operating in Alsace. Thus arises the question: did Frederick II deprive "Germany," whatever that meant in his day, of a golden opportunity to regain the lost city and its surroundings? [38]

It is true that after their victory at Dettingen in June 1743 Maria Theresa's western army and the Anglo-German "Pragmatic Army" under King George II drove the French back to the left bank of the Rhine. At a conference in Hanau the following month, King George and the imperial commander, Prince Charles of Lorraine, agreed on further operations to the south and west. The British-led forces actually crossed the Rhine at Mainz, and a cavalry spearhead was thrust forward all the way to Saarlouis, only thirty-five miles from Metz. From this advanced position, the commander of the flying party, Colonel Menzel, rather grandiosely announced the imminent "liberation from the French yoke" of Alsace, Lorraine, the Three Bishoprics, Franche-Comté, even Burgundy. In early September, however, Prince Charles' effort to cross the Rhine near Breisach, above Strasbourg, was successfully repelled by the French. At this point, the King of England suddenly announced he was taking the Pragmatic Army into winter quarters and headed north to the Austrian Netherlands. No one but an elated cavalry colonel had proposed the permanent reconquest of Alsace.

The supposedly crucial year was 1744. By that spring France was officially at war with Austria, no longer posing merely as a disinterested ally of the Wittelsbach "emperor" against rebels within his realm; and the Anglo-Austrian alliance decided on simultaneous attacks to be launched from the Netherlands and from the Rhine.

With the best French units in Flanders, accompanying Louis XV, it was no great task for Prince Charles to bring his imperials across the river into southern Alsace. From the first day of July until mid-August he moved swiftly, if somewhat aimlessly, about the province. These six weeks, then, represented the Empire's, or more precisely the Hapsburgs', "great opportunity," before the Lorrainer was ordered east to meet the advance of the newly recommitted Prussians in Bohemia.

But did this campaign really signify much? In actual fact, neither military nor diplomatic circumstances at the time pointed to a possible German recovery of Strasbourg, let alone the whole province. Prince Charles was already in trouble, had indeed already lost the battle of Wissembourg, before he and his army were recalled by Vienna. The French had unquestionably been startled by news of the invasion in July, but they had been able to send a force from Flanders which was much stronger than the imperial units in Alsace and which had just begun to deploy when the latter departed.

As for the definition of Maria Theresa's war aims, these do not seem to have had much to do with the Upper Rhine. The queen hoped to find an equivalent for Silesia in Bavaria, whose ruling house she was now fighting. Ideally, however, she would have chosen to recover Silesia itself, in preference to any other territory in sight. Equally important, she had told her advisers as early as August 1743 that she hoped for a *rapprochement* with France; and she would not have wished to prejudice this possibility by seizing Alsace.[39] The diplomatic revolution of the next decade was already being prepared; the long Hapsburg-Bourbon conflict was drawing to a close. At no time in his campaign did Prince Charles ever proclaim the annexation of any French lands.

Needless to say, Frederick II of Prussia was as indifferent to the ultimate disposition of Strasbourg as Maria Theresa was cautious. His motives were characteristically cold-blooded. He felt endangered in his newly won position from the moment in December 1743 when he learned of the Austrian-Saxon alliance. The news of the next summer, that imperial troops had crossed the Rhine, triggered his decision to attack Hapsburg power again, not because of any devotion to French territorial integrity in itself, but because he could not afford to see Louis XV forced into an early peace with Vienna. Alsace and Silesia were closely connected in his mind, as he later revealed in his *Political Testament* of 1752:

> Prussia cannot calmly stand by and watch France lose Alsace and Lorraine; and the diversions which Prussia can undertake, for the benefit of France, are substantial. . . . For the same reason, France cannot suffer Austria to recover Silesia; for that would too greatly weaken a French ally.[40]

If this judgment makes strange reading, in the light of Prussia's later significance for Alsatian history, it was nonetheless consistent with another of Frederick's pronouncements: "One must follow blindly the interest of the state and ally oneself with the power whose momentary advantage corresponds most closely with one's own." [41]

Thus the "liberation effort" of the 1740's will scarcely support the weight of argumentation subsequently loaded upon it. Strasbourg was not even close to reëntering the Empire in 1744. It certainly had been in 1696–1697 and again in 1709–1710, but thereafter it was almost forgotten by the diplomats of Europe, including those of Vienna and Berlin. Neither the Austrian nor the Prussian leaders had any conception of the kind of Germany which would one day seek to judge them by nationalistic standards.

It may be added, merely as an epilogue, that in the longest and most widespread conflict still to be fought by the European powers under the old regime, the Seven Years' War, Strasbourg's fate was neither a military nor a diplomatic issue, for the very simple reason that in 1756 Bourbon and Hapsburg armies took the field as allies. By this time Alsace was a compact defensive area, comprising eleven permanent military bases, from Huningue in the south to Landau in the north.[42] Furthermore, Lorraine at the province's rear had at last ceased to be a cause for uneasiness. Even before 1766, when the

Dauphin, the future Louis XVI, inherited the duchy from his great-grandfather, Stanislaus, French strongholds and military roads extended uninterruptedly from the Rhine to the Atlantic. No longer a periodically isolated outpost, a trading piece tossed on the conference table, Strasbourg had become a French garrison city, like Besançon or Metz or Valenciennes. Only in that setting can its evolution during the eighteenth century be understood.

CHAPTER FOUR

The King's Rule

I

One of the first things Louis XIV did, after annexing Strasbourg, was to put the city, quite literally, on Paris time. A century before, the local Council of Thirteen had defied the Holy Roman Emperor by refusing to accept the Gregorian calendar reform, and, like most of the rest of Protestant Europe, it stayed with the old Julian system, despite the problems of dating correspondence with Catholic states. What the Hapsburgs had never been able to enforce, however, the French monarchy imposed with a minimum of delay. On January 23, 1682, a letter from Louvois was read to the Thirteen, advising that body of the king's desire for immediate adoption of the revised calendar. The Council voted to protest, citing the difficulties and even injustices (to debtors, for example) which would follow a sudden abandonment of the Julian dating. Back from the minister came a brusque order to comply, accompanied by one of his chilling requests for the names of any Thirteeners disposed to resist the royal will. The councilors had no choice but to yield, decreeing on February 11 that the next day would be not the 12th, but the 22nd. Henceforth, when it was January 1 in Protestant London, Amsterdam, and Frankfurt, the accepted date in Strasbourg, as in Paris, Vienna, and Rome, was January 11 until 1700, and thereafter January 12.[1]

This illustration serves as well as any to introduce the problem at hand. The terms signed at Illkirch on September 30, 1681, provided for the old civic constitution to remain in force. That December, Louvois announced there would be no royal interference in the approaching elections to the Magistrat, insisting only that the official oath be revised to include a pledge of allegiance to His Majesty.[2] The voting went off as usual in the first week of January 1682, with Jakob Wencker duly chosen ruling Ammeister, as his father had been in earlier years. The privileges guaranteed the town under its capitulation were subsequently confirmed by Louis XIV in 1698, after Ryswick,[3] again in 1716 on behalf of the new King Louis XV, and several times in later years, to justify demands for financial gifts to the crown.

No amount of formal continuity, however, could hide the fundamental change which had occurred. Time was to show that while the royal authorities would tamper no more than necessary with the internal operations of local government, the entire power structure of Strasbourg had been altered. In order to see how this took place between 1681 and 1789 — how Strasbourg's constitution was modified by the time of the Revolution — several different kinds of change must be examined.

II

Beginning with the entry of Montclar's cuirassiers and infantry in 1681, Strasbourg saw superimposed upon its ruling class a wholly new element, the French military commanders. Seldom inclined to take the initiative in civil administration, save where it touched defensive security or logistical support for their troops, these commanders nevertheless controlled the force which lay behind every decision of the royal government. In addition, they constituted a whole array of privileged individuals on the spot, sometimes arrogant, sometimes condescendingly gracious, always expensive.[4]

The highest in rank of all the king's representatives in Alsace was the governor general of the province, frequently a marshal of France. Next to him, and more commonly in residence, stood the provincial commandant (*commandant pour le roi*), assisted, from 1708 on, by a deputy commandant. Actually, however, these and other local positions were often held by the same men. Marshal d'Huxelles, for example, having been provincial commandant since 1690, was promoted to governor general in 1713, and then, from 1715 to 1730, combined that office with the military governorship of the city of Strasbourg. During these years he occupied the residence provided for holders of the latter post, relinquishing the Hôtel du Gouvernement to the provincial commandant, Du Bourg. The Duc de Coigny, to cite another example, was simultaneously governor general and provincial commandant from 1743 to 1759.

Theoretically distinct from the provincial army leaders was the fortress staff of Strasbourg proper: the military governor, the *lieutenant du roi* or deputy governor, the major of the guard and his two aides, three gate captains, five artillery, and at times as many as eleven engineer officers. Still a third, separate, command center included the governor of the citadel, his staff, and the commandants of the two wall forts. To these, furthermore, must be added the actual troop commanders for the regiments occupying the city at any given time, not to mention a number of inspectors, quartermasters, and field surgeons. Taken together, the provincial, city, and citadel staffs, the medical, quartermaster, and ordnance personnel, and the line officers, whether serving with garrison units or just temporarily assigned to Strasbourg for rations and quarters, made up a total of anywhere from six to eight hundred individuals.

Far more important from the point of view of the local government, of course, were the civil administrators appointed by the crown. The first to appear, though eventually far from the most important, was the "royal syndic." On November 9, 1681, Intendant La Grange presented to the Senate-and-XXI the first bearer of credentials for this office, none other than Christoph Güntzer, the erstwhile town secretary who six weeks before had played such an active, if subordinate, role in the capitulation. Güntzer had been quick to cultivate the good will and reliance of Louis XI's representatives, not least by announcing his conversion to the Roman Church. His new duties were to include attendance at all civic councils, conveyance of orders from the crown, and close observation of proceedings which might interest royal authorities. In fact, though he had no vote in any body, he was entitled to give his opinion ahead of regular members of the Magistrat whenever he considered it advisable to express recommendations or objections. He was also director of the municipal chancellery, thus controlling official correspondence. During the first, confused period after the capitulation, when a knowledge of both French and German was itself a source of power, the syndic, who spoke both, unquestionably wielded considerable influence, seeing to matters as important as the costs of the fortification program and as insignificant as the appointment of a bass viol player for the cathedral orchestra.[5]

Güntzer, however, was too inconsiderable in himself and too limited by the hostility of his former superiors in the oligarchy to be an altogether satisfactory spokesman for the crown. Thus, under letters patent issued at Versailles in March 1685, a higher official was created to represent the king in Strasbourg. This was the "royal praetor," entitled to speak even before the royal syndic whenever he chose to attend a council meeting and in all things "to observe and be sure that nothing occurs contrary to His Majesty's interests." Unlike the syndic, he had a full vote in the Thirteen, the Fifteen, and the Senate-and-XXI. His annual salary and emoluments had by 1789 reached twenty-three thousand livres, plus fifteen hundred bundles of kindling, forty cords of beech and forty cords of oak, ten sacks of wheat, and twelve casks of old wine, or about six times as much as was disbursed to a Stettmeister-Thirteener, highest paid of the native Magistrat.[6]

This position was clearly a rich plum for its occupant, as well as an important agency of control for the crown. Significantly, the first royal praetor to present his credentials to the Senate-and-XXI, on April 30, 1685, was Dr. Ulrich Obrecht, son of the Georg Obrecht beheaded in 1672 for having charged the city's governors with pro-French treason. Obrecht *fils,* a professor at the university, had himself been viewed with some suspicion by the conquerors in 1681, because of his previous writings on the history of Alsace. In 1682, however, he obtained Advocate Binder's place as one of the legal counselors to the Magistrat, and in the autumn of 1684 he journeyed to Paris, there to enter the Catholic church under the guidance of Bossuet. He thus convinced the royal government that he would be both a dependable and an able servant.[7]

In all, Strasbourg had nine praetors before the office was eliminated in 1790. Ulrich Obrecht was succeeded at his death in 1701 by his son, Jean-Henri; and when the latter resigned on orders from Versailles, just five years later, the then royal syndic, Jean-Baptiste Klinglin, moved up to the praetorship. After this first Klinglin and his son, disgraced in 1752, the office passed to one of the bishop's officials, the Abbé de Régemorte, then in succession to two Gayots in the 1760's, to a nephew of the second one, Baron d'Autigny ("Baron" in this case was not a title), and finally in 1781 to another former syndic, Alexandre-Conrad de Gérard, newly returned from Philadelphia where he had served as the first French minister plenipotentiary to the United States.[8]

Above both praetor and syndic in the hierarchy of civil ranks stood the Intendant of Alsace. After the Peace of Westphalia, this intendancy was established at Breisach. There it remained until 1681, when Jacques de La Grange was finally able to settle his headquarters in Strasbourg. He and his successors were provided by the Magistrat with an official residence, as well as with offices for the permanent staff: the *subdélégué général* (really a deputy intendant), two first secretaries, a *subdélégué* for the local district, and the inevitable clerks.[9]

Strasbourg naturally contained other civilian officers of the king, and, at times, seemed in danger of invasion by many more. Especially during Louis XIV's later years it paid dearly, in lump contributions, to avoid the threatened mushrooming of venal offices, which would have brought Louis cash proceeds when sold but would at the same time have saddled the town with a horde of superfluous royal advocates, assessors, collectors, recorders, and the like.[10] Even without the sinecures thus aborted, there were still several provincial administrators in residence, including two *réceveurs des finances* and their staff,[11] as well as the *Maréchaussée,* or territorial police, under the provost general for Alsace, appointed in 1720. These personages normally had little to do with the Magistrat. The city itself was, in fact, exempt from most of their activities. Nevertheless, by increasing the size of the French official population, they helped to change the political atmosphere.

III

The history of royal administration in Strasbourg should warn anyone tempted to view the last hundred years before the French Revolution as a static period that he is wrong. In the beginning, theoretically, there existed a clear division of labor, among the intendant, with his general tasks in the province as a whole, the praetor, with his special authority over local policies, and the syndic, with his more immediate responsibility for the details of business transacted at the town hall. The privileged status of the municipality doubtless helped to sharpen these distinctions, the intendant being content, during the busy period just after 1681, to keep clear of specifically local worries and to give his attention to his nine big territorial districts.

Under the circumstances, it is not surprising that the first major test of authority occurred between the royal syndic and the royal praetor. There was always some tension here, and jealousy often erupted into open conflicts of competence. The praetor was clearly higher in titular rank, but the syndic, at first, possessed definite advantages of his own, including especially his direct control over the municipal *Kanzlei* or secretariat. The resulting competition began to show itself in bitter quarrels, as soon as Obrecht was appointed over Güntzer.[12] The decisive collision, however, occurred after the turn of the century.[13]

Jean-Gaspard de Hatzel becamse royal syndic and chancellery director in 1706, succeeding Jean-Baptiste Klinglin when the latter was elevated to the praetorship. The new official had one asset in his family connections with the membership of the Sovereign Council at Colmar and another in the good will of the then intendant of Alsace, Le Pelletier de La Houssaye. He appears, however, to have

been an ambitious troublemaker who managed almost at once to
alienate Praetor Klinglin, and then, after 1716, the new intendant,
d'Angervilliers. The latter's correspondence on the subject bristles
with dislike of Hatzel, not only for insubordination to the praetor
but also for having tried to go over the intendant's own head to
Chancellor Voisin and to La Houssaye, now back in Paris.[14]

Klinglin, with the support of d'Angervilliers, was obviously eager
for a pretext to oust the syndic. Hatzel supplied just that in 1714,
when he accepted the additional post of "lieutenant to the grand
bailiff of Haguenau," i.e., deputy to the feudal suzerain of the
Décapole towns. Three years later, in 1717, the praetor demanded
Hatzel's suspension from office in Strasbourg, because of the incompatibility between his two sets of duties which theoretically
required residence in different places. When the central government
acceded to this demand and revoked the brevet of office held by the
syndic, the latter promptly entered an appeal against the decision,
and a quarter-century of litigation ensued. The intendant wrote in
1718 to Marshal d'Huxelles at Paris that there were plenty of
charges which could have been brought forward, including that of
financial corruption, but the incompatibility issue seemed sufficient.[15]
The outcome, in legal terms, was far from clear. At one point, in
1736, Cardinal Fleury intervened with a financial judgment very
favorable to Hatzel; and this worthy, though forbidden to exercise
the functions of syndic, was still enjoying his old title and salary in
1740, when his six relatives in the Sovereign Council of Alsace were
obliged to absent themselves from hearings on his appeal to Colmar.
He was, in fact, paid a sizable pension by the city until his death
five years later.[16] In practice, however, no holder of the title after
1717 played a major political role. Finally, in 1781, Praetor Gérard,
with the support of both the intendant and the local Magistrat,
prevailed upon Louis XVI's government to abolish the hundred-year-
old office. At that late date, the disappearance of the royal syndic
represented little more than a tardy adjustment of theory to facts.[17]

The fading of another line, that which originally separated the
powers of the praetorship from those of the intendancy, does not

seem to have been the result of any sustained encroachment on the intendant's part. In 1716, for example, when Ammeister Gambs, having been barred from office on grounds of insanity, appealed to the Regent's Council of the Interior in Paris, Intendant d'Angervilliers answered inquiries from that body by upholding the praetor, Klinglin, and recommended that Gambs be ordered to pursue his case with the proper *local* authorities. A few years later, we find d'Angervilliers again advising the central government that the Magistrat, under the praetor, was in the right, this time in a financial dispute with the citadel staff.[18] Yet throughout the century, one can follow at Strasbourg a dual evoluton in the position of the intendancy which modern scholars have discerned in the French kingdom as a whole: the increasing identification of interests between the intendant and his locality, but at the same time the ever greater reliance by the crown on his direct action throughout the province assigned to him.

In human terms, it was doubtless inevitable that the initial division of authority should become less and less clear. For one thing, the sixteen intendants who successively administered Alsace between 1648 and 1790 were almost without exception capable, while several of them were outstanding — Colbert de Croissy in the middle of the seventeenth century and La Grange at its end, Le Pelletier de La Houssaye during Louis XIV's last years, Bauyn d'Angervilliers under the Orléans Regency, and Blair de Boismont for fourteen years beginning in 1764.[19] They were in close touch with the royal council, their dispatches sometimes taking only three days to reach the distant secretary of state for war, whose department, ever since Louvois, had retained primary responsibility for Alsatian affairs.[20] Throughout the old regime, it was the periodic surveys prepared at the intendancy which constituted the basic source of ministerial information concerning the province.[21] Even before the end of Louis XIV's reign in 1715, moreover, it was becoming customary in Paris to think of Strasbourg as not just a privileged commune, but as the actual capital of Alsace.[22] Hence it is not hard to understand why, although the royal praetor remained important, steadily increasing reliance was placed on the intendant's information and judgment about conditions within the city itself.

As in the Syndic Hatzel case, it took a specific administrative crisis to reveal and at the same time accentuate the change which had been developing for some time. In this instance, the central figure was François-Joseph Klinglin, son of Jean-Baptiste and his successor as royal praetor since 1725. Here, certainly, was one of the most interesting scoundrels to be encountered in the administrative annals of the old regime. Personally charming, shrewd in his distribution of favors and in his cultivation of popularity with the city's lower classes, amazingly supple in dealing with anyone in either the royal or the local government who asked embarrassing questions, Klinglin for more than twenty-five years perpetrated one fraud after another without ever losing his appearance of deep devotion to the public interest.

In 1735, by a combination of gifts and smiling blackmail, he induced the Magistrat to exchange the entire bailiwick of Illkirch-Graffenstaden against his own family's much less valuable domain at Hoenheim.[23] Between 1730 and 1736, using the city's materials and labor, plus liberal helpings of cash, he built himself the lovely mansion which is today the Préfecture, then sold it to the municipality in 1744 at an outrageous price, and finally accepted it back free of charge as an official residence for the praetor, i.e., himself. It is literally impossible to unravel all his complicated manipulations of Strasbourg's various civic assets for his own profit. Several efforts by enraged citizens to expose him bogged down hopelessly in a mire of genial mendacity and rigged bookkeeping.[24] Yet he ended with both hands so firmly planted in the municipal till that not even he could extricate them quickly enough when at last the lights went on.

The praetor's downfall was actually only an incident in the struggle at the court of Louis XV between the minister of finance, Machault, and the secretary of state for war, d'Argenson, brother of the famous memoirist and Klinglin's most influential protector. Machault, who could count on Intendant Mégret de Sérilly at Strasbourg, was determined to expose the corruption there for purposes of his own; and in January 1752 Councilor Courchetet d'Esnans of the Parlement of Besançon arrived in Alsace as a royal commissioner to investigate the situation. Within a month Klinglin was in prison, where he shortly died, while his son and designated successor also died in confinement at Grenoble not long thereafter.[25]

The most positive result of this explosion was the *règlement* concerning Strasbourg's administration signed by Louis XV at Versailles in June of 1752.[26] The law runs to thirty-one articles and represents the most serious effort at regularization imposed on the city by the Bourbon monarchy. Besides abolishing several superfluous commissions and boards, it forbade the Magistrat ever again to borrow sums of over six thousand livres, assess new taxes, or alienate any rights or properties without royal consent. The enactment also extended the authority of the Chamber of Economy (actually established twelve years earlier) over all municipal expenditures, though it was still to be recruited within the regular Magistrat, which thus managed to retain control over its own bookkeeping. The offices of syndic and praetor were confirmed and the latter's political authority actually somewhat expanded, though its incumbent's access to local funds was sharply reduced. The Illkirch-Hoenheim exchange with Klinglin was finally annulled in 1765.

It would be a mistake to think that the royal praetor followed the syndic into political oblivion. He could still, on occasion, take an active and influential part in affairs. It is nonetheless true that by the latter half of the eighteenth century the praetorship had been converted into something quite different from the office it was in 1685. Its occupant spent more and more of his time in Paris or in following the court (during the 1780's the ailing Gérard was away from Strasbourg more than he was there). When on such trips, the praetor functioned less as an administrator than as a representative of local interests in dealings with the crown. Furthermore, after 1752, the praetor, like the Magistrat beneath him, was accountable in financial matters to the central government, which for practical purposes meant to the intendancy. No praetor following Klinglin could have recreated the cat's cradle of graft which was his monument. One of his monuments, that is. The other one was his fine mansion — and that, significantly, was after 1753 the official residence of the intendant.

The changes which had taken place between the late seventeenth century and the late eighteenth were significant. In earlier years, there was an intendant concentrating on questions which affected Alsace as a whole, leaving to the praetor specific authority over and responsibility for Strasbourg, while the royal syndic supervised a variety of administrative details. On the eve of the Revolution, the picture had become very different: no more royal syndic, the praetor clearly subordinate to the intendant, who in turn felt directly concerned with what was now beyond all question the capital of his province.

IV

Below the layer of royal controls which were set up in 1681 and in the years immediately following, the old Magistrat of Strasbourg continued to function.[27] Each January, right down to 1789, the oath to the Schwörbrief, and to the king, of course, was repeated in front of the cathedral. Physical changes occurred. The Chancellery burned in 1686 and was rebuilt with modifications. The ancient Treasury Tower, the *Pfenningthurn,* was torn down in 1745. So too, in 1781, was the old Pfalz or town hall, a medieval structure which had stood near the "new" Pfalz of the sixteenth century. The latter, however, still housed the local government in 1789, as it had for two hundred years. Military orders might originate in the Hôtel du Gouvernement and reports to Paris in the Hôtel de l'Intendance, yet to outward appearances the Pfalz remained Strasbourg's political center, the symbol of all that had survived from the past.

An important aspect of this continuity in the midst of change was the human material of which the Magistrat was composed. On this score, an observer is apt first to be impressed by some notable

disappearances and replacements in the personnel of the town administration immediately after 1681. Several influential figures emigrated. For example, of the four chief legal advisers to the Thirteen,
Advocate Binder eventually became a privy councilor in Vienna and
Stoesser found his way into the service of the Elector of Brandenburg. Friedrich Schrag stayed on in Strasbourg as a professor of law
until 1698, but after Ryswick took a post as assessor at Wetzlar.
Frantz, who lived out his life without emigrating, was replaced in
1681 by Syndic Güntzer as director of the chancellery. Later Frantz
declined a seat in the Thirteen on the grounds of anticipated French
objections, accepting instead the less sensitive office of Fifteener.
Professor Johann Georg Kulpis became *Advokat* in 1683, but in 1686
transferred his residence and his allegiance to Württemberg. The
most famous of the new master's political victims was the once
powerful Ammeister, Dominikus Dietrich, who was summoned to
Paris in 1685 and commanded to renounce Lutheranism. When he
refused, he was deprived of his office, exiled first to Guéret in central
France, then to Vesoul in Franche-Comté, and only in 1689 permitted
to return to his own home, under virtual house arrest, all on Louis
XIV's orders.

However, these well-publicized cases, though certainly not negligible, threaten to obscure the much more numerous instances of
political careers which were quietly continued. Franziskus Reisseissen, whose writings have been frequently referred to, became
ruling Ammeister for the second time in 1683, and filled the office,
following the customary rotation, every sixth year thereafter down
to 1707 (he died in 1710). With him, in the circle of Ammeisters,
even after Dietrich's exile, remained men with familiar names:
Wencker, Froereissen, Staedel, and the like. The often confusing
record of Strasbourg's governing personnel entails changes during
the eighteenth century, some of which relate more specifically to
the city's religious and social than to its administrative history. It
is fair to say, however, that old families in the Magistrat gave way
to new ones only gradually; that, in fact, there was never anything

approaching a complete turnover before 1789, and that even recently recruited members had ample opportunity to fit themselves
into, and identify themselves with, the traditional institutions.[28]

A misleadingly similar impression of continuity emerges from a
first glance at the institutions themselves. The names of the main
executive, legislative, and judicial organs did not change, either in
1681, or in the years between then and 1789, though parallel French
titles were sometimes used in correspondence with Paris — "préteur"
for Stettmeister, "consul" for Ammeister, "sénateur" for Ratherr.
Down to and including 1789, the official almanac was still published
each year with officials listed by seniority in the Thirteen, the
Fifteen, the Twenty-one, the Senate, the Assembly of Three Hundred, and a host of supervisory commissions surviving from the
seventeenth century. True, there were some alterations in the 1680's,
in accordance with the place now assigned local authority — the
creation of the Billeting Council in 1682, for example, to service the
garrison. Several short-lived expedients, such as the executive board
established in 1689 under the name of *Niedergesetzte Herren,*[29]
reflect the crown's recurrent impatience with Strasbourg's ponderous
and expensive administration, as does the reform law of 1752.

Particular expedients and modifications, however, did not greatly
alter the theoretical structure of the local constitution. For the most
part, after only a few experiments in innovation, the royal government held to the policy on which it had settled by the late 1680's: to
introduce French controls at critical points, to make clear that the
old institutions would remain henceforth under surveillance by
representatives of the central power, but otherwise to disturb local
traditions no more than necessary. It is for this reason that no one
can appreciate the political changes which did take place under
Bourbon rule unless one looks beyond the lists of officeholders and
asks what these people actually did once they were installed.

When we turn from institutional titles to the records of the
Magistrat in action, any appearance of unruffled continuity dis-
appears. Here, certainly, is change, beginning with the capitulation
and continuing throughout the next century. The volumes of official

minutes, great bulging folios for each year of the seventeenth century, get progressively thinner from the 1680's onward. The *procès-verbaux* of the Council of Thirteen run to 766 pages for 1683, 438 for 1685, 194 for 1703, and only 104 for 1756. Not only this, but the proportion of these pages devoted to mere copies of correspondence with royal officials, in French, increases steadily. Since the secretaries went on using German for the protocols proper, the mixture of languages and handwritings grows increasingly bizarre.

One body, the Assembly of Three Hundred, had seen most of its power slip away even before the annexation. In the eighteenth century the Assembly, in fact, was all but defunct, until the first stages of the Revolution suddenly jerked it back into prominence. The Senate, without the Twenty-one, also seemed to exist, save in judicial matters, primarily for the sake of its members' self-esteem. Mere Twenty-oners never enjoyed much power; and there were seldom more than four of them at any one time, all awaiting promotion to the two functioning councils. The Fifteen, although it still had a certain amount of business, slid toward complete dependence on the initiative and authority of royal spokesmen in all major questions.

What is most revealing, however, is the evolution of the Council of Thirteen, since it had long been the most influential, and, even after 1681, remained the most prestigious, of the town's deliberative bodies. Before annexation, it made decisions of peace or war, acting on reports from its Superior Military Commission (*Obere Machtherren*) and its Fortifications Commission, calling on the Fifteen and the Senate-and-XXI to take internal measures in support of foreign policy. It exchanged official correspondence with emperors and kings, princes and city-states; but once Louis XIV's army moved in, the Military and Fortifications Commissions were abolished and replaced by a Billeting Council, whose very name bespoke subordination.[30] Thereafter, the Council of Thirteen, which before the capitulation had sometimes held as many as five long meetings in a single week, was by 1700 convening only a few times per month, and by the middle of the eighteenth century it occasionally went six weeks without being convoked at all, though this was admittedly unusual.

The Thirteen's relationship to royal diplomacy and military operations is especially significant. Peace settlements or French victories in battle were regularly noted, of course, and *Te Deums* ordered sung. During the violent period between 1689 and 1714, when fighting swirled in and around Alsace much of the time, the council frequently met to discuss demands by the crown for grain, gunpowder, and other supplies. But during the eighteenth century, the military coming and going seemed most remote. In 1756, for example, the Thirteeners voted to express a somewhat vague joy "at the happy conquest of the fortress of Saint-Philippe, which the royal troops have taken on the Island of Minorca." [31] In the volume of minutes for 1778 there is not a single mention of the crown's declaration of war on England or of its support for the rebel colonists in North America. Even in 1744, when Maria Theresa's *Panduren* were campaigning in Alsace and genuine anxiety gripped the city, the Magistrat could only wait for news of the decisions taken by Louis XV and his generals.

All in all, the history of the Thirteen after the capitulation typifies that of the town government in general. It is a history not so much of external crumbling as of gradual, relentless, hollowing out, until by the end of the eighteenth century one beholds scarcely more than the shell of a once living organism. Where formerly there had been real power, there now remained, for the most part, only theoretical jurisdiction, accompanied by appropriate titles and emoluments, but with actual decisions reserved to men in Paris or at the intendancy — men who would not have been greatly interested in the minutes of the Magistrat, even if they could have read the German script.

V

Common sense alone is enough to warn us that this draining away, as it were, of the substance of local autonomy could scarcely affect all the functions of the municipal government to quite the same degree.

There is, in fact, clear evidence that in one area, that of judicial affairs, Strasbourg's town officials retained somewhat greater authority after 1681 than they did in administration and legislation. Even here, however, they were immediately forced to acknowledge royal authority and subjected to jurisdictional competition from several different quarters.

The municipality retained throughout the eighteenth century most of the tribunals it had had in the seventeenth.[32] Its ruling Ammeister still disposed of petty claims, as did its bailiffs in the rural domains. Special courts survived for cases involving marriage, guardianship, handicrafts, and resident aliens, respectively. The Police Court, which in 1688 absorbed the old Morals Court, was composed of four members of the Secret Chambers, two Senators, and four guild Assemblymen. There was an established civil court of first instance, the Lesser Senate.[33] The Senate itself continued to discharge judicial functions, especially in major criminal cases, while the Fifteen occasionally heard suits involving city administration. At the top of the hierarchy, the Council of Thirteen, when sitting as a court of appeal, still called itself the *Hochpreissliche Delegirte Cammer-Gericht,* as it had ever since 1495. Local independence was particularly marked in criminal judicature, since no appeals against penal sentences could go beyond the municipal level, save theoretically to the king's personal clemency. Even capital punishment was normally carried out by order of the Senate alone.

The rest of the picture, however, necessarily qualifies this initial sketch. Strasbourg, under French rule, contained a number of other courts besides those responsible to the Magistrat. Letters patent issued by Louis XIV in 1681 empowered the Directory of the Immediate Nobility of Lower Alsace to hear civil cases involving any of its members, up to a value of five hundred livres. At the Maréchaussée, the provost-general could dispense summary justice to accused highwaymen brought in by his patrols. The military governor had jurisdiction over most charges against soldiers of the garrison, while a separate royal judgeship was created for the citadel and the city's two wall forts as early as 1682. Shortly thereafter, in 1693, a small

Tribunal des monnaies was established for Alsace, sitting in Strasbourg, to hear cases concerned with counterfeiting or exchange rates, under the general authority of the *Cour des monnaies* in Paris.[34]

These special jurisdictions might be dismissed as too limited in competence to represent any major encroachment on the old authority of the town government. The same could not, however, be said of the two courts answerable solely to the bishop. One of them was that of the *officialité,* revived under the vicar-general of the diocese in 1681, and given the power to judge all future cases touching alleged breach of promise and all petitions for annulment of marriage between Catholics. The second episcopal tribunal appeared in 1704 with the installation of a magistrate in the bishop's palace to judge not only disputes over ecclesiastical discipline, religious vows, or administration of the sacraments, but also — and here the lay population came within his purview — charges of sacrilege and allegations of apostasy or false conversion.

Side by side with these competing courts, a second limitation on the Magistrat's judicial authority occasionally made itself felt: direct interference by the power of the crown. The most important such instance occurred in 1690, when the Strasbourg Marriage Court, already restricted in its competence to cases involving Lutherans, aroused indignation in some Catholic circles by authorizing the remarriage of a man to whom it had granted a divorce on the basis of his wife's conviction for adultery. Louis XIV became interested in the matter, and the Council of Thirteen was shortly informed by Praetor Obrecht that he had received the following message from Louvois:

> You will advise the magistrates of Strasbourg that it is not the King's pleasure that they render any future decisions permitting inhabitants of the city who are separated on grounds of adultery to remarry, and that if, having been informed of the will of His Majesty, they should fail to observe it, whoever presided over the deliberations will be put into prison and all his belongings confiscated.[35]

A third and final restriction originated with the terms of the capitulation, which provided that any decision of a city court in a

civil case involving over two thousand livres could be appealed to
the Sovereign Council of Alsace. This tribunal had first been established in 1658 at Ensisheim, site of the Hapsburgs' old domanial
court, transferred to Breisach in 1674 and finally, in 1698, to Colmar,
where it eventually grew to include some thirty presidents and councilors. Its name theoretically included only the designation "superior"
until 1776, when it became officially *Conseil Souverain;* but it always
called itself "sovereign" and was generally called that by other
authorities as well, even prior to 1776. In any event, throughout the
eighteenth century, Colmar served as the judicial capital of Alsace.
Hence Strasbourg, which was the center of the province for all
other governmental purposes, was compelled to see numerous suits
transferred forty miles to the south before they could finally be
settled.[36]

Yet for all the limitations imposed by competing courts in town,
by acts of royal caprice, and by the appellate role of the Sovereign
Council of Alsace, Strasbourg retained a considerable degree of legal
and judicial individuality. The crown itself supported the Magistrat
time after time when the latter complained of unwarranted encroachments by the Colmar tribunal.[37] The city courts could thus
boast of a recognized, if never wholly clear, set of prerogatives within
the always confusing jumble of French judicature under the old
monarchy. It was perhaps natural that local discretion played an
uncommonly large part in the administration of justice, so much
less centralized in pre-1789 France than were most other public
functions.

The practical implications of this situation manifested themselves
not only in the residual authority of municipal courts, but also in
the procedures and even the language there employed. Whereas,
from 1685 on, all pleading before the Sovereign Council in Colmar
had to be in French, the Strasbourg courts clung exclusively to
German until well into the eighteenth century, and even in its latter
decades still used a mixture of the two languages. Although two royal
notaries were licensed by the crown to certify and record documents in French, no fewer than twenty other notaries, holding their

licenses under the Magistrat, went on writing out testaments and deeds in German legal idiom.[38]

German (Swabian) customary law had constituted the sum total of jurisprudence applied by local courts until the introduction of the imperial code or *Carolina* in 1532 and the Senate's adoption of Roman principles as its theoretical guide in 1555. The lower courts had gone on using a hodge-podge of German custom, imperial statutes, and half-understood Roman axioms. Hence, the procedures and principles employed at Strasbourg appear to have struck royal officials as peculiar and sometimes baffling. Just after 1700, the survey of Intendant La Grange, as summarized by La Houssaye, contained the following:

A very important observation concerning the civil and criminal jurisdiction of the city of Strasbourg . . . is that neither the [French] civil ordinance of 1667 nor the criminal of 1670 is observed here. To date we have left the Magistrat . . . to its old judicial system, different in many respects from that of France.

As for criminal law, this is less disturbing, because the Magistrat has full competence over it and judges without appeal. But for civil matters, where appeals . . . are carried to the Superior Council of Alsace, it is assuredly strange not to have the courts of first instance observe an ordinance which higher judges are obliged to apply.

The intendant's conclusion, however, has a characteristic ring: "It does not seem advisable at present to change anything in this usage, especially until the French language becomes more familiar in Strasbourg." [39]

So the old ways persisted. Condemned criminals, for example, went to meet death amid age-old ceremonies. The victim was still dressed, as for centuries past, in a white shirt and a white cap edged in black when he was led into the square before the town hall. There he and the onlookers heard the sentence read aloud by the ruling Ammeister, who ended by snapping a white stick and dropping it on the ground. With the Penitents' Bell tolling from atop the cathedral, the city guardsmen then marched the prisoner away, preceded by a Stettmeister on horseback and followed by the Senators, as official witnesses. On the long walk to the Saverne Gate, the usual place of execution, the condemned was allowed to pause just once, for a final meal. In an occasional instance of a particularly atrocious crime, he might end by being broken on the wheel or drawn and quartered. During the eighteenth century, however, he was generally either hanged or lashed into a chair and decapitated by a horizontal stroke.[40] The only modification imposed by royal authority came in 1729, when it was decided to suppress the custom of having the accompanying Stettmeister ask the prisoner one last time to confess his guilt. The Magistrat was advised by the royal spokesmen that this usage was contrary to French criminal law and was unwise in any event, since "the prisoner's denial might awaken unrighteous thoughts in the minds of the citizenry."[41] From the standpoint of the condemned, the change was not a major one.

VI

If by the mid-1700's the main lines of authority had been drawn between the leading royal representatives in Strasbourg, there remained a variety of unresolved rivalries within the native Magistrat. One of these, the old conflict between the ordinary Senators and the personnel of the Secret Chambers, which had taken over so much of the Senate's original authority, broke into the open in 1776 over the apparently trivial question of faggots. A manuscript volume in the local university library permits us to follow this dispute through the four years it lasted.[42]

The clash began when the Senate-and-XXI, dominated as always by the latter component, voted a ten per cent reduction in the pay of the permanent councilors, but also abolished the allowance of five hundred bundles of kindling per year which the city had previously delivered to every ex-Senator. By 1778 the regular members of the Senate organized themselves to protest, appealing to the king to send a commissioner, asking support from Cardinal de Rohan in Paris, and writing to various ministers, including Necker. The memoranda all review the decline of the Senate from its late-medieval apogee, then go on to charge the Thirteeners, Fifteeners, and Twenty-oners with arrogant disregard for their colleagues, as well as for the edict of 1752. There is even a coating of liberal theory on these complaints, for the Senate claims to represent "the people" against avaricious oligarchs. It is pointed out to the crown that, while the members of the Secret Chambers wax fat on rich incomes, the ordinary Senator in office receives only two hundred livres per year and then faggots worth a mere forty-five livres per year for the rest of his life. And now even the faggots are to be withheld!

Specifically at stake was only a small matter of the honorific distinction represented by the regular delivery of kindling. Actually, however, a more important question was posed: would or would not the royal government intervene to reverse the drift toward complete eclipse of senatorial prerogatives by the executive chambers? [43] The answer, as usual, was qualified. Having somewhat wearily consulted the intendant and the royal praetor, the Prince de Montbarey at last wrote from the war ministry in 1780 that the Magistrat was to restore the allowance of faggots to former Senators, but added that this represented no general decision as to the proper distribution of powers and emoluments within the town government. The Secret Chambers yielded the special point at issue. The Senate in itself, however, continued to represent a negligible political force.

In the last decade before the Revolution there arose a different kind of dispute. This one involved two distinct relationships, one between Magistrat and guilds, the other between the Council of Fifteen and the rest of the town officials. The Fifteen, as noted earlier, had in some ways suffered less diminution of responsibility under French control than had the theoretically superior Council of Thirteen. It still had a variety of administrative tasks, subject to the authority of the praetor and the intendant; and its decisions might on occasion affect city life more tangibly than did those of any other portion of the Magistrat. In 1779, for example, the Fifteen finally pushed through the introduction of street lights, after more than fifty years of public resistance to the cost involved.[44] In 1785, it imposed the systematic numbering of houses.[45] Now, in 1787, it suddenly precipitated a general furor by arresting several local butchers for continuing to defy what seemed a reasonable enough reform, the establishment three years earlier of a regular system for the inspection and standardization of meat scales.[46]

What turned this into a general fight was the decision of the butchers' guild to appeal to the full Senate-and-XXI. The Senate alone, though it ordered the prisoners' release, had no power to change the ruling; but the guild's action automatically introduced into the debate the opinions of the Thirteeners and Twenty-oners, as well as those of the legal counselors or *Advokaten* not attached to the Fifteen. That body thus found itself touched at a particularly sensitive point, the distinction between its own prerogatives and the powers of the Thirteen.

In the first hearing before the Senate-and-XXI, Advocate Mogg began by opining that the Fifteen might very possibly have exceeded its authority in attempting to legislate about "the tools of any craft." One of his colleagues on the legal staff of the Thirteen, Advocate Holdt, took a more cautious line, asking that a committee be appointed to study the butchers' protest; but the third of the counselors to speak, Advocate Fischer, resumed Mogg's attack on the Fifteen, adding that the printed announcements of the reform "had endangered the good name of an honorable guild." What if the citizenry were to decide that the weighing of meat had not been strictly honest in the past? Secretary Widt at last got the floor to read a prepared statement claiming that the matter was the business of the Fifteen alone, since it concerned trades and handicrafts. The Senate-and-XXI had no right, he argued, to entertain a petition from any source on such a subject. Stettmeister Wurmser, apparently unnerved by all this uproar under his chairmanship, turned once again to Mogg, who promptly denounced the Fifteen's rebuttal as out of order. Two other Stettmeisters, Neuenstein and Haffner, however, recommended referring the question back to the Fifteen for study. And so it went, with individual members of the Magistrat either supporting or criticizing the Fifteeners.

When the meeting broke up without having reached any decision,

the Council of Fifteen hurriedly drafted letters to the intendant and
to Praetor Gérard in Paris, pointing out the injustice of Mogg's and
Fischer's charges, insisting that the problem was one over which
neither the Senate nor especially the Thirteen could claim any
jurisdiction whatsoever, and appealing for royal backing against
"the indecent slanders to which we have been subjected." Excitement
ran especially high since a variety of individuals within the local
population began to attack the Fifteeners as the agents of high-
handed authoritarianism. Once again, the central government tem-
porized, doubtless hoping that this far-off dispute would settle
itself. Perhaps it might have in time; but it was still in progress,
still mired in legal technicalities and multilateral ill will, when
the far greater agitation of 1789 swept over the city. Even then, the
lingering echo of old rivalries and resentments did not die out at
once. In the crowds which surged through Strasbourg after the news
arrived that the Bastille had fallen, there were to be some, not all
of them meat dealers, we may assume, who shouted "Death to the
tyrants of the Fifteen!" and "Long live the butchers' scales!"

VII

Strasbourg on the eve of the Revolution continued to occupy a
unique place in the French kingdom. Its citizens were, in fact, a
rather special category of royal subjects. A Strasbourger paid taxes
only to his local government, which in turn negotiated over payments to the king's treasury. He was exempt from militia duty. He
enjoyed the privilege of *non evocando,* which is to say that he could
be tried and sued in first instance only in one of the courts of his
own municipality, whatever appeals might later be carried to Colmar
or Paris.[47]

The Magistrat continued to control its own budget within broad
limits, even after the reorganization of 1752, whereas most French
cities had long been accountable to detailed administrative and
especially financial surveillance or *tutelle* by royal agents. Strasbourg,
as a vassal of the king, went on ruling its five rural bailiwicks,

which by 1789 contained a population of some 17,500.[48] It administered its own censorship and the licensing of all publications printed
locally.[49] It could ordinarily count on the backing of the intendant
when it sought to collect city taxes even from representatives of the
crown — in 1720, for example, Intendant d'Angervilliers advised
Paris that the officers of the royal mint at Strasbourg were properly
subject to the traditional duty on consignments of wine, from which
they had been demanding exemption.[50]

Any comparison between the Magistrat of Strasbourg and the
Capitouls of Toulouse or the *Jurats* of Bordeaux serves to emphasize how much of the old free city's former independence had survived to distinguish it from the cities of the interior. The differences,
it might be argued, were only matters of degree; since in the last
analysis it was the central power which had either to make or to
approve all major decisions. Yet these same differences contributed
strongly to Strasbourg's political personality during the last period
of the old regime.

It is when we face the other way, toward the remaining free
imperial cities of Germany, that we can best appreciate the political
changes wrought by French rule in Strasbourg. Unlike Frankfurt
am Main, Nürnberg, and their sister urban republics, Strasbourg
no longer made its own alliances or levied its own troops. Instead
it built barracks, housed royal officers, and contributed to the support
of military forces over which it had no control. It had quickly lost
the right to issue its own coinage. It no longer had full authority
to determine its own religious policies, but depended instead on the
forbearance of the crown for such Lutheran privileges as continued
in force. Whereas Frankfurt still received a new Holy Roman
Emperor as an invited guest, for the sole purpose of his coronation,
a King of France could simply announce, as Louis XV did in the
autumn of 1744, that he had decided to visit his "loyal city."

It would not be correct to say that French influence corrupted the
town government. Anyone who observed the ruling cliques of still
free cities in the Empire — the Frankfurt oligarchy of Goethe's
time, for example — could scarcely have charged Strasbourg's Magis-

trat with peculiar vices. For just this reason, I referred in an earlier chapter to certain tendencies antedating 1681, tendencies toward proliferating bureaucracy, toward aristocratic exclusiveness in the governing class, toward a declining level of official morality. Admittedly, all these things became more marked in Strasbourg during the eighteenth century; but this was equally true of city-states all the way from Hamburg to Venice, far beyond the boundaries of France.

No, the changes in Strasbourg's governmental system which may be attributed directly to the capitulation to France must be stated in other terms. The Catholic-Protestant mixture and the infiltration of French-speaking elements into ruling circles were important modifications. It seems clear also that imitation of French salon manners tended increasingly, from the time of the Regency onward, to alter the tone of the local oligarchy. As Louis Spach dryly remarks: "A new spirit had breathed upon the ancient ways — I shall not pretend that in polishing them it had exactly improved them." [51] Lassitude and cynicism, however, reflected more than just a new ideal of social elegance. These traits had their origin in, and were constantly reinforced by, a general awareness that both final authority and final responsibility had passed out of the hands of the once proud ruling families into those of distant ministers.

The whole task of the oligarchy, defined purely in terms of its own self-interest, evolved steadily toward something fundamentally different from what it had been before 1681. Previously, the aim of Strasbourg's leaders had been to keep themselves and their class in power by assuring the external and internal security of the city, while maintaining at least an appearance of accountability to the population in general and the guilds in particular, so that there would be no general uprising. Now, under the French crown, the successors of Jakob Sturm and Dominikus Dietrich had to operate within a radically altered system of power and answerability. They still observed most of the old formalities governing elections and deliberations. They sought to avoid the kind of popular indignation which might undermine their personal credit with the king.

Most of all, however, they had to recognize that they were accountable to the central government, which in turn represented the external force indispensable to their own survival. It is only in terms of the conscious, the increasing identification of interest between the monarchy and the Magistrat that we can understand how national and local issues could merge so quickly after 1789, and why monarchy and Magistrat went down together in the wreckage of the old regime.

CHAPTER FIVE

Catholics and Protestants

I

Dom Ruinart, O.B., visited Strasbourg in September 1696 and made the following entry in his travel notes. It takes us back, abruptly, to the seventeenth century, but that is where we must pick up the religious record:

On the 24th I betook myself to the largest of the Protestant churches, the *Temple-Neuf,* which once belonged to the Dominican Order. I was curious to observe the rites of their cult, and I was able to do so perfectly, being seated high up.

What ensues, concerning the Lutheran service, is couched partly in the language of an anthropologist commenting on the tribal customs of some newly discovered aborigines, but partly too in terms of admiration, for the choral music at any rate.[1] Here, more than a decade after the Revocation of the Edict of Nantes and almost two decades before the end of Louis XIV's reign, a learned Benedictine monk looks down on German-speaking subjects of the king, reasserting by the very form of their worship their independence of the Roman Church.

Obviously, the Revocation itself did not extend to Alsace. This had been made clear by no less an authority than Louvois in a letter to Intendant La Grange on October 18, 1685:

You will shortly hear reports that the King has caused to be published a declaration which forbids the exercise of the so-called Reformed Religion throughout the kingdom; and, as you will receive no order from His Majesty on this point, I am advising you not to be surprised about it, inasmuch as H. M. has decided to leave religious affairs in your department as they have been in the past.[2]

It is sometimes said that in 1685 the Revocation had no meaning for areas which had not yet been parts of France when the Edict itself was issued in 1598; but that criterion would have exempted Franche-Comté, Roussillon, and much of French Flanders, where Protestants were in fact persecuted relentlessly under Louis XIV. Actually, the special position of Alsace, and of Strasbourg within Alsace, rested upon a combination of royal prudence and avowed respect for explicit agreements — for the king was a great legalist when he felt he could afford to be.[3]

The Westphalia settlement, which in 1648 had given the French crown its initial hold on the province, had confirmed the principle of *cuius regio, eius religio,* theoretically assuring territorial rulers religious sovereignty as well. At the same time, however, the Treaty of Osnabrück had committed various princes, including the King of France, to grant the areas ceded to them such freedom of conscience as had existed in the "normative year" of 1624. The multiple pressures subsequently applied by the monarchy in Lower Alsace, with its large Protestant population, unquestionably violated the spirit of this treaty. Nevertheless, even in 1685, as Louvois' letter shows, royal policymakers recoiled from a show of complete disregard for the legal guarantees and, even more, from the danger of a mass religious revolt in a strategic area so vital and so exposed.

Strasbourg itself had a still more concrete claim to toleration for Lutheranism. Article Three of the capitulation signed in 1681 read:

His Majesty will leave the free exercise of religion as it has been since the year 1624 up to the present, with all the churches and schools, and will permit no one to make demands on them or on ecclesiastical properties . . . but will guarantee them in perpetuity to the city and its inhabitants.

In the margin Louvois had scribbled his response on behalf of the crown:

Granted, as regards ecclesiastical properties, in accordance with the Treaty of Münster, except for the body of the Church of Notre Dame, otherwise called the cathedral, which will be returned to the Catholics. His Majesty being pleased, however, to permit [the Lutherans] to make use of the bells of said church for all purposes for which they have been employed heretofore, except for ringing their prayers.[4]

Such, at the outset, was the contract under which the two confessions were supposed to coexist in Strasbourg. As we already know, however, the precise meaning of the terms was subject to interpretation by the crown, and the arrangements originally envisaged changed considerably between the date of the annexation and 1789. Thus, the question arises: how did religious partition, once established, actually work out?

II

To sketch a picture of the rival church organizations in the city would be more difficult if anything like general toleration had been agreed upon in 1681. Instead, Calvinist worship was still forbidden; and the French authorities could count on the Lutherans to keep these Protestant rivals in their place, i.e., permitted to live in Strasbourg but compelled to hold services in the rural church at Wolfisheim. All Jews still had to leave the city at sundown. Anabaptists and other splinter groups were excluded from royal and municipal offices alike. So far as legal, public worship was concerned, until the last years before 1789, the equation had only two terms: Catholic and Lutheran.

After the capitulation, as before, there were seven Lutheran parishes. When the cathedral had to be surrendered, its former congregation moved a few hundred yards north to what in medieval times, as Dom Ruinart noted, had been the Dominicans' *Prediger-kirche*. A general collection paid for clearing and redecorating this edifice; and in December 1681, under the name of *Neue Kirche* or *Temple-Neuf,* it formally assumed what had been the cathedral's role as chief parish. Its choir continued to house the university library; its auditorium, the public academic ceremonies; its cloister, both the Gymnasium classes and the student boarders or "Wilhelm-ites" who held scholarships for theology.[5]

Four other parishes — St. Thomas, St. William, St. Nicholas, and St. Aurelia — underwent no physical change. The remaining two, however, Old St. Peter and Young St. Peter, were modified in a curious manner. These were both collegial churches; and for 150 years the Magistrat had honored the claim of the exiled Catholic chapters to the income from their prebends. In 1681 the French crown, pointing out that the choir of such a church is the special preserve of the chapter, awarded that portion of each of the two buildings to the Catholics; and in each a wall was erected to separate the places of worship. Late in the nineteenth century the Catholic parish of Young St. Peter was to build its own church of that name, leaving to the Lutherans the ancient original. Old St. Peter, on the other hand, remains to this day day an "L"-shaped edifice, with the Lutheran section still occupying the early fifteenth-century nave, while the Catholic part comprises the old choir plus a modern nave jutting out at a right angle to the rest.[6]

The Convocation or *Kirchenkonvent* continued after 1681 to be the common assembly of pastors, vicars, wardens, and teachers. Ultimate control of the Lutheran ecclesiastical polity, however, had to be modified, since the Magistrat as a whole would never again be exclusively Protestant. Hence, a board of seven Superior Church Wardens was established, one from each parish and all of them necessarily members of the city's Secret Chambers. It was these *Obere Kirchenpfleger* who henceforth were to exercise the religious authority formerly vested in the full Senate-and-XXI. Finally, the pastors of the seven parishes, under the President of the Convocation, made up a consultative college of preachers.[7]

Turning to the resurrected Catholic organization, we encounter a bishopric still governed by the German concordat of 1448. Under François-Egon de Furstemberg, who died in 1682, and his brother, Guillaume-Egon, who occupied the see until 1704, episcopal admin-istrative machinery was quickly reëstablished: a chancellery, an *officialité,* and, from 1695 on, an eight-member *Chambre Ecclésias-*

tique to assess and administer funds collected from the clergy for "free gifts" to the crown.[8] Also returned from exile, though they were almost never in the city except for the election of a bishop, were the twelve voting, or capitulary, canons and the twelve associate canons of the cathedral chapter. Known far and wide as the "noblest in Europe," this chapter was exclusively composed of princes or counts of the Empire until 1687, when Louis XIV decreed that in the future one-third of the places should be reserved for French noblemen.[9]

Inside the city, during the hectic period of adjustment after 1681, the Catholics created the parish of St. Lawrence at the cathedral, two more in the choirs of the Old and Young St. Peters, and an additional three — St. Mark (shortly renamed St. John), St. Stephen, and St. Louis — in churches idle since the mid-sixteenth century, but now returned by the Magistrat under royal pressure. By the late 1680's these six parishes were all established; and as in the case of the Lutherans' seven, their number remained constant throughout the eighteenth century.[10]

It was the return of the various orders of regular clergy, however, which did most to dramatize the changed conditions of local religious life. The nuns of St. Margaret and those of St. Magdalen, with a handful of priest-knights of Malta (Johannites), were the only such groups already represented within the walls when the French troops arrived. A few weeks later the first of many reinforcements, three Capuchin monks of the Swiss province, rode in to establish a community especially charged with spiritual care in hospitals, prisons, and other such institutions. By 1686, at the completion of the new Capuchin cloister between the citadel and the walls, there were twenty friars ready to occupy it; and in 1738 they expanded into an additional cloister and chapel in the center of town.[11] Meanwhile, other Franciscans, the *Récollets,* had taken over religious guidance of the military garrison. Perhaps most important of all were the Jesuit teachers and missionaries, who, from a small local beginning in 1682, grew into the largest corps of regular clergy established anywhere in Alsace.

To these must be added smaller communities of Antonites and Augustinians, numerous sisters of the Congregation of Notre Dame, and the band of French *Visitandines* who in 1702 took over the nunnery attached to St. Stephen, formerly a convent for Lutheran noblewomen. As of 1789 the number of secular priests assigned to parishes in Strasbourg stood at 38, the number of friars at 131, and that of nuns at 132.[12] Earlier in the century, before the expulsion of the Jesuits and the submersion of the Antonites in the Johannite Order, the total had certainly been larger;[13] but even the figure of three hundred on the eve of the Revolution seemed gigantic when contrasted with the sparse personnel of the Lutheran establishment.

Admittedly, a mere numerical comparison between the local clergies of the two sects could be misleading, unless it were borne in mind that one of them regularly used ecclesiastics for a variety of services normally performed, for the other, by laymen. This is particularly true of education; since the Lutheran schoolmasters, Gymnasium teachers, and university professors actually constituted a major component of the Protestant church organization. The Catholic parishes too had their schools, while the Sisters of Notre Dame and the Visitandine nuns concerned themselves particularly with the religious education of girls. After 1684 the *Collège Royal* offered direct competition to the old Gymnasium. Finally, for higher studies there was the seminary, established by Bishop Guillaume-Egon in 1683, and the episcopal university created in 1701, when the former Catholic University of Molsheim was moved into Strasbourg and combined with the royal college. Yet for all the diligence of the Jesuit professors, these institutions never managed seriously to challenge the prestige of Strasbourg's Lutheran Gymnasium and university.

It was in the social organization of laymen that the Catholic clergy made up for the Protestants' superiority in advanced education. Both the Capuchins and the Récollets developed large chapters of the Third Order of St. Francis. As the Catholic population of the city grew, a host of lay sodalities took form, under the guidance of priests and friars: in 1698 for French-speaking citizens (*Sodalitas*

Civium Gallorum), in 1707 for journeymen laborers, in 1717 for German-speaking citizens, and so on. Some of them were devoted to penitence and exemplary living, as in the cases of the Brotherhood of the Terror of Death, the Marian League of Absolution, and the Sorority of the Immaculate Conception. Others, such as the Girl Debaters (*Kontroversjungfern*) and the Brotherhood of St. Francis Xavier, were frankly proselytic in character. Whether dedicated to such specific tasks, however, or simply committed to attendance at evening meetings and group participation in religious processions, these societies constituted an elaborate network of contacts between Catholic clergy and laity, a network which could not fail at times to impress the Lutherans with their own corporate weakness in the struggle of faiths.[14]

III

This struggle itself was destined to undergo an evolution in which changing local conditions, church politics, governmental policies, and public attitudes all played their parts. One cannot impose an elaborate periodization on such complex material, because at no point in Strasbourg's religious history between 1681 and 1789 was there a sharp break. At the same time, it is both helpful and perfectly valid to distinguish between the period of extreme tension which lasted as long as Louis XIV was on the French throne and the progressive relaxation of active, though not of theoretical, hostility after 1715. Furthermore, by the latter half of the eighteenth century both of these earlier phases had given way to a third, marked by compromises and concessions which would have seemed unthinkable to king, clergy, or laymen a hundred years before.

Certainly the 1680's offered little promise of interconfessional forbearance. Six weeks after the capitulation, the Marquis de Chamilly decided on a formal procession to the cathedral for prayers on behalf of his ailing father, the Host to be escorted through the streets by some eleven hundred officers and men of the garrison, who carried not only torches or candles but sabers as well. At the town hall, where the nervous Magistrat had chained the doors shut, the governor paused long enough to have the locks opened under the eyes of his troops. In those first years it was as though every public display of Catholic worship served only to remind Lutherans on whose side the military power now lay.[15]

Countless Protestant historians have recorded with great exactitude the measures taken by the crown to favor the Church of Rome in Strasbourg and to penalize those who rejected its communion. In opposition, Catholic scholars have argued that, by the standards of the day, remarkably little violence was employed in the effort to restore the city to the king's own faith. In one sense or another, both sides are right. Except for occasional kidnapings and some sporadic use of billeting privileges to make life unpleasant for Lutheran householders — a pale and soon abandoned imitation of the *dragonnades* — there was in fact little physical mistreatment of old residents. What the royal authorities did do was to offer tempting rewards for abjuring Lutheranism, while placing a variety of obstacles in the way of countermeasures by the Protestant leaders.

In rural Alsace, including Strasbourg's outlying bailiwicks, the methods adopted were much harsher — Lutheran village officers deposed, the local church divided between the two sects as soon as seven Catholic families could be counted in residence, the same church closed to Protestants whenever and wherever Catholics numbered two-thirds of the population. Within Strasbourg, save in the case of the cathedral, no Lutheran congregation was wholly excluded from its place of worship, despite repeated appeals to the crown on the part of the Roman clergy.[16]

The most irritating royal measures were those relating to the question of conversion. Converts to Catholicism were guaranteed three years' exemption from taxes and billeting responsibilities, as well as a moratorium on their personal debts for the same period, the bargain already familiar in the interior. Lutheran ministers were forbidden to give public lectures of a missionary nature, on pain of transportation to the galleys. Lutheran parents were technically estopped from interfering with Jesuit visits to children more than

seven years old, if the latter had indicated any interest in a possible
change of faith. Abjurations could not work in the other direction,
however; since, as elsewhere in Louis XIV's realm, harsh penalties
were provided for the individual who relapsed after having once
been listed as a Catholic.

It is easy for anyone living in a secular society to concentrate on
the religious compulsion practiced by governments in the age of
absolutism and to ignore all other factors. Louis XIV doubtless combined genuine piety, as he grew older, with that petulant desire
for uniformity which Louvois personified in its most brutal form.
As seen from Versailles, Strasbourg's Protestants were an affront,
a challenge to calculating statemanship, which sought to merge
bribery and punishments into a single technique of authoritarian
persuasion. On the local scene, however, the drama involved much
more than that. On one side stood the Lutherans, including the
haughty and itself intolerant ruling class of the imperial era, but
also thousands of men and women honestly convinced that their
personal integrity, their whole relationship to God was jeopardized
by what they viewed as alien idolatry. On the other side stood
Catholic clergymen, most of them sincere, unselfish, and imbued
with a sense of responsibility for the salvation of their new fellow-
citizens. It was exasperating for these men, impelled by such an
urgent motive, to encounter stubborn resistance from Christians
whose basic beliefs, as seen by the priests and friars, included so little
to preclude a joyous return to the old faith, with all its warmth and
color and certitude.

A tormenting conviction, this belief that the Protestants had only
a little way to come, that they were clinging blindly to a few
accidental errors into which their ancestors had fallen. With that in
mind we can appreciate the confidence which Jesuits and Capuchins
brought to their public lectures in the cathedral, as we can comprehend the optimism of Father Dez, S.J., publishing in 1687 his long
tract, *The Reunion of the Protestants of Strasbourg to the Roman
Church, Equally Necessary for Their Salvation and Easy According
to Their Principles*. Where theological and historical arguments

would not suffice, the Jesuits, in particular, were prepared to issue threats, invade private homes, and otherwise apply pressure on the resentful Protestants. Any measure, the Society argued, was justified if it served to hasten what must be assumed to be the inevitable solution of the whole problem. A good example of such policies was the memorandum submitted to Praetor Obrecht by Father L'Empereur, S.J., early in 1686 — an outline for "mild violence" to be applied under royal auspices in a series of increasingly rigorous stages.[17] Obrecht and his superiors refused to adopt these elaborate and sweeping methods, but the campaign went forward at every possible level, through ecclesiastical action.

The actual record of conversion is extremely hard to make out, because the various Catholic agencies, even when they sought to tabulate their own particular successes, did not pool the separate figures to provide annual or periodic summaries.[18] The issue is further confused by the great acclaim which greeted certain individual acts of abjuration. Abbé Fléchier wrote to Madame Des Houlières as early as October 26, 1681, describing the pomp with which a public conversion was celebrated in the cathedral while Louis XIV and his entourage were still at Strasbourg:

> I have received the abjuration of a very pretty girl, sister to the king's resident, concerning which you will apparently be seeing an article soon in the *Gazette*. As this was the first convert since our religion was reestablished here, the Queen and Madame the Dauphine attended the profession of faith, with a large and august company.[19]

So great were the political opportunities offered those who embraced the royal religion that a number of the Magistrat's oldest families saw at least some of their members repudiate Lutheranism. Richshoffer, Kageneck, Leitersperger, Brackenhoffer, and several other familiar names joined those of Obrecht and Güntzer on the Catholic rolls.[20] Though these families generally retained Protestant branches, the excitement caused by conversions within the oligarchy spread quickly throughout Lutheran Germany. In February 1682, the Senate-and-XXI already felt called upon to send a formal protest to Frankfurt over reports published in a newspaper there to the effect that "many leading citizens had turned Catholic in Strasbourg." [21]

Yet the number of conversions, taking the town population as a whole, never approached the early hopes of the crown and the Catholic clergy. Even in the strongly tempted governing class, for every Richshoffer there were several Wenckers and Reisseissens who unostentatiously maintained their previous affiliation. Against the royal government's joy over the conversion of Ulrich Obrecht in 1684 must be set its chagrin the next year when the far more influential Ammeister Dietrich refused to follow suit. As a matter of fact, the first team of ecclesiastics to enter the city for avowedly missionary purposes, a handful of French Oratorians, had by 1686 despaired of success and left town. That same year the Anglican bishop, Gilbert Burnet, passed through Strasbourg and jotted down in his notes an estimate of two hundred abjurations since the annexation.[22] The records of the large and strategically placed Capuchin community show that that order converted twelve persons in 1684 but only three in 1694 and one the following year. For the period 1682–1724 the Capuchins claimed a total of 118 native Strasbourgers converted, or an average of under three per year. In 1697 Intendant La Grange wrote:

> The original inhabitants of the city, noble and otherwise, profess the religion of Luther. . . . There are few native Catholics, the majority of these being converts who have abjured only to obtain offices.[23]

IV

The question of Catholics in the Magistrat deserves special attention. A *lettre de cachet,* signed by Louis XIV at Versailles on April 5, 1687, was destined to become one of Strasbourg's fundamental regulations the moment it was delivered to the Council of Thirteen:

> Very dear and well-beloved: Having been informed that there are now in Strasbourg a considerable number of Catholic citizens and esteeming

that it would not be just for said Catholic citizens to have no representatives in the Magistrat of the city, . . . We are sending you this letter to advise you that Our Intention is that henceforth . . . positions in the said Magistrat should be *alternately* filled by Catholics and Lutherans, in such a manner that there will always be in the said Magistrat and in the other offices and places of the municipality a number of Catholic and Lutheran citizens and inhabitants proportionate to what there will be of the one and the other religion in the city. . . . And having no doubt that you will conform to our will in this matter, We shall not make these presents longer or more explicit. Do not fail in this. Because such is Our Pleasure.[24]

It has seemed worthwhile to quote this document at length, because the text itself best indicates the significance of the policy being announced, as well as certain practical problems involved in its enforcement. Even more important, this first statement offers a basis for judging the extent to which the *Alternative* was later pushed beyond its original limits.

However indignant they might be at what they considered an exaggeration of the actual number of Catholics in the city as of 1687, contemporaries like Reisseissen could scarcely deny the equity of the principle involved, always provided that genuinely proportional representation remained the goal. When the Alternative was introduced in 1687, although the formerly Protestant bailiffs of the Magistrat's rural domains had long since been either converted or replaced, there was not a single Catholic among the elected members of the city government. One difficulty was that ten years' previous citizenship was required for election, even to the Assembly of Three Hundred; and since no Catholic could yet satisfy that stipulation, a second *lettre de cachet* abolished it. There remained, however, the question of numbers. In January 1688, when two Catholics were chosen Senators and four others Assemblymen by their guilds, Louvois wrote angrily to Obrecht that this was insufficient and that the three Lutherans named in the letter must immediately be replaced by three designated Catholics, bringing to seven the total number of Assemblymen of that faith. The same year, Georg Streitt von Immendingen, a noble previously in the service of the Archbishop of Cologne, became Strasbourg's first Catholic Stettmeister since the Reformation; and a coreligionist of his, Lucas Weinemer, was elected to the Fifteen. Two years later, this same Weinemer became Ammeister, filling the place which would normally have been Dominikus Dietrich's during 1690.

By this time the Lutherans were discovering that the Alternative would be used to produce not proportional representation but full parity between Catholic and Protestant officeholders. In 1691 a significant conflict of interpretations arose over the vacancy created by the death of a Lutheran Thirteener named Volz. Since the most recent preceding election to the council had been that of the Catholic Weinemer, the Protestants insisted that another Lutheran should replace Volz. Obrecht, however, replied that the king's intention had been alternation not in elections to a governmental body taken as a whole, but in direct succession by individuals, the replacement always to be of the opposite faith from the man he succeeded. Quite aside from the question of technical application, Reisseissen indignantly tells us that the choice of a Catholic would bring the total of such in the Thirteen, including Obrecht, to four, well beyond the proportion of Catholics in the town population.[25] Resistance was futile, however; and a Kageneck of the Catholic branch had to be promoted directly from the Senate, since there were currently no Catholic Fifteeners or Twenty-oners.

At all levels the movement toward parity progressed so fast that by 1694 fifteen out of the thirty Senators were Catholics, a balance which was to be maintained from then on. Within a few years thereafter, deaths and replacements had produced the same result among Stettmeisters, Ammeisters, and members of the Secret Chambers. Sometimes the crown insisted on one Catholic's being succeeded by another, thus violating the very principle imposed by Obrecht in 1691. These occasional fiats, however, occurred only in cases where the luck of succession was threatening to block the program's whole purpose, and were matched by some flexibility even in the replacement of Lutherans. It was conceivable that absolutely rigid alternation, untempered by common sense, might produce not simultaneous representation for both sects, but instead a series of generations of officeholders now predominantly of one religion and a few years later overweighted in favor of the other.

However bizarre the operation of the Alternative sometimes appeared, given the complexity of Strasbourg's town government, the religious partition of that government had been achieved by the time Louis XIV died. It had brought some new elements into the oligarchy, but the conversion of some of the old ones had prevented any complete revolution in personnel. Disputes recurred periodically, as in 1751 and 1768, when the Catholics sought without success to extend the rule to faculty appointments in the university.[26] The confusions implicit in Louis XIV's original decree were long unresolved, but, after the early wrangles, the general pattern became less and less a source of active animosity or debate, as even the most curious arrangements tend to do when a society has lived with them a while. Furthermore, the eighteenth century was to see disappear the most obvious injustice in the balance established by the Alternative. For parity in the Magistrat was unfair only so long as Catholics were a local minority. It ceased to be so when they achieved numerical equality with Lutherans in the population at large.

V

The first major increase in Catholic numbers is revealed in the figures obtained by the royal praetor, when in November 1697 he took the unprecedented step of conducting a local census.[27] These figures include all inhabitants, whether citizens or not, except noblemen, soldiers, and Catholic clergymen:

Lutherans	19,839
Catholics	5,119
Calvinists	1,523
Total	26,481

Though still constituting less than twenty per cent of the town's population, the Catholics had already become an important minority.

This had come about almost entirely as a result of immigration. Recalling the previously quoted remarks by Intendant La Grange concerning the paucity of conversions, we need attach little quantitative importance to Lutheran abjurations. It was the influx of new settlers which made the difference. Louis XIV offered rewards in land, money, and privileges to Frenchmen willing to move into Alsace — his aim was primarily economic and political, but since Protestants were excluded from the invitation, the effect was inevitably religious as well. Similarly, by forcing Strasbourg's Magistrat to admit numerous new citizens,[28] he made it easier not only for French subjects but also for German Catholics from Protestant states like Württemberg and Saxony to establish themselves in the city.

By 1726, when the town's population had reached 34,821, a new survey revealed 10,480 Catholics, 22,841 Lutherans, and 1,500 Calvinists.[29] By the late 1730's Catholic births had overtaken those in Lutheran families, surpassing the latter by a slowly growing margin in the decades that followed.[30] In 1789, by which time the city had almost precisely 50,000 inhabitants, Catholics outnumbered Lutherans by about 3,500.[31] The former had taken up nearly all of the over-all growth in Strasbourg's population under French rule.

On the eve of the Revolution, Protestants still constituted an overwhelming majority of full guild members: 4,861 to only 1,997 Catholics, the latter faith being most strongly represented among unincorporated labor.[32] It should also be said that the nature of immigration had changed during the eighteenth century, until the figures for reception of new citizens in the four years 1781–1784 show 245 Protestants, as opposed to 204 Catholics.[33] Yet these necessary qualifications of the simple population totals do not alter the significance of the totals themselves. In 1681 Strasbourg had been for all practical purposes a Lutheran city. By 1789 it was half-Catholic and was on its way to becoming predominantly so, though it is to this day the home of the largest urban mass of Protestants in France. By the 1790's equal representation in the Magistrat might have begun to seem unfair to the Catholics themselves. It might have, but it didn't, for the very good reason that by the 1790's the Revolution had swept away the whole principle of confessional representation, as embodied in the Alternative.

VI

Some may find it paradoxical that the years after 1715, the very period which witnessed great numerical gains by the Roman Church in Strasbourg, should also have seen the Lutherans emerge from the defensive and sometimes frightened state into which the capitulation to Louis XIV had thrown them. There were several reasons for the change, including the behavior of the Catholics themselves. The latter, as a small minority at first sustained only by the royal army, had also known insecurity, frustration, and resentment. Hence, in human terms, it is not puzzling to find them speaking more softly as they became more firmly established. This softer speaking, be it added, appeared so only in contrast to the shrill and threatening tones of the late seventeenth century.

The progressive waning of the old intensity was personified by the bishops themselves, the four princes of the house of Rohan who from 1704 to the Revolution occupied the rich see of Strasbourg in an uncle-to-nephew succession. The Furstembergs had been courtiers too, but above all Catholic politicians, trained at Cologne, and dependent on the pious royal master at Versailles. The Rohans, all four of them, were truly *grands seigneurs,* fixtures of an urbane and indolent court, interested in the revenues of the diocese but not greatly concerned over its lack of religious uniformity. They were frequently in Paris, and much of their correspondence with their subordinates or with civil officials reflects a bored desire to get various disputes settled with a minimum of uproar and exertion.[34] The last of the four, Louis-René-Edouard, who became bishop in 1779, found it particularly hard to find time for Alsatian affairs. The enterprises of his protégé, Cagliostro, and adventures such as the purchase of a diamond necklace for the queen taxed his rather mediocre faculties to the limit.

Still more important in the changing situation was the gradual abandonment by the governmental authorities of strongly confessional policies. In this respect, Louis XIV had by the time of his death begun to appear something of an antique curiosity. During the regency of the Duc d'Orléans and the remainder of Louis XV's long reign, French subjects might still eye one another with hostility and suspicion; but whatever formal gestures it might make from time to time, the crown would never again apply the old ruthlessness on behalf of any church.

The change was neither sudden nor quickly apparent. Especially in the early part of the eighteenth century, some of the authorities in Alsace continued to act as though the late king might still call them to account. Strasbourg's Lutherans were permitted no public observance either in 1717, bicentennial of the Ninety-five Theses, or in 1721, the centennial of the Protestant University. The Comte Du Bourg, provincial commandant, was especially eager to demonstrate his orthodoxy by imposing military imprisonment on alleged violators of church regulations.[35] Repeatedly, the Sovereign Council at Colmar drew reprimands from intendants and royal ministers for excessive harshness against non-Catholics.[36] Nevertheless, a single case drawn from the municipal archives will suffice to illustrate the shift of emphasis which took place after Louis XIV's passing. It revolves around a domestic drama, but one which attracted the attention of royal officials all the way up to the Regency Council.[37]

One Maria Salome Blanck, widow of a local baker, had apparently, after the death of her husband, fallen into such a notoriously "wild, lewd, and shameful" life that in the summer of 1718 the Senate of the city had transferred the custody of her four children to her father, who was an established butcher named Magnus, and their Lutheran tutor, Johann Jakob (or Jean-Jacques) Wagner. On November 24 of that year the Senate was startled to receive from the diocesan chancellery a petition drawn up in the name of widow Blanck. It attested to her conversion some two weeks before, as proven by the attached certificate of abjuration signed by Father

Scheffmacher, S.J., and demanded the return of her children so that they might receive proper religious training. When invited to reply, Magnus and the tutor submitted a counter-memorandum to the effect that no one could object to the woman's conversion, that in fact they both hoped it indicated genuine contrition, but that they feared it actually represented only her desire to escape all paternal control. She had, they asserted, already managed to dissipate her dead husband's legacy, still spent her time consorting with actors, drank almost uninterruptedly, and was in all respects unfit to care for a family. Furthermore, she had on several occasions cursed the legal guardians in the most violent terms and had told everyone who cared to listen that she would stab her father or, failing that, burn down his house. This latter threat had been reported to him by his next-door neighbor, who had, as the document sagely points out, "a certain interest in the matter."

With the Magistrat thus pinned between Jesuit demands on one side and the indignation of the Lutheran populace on the other, Praetor Klinglin decided to refer the question to Paris, in a letter of December 9. On the 20th, the secretary of state for war, d'Armenonville, wrote back that the Regent himself had agreed that this was a case demanding a precedential ruling and that the full council had discussed it the previous day. The ministers had decided that no guidance could be obtained from declarations of the deceased Louis XIV concerning the education of converts' children, "which, strictly speaking, concern only subjects of the R.P.R. in the old dominion of the king [i.e., French Huguenots] and not the city of Strasbourg." The council further agreed that the mother's past conduct made her conversion highly suspect and that, in any event, her adoption of Catholicism could not alter a decision previously taken by the Senate, as a civil court acting for the children's welfare. Hence, His Royal Highness was willing that the local government proceed as it thought best. The Regent's only further wish was that the intendant, d'Angervilliers, should attempt with Klinglin's help to induce the present guardians to enter the children in a Catholic school, possibly at reduced tuition. The letter nevertheless concludes: "If neither of you can find a way to arrive at that solution, you will leave the Magistrat free to render its own judgment, as explained above."

On New Year's Eve, shortly after the ruling from Paris reached Strasbourg, d'Angervilliers summoned Magnus and Wagner to his residence for the talk envisaged by the Regent; but, as he explained in a note to Klinglin, "I wasn't able to have any conversation with them, because at the first word I uttered they indicated by gestures that they neither spoke nor understood French." The intendant, in short, must ask the praetor to speak with them. Klinglin did as requested, forwarding to the war minister on January 5, 1719, a report of what proved to be a negative interview. The two guardians insisted on continuing their young charges' Lutheran education. D'Armenonville's subsequent reply is as eloquent of the "Regency spirit" in such matters as any document I have ever seen:

Paris, January 16, 1719

Monsieur,

I have received your letters on the subject of one Blanck in reply to that which I wrote to you on December 20, at the order of Monseigneur the Duc d'Orléans; and I have seen from their contents that M. d'Angervilliers and you have overlooked nothing, each doing his share, in order to spare these children the misfortune of being raised in error. And since we have on this occasion done what depended on us, on behalf of the Religion, the Magistrat of Strasbourg may now give its judgment, as I have previously advised you. I am, very sincerely, etc.

Ten days after the above was written, the Senate confirmed its previous award of custody to the children's grandfather and tutor. This might have ended the matter, if the widow Blanck and her spiritual advisers had been less determined. Even before the Senate's final decision against her, however, she had recovered her eldest daughter — by kidnaping, according to the grandfather — and was now ready to swear that the girl had voluntarily embraced the Catholic faith. So on January 27 Klinglin again wrote to the war minister, explaining this new turn of events and stating that in a conference with him the Lutheran guardians had reluctantly agreed to let this eldest child remain with her mother. D'Armenonville sent a concluding note to the praetor on February 2, congratulating him on having saved at least one girl from heresy. Despite protests from Abbé de Vizé, the vicar-general, this is how the case was terminated. An interesting postscript is the remark Klinglin included in his last letter to Paris on the subject:

I trust . . . that the Jesuit Fathers will discover for themselves that by not observing a certain moderation they will make themselves obnoxious. Otherwise, they are going to injure the interests of the Catholic religion in this city more than advance them by indiscreet zeal.

The mixture of formal piety and essentially political calculation which marks all the official correspondence over the Blanck affair is characteristic of the spirit of the reign, at least down to the 1760's. It was a spirit which sought to exacerbate nothing if it could be left alone, face nothing squarely if it could be sidestepped, solve nothing on principle if it could be solved by an administrative compromise. Under such a regime, restrictive measures against Protestants could and did still create a stir from time to time. In 1727, for example, the secretary of state for war, Le Blanc, informed Intendant Harlay at Strasbourg that the law prescribing Catholic baptism for all illegitimate children, regardless of the parents' faith, must be enforced. (Local records show that in the preceding twelve years alone some 150 such children had been baptized in the city's Lutheran churches.)[38] Louis XV is said to have remarked on one occasion that he personally considered "excessive" his predecessor's doctrine that every bastard in the realm was a child of the king, and Louis XV was no less an authority on this subject than Louis XIV had been. Yet for the time being the old rule remained in force.[39]

It would be a mistake to think of Lutherans as solely preoccupied with Catholic maneuvers throughout the first half of the eighteenth century. Almost as much attention was devoted by the Convocation to the suppression of internal heresies, particularly the doctrine of an inner light which made even their bare Protestant ritual seem pretentious. The apostle of Pietism, Philip Jakob Spener, had been born in Alsace, at Ribeauvillé, educated in Strasbourg's Gymnasium and university, and briefly employed as supernumerary preacher in the then still Lutheran cathedral. His wife was the daughter of a Strasbourg Senator. Yet from 1666, when he left to accept a pastorate in Frankfurt, until just before his death in 1705, his doctrine of intense, introspective, essentially mystical Christianity had been little discussed in the city where he had been educated. Nowhere in the Lutheran world had his *Pia desideria* or his *Explanation of Christian Teachings* awakened fewer immediate echoes. Perhaps this was because during the years of Spener's greatest popularity Strasbourg was wholly concerned with the coming of the French and the return of Catholicism. Or perhaps its Lutheran hierarchy had remained too strong and too orthodox to permit such speculations to gain a foothold.[40]

At any rate, it was not until 1701 that the indignant Convocation and Superior Church Wardens learned of private meetings, being held by small groups of citizens critical of the local establishment for what they considered its pride, bigotry, and superficiality. The suggestion that regular services under permanent ministers were not essential to the spiritual life of the elect was received among Lutheran clergymen with about the cordiality once felt by the Catholic priesthood for Luther's comments on ecclesiastical organization. President Zentgraff of the Convocation dedicated himself fully to a campaign of extirpation, later described in his massive published report.[41] Louis XIV's government, which cannot have felt deeply interested but which automatically condemned any sort of heterodoxy, supported the Magistrat in its decision to exile a theology student, Haug, and two pastors from villages in the rural bailiwicks, Ruopp and Röderer, as well as several laymen who had furnished quarters for their prayer meetings.[42] By 1705 the movement, in its organized form, had been smashed.

But the sectaries of the inner light and the critics of Lutheran orthodoxy were by no means eliminated from Strasbourg. For three decades after the first flareup, cells of Spenerites and Quakers were repeatedly identified by the Convocation. Then in about 1735 the Moravian Brethren began to find support among the local populace, and in 1742 their spiritual leader, Count von Zinzendorf, paid a visit to the city. Again several young clergymen and theology students, including the son of the pastor of St. Nicholas, were banished by the Magistrat. Again arose a champion of the old hierarchy, this time Professor Froereissen, who was, like Zentgraff before him, President of the Kirchenkonvent. It was, however, impossible to prevent individual citizens from sending their children off to Herrnhut in Moravia to be educated at Zinzendorf's school. At one point, in 1745, the Convocation decreed a campaign of "love and tenderness" to convert the Brethren; but ten years later the Magistrat was still passing stern regulations against "secret meetings of anarchical mystics." [43]

At no time did these small defections seriously cut into the total Lutheran membership, any more than did scattered conversions to Catholicism or Calvinism. They served, however, to increase the atmosphere of confusion and uncertainty already created by the religious policies of the crown, conciliatory one moment, threatening the next.[44] The first half of the eighteenth century was not a black time for the Lutherans of Strasbourg, not a time of always clear and present danger, but it was a time of nervous efforts to maintain an old and once seemingly unshakeable position. As things turned out, the last generation before the Revolution was to see a combination of changes, some of which were to be distasteful to ardent Catholics without being wholly comforting to orthodox Lutherans.

VII

On September 27, 1760, Louis XV signed a *lettre de cachet* which at last clarified some old points of confusion in the Alternative governing Strasbourg's Magistrat. His Majesty, having solicited the ideas of both Catholics and Protestants in the local administration, and having "seen with satisfaction that officials of the two religions have agreed in the same views," states that certain positions, including those of royal praetor, royal syndic, and several others more specifically connected with the Catholic establishment, are confirmed as open only to members of that church. On the other hand, the Lutherans are assured in perpetuity all posts of control over the university, the Gymnasium, and historically Protestant institutions in general. They are even entitled henceforth to have one of their own as deputy treasurer of the cathedral's maintenance plant (*l'Oeuvre Notre-Dame*).[45] Most important, it is decreed, once and for all, that in the councils of the Magistrat each vacancy is to be filled by a Catholic or a Protestant, depending solely on the religion of whoever has been chosen in the last previous election to the body as a whole, without reference to that of the official whose death or retirement has created the opening. Thus, almost seventy years after this interpretive problem was first posed, it is finally settled as the Lutheran Thirteeners wanted it to be in 1691.[46]

The above document, like several others which emanated from Paris at about the same time, suggests a growing readiness on the part of the royal government to face a variety of situations long ignored. There is little reason to suppose that the aging Louis XV himself had suddenly changed his whole philosophy of life. He had not. The men around him, however, were considerably more accessible than their predecessors to ideas of religious liberalism and political equity, ideas which encouraged them to break with existing restrictions and to seek rational solutions of current problems, even if not yet to undertake sweeping reforms.

A letter written in February 1762 by the Duc de Choiseul to the intendant, Lucé, in Strasbourg offers further evidence of the same tendency. The king, says Choiseul, sympathizes with the difficulties involved in applying certain pieces of religious legislation inherited from the past. Specifically, the law governing the baptism and education of bastards states clearly that they must be brought up as Catholics. Nevertheless, the minister continues, His Majesty feels that if the parents are subsequently married, "it is very difficult to deny all consideration to the rights acquired by the mother and father over the free education of their child." For the future, therefore, the following rule is to be observed: parents of a bastard who marry before the child is five years old are to be awarded full custody.[47]

This was the same Choiseul, of course, who was connected with another major change in the religious situation at Strasbourg, the expulsion from France of the Society of Jesus. The city's Catholics, largely indifferent to the earlier conflict over the bull *Unigenitus* and the Jansenist-Gallican denunciation of all ultramontane political activities, had been particularly loyal to the Jesuits, whom they saw as heroes in the conquest of this "recovered land." Cardinal de Rohan defended the Society in the council of bishops at Paris in 1761, and even after the edict of expulsion was issued in 1764, the Sovereign Council at Colmar resisted registration for two more years. Nevertheless, though certain Jesuits remained in residence, the Catholic college, seminary, and university of Strasbourg had to be placed in the hands of secular priests, once the measure became law.[48]

Other royal measures of Louis XV's last years offended the town's Lutherans almost as much as they did the Catholics. This was true, for example, of the enforced reception of Jewish residents. There had been just one break, earlier in the century, in the hallowed tradition that no Jew could spend a night within the walls. This had been in 1743, when d'Argenson had written from the war office insisting that Moses Blien and his business associates be permitted to establish local headquarters as purveyors to the royal army. The privilege had terminated with the end of the War of the Austrian Succession, however, and had supposedly been without any force as a precedent. Then, in 1771, a Jewish banker named Cerf-Beer, a special protégé of Choiseul, petitioned for and was granted temporary residence in a house he had bought at Strasbourg through a proxy, the deputy military governor or *lieutenant du roi,* La Touche. Despite repeated efforts by the Magistrat to dislodge Cerf-Beer and his colony of relatives and assistants, he owned no fewer than nine houses by 1789 and had, in effect, founded the first Jewish community Strasbourg had known in over four hundred years.[49]

What the last decade before the Revolution represented in the religious history of the city is easiest to appreciate when one compares several intendants of Alsace as personifications of an evolving official attitude. La Grange, back in the late seventeenth century, had been the "man of Louvois," determined to enforce orthodoxy under the king and Rome to the full limit of political practicability. D'Angervilliers, just after the death of Louis XIV, had represented with great ability the easy-going cynics of the Regency, seeking to relax local tensions without conceding any overt change in general policies. Lucé in the 1760's had acted on the orders of Choiseul, a rational politician inclined to ease repression wherever it appeared flagrantly unjust, but still reluctant to sponsor bold departures from past traditions. Now, in 1778, arrived the last of the intendants, Chaumont de La Galaizière, admirer of Turgot, reader of the Encyclopedists and of Voltaire. With the tide of reformism running strong in Paris, Strasbourg was obviously going to feel a difference.

One sign of a new spirit was the appointment of Baron de Wurmser in 1778 as acting governor general of the province — the first Protestant ever to exercise authority in Alsace in the name of the French king. Another came in 1779, when the Lutherans of Strasbourg petitioned the royal council, with La Galaizière's support, to reëxamine the minimum age limits for legally binding conversions to Catholicism. These limits had previously been twelve for girls, fourteen for boys — already a far cry from Louis XIV's provision for seven-year-old converts. They were now raised to fourteen and eighteen years, respectively.[50] Finally, in 1787, came an "Edict of the King, Concerning Those Who Do Not Profess the Catholic Religion," of which it has been said that it "revoked the Revocation." [51] That is an exaggeration, for Protestants did not recover all their pre-1685 rights. The king restates the customary wish that all his subjects might return to the old faith, his faith; and he confirms the special position of Catholicism as the recognized "public religion of France." Nevertheless, the preamble discourses at length, in the favorite terms of the Enlightenment, on the evils of compulsion and the injustice of inequality. The edict goes on to rescind Louis XIV's old measures against non-Catholics' right to public worship and concedes them full legal status on the *état-civil*. For the Lutherans of Strasbourg, who had never lost the privileges now restored to French Protestants in general, this enactment had little significance; but for another group, the Calvinists, 1787 marked the culminating stage in a long process of liberation.

It is clear enough, in retrospect, that throughout the century the Reformed congregation had benefited from a progressive easing of royal pressure. Louis XIV's early decrees, prohibiting the use of French in the services at nearby Wolfisheim and forbidding Calvinist preachers even to reside in Strasbourg, had lost their force before the end of his reign. Thereafter, sermons were regularly given in both languages, while pastors like Hey, Bischoff, Gernler, and their successors lived quietly within the city itself.

In the decades after 1715, however, local leaders of the two legal denominations fought back at every opportunity. Calvinist sick were still being automatically assigned to Catholic wards at the hospital in 1746, when Praetor Klinglin finally ruled that for the future such patients might opt for a Lutheran ward instead, but even thereafter they were not supposed to be visited by a minister of their own faith. The Convocation was particularly concerned over mixed marriages, as shown by the Magistrat's decree of 1734, confirming the previous rule, that children of a Lutheran and a Calvinist must invariably be raised in the former's church. On this occasion the pastor and seven deacons of the Reformed congregation entered a plea in favor of letting sons follow their father's, and daughters, their mother's, religion, but it was rejected by the Senate-and-XXI.[52]

After mid-century neither the central government nor an increasingly tolerant public opinion would sustain attempts by Lutheran or Catholic authorities to enforce with full rigor the old regulations against Calvinists. The latter went on marrying outside their church. Less and less effective control over the children's education could be exerted from outside the family, though in 1789 the Calvinist *cahier* of grievances still protested against Lutheran pretensions in this regard.[53] By the 1780's the Reformed community included some three hundred relatively prosperous families and could count on financial support, in the amount of two hundred *Gulden* per year, from the Swiss Protestant cantons. Yet the cumbersome obligation to hold services outside the town walls remained, an anachronism perhaps, but nonetheless a lingering symbol of discrimination. Even the famous theologian, Lavater, who came up from Basel on a visit in 1783, was allowed to preach only at Wolfisheim, where the little chapel could hold no more than a third of the crowd.

Hence Louis XVI's toleration edict was greeted by local Calvinists as an unqualified godsend. Citing the royal will in reply to the Magistrat's objections, they immediately began to negotiate for the purchase of a dwelling in town and in August 1788 secured one from the estate of a deceased merchant named Cagnerot.[54] On October 13 of that year, from their new establishment, they sent a letter of thanks to the house of Hesse-Darmstadt, as successor of Hanau-Lichtenberg, for more than 130 years of hospitality in its patrimonial village of Wolfisheim.

VIII

In 1789, obviously, Strasbourg's whole religious aspect was far different from what had first emerged after the capitulation a century before. What once had been a small Catholic minority supported by royal piety was now a slight Catholic majority, but one which had lost the weapon of governmental coercion. Conversely, the Lutherans had come to value the once hated Alternative as their own best guarantee of equality in the local administration. Calvinist services were at last being openly conducted in the city which had excluded them so stubbornly for so long. There was still no synagogue, but at least there were permanent Jewish residents whom the Magistrat was powerless to expel. Both the missionary zeal of Catholics and the tight, defensive orthodoxy of Lutherans had yielded place to rather more comfortable, if perhaps less consciously heroic, attitudes. No spiritual heirs of Jesuits like Dez and Scheff-

macher bombarded the local courts with complicated suits over
conversion or education. To Lutheran fire-eaters like Zentgraff
in the early and Froereissen in the mid-eighteenth century had succeeded spokesmen of the "new era": Blessig, Müller, Haffner, and
other theologians who insisted that traditional beliefs both could and
should come to terms with the century's triumphant reason.

Yet what remained of the old should not be overlooked in considering what had appeared of the new. The parish organization of
both Catholics and Lutherans was just as it had been by the end of
the 1680's.[55] Even the disappearance of the Antonites and the Jesuits
had not radically altered the Roman ecclesiastical organization in the
city. Lutheran worship proceeded along lines incorporating only the
most minor changes of ritual, whatever new theories might be discussed in the Convocation.[56] The Superior Church Wardens — Ammeisters Lemp and Turckheim, Thirteeners Hennenberg and
Brackenhoffer, Fifteeners Gangolff, Flach, and Mogg — were still
deliberating very much as their predecessors had deliberated for a
hundred years past.

In striking the balance between change and continuity, one
survival is particularly worth bearing in mind. That was the
awareness, which no fading of actual conflict and governmental
pressure could eliminate, of the difference between Protestants and
Catholics. Every time a *Te Deum* was to be sung or funeral services
conducted for a public figure, this difference was dramatized anew;
for the members of the Magistrat came out of the town hall together,
then split into two lines, one marching off to the cathedral, the
other to the Temple-Neuf. Even Louis XVI's toleration edict of 1787
had produced, as palliatives so often do, the double result of raising
the status of Protestant subjects in general but at the same time
making them all the more resentful of such discrimination as
remained.

There was, in short, the feeling on both sides that the existing
order was still a Catholic order, in which Catholic intendants and
praetors, not to mention a Catholic king, continued to hold decisive
power, no matter how many concessions they might make.[57] Only

if we recognize this residual attitude can we understand why otherwise conservative Alsatian Lutherans and Calvinists should have
greeted the Revolution, when it came, as *their* Revolution, why from
the pulpits of the Temple-Neuf and St. Thomas and St. Nicholas
enthusiastic voices welcomed the dawn of a new age — even as
Cardinal de Rohan was preparing to move to the Baden portion
of his diocese, across the Rhine.

CHAPTER SIX

The Economics of an Anomaly

I

In no area of local life were the peculiarities of Strasbourg's position, following annexation by Louis XIV, more apparent than in that of economics. After 1681, the city's famous semi-annual fairs went on as before, symbolizing continuity with the past as clearly as did the still functioning Magistrat and the Lutheran parishes. In January 1699, for example, Cabart de Villermont in Paris received a letter from a French correspondent in Strasbourg, containing the following paragraph:

The fair of this city opened last Monday; and according to what I have been told by one of the leaders of the Magistrat, it has been noted that more foreign merchandise and merchants have arrived than there have been for fifty years past. . . . I shall look carefully for that marbled paper and let you know about it.[1]

Despite the repetition of this familiar scene, however, French rule brought with it numerous changes, to be superimposed upon or merged with no less numerous survivals. Thus, the record of Strasbourg's currency, tariff situation, commerce, and industry is an important element in its whole evolution under the old regime. The paradoxes involved are often baffling to a modern observer, but in combination they help to delineate the unique position which the community occupied within the kingdom of France during the eighteenth century.

Alsace had been treated in Colbert's tariff ordinances of 1664 to 1671 as one of the *provinces à l'instar de l'étranger effectif,* that is, the marginal areas equated in many respects with foreign soil.[2] As such, it paid import and export duties on its products when they entered the interior zones set up by Colbert, but paid a maximum of one-half the regular French rates (none at all for many commodities) on shipments to or from Germany, Switzerland, and other lands beyond the monarchy's political frontiers. Strasbourg, in turn, constituted a special enclave within the province itself, after as before the capitulation of 1681. Goods entering the city from the Holy Roman Empire paid no royal customs. If they were sent on across the Vosges, they still paid nothing upon entering Lorraine, actually foreign until 1766 and generally considered part of the *étranger effectif* thereafter. On leaving Lorraine, however, and crossing into Champagne, i.e., into the central zone of France, the "Five Great Farms," goods from Strasbourg were assessed the full external duties. Similarly, if they went directly southwest through Alsace, they were taxed as though then entering the realm when they reached the border of Franche-Comté, one of the intermediate "provinces reputedly foreign." Finally, one-half or less of the domestic tariff was charged for shipments from Strasbourg into other parts of Alsace.

Thus, when a freight wagon rumbled over the Rhine bridge, westbound, or when a barge docked at the Boatmen's Quay, the Magistrat's own agents would collect the regular local fees at the *Zollkeller,* but what the shipper had to pay the farmers of royal customs depended entirely on where his goods were ultimately delivered. If they were disposed of inside Strasbourg, the central collectors would receive nothing. If they were going only to Colmar or some other Alsatian town, representatives of the farmers-general, stationed at the city gates, would assess up to 50 per cent of the normal French tariff on some items, but others, especially foodstuffs, passed duty-free. If the consignment was for Paris or Besançon, it would pay the full rate, later, at the customs frontier. The same regulations theoretically applied to shipments eastbound, out of the interior, from Alsace, or originating in Strasbourg. A complex system of deposits and clearance slips was designed to protect the royal farmers against fraudulent declarations of destination.

If Strasbourg remained a German city under French rule as regards commercial tariffs, it quickly became a complete hybrid with respect to its circulating coinage. Although royal officials were established in the town mint from 1694 onward,[3] traditional units survived alongside the French ones. Louis XIV established a *livre d'Alsace* (fixed at ten-elevenths of the value of his *livre tournois*) but abandoned it in 1716. Strasbourg's own *Pfund,* worth four French livres tournois, remained an alternative to the latter as a local money of account throughout the eighteenth century. The term "franc" for the livre tournois was already common in Alsace in the early 1700's, to distinguish the French pound from Strasbourg's.[4] Since neither a livre nor a Pfund was an actual coin (they were merely accounting terms), there was the problem not only of translating values from one into the other, but also of figuring their equivalents in various combinations of specie.

In 1715, for example, when a new *louis d'or* was fixed at fourteen livres in Paris (earlier ones differed in value according to the year of minting), it was worth seven *Gulden* in Strasbourg. The French *écu,* at three-and-half livres, was worth one Gulden, seven *Schillings,* and six *Pfennige.* Add to all this the circulation of imperial, Swiss, Dutch, even Italian and Spanish coins, and you have some idea of exchange problems in the "royal free city." A receipted bill for two hundred livres settled there in 1781 might show that this sum had been initially recorded as fifty Pfund and ultimately paid in some such combination of coins as five new louis d'or, three German *Laubthaler,* twenty twelve-sol pieces and 150 *Batzen.* Or again, a banker might lend a local merchant sixty Gulden one year, in the form of forty French-minted écu pieces, and receive it back the next as a sack of nine hundred native Batzen, with two hundred forty *sols* in interest.

Such examples as the preceding two reveal a complexity of monetary units which is further illustrated in successive editions of the merchant's handbook published in Berlin by Nelckenbrecher.

His fifth edition, dated 1781,[5] gives the following table for conversion of common currency in Strasbourg. Read across for equivalents:

Ecus	Florins*	Livres	Schillings	Batzen	Sols	Kreuzer	Pfennig†	Deniers
1	1½	3	15	22½	60	90	360	720
	1	2	10	15	40	60	240	480
		1	5	7½	20	30	120	240
			1	1½	4	6	24	48
				1	2⅔	4	16	32
					1	1½	6	12
						1	4	8
							1	2

* I.e., Gulden.
† Halved in value by the late eighteenth century.

The task of this chapter, however, is not simply to characterize the anomalies of Strasbourg's coinage and tariffs before the Revolution. It is even more important to discuss the growth and development of Strasbourg's economy under French rule. We shall have no concert of scholars to help us. Some German historians have painted a picture of almost unrelieved decline in local prosperity between 1681 and 1789. Yet the same period saw the population of the town rise from about 25,000 at the annexation to some 32,500 in 1709 and almost exactly 50,000 by 1789, though the annual figure for births seems to have increased little from about 1750 until the Napoleonic era.[6] The guilds grew steadily in size, until in 1789 their combined membership totaled 6,858 as against 3,322 in 1681.[7] Marquet de Bourgade's commentary of the mid-eighteenth century refers to a "large and rather beautiful city . . . well-populated, rich, and very busy commercially." [8]

On the other hand, French pride has sometimes exaggerated Strasbourg's expansion under the Bourbon kings. Several other cities of the realm grew even faster, both in population and in wealth. Its special position involved strains and confusions which offset some of the advantages seemingly guaranteed by privileges and exemptions. The very continuity of its political organization and its relatively remote dealings with the central government posed obstacles to the rapid exploitation of new methods and markets. The difficulty of reaching a fair, comprehensive judgment is obvious; but the effort, I think, needs to be made.

II

One approach to the problem is to consider the state of the city's own finances. The most important new item after the capitulation, of course, was the obligation to make financial contributions to the crown. In the first years, such sums were negotiated *ad hoc:* seventy-five thousand livres in 1683 and again in 1686 for barracks, forty-five thousand per year from 1689 for a five-year moratorium, repeatedly renewed, on the town's foreign debts, three hundred thousand in 1692 as a "free gift" to prevent the creation of a flock of venal offices, and so on. Always there were the standing military expenses: upkeep of fortifications, billeting, barracks supply, and housing for staff officers. The total military contribution rose from 120,700 livres in 1685 to 196,200 six years later, in wartime, then climbed unevenly until by 1764 it had reached its eighteenth-century peak of almost 290,000.

Two scholars have arrived independently at about the same figure for the total of all of Strasbourg's various payments to the monarchy in the years 1682 through 1788. One of them, Engel, sets this comprehensive figure at just under 53,500,000 livres,[9] while the other, Müller, fixes it at slightly over 54,000,000, plus some 3,000,000 in miscellaneous gifts, bribes, and pensions.[10] In any case, a yearly average of roughly five hundred thousand livres is indicated, with military costs, again on an average, amounting to one-half of that figure. Actually, however, the annual total rose from much less than a half-million livres in the 1680's to well above that amount in the last decade before the Revolution. In 1788, the total contribution to the central government amounted to 969,424 livres, under ten different headings, with military expenses making up only a quarter of the total.

Now, if you accept La Grange's assertion that the Magistrat's annual income in the 1680's and '90's was approximately five hundred thousand livres,[11] or especially if you take Reisseissen's somewhat lower figure,[12] you may get the startling impression that, over the whole period from then until the Revolution, the crown each year took as much as the city itself was collecting from all sources. Such a conclusion, however, would be completely unfounded; for it would leave out of account not only the uneven increase in royal exactions from relatively modest demands at the outset, but also the expansion in the city's own revenues. Finally, it would be overlooking the general movement of money values.

When Louis XIV first began to collect lump sums from the local Magistrat, those sums were primarily for fortifications and billeting expenses which in effect replaced the previous costs of the town's own military establishment. This is not to say that the early demands of His Majesty were either welcome or easily met, but it does mean that they cannot be thought of as having been simply added to the pre-1681 budget. Other items, like the three hundred thousand livres to avert the sale of new offices in 1692, required extensive borrowing by the Treasury Tower; and during the wars of that epoch, emergency demands for money, grain, and other supplies sometimes hit the Magistrat with painful suddenness. Yet the manipulations required to cover such payments at least rested on that all-important intangible — improving prospects. The busy fairs at the end of the seventeenth century not only impressed visitors such as Villermont's friend,[13] they also encouraged the townsmen. Anyone who reads the official and unofficial sources surviving from that period can scarcely fail to be impressed by the difference between the grumbling which admittedly runs through them and the blank pessimism which fills comparable material from the 1660's and '70's.

The municipality's financial resources were actually increased in certain respects not only by the continuing moratorium on pre-1681 foreign debts, but also by the very nature of local dealings with the royal fisc. The *gabelle* on salt, for example, did not apply in its usual form. Instead, the city government bought salt wholesale from the French *greniers* and resold it to the citizenry at a profit, though still at a price far below what a Breton or a Picard had to pay in his home province. Later, when the *capitation* was introduced in 1695, the town authorities at once offered the king a lump sum and themselves collected this tax each year within the city, generally with a clear margin of gain for local uses. In cases such as these, Strasbourg's Magistrat was in effect functioning as tax farmers did elsewhere in the kingdom and reaping the benefits otherwise enjoyed by private contractors. It was not the only commune granted this privilege, for other French municipalities were sometimes permitted to administer specific royal taxes, but no other was so nearly independent of tax farmers. Only once, in 1686, did the crown try to insist on general use of the latter in Strasbourg. On orders from Louvois, the Magistrat had to place on sale farms for fourteen different sources of income, each contract to run for three years.[14] The system, however, was neither popular with the burghers nor favorably viewed by the town government, and after the initial term it quickly lapsed. There remained farmers for certain royal revenues, such as that from the mint, but not for strictly municipal ones.

Much more important than new sources of income was the increased yield from old ones.[15] The *Stallgeld*, the annual property tax, went on being paid by the citizenry on the basis of each individual's declared assets, with such returns ultimately subject to verification through the compulsory inventories of testamentary estates. This may seem to have left the door open to evasion over whole lifetimes; but custom, the fear of posthumous disgrace, and the threatened lien against his estate made the average Strasbourger careful to discharge his Stallgeld in the proper amount. Fines, chancellery fees, and various dues from the rural bailiwicks rose gradually with the number of inhabitants. Certain other items, such as the *Umgeld* on incoming wines, grains, and vegetables; transit duties; bridge tolls; dock charges; and rentals for storage space, mounted at a much sharper rate as trade revived. All in all, the municipal revenues stood at 1,000,000 livres by 1750 and over 1,400,000 by 1789.[16]

The one additional control which needs to be applied to the Magistrat's budget, as recorded in livres, is the evolution in the real value of that unit itself. Not all of the city's income, to be sure, was received in cash. The municipal granaries and wood bins formed an integral part of its treasury; and in 1774, a census of wine barrels in the cellars of the government showed a total storage capacity of over ten thousand gallons, a sort of built-in cushion against excessive despondency in ruling circles.[17] Since, however, official salaries for everyone from the royal praetor to musicians in the city orchestra were also paid at least partly in wood, wine, and grain, the receipts and expenditures in kind tended to cancel each other out, leaving us with money values as the one real variable.

The livres demanded by Paris in the 1780's, like those entered in the town's ledgers as revenue, were unquestionably worth less than the livres received and expended a century earlier. How much less is not so easy to say. Though Strasbourg appears to have known rather more monetary stability during the eighteenth century than did the French kingdom as a whole, the general movement was the same on both sides of the Vosges. In his *Notices,* written at the end of Napoleon's reign, J.-F. Hermann, who throughout his life had been well-situated to know such things about his native city, set down a number of commodity prices for the first half of the eighteenth century, for 1756, and for 1789.[18] Over this time span, a pound loaf of bread of good quality went from two sols five deniers, to two and eight, and finally to three sols — an increase of about 25 per cent. Retail beef started at a statutory four sols per pound and ended at six sols just before the post-1789 inflation — up 50 per cent. The best sugar crept upward from seventy livres to ninety, for a hundred-pound sack, while butter was much steadier, going only from about eight sols ten deniers a pound to ten and five during the same period.

Reducing Hermann's lists to a meaningful generalization about the movement of prices necessarily involves some arbitrariness in weighting the various items he mentions. The best I can do is to say that his figures, together with contemporary newspaper listings and the coefficients later worked out by Hanauer for the province as a whole,[19] suggest a slight rise in the local buying power of the livre in the first third of the eighteenth century but a net decline of about 25 per cent between 1681 and the beginning of 1789. If the change in monetary values is now applied to the bare figures of the city budget, the latter's expansion during the same century obviously appears reduced. For example, the royal exactions of almost 970,000 livres, in the money of 1788, represented only about 775,000 for purposes of real comparison with the demands of the 1680's. Similarly, to take an item of municipal income, the Stallgeld rose from 72,000 livres in the earlier decade to about 128,000 a hundred years later; but this apparent increase of some 77 per cent actually represents a rise of just over 40 per cent, in terms of what the Magistrat could buy with it.

Once more we are obliged to stand back from the details and ask: does the record of Strasbourg's civic expenditures under Louis XIV, XV, and XVI, especially its payments to the crown, justify portraying its economy as sick and getting worse? I do not believe so. The rising demands were met by growing resources. The local budget, it is true, showed a deficit of slightly over 132,000 livres, or about 9 per cent of income, for 1789;[20] but there had been other such deficits in earlier years, often followed by surpluses for substantial periods. Whatever part financial concern played in the pre-Revolutionary unrest was not, I think, the result of any long-standing belief that royal demands were unbearable. The municipal deficit of 1789 took on special significance only against the background of general uneasiness and distrust — the suspicion that funds delivered to the monarchy were being employed either foolishly or fraudulently, or both — which had been spreading all over France since Necker's revelations in 1781.

III

Governmental finances, regardless of their condition, doubtless impinged much less on the consciousness of the average Strasbourger than did the apparent course of trade. The latter might impress a contemporary in any of several ways, depending on how his private fortunes looked to him at the time; and the modern observer is equally a prey to conflicting judgments, based on the various glimpses he may get into the whole complex of Strasbourg's commercial life under the old regime.

As for external trade, the pre-1681 pattern had revealed three principal characteristics: heavy dependence on local commerce with surrounding Alsace and nearby Baden; scarcely less heavy dependence on a number of vital exchanges with German territories farther east and north; and finally, a special stake in carrying and transshipment for the whole Rhine valley.

Representatives of the Magistrat, as well as every intendant or royal praetor who had been in office long enough to size up local conditions, spent a good deal of time explaining to Paris how badly Strasbourg needed to maintain its role as clearing house for Alsatian wines, cereals, hemp, flax, saffron, indigo, and numerous other products eagerly sought in the Holy Roman Empire and Switzerland. In 1716, d'Angervilliers wrote from the Intendancy to Marshal de Villeroy and the Regent's financial council to urge the immediate lifting, in Alsace, of all restrictions on grain exports from the kingdom. The province has a large surplus, he points out, and at a time when the Germans and Swiss are anxious to buy, the price of wheat, rye, oats, and barley are badly depressed on the Strasbourg market, because of the artificial blockage left over from the end of Louis XIV's wars.[21] Documents of this type — for d'Angervilliers' letter is typical of many such statements during the eighteenth century — reveal the great extent to which the old pattern had carried over into the French period.[22]

Eighteenth-century Strasbourg naturally drew most of its own food supplies and raw materials from agricultural Alsace,[23] but certain commodities had to come from abroad. In the above letter from d'Angervilliers to Villeroy there appears the flat statement that "the city . . . cannot get along without bringing in livestock from Germany and Switzerland." [24] A memorandum of 1731 explains that at that date Strasbourg still imported most of its wood, for building and bridge maintenance, from across the Rhine.[25] Some manufactured items too were chiefly supplied by foreign sources. When in 1718 Praetor Klinglin was asked to report on glass products, for example, he replied that Strasbourg got most of its window panes from Gengenbach in Baden, its drinking glasses from Bohemia and Lorraine, its best mirrors and carriage windows from Venice. There were no Alsatian sources, he added, which could even begin to meet the urban demand.[26]

At the time of its annexation Strasbourg still occupied a commanding position in Rhine shipping; but just before the royal troops marched in, a century of troubles in the river trade began. The boatmen's guild, the "Anchor," had long enjoyed advantages first won in the Middle Ages, partly as a reward for their efforts in clearing the channel, and later consecrated by a network of special treaties with potential competitors. Under this earlier dispensation, a boatman from a downstream town, such as Mainz, could bring a cargo into Strasbourg, but if he had not found a return cargo within three days, he was required to leave anyway. Boats from the upstream ports lacked even this limited right of outbound hauling, they could not leave Strasbourg with any cargo at all if a single "Anchor" member was available to make the trip to Breisach or Basel.[27]

The disintegration of Strasbourg's once uniquely favored position began in May 1681, when the Elector of Mainz announced the first of a long series of enactments limiting the right of foreign crews to enter the Main or to take cargoes back up the Rhine from his capital. Not until seventy years later was a compromise arranged; and even after the 1751 treaty between the Elector and the King of France, Strasbourg could haul upstream from Mainz only during the month of January and for six weeks at the time of each of Frankfurt's semiannual fairs. During the remaining eight months per year, Strasbourg boats might unload in Mainz, but could not go beyond and even had to return empty, as far as Speyer at least. Meanwhile, in 1711, Basel had at last won from French royal authorities the permission for its boatmen to carry cargoes upstream from Strasbourg to Switzerland. By the 1720's, Mannheim's crews, no longer willing to be confined exclusively to traffic on the tributary Neckar, were competing actively on the Rhine, as were those of Breisach in the south.

For the first three-quarters of the eighteenth century, this growing rivalry was less harmful to Strasbourg than its traditionalists,
nostalgic for the old hegemony, said it was. The local boatmen were
apparently kept busy carrying goods for local merchants and for the
royal armies. Even in 1789, after more than a decade of undeniable
depression in their craft, the members of the "Anchor" still numbered
230, as compared with 160 in 1681. However much they might com-
plain, the boatmen prospered under the new and more open conditions, as long as Strasbourg remained the greatest *entrepôt* on the
Upper Rhine, its wharves and warehouses constantly jammed with
goods in transit.

For just this reason, the emergence of a rival port directly across
the river was a far more serious blow to the city's boat operators, as
it was to the merchants and the toll collectors of Strasbourg, than the
mere entry of foreign craft had been. The Baden government's effort
to build Kehl, once no more than a little bridgehead for Strasbourg,
into a major trade center unquestionably constituted a severe blow
to the old city's economy in the years just before the Revolution.
Successive margraves had been drawn to such an enterprise ever
since 1699, when Kehl had passed under the control of Baden-Baden;
but for a long time they had been hampered by the existence of
various reciprocal agreements between Strasbourg and other Rhenish
towns. Furthermore, the French crown had occasionally acted to
protect its subjects along the river. As late as 1773, for instance, the
royal control bureau at Fort-Louis, downstream from Strasbourg,
had seized three "illegal" boats of Baden registry and sold them at
public auction.

Then, in 1775, the Elector of Mainz suddenly upset the whole
existing state of affairs when he announced that his subjects were
henceforth free to ship by whatever means and route they preferred,
saving always the right of his own chartered boatmen. In other
words, he would impose no further privileges in favor of any other
locality. The traders of Mainz, who controlled most of the big
consignments from farther north, promptly began switching to Kehl
as a transshipment point offering considerably lower customs duties

and port taxes than Strasbourg did. Within a year, the latter's
share in the handling of goods bound for Switzerland and Italy
from the Low Countries, Cologne, and Frankfurt had declined by
fully a third. Anyone strolling past the quays along the Ill could see
the startling change. Agonized appeals to Paris brought formal
representations to Mainz, and finally, in 1786, the elector rescinded
his earlier decree. He did not, however, reëstablish all the old
provisions in favor of Strasbourg; and he informally interpreted his
latest ruling in terms so flexible as to leave Mainz shippers free in
most cases to use right-bank ports. By 1787, when the Provincial
Assembly of Alsace heard a report on the problem, shipments to
Switzerland via Kehl and nearby Schreck had reached an all-time
high. The fruitless litigation over Kehl was the last, and for Strasbourg the most depressing, chapter in the general struggle for
Rhenish trade under the old regime. Neither this specific contest
nor the broader one had been settled when the Revolution swept
over the great valley.[28]

IV

If the time-honored pattern of Strasbourg's commercial dealings
with Alsace, Germany, and Switzerland had merely persisted rigidly
down to 1789, while the city's grip on the river trade got progressively
weaker, we should have to conclude that the eighteenth century
was indeed an era of local economic decline. But the picture is not
that simple. Instead of blacks and whites it presents us with a variety
of shadings, becoming brighter in some areas as they became darker
in others. What the town gained by virtue of even partial inclusion
in a larger unit, the French kingdom, must be taken into account,
as must its troubles with the distant bureaucracy in Paris and
with certain obstacles inherent in the commercial and fiscal policies of
the Bourbon monarchy.

Admittedly, the French customs system could be frustrating, as is
shown by a petition which Jean-Georges Schertz addressed to the
Council of Fifteen in 1777.[29] Schertz was a wholesaler who dealt in

Hungarian, Bohemian, and South German wool, among many other things; and the initial portion of his long memorandum contains proposals for simplifying the town's own customs procedures affecting that commodity, especially in view of the competition from Kehl. It is when he turns to the problem of dealing with the farmers-general of royal import and export duties, however, that he is most enlightening.

The root of the trouble, he asserts, is the customs farmers' "arbitrary indecision in treating Strasbourg as now foreign, now French, depending on what they find suits their interests." Shipments "into the kingdom," as he puts it, are hurt by high duties. Since 1771, for example, starch manufactured in Strasbourg has been assessed four sols per livre, or 20 per cent *ad valorem,* even when entering Franche-Comté, where it was previously exempt from duty, whereas starch coming from the Five Great Farms pays only two sols per livre at the frontier of that province. It seems clear that Schertz, who certainly wants Strasbourgers to retain their unique freedom of exchange with Germany, but would also like them to enjoy equality with Frenchmen of the interior when trading with Franche-Comté, is himself not above making the city "now foreign, now French," according to the advantages offered.

His interest, however, is focused on commodities shipped all the way *to* Strasbourg from Paris or elsewhere in the Five Great Farms, and here he appears to have a valid complaint. He points out that if an item is subject to a consumption tax, payable by French subjects, then a Strasbourg wholesaler has to pay it at the time of purchase in the old dominion. If, on the other hand, the product in question is one which Frenchmen can buy free of tax, but which only Frenchmen can retail within the kingdom, a Strasbourg merchant immediately becomes a foreigner in the eyes of the customs farmers and must post a bond, as well as pay the fee for a clearance slip, which is turned in when his consignment crosses the customs frontier. Thus, for tax-free items he is no better off than a German or Swiss importer, while for internally taxed goods he is decidedly worse off;

since the latter can be taken out of France by real foreigners under the clearance slip system, without payment of any consumption tax.

Schertz goes on to explain two methods by which a Strasbourg native can escape the purchase tax on products subject to it, adding that both these methods are cumbersome and that the second actually benefits the rival across the Rhine. He can have his shipment first sent from the interior only as far as Nancy or Montbéliard, in which case the farmers-general must exempt it from internal taxes and issue the regular foreign clearance slip, these destinations being treated as wholly outside the French customs net. After delivery in either town, the goods can then be reloaded and sent on to Strasbourg without further interference, but with the expense of the stopover added to the cost of what ought to be a single, direct journey. He pauses to underline the inconsistency of treating Nancy as foreign, with respect to export duties, when for salt and tobacco taxes it is Lorraine and not Alsace that is considered part of the kingdom.

The second technique for evading "the farmers' cupidity" is less expensive but also less patriotic. It is to declare the shipment's destination as Kehl in Baden, right from the start, and then, having turned in the exit stub of the clearance slip upon crossing the Rhine, to swing the wagon around immediately, so that it can come back over the bridge into Strasbourg like any other arriving from Germany. As such, it is exempt from royal customs. What worries him, he says blandly, is that under the present arrangement the farmers are gaining nothing, while the fee required by the margrave's agent in Kehl, though small in itself, nevertheless helps to "nourish this entrepôt which the Magistrat of Strasbourg is eager to destroy."

The Fifteen requested the royal praetor to take up with Paris the indicated modification of existing rules, so that local merchants would no longer have to resort to such expedients as Schertz had described. So far as I have been able to discover, the matter had not yet been settled when the Revolution obliterated the whole patchwork of tariff zones; but the petition's documentary value is scarcely diminished by our uncertainty as to what might have come of it under other circumstances. Here, among other things, we see a businessman engaged in that "war with the fisc" which has had important consequences for France down to the present day.

Now, against such difficulties as Schertz complained of, what can be cited as advantages of French rule? One which certainly deserves notice was the gradual expansion of market opportunities. Strasbourg may have been outside the kingdom in many economic respects; but politically it was part of the realm, and buyers to the west had reason to prefer a source of supply which was legally subject to the royal courts, as against other towns offering products from the Rhineland. The result, from a Strasbourger's point of view, is reflected in the account books of Philippe-Jacques Ebert, general wholesaler, for the years 1723–1743.[30] Ebert dealt with merchants in Basel, Mulhouse, Frankfurt, and Worms, as well as numerous other Rhenish towns, shipping them everything from wax, starch, and dyestuffs to hardware and salt fish. There is no question that the proportion of his bills of sale drawn up in German far outnumber those written in French. The latter, however, are for considerable amounts, since he had several big customers in Besançon and Lyon. Besides consignments via Rhine boat or *Kutsche* into the Empire, he sent off countless barrels, bales, and crates with the *rouliers* of the French cartage franchises.[31]

This calls attention to the steady improvement of Alsatian roads and the increased volume of land traffic, which represented a clear gain under the monarchy. By 1746, a printed announcement of that year informs us, Paris stages entered and left town six days a week.[32] Three times per week public coaches arrived from and set off to Lyon, while on three other days there were arrivals and departures connecting Strasbourg with Nancy and the Three Bishoprics of Metz, Toul, and Verdun. In addition, numerous coaches made daily runs to other towns in Alsace. The regular German stage, on the other hand, was still limited at this date to two trips per week, though by the 1780's it arrived and departed daily. These scheduled services, in all directions, were far outnumbered by chartered trips of rented carriages or saddle horses over various routes where the fixed points for turning in or exchanging vehicles and mounts constituted units for the computation of charges. All the above were essentially passenger services, though they carried mail and parcels, as did most of the drivers of rented carriages. Heavy overland hauling was dependent on larger, slower, but less expensive wagons.

It must be said that the movement of passengers, mails, and freight over the post roads was subject to conflicts and uncertainties until almost the end of the old regime, because of the welter of patents and theoretical monopolies sold by the crown to various contractors. As early as 1683 the "Farmers of Coaches and Carriages from Paris to Strasbourg" were engaged in angry litigation with the "Royal Farmers of Freight Transports." In the ensuing decades, special charters went on being issued, compounding the confusion. In 1775, however, the Council of State at last decided that some order had to be brought out of the existing chaos; and its survey of all legal claims by competing firms, followed during the next two years by a series of regulatory decrees, greatly improved the situation.[33] In the 1780's Alsatians enjoyed the benefits of communications as rapid and dependable as any Europe was to know until the advent of the railroad.

The improvement in roads and the expansion of overland transport were especially important for a city which had seen a sharp diminution of its river trade. By 1787, when Thirteener Hennenberg gave his report on local commerce to the Provincial Assembly, he was able to state that more than a thousand tons of goods now moved each year in the big, three-span wagons over the highway from his native city to Basel, instead of plodding upstream against the swift Rhine current.[34] Hennenberg's figure of twenty to twenty-five thousand hundredweight is especially significant since it amounts to a little more than the volume of water hauling to Switzerland which Strasbourg had lost since Kehl's competition began to be acute in 1775. Not all the carting to Basel had appeared just since the river crisis broke, of course; but there is more than a hint here that profits from wagons on French highways built or improved during the eighteenth century were helping to offset losses sustained on the water route, however slight such consolation might appear to guild boatmen at the "Anchor." [35]

V

Turning from commercial to specifically industrial questions, we encounter one important distinction which needs to be made at once. The city had long had an active carrying and handling trade, save for periodic setbacks in wartime; and in consequence, the changes after 1681 were superimposed upon a relatively impressive base of previously established commerce. Manufacturing for export, on the other hand, with only scattered exceptions, had not been a major feature of the old free city's life, which had been marked by closely controlled guild production for local consumption long after certain other towns had begun to acquire continental reputations for their products.

One German historian, Fritz Kiener,[36] has offered a possible explanation for this industrial lag, which was not fully overcome — though more progress had been made than he seems willing to allow — until Napoleon's time. Kiener's theory is that the absence of a technically under-developed hinterland tended to inhibit extensive manufacturing in Strasbourg. It is certainly true that whereas the Swabian and Franconian cities were supplied with agricultural and mineral products by the Austrian domains and Poland, in turn supplying those areas with finished goods, Strasbourg was wedged between the other Alsatian towns, with their own guild systems, and the equally industrious populace facing it across the Rhine.

Whatever the reason or reasons, we are dealing here with a degree of industry so limited at the outset that there is some danger of exaggerating the scale of such manufacturing enterprises as were established between 1681 and 1789. It is especially important to remember that Strasbourg entered the Revolution still primarily a guild town, with dozens of crafts grouped within the twenty corporations. The latter had grown in size and had kept themselves solvent,[37] but they were cautious organizations, deeply suspicious of all innovation. Against this background of small-unit production for a closely controlled local market, any invasion by industry under capitalists who looked beyond the walls stood out as a change which could impose itself only slowly, uncertainly, and always with more or less difficulty.

In the decades just before the annexation, Strasbourg's craftsmen had been exporting relatively small quantities of building tile and crockery, woolen textiles, leather goods, barrels, gunpowder, fire-arms, and a few other products. It was only after about 1690, how-ever, that beer and tobacco production expanded so sharply as to make these major items. From a modest beginning in 1620 at Robert Königsmann's *Englischer Hof*, "tobacco spinning" grew rapidly in volume only after the capitulation to France, though presumably not because of it. By 1789 the city had no fewer than forty-five such factories, most of them small, but together employing a total of over a thousand persons on at least a part-time basis.[38] Tobacco had by that date, furthermore, built several great fortunes in the city, including that of the devoted patron of the arts, Pierre Mayno. Similarly, although certain brewmasters had exported a fraction of their output before 1681,[39] it was the eighteenth century which saw the emergence of big firms like that of the Hatt family, whose brewery still produces the well-known "Kronenbourg" beer.[40] To take another example, the carpet factory of Basel-born Niklaus Herff, though established before the coming of the French, received a new impetus from the royal privilege of 1683 and attained its highest production in the 1690's.

The relatively tranquil years after the end of Louis XIV's great wars saw the addition of other new enterprises, none more im-portant than the Hannong works. Charles-François Hannong, a Dutch immigrant who founded a clay pipe factory in Strasbourg in 1709, was joined in 1719 by an associate from Ansbach who knew Saxon methods for making earthenware; and within a couple of years Hannong faïence dishes were being shipped from one plant in the city itself and another in Haguenau.[41] French immigrants too brought a considerable variety of new techniques, though only a couple of examples can be cited here. In 1744 the Council of Fifteen approved the petition of Jean-Joseph Lamiral, "late of the royal factory of the Gobelins," for a ten-year exemption from duties on raw materials needed to produce tapestries.[42] Another newcomer, a Provençal named Félix, asked permission in 1749 to begin manufacturing vermicelli in the town. The wording of his appeal makes it an ominous forerunner of the billboards and radio commercials lying in wait for a later epoch. These little noodles, he assures the Fifteen, will be marketable over a wide area, since they "are recommended by doctors for the sick . . . a food as healthful as it is inexpensive and easy to prepare." [43] Strasbourg's economic future did not hinge on vermicelli production; but the enterprising Sieur Félix was representative of a genuinely new species, the small manufacturer who nevertheless had his eyes fixed from the outset on export possibilities.

If all the projects submitted to the Magistrat and especially to the royal praetor during these optimistic decades had become successful undertakings, the city would have encountered a massive labor shortage. Beginning in 1745, with the proposal drawn up by a Sieur de Barry (who incidentally wanted to offer asylum to Protestant workers from southern France), the local government itself invested in the silk business, importing the precious worms and almost fifty thousand seedlings for mulberry trees to supply them with food. Alsace, however, proved to be not very invigorating for silkworms, and the enterprise died a lingering death amid loud recriminations from various former enthusiasts.[44]

In 1775 appeared another instance of ambitious planning when one of the Wencker family presented to Praetor Baron d'Autigny a proposal which speaks volumes concerning the economic practices of the day.[45] Wencker, while on a vacation trip in Baden, had stumbled upon a remarkable cutlery works at Pforzheim, with some three hundred workers, the leading ones all immigrants from

Great Britain. Their polished steel products, he says in his memorandum, "happily combine French taste with English skill." Wencker now proposes to bring these workers to Strasbourg, if the crown will first issue an edict placing such high duties on their present output as to shut off the Paris market and thus ruin the Baden factory. One of their leaders has already agreed to come, provided he and his fellows can be assured of certain tariff and tax concessions until their production is well established in the city. Unfortunately for Wencker, as the praetor shortly informed him, the royal council had just that summer issued a decree making cutlery a free item, with respect to both importation and manufacture. The new doctrines being applied by Turgot thus left the hated margrave in possession of his foreign team at Pforzheim.[46]

This local setback, related as it was to economic liberalism, seems rather ironic in retrospect. Certainly the obstacles to industrial expansion in eighteenth-century Strasbourg were much more commonly matters of restriction, both municipal and royal, than of its opposite. The Magistrat and the guilds fought hard to prevent expansion, especially when projected by immigrants. Sometimes the vested interests had to yield, as in 1753, when the stockingmakers tried in vain to prevent the establishment of a silk-weaving shop by Sieur Rouquairol,[47] or in 1778, when the Oberherr of the weavers' guild, Thirteener Staedel, was compelled by the royal praetor to sponsor before his fellow guildsmen a demand for thirty-six journeymen badly needed in Monsieur Gau's royal sailcloth factory.[48] In many other cases, however, the town fathers and master craftsmen held their own in defense of the old economic order.[49] The royal declaration of 1755, demanding liberalization of the rules governing admission to crafts and trades in most of the kingdom and denouncing guild membership quotas, drew an answer from the Magistrat which pointed out the city's special status under its capitulation and asserted that it must, like Paris, be considered an exception to the new provisions.[50] Even in the 1780's after Turgot's reform efforts and at a time when no resistance could completely block the rush of new enterprises, a disgruntled textile manufacturer at Strasbourg sent the praetor a long memorandum charging the town authorities with obstructionism in refusing to permit a genuinely free labor market among weavers and in clinging to antiquated methods of inspection and taxation.[51]

Not all the resentment of the rising capitalists was centered on local prejudice or on the guild system they were seeking, for their own profit, to break through. The letter just mentioned also denounces the hodge-podge of royal restrictions and sometimes even specific new legislation which threatened to cancel the effect of the crown's avowed eagerness to encourage economic growth. It might on occasion be only a single, excessively officious agent who made the trouble. In 1785, for example, Praetor Gérard in Paris succeeded, without much delay, in getting the comptroller general to release the stocking machine which had been bought in the old dominion by a Strasbourg manufacturer but impounded on arrival at Châlons by the customs inspector there, under an old law against the exportation of machinery.[52] In certain other instances, however, the problem was more complicated and the central authority less conciliatory.

A case of this latter variety involved no less an establishment than that of the Hannong family. Already possessed of a European reputation for the quality of his faïence, Paul Hannong, the elder of the founder's two sons, had begun in 1751 to produce porcelain as well, taking the china of Meissen as his model.[53] Only three years later, just as he was beginning to earn appreciable profits from his new product, he was informed that he was violating the royal monopoly enjoyed by the factory at Vincennes (subsequently at Sèvres). After having protested in vain that Alsace should not be affected by a monopoly in France proper, he abandoned porcelain and actually moved his personal headquarters into Germany, to Frankenthal in the Palatinate. Upon Paul Hannong's death in 1760, however, his son, Joseph, representing the third generation of the dynasty, decided to sell the Frankenthal works to the Elector Palatine and return to Alsace. He resumed full production of faïence in Stras-

bourg and Haguenau; then, when the Sèvres monopoly expired in
1766, he moved back into the manufacture of china once attempted
by his father. Five years later, after heavy, ultimately ruinous borrowing, he marketed his first porcelain.

Now began the second, and decisive, collision between the Hannong enterprise and the central authorities, this time the farmers-
general of customs dues. By a ruling of the royal council, dated
July 20, 1774, the *Bureau des Fermes* was suddenly empowered to
collect not three livres per hundred pounds gross weight on pottery
entering the Five Great Farms from the "foreign" provinces, as
provided in 1723, but twenty-eight livres per hundredweight, the
amount previously assessed only upon really foreign earthenware.
For Alsatian porcelain, the duty was just as abruptly raised to 140
livres per hundredweight. In his written protest,[54] Joseph Hannong
explained that this would mean any of his products shipped to Paris
would be taxed more than the equivalent of their original sales
price. For example, he says, a dozen faïence plates of medium quality
cost four livres in Strasbourg. They weigh about twenty pounds
when packed and so are now subject, upon entering the Five Great
Farms, to a duty of five livres twelve sols. In the case of a dozen
china plates initially priced at twenty livres, the duty is twenty-eight
livres at the customs boundary, so that with transportation, insurance,
and local fees their price may be as high as eighty livres per dozen
at Paris. Insisting that the crown has never wished to penalize its
subjects outside the Five Great Farms and asserting that he is
currently faced with ruin, he asks for immediate exemption from
the new schedule. He ends on a particularly plaintive note, demon-
strating statistically that "the Chinese manufacturer in Kingts-
tsching, who lives under another sky," receives better treatment for
his products in France than does a maker of dishes at Strasbourg.

Hannong was not exaggerating the financial difficulties he faced.
His principal creditor had been the late bishop, Cardinal Louis-
Constantin de Rohan; and in the summer of 1779, the heirs of this
prelate, including his nephew, the new cardinal-bishop, had the
famed manufacturer imprisoned for debt. He was released after

more than a year behind bars, but he still owed two hundred thousand livres to the Rohans. Then, in November 1780, his local factory was seized by order of the secretary of state for war, on charges that its owner had been abusing his privileges by selling exclusively outside the kingdom. This was the end of the Hannongs at Strasbourg, for Joseph moved away to Munich in 1781. The smaller plant at Haguenau remained in operation, but under heavy mortgages and restricted to faïence production.[55]

Yet even the loss of this prestigious firm could not, by the date of its occurrence, wipe out the city's share in the luxury trade of the interior, as it practically would have a half-century earlier. In that same 1780, when poor Hannong saw his factory occupied by the gendarmerie, an observer jotted down the following in his travel notes:

> The ordinary artisan is jovial, hard-working, and accorded a great reputation for honesty. He has no flare for invention, but he imitates with care and enthusiasm. Many sellers of gowns in Paris send their new designs to Strasbourg and have the work done there. It is well known that the carriages made in Strasbourg are the latest thing in Paris, and much lower in price. . . . In France, gilt decorations from this city are preferred to all others.[56]

VI

Whatever disagreement may exist over the proper balance to be drawn between Strasbourg's material progress under French rule and the difficulties which continued to hamper such progress, there are certain features of its situation in 1789 which seem clear enough. The city, like the surrounding province, was still outside the full French customs systems, though the original appellation of "effectively foreign" had tended increasingly during the eighteenth century to be confused with the status, "reputedly foreign," enjoyed by such provinces as Franche-Comté and Dauphiné; and the precise conditions applicable to even this latter category were often called into question by the central government. Modern historians have at times appeared to be clearer in their minds about the exact differentiation of tariff zones outside the Five Great Farms than eighteenth-century officials were. The fact that some differentiation remained is nonetheless important.

The century had brought a regularization, as well as a substantial increase, in the municipality's annual payments to the crown. Yet the Magistrat of Strasbourg was until the Revolution a fiscal entity considerably more independent than any of the city governments of the interior. It audited its own accounts, collecting and delivering the specified contributions to Paris. It was, in short, enough of a buffer between the local taxpayer and the royal treasury so that genuinely national taxes were destined to come as something of a jolt to Strasbourgers during and after the Revolution.

The old regime never solved the economic problems inherent in narrow, monopolistic conceptions of privilege, in restrictive guild practices, in unclear or outdated regulations, and in the extortionate behavior of farmers of royal income. Nevertheless, if one looks back to the depressed condition of the city just prior to 1681, he can scarcely denounce the annexation as a source of material retrogression for Strasbourg. Commerce with Germany expanded thereafter, while an almost wholly new commerce with France was born. An increased scale and variety of industry, indeed a changing definition of what industry should be, invaded the town, as it did most of the rest of the European world, in the late seventeenth and especially in the eighteenth century.

Even the oft-repeated charge that Strasbourg suffered as a Rhine port *because* of its capitulation to France impresses me as the product of peculiar reasoning. What the city lost in river trade between 1681 and 1789 it lost to Swiss and German rivals who would scarcely have been less aggressive if their adversary had still been a little republic within the Empire. The Margrave of Baden, the Elector of Mainz, the Magistrat of Basel, to mention only the three most serious competitors, abided by the old restrictions only so long as they had felt unable to repudiate them. That they felt increasingly able to do so in the eighteenth century was the result partly of developments within their own territories and partly of very broad changes taking place in the economy of the whole valley. Later history suggests, in fact, that Strasbourg prospered more when it was the single major French Rhine port than when it was simply one of many competing river towns under German rule.

For all the undeniable growth of the city during the eighteenth century, however, there is one final twist to its economic history in that period which must not be overlooked. This has to do with the specific deterioration of certain conditions in the years just prior to 1789. The worst Rhine shipping crisis broke, as we know, in 1775 and remained serious thereafter, despite the rapid increase in overland hauling. The financial predicament of the central government began to be generally recognized early in the 1780's, and the local budget felt the strain of desperate demands from Paris. The simultaneous jump in various commodity prices, analyzed by Labrousse for the kingdom as a whole,[57] was less severe in Strasbourg than in Paris; but its effects were by no means negligible even in Alsace. If one is asking how much economic conditions had to do with producing revolutionary tension on the Upper Rhine, he is well-advised to balance the very considerable advances of the century before 1789, taken as a whole, against a combination of setbacks during the last decade of that century. This conception is no longer novel, but it is worth calling to mind, since it makes sense in terms of social psychology, while for Strasbourg, at least, it fits all the evidence concerning commercial profits, which were down, and taxes and food prices, which were rising.

Quite aside from popular discontent, the sentiments of the well-to-do businessman, including particularly the manufacturer, were not irrelevant to the sharpened tension of those last years before the explosion. The century had seen business, as a social and political force, achieve unprecedented importance; but it had not seen disappear the institutions and traditions of the old regime which hampered the entrepreneur at every turn. Royal reforms had intermittently sought to reduce the growing strain placed on the old framework by new forces. Such reforms had not been enough. The angry makers of porcelain and textiles and tobacco products at Strasbourg were characteristic spokesmen of their class. It was men such as these who made 1789 at least partly "the capitalists' revolution."

CHAPTER SEVEN

Social Changes

I

Social history, most broadly conceived, is practically limitless. It is in one sense the record of how the people of a given community lived, and that necessarily includes their government, churches, trade, and taxes, as well as travel and ideas and works of art. Hence, in the present case, there is no point in trying to isolate all the social changes which occurred in Strasbourg between 1681 and 1789 from developments already discussed or from others still to be considered. Such separation, to adapt a useful epigram, is not necessarily un-desirable — it is merely impossible.

There are, nevertheless, problems of ethnic composition, group behavior, and class structure which are bound to arise in the course of any general study. They demand and deserve separate attention, because they offer additional angles from which to view the material at hand. If, with such considerations in mind, we ask the question previously stated in political, religious, and economic terms — how did Strasbourg change during the first century of French rule? — we can discover some further elements of what must finally be a composite answer.

The point of departure is local society as it existed just before the annexation, a society divided into a few relatively compact groups. At the top were the *Constoffler* or citizen-nobles, equal in social status with those other members of the Immediate Nobility of Lower Alsace who lacked political rights in the municipality. Next came the enfranchised bourgeoisie, ranging from proud families of the ruling oligarchy all the way down to the humblest guildsmen of the twenty corporations. Below the voting line was another major group, the registered non-citizens under the *Schirm* or protection of the town. Living around and among all the above were the temporary residents: foreign merchants, travelers, university students, mercenaries in the municipal garrison. Finally, there was the floating population of the daylight hours when the gates were open: beggars dodging the redoubtable *Fausthämmer* of the constabulary, peasants in from rural Alsace or Baden to market their produce, Jewish peddlers with their incessant call: "Nix ze handle?"

There is, it must be admitted, some danger of exaggerating the simplicity of this older structure, the danger of overlooking, for example, the then still close liaison between the most prestigious middle-class officials and the Constoffler, or the special situation of lawyers, doctors, professors, and Lutheran clergymen. All the same, it is impossible to compare the late seventeenth century and the late eighteenth without being struck by the much greater social complexity of the latter period: more groups, more gradations within groups, hence more lines of connection and division. This increasingly intricate network of distinctions in manners, in status, in wealth, in power, was certainly not wholly the product of French rule, for it was matched by developments throughout Europe in the century preceding 1789. What the capitulation had done, however, was to create at a stroke an altered political setting, then introduce human elements and social values which would have figured much less prominently, or not at all, in the city's evolution if it had remained a little German republic.

II

Subjection to Louis XIV grafted on to local society three important new groups: French administrative officials, royal troops, and Catholic clergy. Of these, the first took their places fairly quickly at appropriate levels in the city's class structure, as it emerged under the changed circumstances. An intendant, born to the *grande robe,* trained in Paris as a *maître des requêtes,* and capable of going on

later, as did several of those who served in Alsace, to a ministerial
post in the central government, or a royal praetor, boasting powerful
family connections in the province and bearing the title of "councilor
of the king in his councils," naturally moved with ease among the
nobles, prelates, and military commanders resident in the city.
Other principal French agents, at the intendancy, the praetor's
office, the *Chambre des Monnaies,* and so on, were comparable in
prestige to the native members of the Magistrat itself. It would
take time for personal familiarity to catch up with official association;
but from the very first, the activities and, be it added, the civilian
dress of royal administrators made them less obviously distinct from
the old population than were the priests and soldiers.

The Catholic clergy, too, represented within itself a variety of
backgrounds and degrees of family pride. The eighteenth-century
bishops, all four of them, sprang from a Breton dynasty whose
trenchant motto read: "Kings we are not. Dukes we seek not to be.
We are the Rohans." Scarcely less haughty than this clan of cardinals and generals were the holders of places in the grand chapter
of the cathedral. After the annexation, as noted earlier, Louis XIV
decreed that one-third of the twenty-four canons should be of French
origin; and in the century that followed, princes of Soubise, Tré-
moille, and Croy shared honors with those of Hohenlohe, König-
seck, Truchsess, and other great houses from beyond the Rhine.[1]
These aristocrats were actually in town only for brief periods, the
Rohans, for instance, having a château at Molsheim, a more lavish
one at Saverne, and a great hôtel in Paris, in addition to their palace
at Strasbourg. Even when the bishop or one of the chapter was in
residence, he moved only in the rarified air of the social heights.

Among the lower clergy, the Johannites too were noblemen,
Knights of Malta; but the rest were recruited primarily from bourgeois or even peasant families. In one respect, that of geographical
origin, the Catholic ecclesiastical personnel drew closer to Strasbourg
society after the opening decades of French rule, when the priests,
friars, and nuns had swarmed in not only from other towns in
Alsace but also from Champagne and Paris, Switzerland and Ger-

many. After that first generation, when a priestly or monastic habit had dependably signified an alien, local recruitment gradually increased until, a century later, Strasbourg was supplying most of its own parish priests. The composition of the regular clergy remained more complex. The list of sixty-four Jesuits resident in Strasbourg when their Society was outlawed in 1764 shows that thirty-eight of them had been born elsewhere in Alsace, thirteen in the French interior, ten in Lorraine, one each in Luxembourg and distant Silesia, and only one in the city itself.[2] Even if a friar or nun had sprung from a local family, however, the very nature of the calling removed a novice from what would otherwise have been his or her placement in society. Hence, the question of origin was much less important in the case of the regular orders than in that of the familiar parish priesthood.

Finally, there was the garrison. Here again, we must distinguish internal gradations, not so much of military rank as of social background. The two were related, but not interchangeable; for the scion of a great family might be stationed at Strasbourg as only a young ensign, yet enjoy an assured welcome in the city's most exclusive salons. Some of the highest officers did not really fit into the local hierarchy at all, being in effect suspended above it. Within a single decade, the 1730's, for example, we encounter a Duc de Coigny as governor-general, a Duc de Broglie as provincial commandant, and a Duc de Berwick (illegitimate son of King James II of England and Marlborough's sister, Arabella Churchill) as military governor.

Figures such as these were scarcely visible to the town population save on great occasions. Much more important in the citizenry's scheme of things were the junior officers. Various memoirs give us an idea of how these young men, often chevaliers, barons, counts, or marquises themselves, moved between the military and the civilian milieux.[3] They supported the French theater, populated the livelier salons and balls, sought to cultivate bourgeois families which included handsome daughters, and provided all the city's dueling fatalities in the eighteenth century,[4] as well as many of the bad gambling debts. As for the enlisted men, they seldom had access to civilian homes, but filled the streets and the taverns during off-duty hours, their lives being divided between the barracks or citadel and the less costly of the town's available pleasures.

The number of troops in the city at any one time varied with the international situation in general and the degree of danger on the Rhine in particular. From early October 1681, when several battalions were added to the original occupation force, the garrison normally stood at between nine and ten thousand men throughout the rest of Louis XIV's reign (though for a brief period in 1694 it was down to only about one thousand). After Utrecht and Rastatt the average figure was somewhat lower than it had been in the age of blood and glory. The situation during the Seven Years' War offers a good example of the military sociology of eighteenth-century Strasbourg. When fighting began in 1756, the place — always including the citadel — contained some 7,600 soldiers, including 1,600 cavalry and 720 artillerymen. Thereafter, countless regiments stopped for longer or shorter periods as they passed through en route to the battle zone in Germany or fell back for rest and regrouping. After 1758 remnants of the Saxon army, which Frederick the Great had scattered in defeat, were assembled in Strasbourg to form four new regiments in French pay. By 1760 there was another unusual contingent within the walls: around seven hundred soldiers previously captured by the Prussians but returned to France, in excess of the normal exchange of prisoners, on condition that they be kept out of action and simply brigaded for guard duty. After the end of operations, in 1762, the royal armies were swiftly reduced until the garrison leveled off at 5,500, approximately the figure maintained until the Revolution.[5]

The presence of all these troops could not fail to create difficulties, especially during the first years after the capitulation. There were repeated instances in the 1680's of insults and injuries to native Strasbourgers: interruptions in Lutheran church services, mistreatment of corpses disinterred in the course of excavations for the citadel, even some fatal shootings by sentinels. In fairness to the military governors, it must be said that almost without exception, from Chamilly at the beginning down to Stainville in the late 1780's, they acted promptly and sternly in punishing malefactors under their command.[6]

The sources of bad feeling could never, of course, be wholly eradicated. Aside from the question of discipline, there were numerous other problems touching the military which caused trouble throughout the eighteenth century. The purveyors to the troop canteens were almost constantly under attack from local restaurateurs and innkeepers demanding larger shares of the refreshment trade.[7] The Magistrat protested repeatedly against the Calvinist church services for Swiss troops in regiments like the "Boccard Infantry." Citizens compelled to take soldiers into their homes when the barracks could not accommodate all the units in transit complained of property damage and of inadequate reimbursement from the billeting funds. At one point, even the music teachers of Strasbourg formulated a solemn appeal, in this case against one of the regimental bands, whose members were giving lessons at reduced rates.[8]

Nevertheless, after the particularly ugly years at the outset, relations gradually improved. The passing of a generation of Strasbourgers who had been adults in 1681, like the coming of soldiers who no longer thought contemptuously of this as a conquered city, could not fail to ease the situation. The regular use of German-speaking regiments — "Royal Alsace," "Royal Deux-Ponts," "Royal Hesse-Darmstadt" — the advance of spoken French among the townspeople, and the waning on both sides of the earlier religious sensitivity all worked to reduce suspicion and hostility. By the mid-eighteenth century at the latest, though there were still burghers who glowered impartially at priests and soldiers alike, for most of the population cassocks and royal army uniforms had become accepted parts of the local scene.

III

In this city of soldiers and shopkeepers, of craftsmen and lawyers and clergymen, were to be found numerous visitors as well. Strasbourg always attracted foreign merchants, students, and tourists in large numbers; but even in this regard there were differences between the imperial era and the eighteenth century. These were differences produced partly by the evolution of European society as a whole, partly by the altered status of the town itself; and they contributed in turn to the change in local conditions.

For one thing, Strasbourg was now a Bourbon stronghold, the easternmost bastion of French power. Hence it served as a convenient staging point in royal journeys. It was here, in the summer of 1725, that former King Stanislaus of Poland (not yet Duke of Lorraine) presented his daughter, Maria Lescinska, for her proxy marriage to Louis XV. The exiled monarch, his queen, and the princess were housed at the Hôtel du Gouvernement for six weeks preceding the wedding in the cathedral, where the young Duc d'Orléans, son of the late Regent, represented his royal cousin.[9] It was here, October 5–10, 1744, that Louis XV himself received one of the most lavish receptions of his reign, the streets adorned with specially constructed arches and flag-draped façades, the episcopal palace illuminated as no building in the city had ever been before.[10] And it was here, in 1770, that another future queen, Marie-Antoinette, paused on the long journey from Vienna to Versailles. Amid tremendous pomp (the cathedral tower itself was fully illuminated and a richly furnished pavilion erected for the princess' use on the mid-Rhine island which separated the two main spans of the bridge), she went through the elaborate ceremonies of her formal reception by the representatives of the crown.[11] On all these occasions the city paid dearly for decorations and refreshments. The expense of Louis XV's visit, in fact, was what triggered the financial crisis resulting in Praetor Klinglin's exposure eight years later.

Foreign royalty also came on visits in the supposed incognito so popular with princes of the rococo age. King Frederick II of Prussia rode over from Baden in August 1740, just three months after his accession. The as yet unrevealed military genius seems to have been really desirous of an anonymous look around; but the day after he registered as the "Comte Dufour" at the historic hostelry, *Au Corbeau,* he was recognized by former Prussian soldiers at a review he was watching. He had to pay a formal call on the Duc de Broglie and was to have shared the commandant's loge at the Comédie that afternoon. Instead, he angrily rode off to Landau, dispatching his regrets to Broglie at the theater.[12]

In some other cases the effort to maintain secrecy was purely formal. On April 9, 1777, for example, Emperor Joseph II, calling himself "Count Falckenstein" and accompanied by Counts Colleredo and Cobenzl, arrived in Strasbourg with a suite of twenty-seven servants, including valets, secretaries, messengers, and a cook, all traveling in five carriages. The visitors stayed only a day-and-a-half; but in that time they were shown the ramparts, citadel, arsenal, and barracks, attended "The Barber of Seville," and were guests at a military review before rushing on toward Paris, thus maintaining Joseph's customary pace as a sightseer.[13] The future Czar Paul I, on the other hand, was coming *from* Paris, via the Low Countries, when he arrived in town for dinner on July 30, 1782, accompanied by his wife and using the pseudonym, "Comte du Nord." The grand duke and duchess were bound for Montbéliard on the border between Alsace and Franche-Comté to visit her parents, rulers of that principality. On September 14 the imperial couple returned for a two-day stop-over, in the course of which they visited the cathedral and the citadel and were entertained by French, Russian, and German aristocrats.[14]

If royal visitors did much to set the tone for high society, many less august tourists were equally important for the community at large and especially for its educated elements. Every year they came: doctors from Switzerland, privy councilors from Baden, professors from Göttingen, collectors of antiquities from Paris, and so on endlessly.[15] Just one file of letters of recommendation, those sent by the historian, J.-J. Oberlin, in Strasbourg to his friend, André Lamey, at the Electoral Academy in Mannheim, gives an idea of this passing parade.[16] "Baron Rudbeck and Monsieur Bjornstahl from *Upsaal* in Sweden" (1773); "Mr. Coxe, a learned Englishman who is accompanying Milord Herbert, son of the Duke of Pembroke" (1777);

"M. le Baron de Münchhausen and M. Schonfeldt, his tutor" (1777);
"the bearers of this letter, Spaniards by birth, educated in natural
history and above all in mineralogy" (1778); "Herr Durand of
Metz, an officer in the royal service" (1782); "two Parisians, M.
Bignon and his tutor" (1787); "Dr. Penneck, librarian at the British
Museum" (1788) were only a few of the travelers sent along to
Lamey by Oberlin. On November 29, 1764, to take another example,
Strasbourg's greatest eighteenth-century scholar, Jean-Daniel Schoep-
flin, wrote to the Margrave of Baden-Durlach:

> Monsieur Boswel, the Scotchman, who has passed through here, was
> moved by the kindnesses Your Most Serene Highness heaped upon him.
> This is a young man who will go far. He has many attainments and
> shrewd judgment.[17]

Not everyone, as we know, found Boswell so attractive — he was at
this very time on his way to Switzerland, where his importunities
would send poor Rousseau into a rage. In Strasbourg, however, the
irrepressible Scot took pains to cultivate Schoepflin, enjoyed his
talks with Praetor Gayot, and even wrote a rhymed reply to David
Garrick's criticism of the tradesmen's shops around the base of the
cathedral.[18]

Finally, whether one chooses to class them as visitors or as a
special category of temporary residents, the students at the university
constituted an all-important element, without which the Strasbourg
scene would have lacked much of its cosmopolitan variety. Here,
certainly, we have plenty of evidence of significant changes between
the seventeenth century and especially the second half of the
eighteenth.[19]

For one thing, although the local university had always been
sought out by numerous foreigners, the range of origins and the
commonest reasons for coming were very different by the latter
period from what they had been in the earlier. During the first
sixty years after its elevation to university status in 1621, the institution had a total of slightly over nine thousand students entered on
its rolls. Of these, about 10 per cent were native Strasbourgers,

while just twenty-four individuals were from France (though Mont-béliard and Lorraine sent an additional hundred presumably French-speaking candidates). For the rest, there were contingents of out-of-town Alsatians, Swiss, Scandinavians, even occasional Hungarians and Czechs. But it was the Germans who ran into the thousands. From places like Ulm, Schwäbisch-Hall, Heilbronn, and Esslingen, not to mention Augsburg, Nürnberg and Frankfurt, the Hesses, and the Palatinate, the more distant Brandenburg, Brunswick, Sax-ony, and Silesia, students crowded in, especially to study theology in what was the only university located in an imperial free city.

The change after 1681 was not immediate, except that native-born students represented fully 25 per cent of the total enrollment from then until 1715, a period when French-German warfare cut the overall figure by more than half. Then, during the years 1716–1720, German subjects of the Empire returned in such strength as to repre-sent almost two-thirds of the student body once more. Frenchmen still numbered only a handful: eight Parisians (all taking law) and ten other *régnicoles* over the space of thirty-five years following the capitulation.

The first appreciable changes appeared during the next thirty-five-year period, 1721–1755, when enrollment climbed back to about its pre-1681 level. Swiss students came in markedly increased num-bers. The group of Frenchmen from the interior was still small, thirty-nine in all; but this was an increase, and about a quarter of the 315 Lorrainers and 524 Alsatians used French in matriculating. Germans, however, remained an absolute majority.

In order to appreciate what took place at the university from 1756 until the Revolution, we need to reflect a moment on what it had come to represent. Its Protestant theological faculty was no longer the main attraction. For Frenchmen this had become an excellent place to learn German and, above all, German law, as a basis for diplomatic or administrative careers east of the Vosges. For all other continentals it offered a chance to learn French without having to travel farther west or suffer the Parisian's scorn for any language other than his own. Finally, by the mid-eighteenth century Strasbourg acquired the reputation in medical studies which it has never lost. All the faculties, be it said, were emerging from the doldrums into a new era of genuine excellence.

Now consider the distribution of student origins within the total of over five thousand matriculants between 1756 and 1793, when the university was suppressed. There were 834 native Strasbourgers, 893 other Alsatians, nearly 600 candidates from Lorraine, and 179 from the interior of France. A German historian has put the *Welschen,* as a language group including many of the Alsatians and most of the Lorrainers, at 1,137 during this period, 1,065 of them studying law.[20] In the final five years of "normalcy," 1786–1790, French-speaking subjects of the king represented 25 per cent of the student body — almost exact parity with the Holy Roman Empire's contingent. For the rest, in just these five years, besides German-speaking Alsatians and Swiss, there were 226 students of other nationalities, including eighteen from England, and no fewer than sixty from Russia.

Next to the sharp increase in French representation, this Russian influx, underway since about 1760, had been perhaps the most striking change.[21] The Seven Years' War, disrupting German universities and bringing a friendship pact between the Czarina and Louis XV, induced several Russian princes, led by the powerful Count Cyril Razumovsky, to entrust their sons to Strasbourg. Besides these aristocratic students, numerous young men were sent by the Academy of St. Petersburg with scholarships of two to three hundred rubles (one thousand to fifteen hundred livres) per year, probably the largest grants in aid enjoyed by any members of the student body.[22] Most of them were enthusiastic. In 1777, it is true, Fonvizin complained of the city that its houses were "like prisons, the streets so narrow that the sun never shines on these poor fishermen," but he added that "the cathedral is incomparably more beautiful than our Ivan Veliki."[23] The correspondence of scientists like Lepekhin, Ozeretskovsky, and Sokolov, or historians like Polebov, after their return to Russia, reveals their continuing attachment to various professors at Strasbourg.[24]

The distance separating Russia scholarship students from scions of families such as Razumovsky, Skravonsky, and Stroganov was matched by the noble-bourgeois distinction throughout the student body. German princes like young Karl August, already Duke of Saxe-Meiningen when he came to the university in 1775, lived a life of salons and theater parties, dancing and fencing lessons, and roistering with their peers.[25] If one compares the memoirs of Prince Metternich for his Strasbourg student days[26] with the autobiography of Jung-Stilling,[27] one gets a vivid impression of the extent to which the son of an imperial count and a poor tailor from Westphalia could live in different worlds while attending the same institution. As a matter of fact, the special *Matricula Serenissimorum ac Illustrissimorum* and the hundreds of less exalted titles inscribed on the general register show that Strasbourg in the eighteenth century was more than ever an aristocrats' university. This feature, plus the increased recruitment from democratic strata below the level normally touched in the 1600's, obviously sharpened the sense of extremes and constituted a change no less significant, though much more difficult to measure, than the shift in national origins.

Eminent visitors, passing scholars and sightseers, students from all over Europe — these, like the garrison, constituted the human background against which must be envisaged the local population, itself undergoing important modifications. It is only when changes in the citizenry's own composition, way of life, and social structure are placed in this external frame that their own significance can be properly assayed.

IV

It would be hard to exaggerate the importance for Strasbourg of the process by which its regular inhabitants ceased to be solidly German and became instead elements in a very special amalgam. Not that immigrants from west of the Vosges had arrived with a rush after 1681. At first the municipality's old laws governing admission to citizenship posed so many obstacles that on January 3, 1686, Louvois wrote to Intendant La Grange:

His Majesty would be pleased if you would induce the Magistrat of Strasbourg to reduce to one-third the reception tax which it assesses upon French and foreign families who are going to establish themselves in the city, giving the said Magistrat to understand that if it does not itself [reduce the tax], His Majesty might well abolish [such fees] completely.[28]

Not surprisingly, the town fathers acceded to the suggestion; yet even thereafter immigration for a while progressed so slowly as to excite ministerial suspicion that efforts were still being made to discourage new settlers.

Particular care should be taken not to exaggerate the number of French immigrants by confusing them with all the Catholic ones, since many of the latter, especially at the outset, were of Swiss, Dutch, or especially German origin. This distinction is perhaps easiest to illustrate at the political level where, despite the guaranteed alternation of Catholics and Lutherans in town offices, Frenchmen from the old dominion worked their way into the Magistrat only very gradually. The first of their number to become a Senator was Paul-Roger Sibour, a retail merchant elected from the "Mirror" in 1695. Between that date and 1710 just two of Sibour's compatriots reached the Senate. Thereafter, the incidence of *Welschen* in the town government began to increase, thirty-three of them appearing on the Senate rolls between 1710 and 1760. Of this number, however, only two went on to membership in the Secret Chambers.[29]

It was not until after mid-century that a second and much more considerable rise took place in the number of French patronymics in the Magistrat. In 1762 the number of Senators whose names were printed in Roman type when the yearly almanac appeared (the customary method of distinguishing them from all the others listed in *Fraktur*) reached its high point for the century: eight out of the total of twenty non-nobles.[30] By that time too, the Secretary of the Senate was Charles-François-Antoine Delaurier. Then in 1765 a new stage was reached when François-Joseph Nicart began his first term as Ammeister, an office subsequently attained in 1774 by François-Joseph Poirot, who served two later terms as well.

This slow, but in the long run considerable, modification in governing personnel reflected less apparent changes taking place at the level of the voting population. For the first two or three decades after 1681 there are scattered traces of French settlers' having moved into Strasbourg: a François Joffin of Verdun, for example, petitioning in 1698 to be inscribed at the university as a dancing master, or a Pierre Fumel applying later the same year for a license to sell Burgundy wines.[31] So far as craft production was concerned, however, the records of various guilds reveal how little the basically German character of the citizenry was affected until well into the eighteenth century.

Among the tanners, for instance, we encounter a Jacques Pasquay, admitted in 1695, a Benjamin Formier in 1704, and a François Gagneau in 1706. Then, in just three years, 1707 through 1709, a cluster of seven apparently French-born leatherworkers entered the corporation.[32] This was characteristic of the migration of craftsmen within the kingdom during the worst years of the Spanish Succession fighting and helps, no doubt, to explain why the ethnic pattern of political representation began to change at Strasbourg after about 1710. For at least another generation, however, the *Welschen* remained only a small minority among guild masters. On the rolls of the goldsmiths, to take another example, not one French name appears between the admission of Jean-Nicolas Barbette in 1689 and the year 1704, when Jean-Valentin Poley was initiated, to be followed in 1707 by Jacques Fagard; and in the ensuing twenty-five years only three more French immigrants were among the almost sixty new goldsmiths received.[33] As late as 1751, the 167 members of the weavers' and drapers' guild included thirty-seven Catholics, but of these just three seem to have been from the interior.[34]

Even the admittedly scattered sources available suggest that the mid-eighteenth century — a social and cultural watershed for Strasbourg in so many other respects — was also the point at which the city's population began to change more rapidly, so that by Louis

XVI's accession in 1774 it was already a human compound fundamentally different from that of 1681. This impression emerges from the guild records and from the lists of officeholders, as noted above. It is supported by remarks such as Praetor d'Autigny's in a report of 1776, that the city's craftsmen were still "four-fifths German." [35] The other one-fifth represented a clear margin of change. To that extent Strasbourg was becoming not just a city subject to the king of France, but a city partly French in other and more fundamental respects.

It should be pointed out that, because of intermarriage, family names themselves are data to be used with increasing caution for each successive generation under the old regime. By the latter half of the eighteenth century, German-Alsatian patronymics covered numerous families which now included the daughters of former immigrants from France. Conversely, the election of a Nicart in 1765 or a Poirot in 1774 no longer meant, as it would have in Louis XIV's day, the accession of a new Ammeister speaking only French and wholly strange to the older traditions of the city. The record of intermarriage in the early decades after the annexation is suggested by the register of a single Catholic church, St. Etienne. During 1688, among the weddings held in the newly created but already large parish, there were seven in which the bridegrooms were French, three of them marrying Frenchwomen, three others choosing Swiss brides, and only one taking a wife born in Strasbourg. In 1705, on the other hand, twenty-five Frenchmen were wed in St. Etienne, sixteen to Frenchwomen, three to natives of Germany, Switzerland and Luxembourg, respectively, and six to Alsatian women, of whom five had been born in the city itself.[36] Thereafter, one finds in the archives more and more documents such as the petition presented to the Magistrat in 1753 by the widow of Jean-Philippe Baehr and "le Sieur Barbier, dessinateur, géographe et graveur," her present husband, asking leave to open an embroidery and lace shop.[37]

The line between "French" and "German" citizens had not wholly disappeared by 1789. In fact, it is still visible today. But a combination of immigration and family alliances had by that date produced a town populace quite different from the one Montclar's army had found lining the streets for the march-in of 1681. What would Ammeister Reisseissen have thought of such names as Pierre-Hyacinthe Langhanss or Antoinette-Françoise Klotz!

V

A local society, changing as Strasbourg's was during the eighteenth century, was bound to display some evolution in its prevailing conceptions of comfort and enjoyment. The familiar mixture of tradition and innovation, of tenacious custom and encroaching novelty shows up in the record of pastimes as clearly as in all other aspects of the city's history under the old regime. To this extent, pleasures and even vices become valid matters of interest for anyone seeking to comprehend the metamorphosis by which the city of 1681 became that of 1789.

The social life of earlier times had been punctuated by festivals and games, such as the famous shooting match in 1576, to which the boatmen of Zürich had brought their symbolic cauldron of porridge, packed into sand in their native town at dawn and delivered that evening, still warm, after a downstream dash of over 135 miles.[38] Strasbourg's own boatmen had been noted for the public competitions staged on the Ill in front of their guildhall. Rough and often cruel games they were: logrolling with the aid of cudgels, jousting with staves between men in punts, contests to see who could first pull the head from a greased goose suspended from a line across the stream. It was indicative of the general decline in the guilds' importance as public centers that the river sports were by Louis XV's time scarcely more than occasional exhibitions, put on to entertain visiting dignitaries.

Eighteenth-century Strasbourgers remained fond of picnics and hikes, but even here a certain adaptation to more elegant fashions is revealed in the history of the "Contades." This wooded park, today surrounded by homes and apartment houses, was originally an outlying preserve north of the Jews' Gate, beyond the canal of the

Faux-Remparts. It had been the civic shooting ground of the imperial free city. In 1764, however, the new provincial commandant, Marshal de Contades, ordered its formal landscaping and maintenance as a place for outdoor dances, banquets, and decorous strolls along graveled walks beneath the handsome old trees. When the work was done, the former range for arbalest, arquebus, and musket had surrendered to the promenade.[39]

Musical and dramatic entertainment also took on more formal organization. Soon after 1681, perhaps partly to keep up with the reëstablished bishop, who had his own staff of musicians for the cathedral and palace, the Magistrat abandoned its previous custom of merely hiring a group of instrumentalists whenever the occasion demanded and instead founded a regular municipal orchestra. A contract which has survived from 1747 shows one Pierre Jacquot, first oboe, signing on for life at an annual salary of 610 livres in silver, twelve sacks of grain, three cords of wood, three hundred faggots, and about 144 gallons of wine. For this pay, he agreed to perform whenever needed and not to leave town or perform at private functions without the express consent of the Magistrat.[40] Jacquot was still a member of the orchestra in 1771, when, according to a list in the city archives, it consisted of twenty-five regular members.[41] The larger among the guildhalls, especially the "Mirror" and the "Mooress," continued to be used for concerts; but there were also performances in the French Theater or Comédie, the Temple-Neuf, and the main lecture hall of the university.

As with music, so with dramatics, the center of gravity shifted away from the guildhalls toward larger civic establishments. Back in the early 1600's, the "English comedians" — Sackville, Machin, Robert Browne, John Spencer — had come to entertain the guilds in their lodges. In 1736, however, when the German Theater opened in the renovated Drapers' Hall, it was completely under municipal control, while the *Théatre Français* had by that date already been occupying for thirty-five years the building expressly built for it on the present-day Place Broglie.

Needless to say, the majority of the established population did not simply abandon its traditional pursuits in favor of more formal entertainments in new surroundings. While officers and university students were at the Comédie, and while aristocrats, with such representatives of the middle class as could get in, danced, gossiped, and flirted beneath the chandeliers of the intendancy or the episcopal palace, your average guildsman was most likely to be found either sitting at home or ensconced in a pub. The importance of the guilds' *Stuben* and the growing number of private taverns simply as places to keep warm in winter is commemorated in the French name, *poêles* or "stoves," still sometimes used for Strasbourg cafés.

Gambling, on the Parisian model, was naturally a feature of all the more resolutely stylish salons. In other circles, it had originally been limited to sporting events, especially target shooting, and to intent card players, lingering for hours about their regular table in a Stub', occasionally bursting into noisy arguments, but the rest of the time alternately slapping down their leads or discards and gazing solemnly into the depths of their drinks. For eighteenth-century Europe, however, betting became a more and more serious problem from the point of view of family welfare, and Strasbourg was no exception. A printed municipal ordinance of 1787, after referring to earlier laws of 1741, 1776, and 1780, goes on to forbid contests of "blind luck" (including dice and draw card games), as well as games favoring the proprietor or bank, such as roulette.[42] The sponsor of any such operation is declared liable to a fine of six hundred livres and the participants, to penalties of five hundred livres apiece, with one-third of the total payable to the informer and the rest, most appropriately, to the city poorhouse. It appears that both the variety of games and the intensity of the craze had increased considerably during the preceding couple of generations.

The dietary habits of the ordinary Strasbourger, especially until about the mid-eighteenth century, would scarcely appeal to most of us now. Many families still clung to what was essentially the eating schedule of rural Alsace: a small breakfast of bread and soup at dawn, followed in the middle of the forenoon by the day's single large meal: cabbage, beans or rice with fat pork, beef, or salf fish plus various boiled dishes on the side. The famous *choucroute garnie* of modern times is a relatively refined descendant of such platters; and even it would be hard to face at 10 A.M., though having risen with the sun might help to prepare one for the experience. Gradually, as the century progressed, memoirs and letters tell us the custom of eating somewhat less, at shorter intervals, gained in popularity. Breakfasts of coffee or chocolate and rolls became more common, and fried or grilled foods established themselves beside the exhausted products of long boiling.[43]

Still, it would be an error to exaggerate the local changes in diet before the Revolution. Real delicacies seldom found their way into any but the wealthiest homes. The discovery, or perhaps rediscovery, of *pâté de foie gras,* for example, came only in the 1770's from Pierre Claude, chef to Marshal de Contades; and even thereafter, until well into the nineteenth century, it would rarely have been encountered save on a few lavish menus or in still fewer luxury shops.[44] No, if you are looking for a major addition to the fare of Strasbourgers under the old regime, you will have to pass over the precious goose liver in favor of the humble potato. By about 1770, two decades before Parmentier's crusade had begun to show results in France proper, potatoes had crowded their way onto the Alsatian bourgeois table and ensconced themselves solidly in the midst of the cabbage and dumplings.

This reliance on heavy, and especially on starchy, foods helped the town population maintain its proverbial capacity for liquids. The Strasbourger drank with his meals; he drank socially during leisure time; and in honor of a major festival he was fully capable of drinking all night, especially on those occasions when the Magistrat provided wine for uninterrupted distribution through one or more of the public fountains. After the Peace of Ryswick was formally announced in early February 1698, Marshal d'Huxelles wrote to Barbezieux in Paris:

They will sing a Te Deum next Thursday, after which the town officials have prepared a magnificent bonfire and feast, and you may be sure three-quarters of the city will be drunk on that day. Perhaps, if my health permits, I shall be too.[45]

The intendant, Le Pelletier de La Houssaye, struck a more censorious note some three years later when he remarked:

The inhabitants of Alsace are rather fond of good cheer. . . . They are strongly addicted to wine, which is one of their greatest failings.[46]

By the end of the eighteenth century, beer had become more popular than ever before, and French red wine was a serious rival to Alsatian white; but there is no indication that greater variety was matched by reduced per capita consumption — quite the contrary.

Given the high incidence of drunkenness, it was doubtless inevitable that prostitution should constitute a continuing problem. In medieval times, the whores of Strasbourg, like those of Venice, had been famous for their numbers and their formal organization. Their "guild" had been outlawed by the social ordinances of the Reformation; and since the 1540's, when over eighty brothels had been closed, most harlots had had to solicit business individually. Yet they were not hard to find around the eighteenth-century wine houses, inns, and troop canteens. Furthermore, cases heard by the Police Court revealed that many of the serving women regularly employed in such establishments were engaged in two occupations at once. Since 1503, the *Blatternhaus* or hospital for venereal diseases had been an endowed foundation under the supervision of the Magistrat. It was popularly called *"Zum Franzoesel,"* since Alsatians, following the general practice of naming the disease in honor of some foreign nationality, had long referred to syphilis as "French pox." When the venereal hospital was moved in 1687 to a spot on the Ill near the Covered Bridges, it carried its nickname with it. *Quai de la Petite-France* the location is still called, one of modern Strasbourg's most picturesque and charming spots, where few residents or tourists feel oppressed by etymology.

It would be a mistake to confuse prostitution with the problem of illegitimacy, especially when discussing a society where cohabitation frequently began with the formal announcement of intended marriage. This practice did not enjoy full social or religious approval, to be sure, but neither did it create any particular scandal. The yearly summaries of the *état-civil* regularly showed anywhere from fifteen to fifty births out of wedlock.[47] This, however, was lower than the nineteenth century's average rate; and more important, there are various types of evidence, including official correspondence about the religious education of bastards,[48] to indicate that subsequent marriage very frequently legitimated an initially nameless child. At least until the mid-1700's, even in cases where such legitimation did not occur, bastard children were normally cared for by the mother's family or by church organizations.

The establishment of a civic foundling home in 1748[49] thus emerges as a significant departure, indicative of changing needs. Why should Strasbourg at this late date have set up an institution for abandoned infants, as distinct from its old *Waisenhaus* for the legitimate orphans of citizens? The number of illegitimate births each year was rising, but not, according to official statistics, at a rate disproportionate to the growth in population. What *does* seem to have been alarming was the increase in such births occurring outside the old system of recognized family responsibility, avowed intention to wed, and actual marriage after the event. Inevitably, one thinks first of the garrison, especially since we know that social contact between the troops and the townspeople became progressively closer over the entire century preceding the Revolution. We know too that the problem of seduction by army officers was a favorite literary and dramatic theme from the time of the Seven Years' War onward. When it is recalled that two of the most important products of Strasbourg's *Sturm und Drang* literature in the 1770's, *Die Soldaten* by Lenz and *Die Kindermörderin* by H. L. Wagner, are devoted to this topic, one senses the impact on sympathetic observers of such real-life tragedies, particularly the execution of desperate women who had been convicted of infanticide.

There was more involved, however, than the presence of a French garrison in a town full of burghers' daughters. The garrison had been there for a long time before the appearance of the foundling home. What was taking place by the mid-eighteenth century went far beyond specific encounters, was, in fact, related to very broad changes in the whole fabric of European society. For this society was ceasing to be one of small, close circles — families, guilds, parishes — and of firm customs, some hampering, some comforting. Not only soldiers and students but also tradesmen, day laborers, and clerks came and went at a rate which made the group pressure to acknowledge paternity and its responsibilities much less meaningful than it had been so long as social ostracism of a man had spelled his personal ruin. The brawling energy of the new age would be creative, but its individualism would be ruthless too. Liberation is not necessarily reprehensible in itself, merely because it exacts a price. To the victims of shattered conventions, however, the price must seem very high.

VI

As suggested earlier, one encounters the need to introduce more and more terms and concepts the further in time he pursues the development of Europe's social structure. Certainly Strasbourg's society in the 1780's can only be visualized as a much more complex set of groups, defined in several different ways, then the class and status pattern of the 1600's.

Not all the distinctions applicable to the later period were equally significant, of course, either for the daily lives of individuals or for the eventual course of political affairs. The line between *Welschen* and German-speaking "old Strasbourgers" had long since ceased to provide much cause for animosity. In some mixed families it was already becoming extremely blurred; and though it remained a feature of the local scene, by Louis XVI's time real tension was centered elsewhere. Similarly, while religious differences could still produce bad feeling, could sometimes decisively affect personal advancement or marriage plans, Catholics and Protestants had arrived at a social relationship going beyond mere coexistence. Two other lines had come to be far more significant than were those of creed, language, or national origin. I refer to distinctions in wealth and in honorific status. Each was in itself a potential source of conflict; and in combination, since they cut across each other, they produced at their point of intersection an additional focus of burning resentment.

There had been some prosperous Constoffler, merchants and bankers in seventeenth-century Strasbourg, just as there had been poor guildsmen and Schirmverwandten. A town house such as Stettmeister Mueg von Booftzheim's, inventoried in 1702, with its large and well-equipped kitchen, heavily adorned living rooms, thirty-eight beds, and cherished *Kaysercammer* in which Holy Roman Emperors had slept five times in the fifteenth and sixteenth centuries, obviously overshadowed the narrow tradesmen's dwellings surrounding it in the Rue du Dôme and the Rue des Juifs.[50] Homes like that of Ammeister Dietrich, which housed the Dauphin and Dauphine in 1681, or the fine Boecklin mansion acquired by the Immediate Nobility for its Directory in 1687, bespoke sizable incomes and a rather heavy style of comfort.

What impresses one most, however, about the situation before and for some years after Strasbourg was annexed by France is the evidence of relative homogeneity within its bourgeoisie. Reuss, for example, without seeking to portray an egalitarian utopia, has discussed at length this economic compactness of the seventeenth-century town population in Alsace.[51] The early French officials, seeing with eyes accustomed to the grandeur and the squalor of Paris, swore that here there were no extremes of wealth worth considering. "It must be admitted," wrote La Grange to Pontchartrain in 1692, "that in Strasbourg . . . there is no one who has much more than he needs to live moderately well." [52] Five years later, the same intendant remarked:

They are not attached to quantities of possessions, and great fortunes do not attract them, so that there are only very few rich; the rest of the inhabitants are generally comfortable, there are scarcely any who cannot find a way to make a living, and there are not many paupers.[53]

One may treat with reserve this estimate of economic appetites, but the suggestion of a limited range of variations in wealth turns up too frequently to be ignored.

What occurred during the eighteenth century thus stands forth as an accentuation of the extremes. As we know, a certain number of guildsmen, neither affluent nor destitute, remained in the center; but new commercial opportunities, new combinations of industry, commerce, land, and public securities could with increasing frequency be parlayed into amounts of capital previously all but unimaginable in a provincial city. A family like the Hannongs might create a great fortune in thirty years and lose it in thirty more. Others built more solidly, if no less rapidly, on the profits from tobacco, beer, food and wine exports, textiles, or metal products. Older fortunes too expanded and changed in nature, as families of the oligarchy — the Dietrichs, Wenckers, Staedels, Richshoffers, and others — found that they could exploit their original funds and their political advantages to achieve an affluence with which that of their forebears could not even be compared. Some invested in industry or mining, others in wholesale trade, practically all to some extent in banking operations.

At the other extreme, however, a depressed lower class was growing in size with each passing year of Louis XV's and XVI's reigns. It was not merely that the appearance of larger enterprises created a shifting mass of wage-earners, subject to much more abrupt fluctuations in income than the earlier Schirmverwandten had been. In addition, the withering guild economy, however stubbornly it might hold on to its political influence, was finding its own certified labor force harder and harder to support. Thus, approaching 1789, one can discern an emergent proletariat: a restless array not only of transient laborers but also of increasingly numerous journeymen for whom the supposed distinction of guild membership and the full citizenship which went with it had become a mockery.

Had the obvious attributes of wealth, combined with official position, been the only requirements for public honor, the nature of Strasbourg's social elite on the eve of the Revolution would be easy to portray, as would the possible sources of attack upon the existing order. But the case is not so simple. "High society" had actually come to comprise two different societies, which might appear intermingled when viewed from below but which, in the eyes of noblemen and merchants, was clearly divided by the other crucial line, that of status determined by birth.

The coming of the French, with that extreme sensitivity to rank which had characterized the regime of Louis XIV, had sharpened the distinction between noble and commoner, a distinction made even more apparent by the widespread feudal resurgence in the eighteenth century. It is true that Constoffler remained citizens of the municipality; and families like the Zorns, Wurmsers, Berstetts, and Johams still provided in the 1780's, as they had in the 1680's, their quotas of Stettmeisters, Senators, and members of the Secret Chambers. These people naturally saw a good deal of their bourgeois colleagues in the Magistrat; and political collaboration carried with it some possibility of social contact as well. A list dated 1781 shows the wives and daughters of Stettmeisters, Ammeisters, Thirteeners, Fifteeners, and Twenty-oners, noble and non-noble alike, who were entitled to occupy seats in the Magistrat's special loge at the Comédie.[54]

Even the Constoffler, however, to say nothing of other members of the Immediate Nobility resident in Strasbourg, were increasingly conscious of being nobles and decreasingly proud of being citizens.[55] The memoirs of the Baroness d'Oberkirch, daughter of Baron de Waldner-Freundstein from Ribeauvillé in Upper Alsace, wife of a Strasbourg Stettmeister, reveal how coldly she ignored the wealthiest middle-class families, fluttering instead from the bishop's palace (though she was a Lutheran) to soirées in aristocratic homes, when she was not visiting the court of Louis XVI or hovering about the Württemberg prince and princess at Montbéliard. In 1773 all members of the Immediate Nobility were declared by the crown to be, without exception, at least barons under French law;[56] but long before that they had eagerly asserted their intimacy with titled officers of the garrison, high-born students attending the university, and the august families of German *princes possessionnés en Alsace,* especially the houses of Deux-Ponts (Zweibrücken) and Hesse-Darmstadt. It was these latter two dynasties that supplied colonels for the "German regiments," built palaces in Strasbourg, and provided lavish hospitality for suitable guests. As heir of one of them, Maximilian of Zweibrücken-Birkenfeld would eventually become Elector Palatine and then Bavaria's first king in 1805. His son, the future King Ludwig I, was born in the Hôtel de Deux-Ponts at Strasbourg in 1786.

So the city's own Constoffler pushed themselves more and more fully into the international aristocracy they saw glittering around them. They still went to the town hall, where they argued among themselves about honorific precedence.[57] But how could habitués of the Château des Rohan and all the fashionable gatherings be expected to feel concern over prices at the vegetable market or the finances of the boatmen's guild? They rushed off to Versailles whenever an opportunity presented itself, spent vacations hunting on their estates in rural Alsace or Baden,[58] and accepted commissions from foreign rulers. In 1742, for example, we find Frédéric-Auguste Zorn de Plobsheim writing from Warsaw, where he was King Augustus' chamberlain, to demand that the Senate-and-XXI guarantee his eventual burial in St. Nicholas at Strasbourg.[59]

Two of the formerly bourgeois families, the Dietrichs and the Turckheims, were ennobled (the former by Louis XV, the latter by Emperor Joseph II) and effected a partial change of caste, though the Turckheims retained the right to hold public offices reserved to commoners. An occasional non-noble hostess, such as Goethe's friend, Louise König, might succeed in making her home a popular center for French officials, both civil and military, and hence for some local aristocrats.[60] In general, however, it was difficult for even the proudest Ammeister or non-noble Thirteener to make himself appear socially quite "right." Consider then the chasm which yawned between the wealth of a successful tobacco dealer or brewer and his place on the scale of aristocratic prestige. One could be rich and yet treated as very common, just as one could, especially after a bad run of cards, be noble and still envy Monsieur Mayno or Monsieur Kornmann the profits of vulgar trade.

It was at this precise point, where gradations of wealth and honor clashed, instead of corresponding, that a special tension appeared. The hatred of very poor men for very rich ones was an important political fact. So was the hatred of humble men for those who treated them with contempt. But still another kind of hatred, felt by men who were by no means poor and who did not feel at all humble, was destined to have fateful significance in 1789. For these men's resentment of hereditary privilege merged with their indignation against political disabilities and their anger at what they considered unjust restrictions on their economic ambitions. Out of that combination of sentiments was being fashioned dynamite, all over the kingdom, long before the fuse was laid.

VII

At this point, however, it is less rewarding to pick at the social fabric of Strasbourg on the eve of the Revolution, seeking to identify the threads most apt to ravel it, than it is to see the whole, a composite product of the city's particular experience under the old regime. After the French annexation local society had at first been modified primarily by additions: administrative, military, ecclesiastical. The personnel of the native citizenry had changed little for the first thirty or forty years, and their customary way of life had changed even less. The intermediate stage, roughly the first half of the eighteenth century, had been marked by a slow accretion through immigration from the interior of France and by a much more rapid increase in the number of Catholics. Not surprisingly, the old ethnic and religious distinctions retained their full force during those decades; but many of the active animosities of the first generation after 1681, including that between soldiers and citizenry, were already fading.

Then, after about 1750, as though snowballing from a gradual start, the growth of the French minority, the new cosmopolitanism of the university, the appearance of much greater extremes of affluence and poverty, increased self-consciousness on the part of the nobility, changes in the mores even among "old Strasbourgers" all contributed to a radical alteration of the local scene. Wealth and birth crowded to the fore as the critical determinants for locating a man in society. "Is he rich or poor? Noble or non-noble?" became questions eclipsing in interest those earlier ones: "Is he Catholic or Protestant? A *Welscher* or of the old stock?"

On the one hand, it was ominous that caste and fortune had come to represent such barriers. On the other hand, if we seek for a moment to escape our natural preoccupation with the Revolution and look at Strasbourg in the 1780's in terms of what had already happened, instead of what was about to, we perceive a striking phenomenon. It is the spectacle of a population which, for all its internal variety, had in the space of a hundred years nonetheless acquired a unique personality. Here was a new kind of Strasbourger, as distinguishable from the resident of Augsburg or Frankfurt as he still admittedly was from the resident of Paris.

CHAPTER EIGHT

French Influences
and German Residues

I

The civilization of a border area always looks bizarre to anyone viewing it in terms of one or another of the juxtaposed "national" cultures. Our whole sense of heterogeneity or homogeneity depends on the specific period under consideration and its place in a long sequence of interaction. A medievalist thinks of France as a Latin-Germanic-Celtic compound and of Spain as a meeting place for all those elements with quite different ones of Arabic origin. At the other extreme, historians of modern power politics appear content at times to use national units as solid, sharply differentiated blocks and to treat the fringe areas which resist easy classification as possibly interesting, but nonetheless irritatingly eccentric.

The seventeenth and eighteenth centuries constituted an intermediate stage in this hardening of lines. National cultures had come to possess distinct sets of shared characteristics, but men still lived peaceably with the notion that any continental journey would carry one through countless variations between accepted poles like Paris, Madrid, Rome, Frankfurt, or Amsterdam. Just within the French monarchy, Roussillon on the Spanish frontier, Dauphiné on the Italian, and Flanders on the Netherlandish were all linguistic, and to some extent social, hybrids.[1] As for Alsace, Voltaire adjudged Colmar to be "half-German, half-French, and altogether Iroquois."[2] Nevertheless, the age of the Enlightenment still conceded such areas genuine personalities of their own.

In Strasbourg's case, it is possible to distinguish between the advance of French culture and the survival of German, without losing sight of the fact that the product of the two was necessarily something different from either one alone. It is not my purpose to contribute to the oversimplification of European history by insisting that a jumbled set of "national characteristics" be neatly sorted out and handed back to their parent cultures. On the contrary, the civilization of the old continent owes much of its richness to just such localities as Strasbourg and Brussels, Perpignan and Nice, Trieste and Breslau, which defy arbitrary classification, however pure the colors on a political map may have to be.

For the period here dealt with, however, the powerful civilization which centered in Paris, its impact on wide areas of Europe and especially its influence on Rhenish Germany are such important aspects of cultural history that we can scarcely avoid seeing Strasbourg's experience in terms of its reactions to that civilization. The question of how Strasbourgers talked, how they wanted to look, and what they found beautiful or intellectually impressive after a century of Bourbon rule is only one more, and the most elusive, segment of my general topic. It could scarcely have been posed until the more obvious conditions of civic life had been sketched; and even now, despite the many different kinds of source material available, the reader must at times seek the aid of his imagination. Against a background of narrative and institutional data, however, imagination need not be dismissed as fantasy.

II

Given the conservatism of Strasbourg's citizenry in other respects, we can understand the slowness with which the local use of French costumes and language advanced after 1681. Louis XIV himself had expressed dislike for women's styles in Alsace, calling them both wasteful and unsightly. The crown did not, however, seek to impose complete and immediate acceptance of French dress. The initial ordinance on the subject, issued by the Senate-and-XXI on June 23, 1685, specifically recommended Frankfurt, Hamburg, and Leipzig as models for the comely adaptation of Parisian modes to suit German tastes.[3] It also required the total abandonment of old Strasbourg styles only by brides, who would presumably be buying new wardrobes anyway. A relatively modest fine of twenty livres was to be imposed by the Morals Court for non-observance of the injunction. The failure of this effort was already apparent in September 1686, when a second ordinance was issued in considerably sharper terms.[4] Now the choice was to be simply "la mode françoise" or "la mode de Francfort." Either of these would have meant the abandonment by a Strasbourg lady of the long-billed black bicorn (not to be confused with the great bow of the Alsatian peasant woman) as a holiday headdress, the sleeves she built up out of countless ruffles, and the tightly laced vest which supposedly guaranteed a slender torso. The new law specified the change not only for brides but also for all girls on their reaching the age of nine.

The reaction was defiance, passive but total. It was impossible to fine every bourgeois family in town, and prints of Strasbourg brides dating from a full generation or more after 1681 still show them in their big black hats, their furs and vests and ruffled sleeves. In 1701 Intendant La Houssaye copied into his general survey these words of La Grange:

> The women have one or two German-style outfits, of which one sees no abandonment. Their fashions do not change, and nothing can lead them to any increased expenditure. Novelties bother these people, and they are great lovers of their old ways, good or bad.[5]

Despite this traditionalism, however, certain alterations in costume were beginning to appear even by La Houssaye's time. The memorandum just quoted admits that "the nobility dresses à la françoise," and in masculine dress generally, the emulation of France seems to have begun earlier than it did among bourgeois women. Johann Friedrich von Uffenbach, for example, son of a well-to-do Frankfurt merchant, tells us in his diary that upon arriving in Strasbourg to enter the university in 1712 he found it necessary to keep to his rooming house for several days until a new suit could be made for him, "because my costume was so German that it caused me to be laughed at." [6]

The slower but eventually more striking change in women's clothes began with the 1720's and '30's. That is to say, from those decades onward, ladies began to look distinctly old-fashioned if they clung to completely local styles. By mid-century the unwieldy fur or felt hats had all but disappeared. It was increasingly true that if one could afford to buy an occasional dress from Paris, or at least of Parisian design, one did so; and even if such garments were out of reach financially, one still tried to show enough familiarity with French patterns to avoid looking hopelessly provincial. This was no total surrender. In many families French *couture* was merely adapted, or introduced for occasional wear. A lady who attended the theater in powdered wig, sharp *décolletage,* and modish panier skirt, might for an outdoor supper dance turn up wearing a little round bonnet, straight skirt, and embroidered apron. The latter was an often quite graceful style, far less clumsy than that of 1681 but nonetheless quaint in Parisian eyes.

Language followed a more complex evolution. Though the increased use of French has come up in various connections, it is well to remind ourselves of the general situation of Strasbourg in this regard, as of 1681. The basic line of division between Swabian and French dialects ran then, as it does today, approximately along the crest of the Vosges, placing the free city at least twenty miles inside the German linguistic area.[7] Because of its commercial, political, and scholarly contacts, the town oligarchy had long included some members who could speak French and more who could read it; but the difficulties confronting any royal official who knew no German were nonetheless considerable in the first years after the capitulation.

As with clothing so with language, the crown, by a ruling of the Council of State in January 1685, made a short-lived effort to impose a change, in this instance the adoption of French for all official documents. Some months later, the Magistrat presented a petition to the new praetor, Obrecht, arguing among other things that such a law violated the terms of the capitulation; that Strasbourgers had not yet had time to learn French; that many experienced officials would have to be dismissed if the decree were enforced; that parties to suits would be unable to understand the briefs presented by their own lawyers; that German remained essential for commercial dealings; and that, in any event, affection for a ruler did not depend on language. Obrecht replied, point for point, insisting that language is a right of sovereignty; that enough citizens and officials knew French to permit its adoption (while others could use interpreters); that so far as lawyers were concerned, no one could understand them anyway, in any language; that German could still be used for business purposes; and that the king deserved more of an effort than had yet been made by the populace to master French.[8]

Despite this seemingly adamant reply, the royal authorities did not seek to enforce the law on language. In 1735 Peloux, writing for the intendant a full half-century after the original decree, mentions its having been ignored and suggests that despite the policy of not disturbing Alsace, a new effort should now be made "to oblige the people of this area to speak their sovereign's tongue." [9] Nevertheless, notaries and lawyers went on using German for German-speaking clients, town records continued to be kept in German, save for inserted copies of correspondence in French, and official announcements were regularly published in both languages.

Eighteenth-century newspapers offer interesting evidence of both the gradual increase in the local importance of French and the tenacity of German. The *Wöchentliche Strassburger Frag- und Anzeigungs-Nachrichten,* begun in 1731, was a little four- or sometimes six-page journal which came out each Thursday carrying want ads, notices of sales, and current prices of representative products. From 1742 on, it contained some bilingual advertisements; and in 1754 it actually attempted a French printing in addition to the regular one. It reverted to the old system after only three issues of this separate edition, but by that time the *Wochenblatt,* as it was commonly called, was heavily larded with French items, as well as with French phrases in German sentences. Finally, in 1788, it definitely adopted a double issue, French on Wednesdays, German on Saturdays.[10]

Strasbourg's press was still mainly German in the last years before the Revolution, despite this concession by the old *Wochenblatt*. Aside from several short-run periodicals of varying degrees of interest, there were the *Privilegirte Strasburger Zeitung* (founded in 1744 as the *Wöchentlichen Politischen und Neuen Weltgeschichten*, but renamed in 1764); Seybold's *Magazin für Frauenzimmer* (1782 ff., featuring poetry, continued novels, educational essays, and ladies' fashions); and the *Strassburgische Gelehrte Nachrichten* (1782–1785). Only J.-J. Oberlin's *Almanach de Strasbourg* (1780–1781) and its successor, the *Almanach d'Alsace* (1782–1792), appeared wholly in French. This did not mean, however, that French-speaking citizens were deprived of periodical reading matter, since articles in their language appeared in all local sheets. Many residents also received journals by mail. Finally, in 1786, with the opening of Jean-Chrétien Treitlinger's newspaper reading room at the Swedish Coffee House on what is now the Place Kléber, any subscriber willing to pay a nominal fee could pore over fully twenty-nine current out-of-town papers in French and fifty-four in German, plus the *London Evening Post, Notizie del Mondo* (Venice) and *L'Observatore Triestino*.[11]

Under the circumstances it is hardly surprising that the century produced a new garble of idioms, a *Kladderadatsch* no longer just German and Latin as in the seventeenth century but now including French expressions as well, so that on a petition of 1753 the spokesmen for the merchants' guild could proudly sign themselves: "Die Assessores Eines Löblichen Corps des Marchands hiesiger Statt."[12] Though French began to be a regular subject of instruction in the Protestant Gymnasium only in 1751,[13] it had already been taught for two generations in the Jesuit *collèges* of Strasbourg, Colmar, and Ensisheim. As a conversational and classroom language at the uni-

versity it had overtaken German by the mid-eighteenth century. The
number of French tutors and *pensions* advertised in the local press
increased with each passing year.

Needless to say, class lines were important in the eighteenth-
century language picture.[14] French alone was tolerated in the salons
or the loges at the Comédie. For middle-class people of some wealth
and professional or political aspirations it seemed more and more
important, while most shopkeepers and restaurateurs could use it at
least well enough to communicate with customers before Louis XV's
reign was far advanced. Yet in 1789 thousands of ordinary craftsmen, not to mention most Alsatian peasants, still could neither
speak nor understand much of the king's idiom. Even local scholars
like Schoepflin, Schweighaeuser, Haffner, and, rather surprisingly,
Grandidier, though they used French a great deal, occasionally
prefaced their writings with apologies for imperfections in style.
The story is told of the revered Professor Koch that he was invited
to Paris in 1782 to read a paper on Japanese history before the
Académie des Inscriptions et Belles-Lettres. After having for some
time registered mounting irritation, the chairman finally interrupted
the lecturer with the scarcely hospitable remark:

"Monsieur 'Kock,' we say *le Japon* — not *le chapon!*" In reply to
which his victim came off rather better than many Alsatians before
and since by snapping:

"Monsieur le Président, we say *Koch* — not *coq!*" [15]

III

What Strasbourgers knew about Paris obviously depended not
only on the appearance in their midst of French officials, soldiers,
students, and tourists, the immigration of new settlers, and the delivery of French reading matter, but also on the direct experience of
local citizens who traveled westward across the Vosges, in order to
see for themselves.

Certain of the city's scholars, merchants, and magistrates had
always journeyed far and wide across Europe.[16] Back in 1643, for

example, the future Ammeister Dietrich had visited Paris, as a young man, on an excursion far pleasanter than he was to make in 1685 for the purpose of hearing Louvois' demand that he change his religion. Some representatives of the free city had gone to the French court every year or so, on official business, throughout the 1600's. Nevertheless, travel from Strasbourg before its capitulation had always been much heavier up and down the Rhine, or eastward into Germany, than into France. Language, family connections, economic interests, sometimes religious considerations, all had combined to make travel in the Empire or Switzerland especially attractive to an Alsatian burgher.

What happened in the eighteenth century was not that Strasbourgers traveled less to these familiar areas but that, in addition, they traveled a great deal more within the French kingdom. It was a time marked by immensely increased circulation all over Europe, when the upper social and income groups adopted touring as an integral part of polite existence, and when a higher proportion of businessmen and scholars than ever before in history took trips for professional reasons.

It is worth reëmphasizing that visits by residents of Strasbourg to German-speaking areas, despite a relative decline in importance, probably did not undergo any absolute reduction at all. Merchants went to the Frankfurt fairs as regularly as ever and often pushed on to do business in Leipzig or the Hanseatic towns. Well-to-do gentlemen, including many officers of the Magistrat, took vacations in the resort towns of the Black Forest and farther north in the Taunus. Protestant clergymen or theology students made pious journeys to the Lutheran shrines of Saxony, often visiting Berlin and Potsdam as well.[17]

Strasbourg's own university had by no means absorbed all local students during the seventeenth century. Each year an average of four to five of the city's residents sought fuller educations, and greater freedom from parental control, by going elsewhere. Occasionally the choice fell on Paris or Grenoble or Orléans,[18] rather than on Leyden or Basel. The majority of such students, however, went to other German universities in the Empire.[19] Between 1648 and 1700, a total of sixty Strasbourgers (a large number for the time) went to Leipzig, thirty-five went to Tübingen, twenty-one to Giessen, eighteen to Heidelberg.

After about 1700, as with travel in general, the pattern of university attendance by natives of the city changed in several ways. Many still went to Germany, where Jena replaced Leipzig as the most frequented among Lutheran schools,[20] while Calvinist Heidelberg and Catholic Freiburg led their respective denominations among sons of Strasbourg families. Leyden and Basel also remained relatively popular. There was, nevertheless, an overall decline in the number who attended German-language universities; for only 335 of the city's residents matriculated in such institutions between 1701 and 1800, as compared with 237 in just the preceding fifty-three years. This was partly because the University of Strasbourg itself was managing to draw more and more local support, as the advantages of its French admixture and its greatly improved faculty became increasingly apparent. No less important, growing numbers of Strasbourgers were setting off for Pont-à-Mousson, Besançon, Dijon, Grenoble, and, above all, Paris. No historian has assembled statistics for French universities comparable to Jaffé's for the German ones; but numerous memoirs, letters, and biographies of the period reveal the new academic ties.

Stylish visits to Versailles, scholarly pilgrimages to the capital, military tours of duty by Alsatian officers, business trips — these were all distinct categories of human contact with the hub of French culture. Equally important was ordinary tourist travel to Paris, of which we can form some impression from the entries in the guest book of the Swedish legation's Lutheran chapel on the Rue Jacob, itself presided over from 1742 to 1784 by a Strasbourg-born pastor, Charles-Frédéric Baer. The signatures record the presence of the jurist, Jean Silberrad, and Senator Philippe-Jacques Straus of the "Anchor" guild (in 1739); Jean-André Hammerer, M.D. (1747); Senator Jean-Daniel Kornmann (1752); Pastor Jean-Frédéric Schweighaeuser (1765); Jean-Godefroi Treuttel, bookdealer (1770); Jean-

Philippe Fries, tutor (1773); and Pastor Matthieu Engel (1788), to mention only a few characteristic visitors.[21] These Strasbourgers even had a regular pickup point for letters from home — Kolb's and Zeller's specialty shop near the Swedish chapel and St-Germain-des-Prés. As one student of Alsatian newspapers before 1789 puts it, the number of advertisements appearing in the Strasbourg *Wochenblatt* for printed guides to France in general and its capital in particular suggest the extent to which travel to Paris was becoming "vulgarized" in the eighteenth century.[22]

IV

It is not easy, and perhaps not even essential, to identify "national influences" in the eighteenth-century world of erudition. Learning had for centuries represented the pooled efforts of widely scattered contributors, and the decline in the use of classical tongues had not yet set in so strongly as to sunder the old communications net of European scholarship. At Strasbourg Schoepflin could be a royal historiographer of France, as was Grandidier after him, yet travel incessantly in Germany, corresponding the while in French, German, and Latin with colleagues all over the continent.[23] Professor Nicolay could betake himself to London and thence to St. Petersburg with young Count Razumovsky in 1769, then decide the next year to remain in Russia as tutor to the Imperial Grand Duke — and eventually as privy councilor — without feeling that resignation from his chair at Strasbourg implied desertion of either the French or the German West.[24]

From the profuse correspondence between local scholars and colleagues elsewhere in Europe there emerge two facts of general importance for Strasbourg's intellectual history in the eighteenth century. One is that the quantitative weight of personal contacts, of real familiarity with men, theories, and institutions, lay on the side of Germany — the files of letters in German libraries and archives (or returned from there to Strasbourg) are unmatched for volume by any in France. The other fact, however, is that although it took more effort to keep up contacts with scholars in France, although these contacts tended to be more formal and, as it were, less natural, the effort was made. The average Strasbourg professor, the wealthy amateur of science or antiquities knew Germany better, but he went to Paris eagerly, with a special kind of excitement.

No man of learning could be unaware of Strasbourg's opportunity, and responsibility, as a "clearing house for enlightenment" between purely French and German centers.[25] Over the whole century the number of translations and original works designed to fulfill this function grew steadily with each decade. In just the last couple of years before the Revolution, Germany could be grateful for new translations of Berthollet on industrial chemistry and Montgolfier on aerodynamics, France for the same of Büsching and Krebel on geography, Trebra and Ferber on mineralogy, Euler on physics, and Scheele on chemistry. For German-speaking students in the 1780's Professor Koch lectured on German law in terms of French critical principles, though he wrote his *Table of Political Revolutions* in French. Whereas in the early 1700's the norm for a Strasbourg scholar had still been to publish and to lecture in Latin, corresponding in that language or in German, by the end of the century he was apt to publish, lecture, and correspond in either French or German, with Latin still used but becoming rarer. The reliance on French by specialists outside the university was exemplified by Jean-André Silbermann in his *Histoire topographique de Strasbourg* (1775), Philippe-André Grandidier in his *Histoire de l'Eglise et des princes-évêques de Strasbourg* (1777–1778), and Philippe-Xavier Horrer in his *Dictionnaire . . . de l'Alsace* (1787).

Two examples may suffice to give a purely statistical idea of the importance of French reading matter by Louis XVI's era in this once solidly German community. The works reviewed by the *Strassburgische Gelehrte und Kunstnachrichten* during its first year of publication (1782) were divided into fifteen different groups for purposes of indexing. In all, they comprise 177 German titles, 19 Latin, and 131 French, including a half-dozen translations from English. In certain fields, notably theology and education, the

German preponderance is very great; but in law, philosophy, political economy, history, poetry, drama, and fiction, there is approximate parity, while in the grouping headed "Medicine, Chemistry, and Botany" there are fourteen French as against nine German works. Later yearly volumes of the journal reveal the same general pattern. To take another case, when the enterprising Treitlinger added a lending library to his newspaper reading room in March 1786, he offered a choice of 514 books in German, 413 in French, 23 in English, and 11 in Italian, combining poetry, novels, essays, and scholarly works.[26]

In this cosmopolitan world of learning and in the social circles where it was discussed, strange things could happen. A man with one eye cocked on the all-important approval of Paris found in Strasbourg an excellent sounding board, an entrée to the Parnassus of both scientific and social distinction. He might be an honest searcher after altitude, like the optician, Adorn, who pored over every French report on lighter-than-air craft and solemnly attempted a new balloon ascension of his own as quickly as his fractures from the previous one had knit.[27] He might be a self-hypnotized apostle of magnetism like Dr. Mesmer, who briefly dominated local salon society in 1778 and whose vogue in certain groups survived long after his departure for Paris. Or he might be an intense member of the "Illuminati," a seeker after the common base of all mysticism like Saint-Martin, who after encountering Gnosticism and cabalistic Judaism in Bordeaux, spent three years in Strasbourg, 1788–1791, trying to absorb the differing lessons of Mesmer and Boehme.[28] Finally, he might be a true prince of mountebanks, a Cagliostro.

Guiseppe Balsamo had been born in Palermo in 1743, had learned some alchemy as a student of the Hospitalers in Caltagirone and, after numerous misadventures, had presented himself as "Count Cagliostro" on Malta, where he secured letters of recommendation from the Grand Master of the Order. Following further travels in France, England, North Germany, the Baltic lands, Poland, and Russia — in the course of which he built a seamless web of international introductions as a nobleman — he finally swept into Strasbourg on September 27, 1780, crossing the bridge in a six-horse carriage with his dazzling "Countess" (the Roman silversmith's daughter, Lorenza Feliciani). He was to stay three years, the period of his greatest successes, but also the preface to his ruin.[29]

At Strasbourg he took an apartment and immediately began offering free medical service to the poor. No one has ever denied his cleverness in practical healing. His opposition to the violent purges and bleedings then favored by professional doctors must alone have saved some lives. Above all, however, he was a show-man, playing for the attention and eventually the support of rich and powerful individuals. A memoirist who was an apprentice apothecary in Strasbourg at the time has this to say of Cagliostro:

> The confidence he enjoyed was extraordinary. The military in partic-ular showed a great inclination toward him. . . . Even if many of the methods [he] employed seem strange and unscientific . . . he possessed many kinds of practical knowledge, through which he was able to build his reputation. He was not at the time concerned with animal magnetism. In the chemical treatment of metals he unquestionably had certain knacks, as when he gilded two doorknobs in the palace of Cardinal de Rohan. . . .
>
> He deposited at the pharmacy several of his master formulae, which I was given to prepare. . . . All of Cagliostro's pills weighed five grains and were heavily gilded.[30]

A man of endless fantasy, he convinced Louis-René de Rohan that in time, and given sufficient faith of a type not normally em-braced by cardinals, the prelate's asthma could be cured and endless quantities of base metals turned into gold for his use. Cagliostro startled even the skeptical Baroness d'Oberkirch by his shrewd guesses, or perhaps quietly assembled knowledge, about her family history.[31] He boasted of owning the Philosophers' Stone and let it be understood that in introducing the "Rite of Memphis" into free masonry he was speaking not just as a student of ancient Egypt but as someone who had taken part in the original observances. In-tendant La Galaizière, Praetor Gérard, Marshal Contades, Am-meister Lemp, even Vergennes in Paris pronounced him the apostle of a new vision of philanthropy and vied for his favor. Neverthe-

less, the mounting hatred felt by Strasbourg's regular doctors began
to make life unpleasant for the Count by 1783,[32] and he decided to
push on toward Paris, this time as protégé of the joyously trembling
cardinal. Both were to be dragged down in the fiasco of the Diamond Necklace, though Rohan would only be disgraced until the
Revolution drove him from France, while Cagliostro died in Urbino
in 1795, a prisoner of the Papal Inquisition. He was one of Strasbourg's most curious links with the great world of Paris. At the
same time, he was a striking example of the mobility, both social
and geographical, which made this a lively center.

V

In the realm of graphic and plastic arts, Strasbourg under the
Bourbons witnessed the victory of a consciously French aesthetic,
as did many centers still inside the Holy Roman Empire. As a matter of fact, no small part of the French artistic influence in Alsace,
especially during the first decades after 1681, came by way of
German cities and their craftsmen. Given this complicated route for
some motifs and the distance to be traversed even by those coming
straight from the west, it was doubtless inevitable that successive
"periods" of French art, as Hans Haug has demonstrated,[33] should
have been reflected in Strasbourg with a lag of anywhere from two
to four decades.

That being the case, it is useless to search for a local version of
"Louis XIV" much before the 1720's. The first thirty-five to forty
years of royal domination were marked instead by the continuance
of older techniques and conceptions, with French artists frequently
in residence but never, it would appear, exerting any great influence
over regional preferences. This was true of a sculptor like François-
Alexis Francin from Rennes or a painter like Largillière from Paris.
Artists brought east to decorate the new military buildings kept
strictly to their special tasks, being invited to undertake no others.
The wealthy student, Uffenbach, tells us that in 1713–1714 he knew
a French portrait painter, Janson, as well as a sculptor named

Fosset; but he had two portraits of himself executed, respectively, by the elder Altenwanger and a Dutchman, Kirchberger.[34] Strasbourg's most successful artist of the time was Jean-Adam Seupel, who died in 1717 after having painted Obrecht, Bishop Guillaume-Egon, Chamilly, and numerous members of the Magistrat in a manner not very different from that popular at Versailles but no more "French," on that account, than the ordinary productions of countless other late Baroque portraitists. In decorative arts, including everything from incidental paintings to patterns for the earliest Hannong pottery, the German "curiosities" (monsters, meteors, fantastic plants, and birds) hung on stubbornly.

In architecture, where the most impressive things would ultimately be done and the most striking changes registered, this early period went on producing examples of late "Rhineland Renaissance" houses, consciously Italianate despite local modifications. One can still see a number of them, along the Ill and in the old neighborhood west of the cathedral. As a rule, the main doorway is arched, the window frames square and flush with the wall, the ground floor windows heavily grilled with straight bars, the façade almost invariably four stories high. Always, and this is the surest hallmark of the style, there is a heavy cornice above the top story of the façade, which thus becomes a rather heavy rectangle, as seen from below by any observer too close to perceive above this cornice the more familiar Alsatian line of the steeply sloping roof.

Not until the 1720's did the reception of French tendencies begin to be visible at Strasbourg, in the ornate ironwork and a bit later in pottery designs showing real flowers or not at all real pastoral scenes, even in the bookplates favored by wealthy bibliophiles.[35] In painting, the more graceful, but empty and often saccharine, themes of courtly art began to crowd out the soldiers and the still lifes of fruit or game so dear to the seventeenth century. Again, however, it was architecture which showed most clearly the dominant style. In these first two decades of Louis XV's reign, there appeared the city's first "Louis XIV" buildings, designed by a remarkably mixed group of architects. The Strasbourg-born François-Rodolphe Mollinger still used frankly traditional lines in planning the handsome main unit of the Civil Hospital (1718–1726); but then he and the Franconian, Johann Peter Pflug, built the Hôtel de la Prévôté following standards set by Paris in the 1670's and '80's. Frenchmen did the same, Lagardelle and Saussard for the Hôtel du Grand Doyenné (1722–1728) — now the episcopal palace — and Perdiguier for the Hôtel du Gouvernement. In all these, as in the new butchers' guildhall, the *Commanderie* of the Order of Malta, and numerous private homes, we see the first mansard roofs (sometimes topped by a second, irrepressibly Alsatian one) and protruding, richly molded windows.

This was still, however, only a brief introductory phase when compared with the much longer and richer period, from around 1730 to 1760 or 1765, of what may be called "Regency," making allowance for the inevitable overlapping with earlier and later tendencies. Since in France many characteristics of this art were already gaining currency two decades before the Duc d'Orléans became Regent in 1715, we have here another example of more than a generation's lag at Strasbourg. The productions were nonetheless impressive when they came. Cardinal de Rohan borrowed the king's own architect, Robert de Cotte, to design the magnificent new episcopal palace on the Ill (1728–1742), which Joseph Massol completed after Cotte's death. The same year he began the Château des Rohan, Cotte was also asked by Count Régnier III of Hanau-Lichtenberg to make suggestions for the big Hôtel de Hanau, which Massol, Perdiguier, and Le Chevalier would also work on and which, after having by mid-century become the Hôtel de Hesse-Darmstadt (by inheritance), has served since the Revolution as Strasbourg's town hall. But neither these palaces nor the Hôtel de Deux-Ponts and the Collège des Jésuites of the 1750's present quite the balanced grace of the Hôtel de Klinglin, completed in 1736. Walking over the footbridge which crosses the canal in front of this building, the Préfecture as it is now, most onlookers experience the lift which comes from the fine achievements of any style.

Like the other buildings just mentioned, the Préfecture reveals the simple moldings which had succeeded the ornamentalism of the Louis XIV epoch, the slightly arched lintels of the casement windows broken by masks or plaques in low relief, the *appuis de fenêtre* in delicately wrought iron. Massol and Le Chevalier topped this façade of rose-cream stone with the mansard roof they knew so well; but their German colleague, Pflug — and this is characteristic of much in Strasbourg — flanked the windows of the mansard with rococo scrolls and vases of a type he had learned to admire in Bamberg and Würzburg. Yet the harmony is impressive.

For the remainder of the century, architecture continued to be the best index of French influence. Painting minced through its imitative, cosmopolitan minuet, producing little of lasting value or even of historical interest.[36] About the most that can be said on the latter count is that Joseph Melling's establishment of an art school in 1776 brought to Strasbourg a German-born student of Van Loo and the French Academy at Rome, who as Baden court painter had just completed the ceilings for the new palace at Karlsruhe. There had been several previous efforts since 1760 to found an art school at the "Mooress" guildhall or elsewhere, but all had failed. Melling had better luck, though by 1783 even he had to ask for financial aid from the Magistrat. The latter, in turn, obtained voluntary contributions from most of the twenty corporations, since a school of design had come to be looked upon as essential to the maintenance of elegant standards in all crafts.[37]

There were always sculptors about, to do portrait busts and burial monuments, decorate new mansions, and work on church renovations; but Strohe in the 1760's, Degroff in the '70's, and Wahl in the '80's represented no important tendencies of their own or of any larger school. As in painting so in sculpture, such native Alsatians as acquired any international renown did so, almost without exception, after having emigrated to Paris or London. The only piece of eighteenth-century statuary in Strasbourg which deserves individual notice is the monument which Pigalle executed for the tomb of Marshal de Saxe.

After his death in 1751 the marshal, the only real military hero of

Louis XV's reign, had been interred in France's largest Protestant church, the Temple-Neuf at Strasbourg. Not until 1777 were his remains transferred to their permanent resting place in St. Thomas.[38] For this final tomb the Parisian sculptor created an elaborate allegory in glistening white marble, a prize example of rococo ideals. The marshal himself is at the top of the grouping, calmly descending the steps to the casket below him. On his left is an infant Genius, weeping, and a despairing France, trying with her outstretched arm to banish Death. The latter figure, with its hour glass, is waiting below, beside the sarcophagus, on the other side of which stands Hercules, grieving, but in manfully restrained contrast to France and Genius. There is nowhere any trace of Christian symbolism.

The architects of the middle and later eighteenth century, Parisians like Pinot and Le Mire, Strasbourgers like Werner and the younger Pflug, the Viennese Hiski, the Nassauer Goetz, the Languedocien Ixnard, went on adapting successive French innovations. By the 1760's, recognizably "Louis XV" motifs were in evidence, undulant window lintels, moldings become ornate once more (though lighter than in "Louis XIV"), sculptured bands often separating the stories. In this same decade the first Parisian *entresols* and galleries appeared inside certain new homes. What few specimens of "Louis XVI" are to be seen in Strasbourg date mostly from the Imperial and Restoration eras; but Ixnard's plan for the new "Mirror" guildhall, of which only one wing was actually built (1782–1783), offers us a good example of the much enlarged windows, rather stiffly rectilinear effect, and decreased ornamentation characteristic of the style.

It would be a mistake to assume that all these accretions of French influence encountered no resistance in the city. There were some who found Pigalle's statuary in St. Thomas decadent, if not actually sacrilegious. Even more debated were the activities of Jacques-François Blondel, member of the Royal Academy of Architecture. Blondel first came into contact with Strasbourg in 1762, when he arrived to arbitrate the dispute over the rebuilding of the cathedral's transept cupola.[39] The old *Bischofsmütze* of the fourteenth century had been destroyed by lightning in 1759; and for three years the plan for an Italianate dome to replace it, espoused by the Magistrat's town architect, Werner, had been stalemated by the rival project of Soufflot (creator of the Panthéon at Paris) and his fellow academicians for a Gothic tower — an interesting reversal of what one might expect to have been the division of opinion. All that came of the argument was a supposedly temporary compromise, an octagonal, plain-surfaced cupola which actually remained until the Prussian bombardment of 1870. Now that Blondel had seen Strasbourg, however, he had much greater plans for what seemed to him a city planner's paradise.

In 1764 he returned, with Choiseul's blessing, to work out the widening and straightening of streets, the regularization of squares, and the general "rationalization" of the place. His eventual project, approved by Louis XV in 1768, would have provided for a huge, symmetrical Place d'Armes (of which only the present-day *Aubette* was actually built), a new town hall inspired by the Louvre, and a set of broad avenues giving more space, light, and military advantages. But what Haussmann would later do for Paris, Blondel was unable to carry through at Strasbourg, where the local government found his plans too radical and, still more serious, too expensive. His personal disgrace at court in 1770 guaranteed that there would be no sustained royal pressure on behalf of his still technically approved project.[40]

If this attempt at a structural revolution failed in Strasbourg, as it probably would have at the time in any city of the kingdom, the physical changes completed by the end of the old regime were nonetheless striking. The removal of landmarks like the Old *Pfalz* and the Treasury Tower, the appearance of a dozen or more French-style palaces and scores of less magnificent but still impressive homes, plus the survival, of course, of pre-1681 edifices as the mass of the city's housing, these factors had in the space of a century combined to produce the unique appearance which almost two more centuries have only intensified.

VI

In only one artistic realm, that of music, were French influences unimportant. Some of the older German traditions died out during the eighteenth century, the once-powerful Strasbourg *Meistersänger* shrinking to a mere half-dozen tradesmen and finally dissolving their society in 1780,[41] the four-hundred-year-old *Pfeifen-Brüderschaft* of Alsace losing control over the city's composers and instrumentalists, who in 1788 finally severed all ties with the Brotherhood's headquarters at Ribeauvillé.[42] The continuing power of German music, however, was never matched by any corresponding impulse from the side of France. On the contrary, one of the most successful composers in Paris at the end of the century was a Strasbourger, Erdmann, whose *Ariadne on Naxos* was popular in the 1780's. Back in Strasbourg itself at this time, Franz Xavier Richter was *Kapellmeister* of the cathedral, while another Austrian, Ignaz Pleyel, a student of Haydn, was already Richter's associate in 1783 and was to succeed him in 1789. On the Lutheran side, the Church Music Inspector, Jean-Philippe Schoenfeld, was a product of wholly German training, as was the organist serving under him at the Temple-Neuf, the internationally famous Sixtus Hepp.

Wolfgang Amadeus Mozart arrived in Strasbourg on October 10, 1777, at the age of twenty-one. He was coming from Paris, where his mother had died that summer and where blasé audiences had treated coldly the former boy wonder they had lionized seven years before. Mozart was welcomed in Alsace by a musical elite indirectly known to him through introductions from mutual friends in Austria and at Mannheim. He seems to have been the house guest of the banker, Franck; and he was shown about by Richter, Hepp, and the Silbermann brothers, makers of the famous pianos and organs. Mozart himself gave three piano concerts, one at the "Mirror" guildhall and two, with the city orchestra, on the stage of the Comédie. Only one of the three earned him any money, but all brought him wild applause from select audiences. Near the end of his visit, he wrote to his father in Salzburg:

Strasbourg can scarcely do without me! You cannot imagine how I am honored and loved here. People say that I do everything so nobly, that I'm so composed and courteous and that I have such a fine manner. Everyone knows me.[43]

The young man even hoped for a while to obtain a permanent appointment at the cathedral; but in this he was disappointed, venting his wrath on his compatriot, the poor old Kapellmeister, of whom he wrote to his father: "Richter has cut down on his drinking — instead of forty bottles of wine per day, only twenty now."[44] All in all, however, he felt warmed by Strasbourg's reception; and when on November 3 he caught the Mannheim coach, beginning the long journey to Munich and thence home, it seems to have been with the feeling that here he had been appreciated, as the cruel capital of the French could appreciate no one.

CHAPTER NINE

Two Literatures but One Allegiance

I

The rivalry of two great literatures was central to the intellectual life of Strasbourg, especially in the last twenty years before 1789. Both of these literatures had prior advantages of their own. That of France had dazzled Europe for generations. That of Germany was firmly rooted in Alsatian tradition and entrenched on the popular stage. What gave point to the competition on the Upper Rhine was that by the 1770's, while the claims of Paris to cultural hegemony had not diminished in any absolute sense, the prestige and appeal of a new literary impulse from Germany gave interested Strasbourgers a new range of choice in matters of taste. Here were to be found two clearly competitive theaters. Here the influence of Voltaire and Rousseau and Beaumarchais vied with that of Lessing and Goethe and Herder as in few other European centers. This is an issue of critical importance for the town's history, not only as regards its view of aesthetics in the age of Enlightenment, crossed by *Sturm und Drang,* but also as regards the cultural, and hence to some extent the political, allegiance of the articulate elements within its population on the eve of the Revolution.

During most of the eighteenth century, the admiration for French letters evinced by the cultured classes in Strasbourg matched that to be found among comparable groups all over Europe, from Lisbon to St. Petersburg. Even in the 1730's the oldest surviving catalogues of local libraries showed the esteem in which Corneille, Racine, Molière, Boileau, La Bruyère, La Rochefoucauld, and Fénelon were held. As later figures like Prévost, Montesquieu, and the Encyclopedists gained general recognition, they too were adopted by the provincial cognoscenti.[1]

In mid-August of 1753 Voltaire arrived in Strasbourg after three years of troubles at Berlin and Potsdam and along the way back through Germany. Most recently he had been virtually imprisoned for six weeks in Frankfurt at Frederick the Great's behest, delayed again at Mainz, finally held up for a fortnight in Mannheim by the adulatory Elector Palatine. He crossed the Rhine in a ferocious mood, gouty, still seething with resentment against the King of Prussia, and worried about his chances of ever being permitted to resume residence in Paris. During the month-and-a-half he stayed, before moving to the greater seclusion of Colmar, he occupied a house outside the walls and judging from his correspondence, he left it seldom. Because he was checking his *Annals of the Empire,* he was glad to consult Professor Schoepflin at frequent intervals; but for the rest he politely declined most invitations from the Cardinal, Intendant Lucé, or Marshal de Coigny, and impolitely ignored many others. His letters to his niece, Madame Denis, that August and September show him dejected over the long exile, though not particularly hostile to the city in which he found himself — at least he was back under the French flag! Some time later, from Colmar, he wrote sarcastically of the emptiness and indolence of upper-class society in Strasbourg;[2] but just a month after this outburst, he remarked to Madame Denis that "the city of Strasbourg might please you sometime." [3]

If Voltaire was too embittered to make the most of proffered hospitality in 1753, Rousseau was almost mad with worry when he arrived in Strasbourg on November 2, 1765.[4] It was three years since the Parlement of Paris had condemned his *Emile*; and just that fall, in Switzerland, he had been driven first from Motiers-Travers, then from the Isle de St-Pierre. Both England and Prussia were open to him, but he hoped to be able to remain incognito in Strasbourg for a time. Within a week, however, he received a formal summons at his lodgings to call on Marshal de Contades, who assured him "he was as safe in Strasbourg as he would be in

Berlin." The next day the *Comédie* performed his opera, *Le devin du village,* which he attended in his preferred Armenian costume (Schoepflin thought it was a dressing gown)[5] and in the famous round fur hat.

Rousseau's letters show that, unlike Voltaire, he was at first grateful for Strasbourg's cordiality.[6] Everywhere he went he was almost overwhelmed with applause. Soon, however, the social whirl began to wear on him. His nerves, not very steady at best, became so frayed that he could not forego any occasion for rudeness. At one point a Monsieur Hangardt rushed up to him at a gathering with the enthusiastic avowal that since reading *Emile* he had been raising his son in strict accordance with its lessons. Rousseau, for whom it must be said that he had never intended the book as a literal guide to education, replied curtly: "So much the worse for you and for him." By the latter half of November he was keeping very much to himself, studying botany. Choiseul rejected his request to spend the winter in Strasbourg, but friends at court did manage to secure for him a passport to cross France en route to England. On December 9, after slightly over five weeks in the city, he boarded the stage for Paris, where David Hume was awaiting him.

Far more, of course, than through occasional visits such as these, Paris presented itself to Strasbourg across the candle-reflector footlights of the local Comédie, organized in the 1690's. It is at this point, however, that one encounters signs of competition, because in terms of popularity, the German theater was unquestionably a more considerable institution than the French, at least until the last quarter century before the Revolution.[7] With a few exceptions, the cultural level of the two enterprises cannot be seriously compared. One such exception was the two-month visit in 1736–1737 of the brilliant Caroline Neuber, Gottsched's protégée, who brought even the French elite of Strasbourg into the German theater, since she was crusading for German translations of Molière and Racine. Another was Madame Abt's performance of *Minna von Barnhelm* in the early 1770's, when Lessing was already being played in French as well. A third, in 1781–1783, was the troupe of Karl

August Dobler, which brought Shakespeare to German-speaking Strasbourgers, though they left the performance of *Lear,* according to one witness, grumbling: "There wasn't much to laugh at . . . the fool wasn't on long enough . . . too few soldiers . . . it's not natural!" [8] In general, despite these high points, the Deutsches Theater played host to one burlesque after another, each seeking to outdo the preceding one in heavy, more or less obscene, humor.

The "Comédie Française de Strasbourg," on the other hand, was long a good theater with an inadequate clientele. [9] Until the middle of the eighteenth century it was almost wholly dependent on the subscriptions of garrison officers and occasional largesse from royal officials and local aristocrats. When the famous Swiss doctor, Haller, passed through in March 1728, he found an audience of only about thirty at a performance which he personally found excellent. [10] Klinglin's short-lived project of 1750, for the Magistrat to receive the garrison subscription and to take over the administration of the theater, was liquidated after the praetor's imprisonment and death. It was an expensive institution at this date, with salaries alone, for an orchestra of four violins, two cellos, two oboes, and a bassoon, a dramatic corps of fifteen and dance group of ten, costing close to fifty thousand livres per year, while the army officers' compulsory support came to only twenty thousand. [11] Until about this point, for all the talent and beauty of an Adrienne Lecouvreur, the Comédie had looked like a very sickly hothouse plant indeed.

A factor, however, which might be overlooked is the exceptionally early founding of Strasbourg's French theater, precisely because royal officers had felt it was needed in these German surroundings. Most French cities lacked regular theaters, and probably could not have supported them, until the latter half of the eighteenth century, which is when Strasbourg's Comédie became a successful enterprise. By the 1770's Molière, Racine, Marivaux, Voltaire, Beaumarchais, and translated foreign greats crowded one another in a full and varied répertoire. Not only officers but burghers came in growing numbers, while the ever more French-conscious student body offered enthusiastic support. So did numerous tourists. In the summer of 1786, a young Parisian attended *Richard-cœur-de-lion* in the theater on the Horse Market, then wrote in his journal:

> The Comédie at Nancy had given me a low opinion of provincial spectacles, but that of Strasbourg has proved to me that Paris is not the only place where talents come together.[12]

II

If one could close the record with just a summary of French influences, Strasbourg's place in the history of eighteenth-century European literature would be easy to summarize — and quite uninteresting. The story, however, is not so simple. For just when the city seemed most taken with its view of Paris from the east, it received into its midst a remarkable group of young German writers. The name of Strasbourg looms large in every account of the *Sturm und Drang* in the 1770's, but it is not for that reason that Goethe, Herder, and Lenz must be considered here. The real reason is that these were authors of undeniable talent, who either brought with them or developed upon reaching Alsace a self-conscious, and in varying degrees anti-French, ideal of cultural nationalism. They exalted the local cathedral and waxed rapturous over Alsatian folklore. They talked to, and were for a time much admired by, numerous members of the city's native literati. To that extent, they contributed still another element to the French-German mixture already examined under various headings. If their pleas and their example failed in the end to dissuade these brethren on the left bank of the Rhine from admiration for Parisian standards, their challenge to such standards was nonetheless, like the continuing claims of German music, an important contrapuntal theme.

Goethe was a Francophile before he first left Germany. He became, for a while at least, a German patriot after arriving in the kingdom of France. For three years, 1765–1768, as a teen-age student in Leipzig, he had immersed himself in French manners and language. He destroyed boyhood poems in German and replaced them with *vers galants* addressed to numerous ladies, real or imaginary. Between the young fop in Leipzig, however, and the Strasbourg student of 1770 intervened almost a year and a half of desperate, at times seemingly hopeless, illness, while Goethe lay in an upstairs room of his father's house in Frankfurt, wondering whether the malady would ever abate. He wrote letters, pessimistic or resolutely flippant, depending on his mood. He turned to the Pietism of his mother's friend, Fräulein von Klettenburg. Then, in the final weeks of 1769, the illness began to wane. The constitution which would carry him to the age of eighty-two demonstrated its vitality. With returning health he managed, as in the past, to infuriate his father by twitting that impatient patrician on the furnishings of both his mansion and his mind. The plan to send the convalescent to study law at Strasbourg was at least partly inspired by the need to keep peace in the family.

On April 4, 1770, he climbed out of a coach in front of *Zum Geist* (or *L'Esprit*), a famous hostelry on the Ill.[13] He was twenty-one, gaunt after his long siege, but eager, as always, to devour whatever new sensations his locale might provide. He knew exactly where he wanted to go first. No sooner were his bags deposited than he was off, hurrying through the streets on his way to the cathedral. From the dizzy height of its tower he looked down through the spring twilight on the panorama which he could still, forty years later, describe so eloquently in the passage of *Poetry and Truth* which is perhaps the most beautiful word painting ever inspired by the Alsatian landscape.

Since the poet had introductions from Frankfurt and others from Darmstadt, it did not take him long to find new acquaintances or to locate permanent quarters. The latter he rented in a tradesman's house "on the sunny side of Old Fishmarket Street," i.e., the east side of the Rue du Vieux-Marché-aux-Poissons, just a short distance from the cathedral. On April 19, 1770, Goethe wrote to the poor, half-blind theologian, Johann Christian Limprecht, in Leipzig:

I've been here a fortnight and find Strasbourg neither a hair better nor worse than anything else I've seen in the world, that is to say, very mediocre, but yet possessed of certain qualities which can set one in motion for good and evil and can bring him out of his usual state.[14]

This was assuredly no outburst of enthusiasm; but the entire letter maintains a piously critical tone intended no doubt to please its recipient. In any event, the initial period of getting settled was almost over; the university's summer semester was about to begin. On the preceding day, April 18, "Joannes Wolfgang Goethe, Moeno-Francofurtensis," had inscribed himself in the general matriculation register.[15]

An eighteenth-century student at Strasbourg, if he were of a princely family, ordinarily had his meals served in his rooms. If he was a "Wilhelmite," on a theological scholarship, he shared the limited fare of a common refectory. The great majority of students, however, relied on *pensions,* boarding but not rooming houses, where private families or single ladies provided at least the principal, noonday meal to regular groups of subscribers. Such an eating club was run by the sisters Anne-Marie and Suzanne-Marguerite Lauth in a room over their delicatessen; and it was here that Goethe became part of what has entered literary history as the "Salzmann circle." [16]

The man who gave his name to this group, Jean-Daniel Salzmann, was forty-nine in 1770, the product of a merchant family which since the mid-sixteenth century had given Strasbourg countless scholars, clergymen, and civil servants. A lawyer by training, he had in 1753 been named permanent secretary or *Actuarius* of the city's Wardship Court, and he was normally called "the Actuary" by his wide circle of friends. He was in every sense a man of the Enlightenment, humane and conscientious in discharging his official responsibility for orphans and widows, fond of discoursing mildly on Reason, Virtue, and Beauty. His letters reveal neither great erudition nor depth of perception, but a benevolent interest in acquaintances as distant as the Marburg professor of medicine,

Michaelis, or the jurist, Hufeland, in Danzig, and as near at hand as the young men around the table in Strasbourg.

The unmarried actuary ate his noon dinners at the Lauth pension long before 1770 and continued to do so long afterward; but that year marked the formation around him of a particularly memorable cluster of students (about ten when Goethe arrived, nearer twenty throughout most of the following fall and winter). Besides the sage actuary, arbitrating disputes and on occasion prescribing less wine, there were several other native Alsatians: the good-humored theology student, Lerse, who became Goethe's closest friend in Strasbourg; the studious Jean-Conrad Engelbach (a member of the group until he left to become councilor to the Prince of Nassau-Saarbrücken); the medical candidate, Weyland; and three or four others.

Johann Heinrich Jung, a struggling medical student from Westphalia, better known, because of his autobiographical pseudonym, as Jung-Stilling, was a particularly intense youth.[17] He later became successively professor of medicine at Marburg and at Heidelberg, then privy councilor to the Margrave of Baden; but when Goethe befriended him in Strasbourg he was an impecunious scholar, in Vermeil's words the epitome of "Pietistic sentimentalism,"[18] who believed that the fortuitous loans which saw him through the university were gifts from a Divinity specifically concerned with his academic progress. Then there was Meyer von Lindau, a handsome, gifted rake, as were several of his peers around the table. One in particular, identified in *Truth and Poetry* only as an aging Chevalier of the Order of Saint Louis, shocked Jung-Stilling and delighted Goethe with scandalous stories from Strasbourg's history, including the adventures, both fiscal and erotic, of ex-Praetor Klinglin. Finally, there were two extreme *Stürmer und Dränger,* Henri-Léopold Wagner from Strasbourg itself, but very different from the group of Alsatians mentioned earlier,[19] and, beginning in April 1771, the stormiest figure of them all, a doomed spirit from faraway Livonia, J. M. R. Lenz.

It was not at all a solid or dependably fraternal group. A libertine remark might offend Lerse or Jung, or an unusually critical comment touch the immense vanity of Wagner, while many of the peripheral individuals seem to have come and gone without particularly impressing the "regulars" one way or another. Yet the calm leadership of Salzmann, the ebullient humor of Goethe, and the fluency of Lenz gave a certain style to those meals which the participants would later recall with appreciation.

Such a circle obviously could not absorb all its members' time and interests. Jung-Stilling was establishing himself as Spielmann's and Lobstein's best pupil in surgery, while offering a free public lecture course in religious philosophy and reading English literature at Goethe's urging. In June 1770, Goethe accompanied Engelbach on the long ride, over the Vosges and through Lorraine to Saarbrücken, that is described with such fervor in *Poetry and Truth*. He also, that spring and summer, explored the Alsatian countryside on various shorter excursions. As for his studies, he wrote to Fräulein von Klettenberg in Frankfurt, with transparent exaggeration:

I am beginning to like jurisprudence very much. With everything it's just as with Merseburg beer — the first time, one shudders, and then when one's drunk it for a week, he can't get along without it. Chemistry is still my secret love.[20]

Goethe crammed for the examinations, with the help of a tutor and the lecture notes loaned him by Engelbach, so that on September 22, 1770, he was able to register as a "candidate in law" wishing to be tested.[21] On the 25th, in the old chapter room at St. Thomas he passed the general oral examination, *cum laude,* and, as was customary, received an assignment of two texts, one in civil, the other in canon, law on which he commented at his special examination two days later.

He was now free either to prepare a public disputation of theses for the *licence* or to write a dissertation for the doctorate. His father, himself a *Dr. Jur.,* urgently demanded that the young candidate work for the higher degree. Thus, less than six months after arriving in Strasbourg, Goethe began the second and longer portion of his education there, the composition of a thesis on the proposition "that the legislator is not only entitled but obliged to establish a specific cult, which neither clergy nor laity may reject." In addition, he attended further lectures on law, natural history, classics, and history. And always he read about and discussed medicine, with the restless, devouring passion for new ideas which made sustained work on a legal dissertation boring, but which would conceive and comprehend the image of Faust.

Poetry and Truth contains numerous reflections, some critical, some enthusiastic, on Strasbourg itself — the decay of the municipal constitution, the evils of oligarchic reliance on royal power, the curiosities of the local religious situation, the liveliness of the people, the physical charm of the outlying parks and hamlets, the tapestries in the island pavilion for Marie Antoinette. Subsequently, in his reminiscences, Goethe suggested that he recognized the significance of changes in lower middle-class life, seeing in them both danger and the possible source of a new culture. As revealed in letters and notes written at the time, however, the young man of 1770–1771 seems to have been less concerned over city politics and social conditions than over the experiences he himself was having.[22]

His friendship with Salzmann, Lerse, Jung, Lenz, and the rest of the *Tischgesellschaft* continued unchanged during the "thesis year." Two other people, however, affected Goethe's life more powerfully in his Strasbourg period than did any of those at the boarding house. One was Johann Gottfried Herder, who gave him a new conception of art. The other was Friederike Brion, who inspired as high a level of purely lyrical production as he ever attained.

III

Herder arrived in Strasbourg five months after Goethe.[23] In May 1769 he had resigned his post as associate pastor of a Lutheran parish at Riga and left his Baltic home on a ship bound for France. After sojourning in Nantes and Paris, he accepted an invitation from the Prince Bishop of Lübeck to accompany the latter's son on a grand tour. This necessitated doubling back into northern Germany; but by early September 1770 the young prince's party reached Strasbourg and settled down for the winter.

Herder's period there was exceptionally tense and bitter. Homesickness and dislike for his tutorial position would have been enough, but at Strasbourg they were combined with physical pain. On arriving in town he consulted Lobstein at the university about an old eye ailment, and the decision was taken to operate, drilling a hole into the nasal cavity to provide additional drainage for the left tear duct. Such a prospect, without anaesthetic, was enough to fill anyone with dread. Herder, who had previously reserved his special abomination for Paris, now turned his full wrath on the city where he was marooned in suffering:

> Strasbourg is the most miserable, most desolate, most unpleasant place which, speaking carefully and cautiously, I have ever come across in my life. I don't want to think of people. Here there is no grove, no place where one can lie in the shade with his book and his thoughts [the exact opposite of Goethe's impression].[24]

Very early, probably before the end of September, he met and quite overwhelmed Goethe. Herder was already enough of a personage — his *Fragmente über die neuere deutsche Literatur* (1767) and his *Kritische Wälder* (1769) were being much discussed — so that the young law candidate was thoroughly in awe of him. Goethe, in fact, was present when Lobstein performed the excruciating bone puncture in October; and in *Poetry and Truth* he has left a tribute to Herder's courage. Throughout the winter of 1770–1771 the two spent several evenings a week together in the invalid's room. Herder's pampered princeling went in without him, while he himself worked on the *Archaeology of the East* and *Origins of Speech*. From the time of his first surgery until his departure for Bückeburg soon after Easter 1771, a period of six months, his sole pupil and only regular contact, save for a Russian friend, Begrow or Peglov, was Goethe. What that meant to Herder is difficult to say. One can only infer from the care he took that he knew this was no routine acquaintance. What it meant to Goethe is as clear as such things can ever be.

Aside from his scathingly critical comments on the younger man's literary drafts, Herder imparted a set of views on history and nationality which he had been developing for several years but which first reached the stage of systematic argumentation in Strasbourg. For this "empty French-German place" inspired him by repulsion, as it inspired Goethe and Lenz by attraction. The humane, universalist Herder of 1784, who would insist in his *Ideas for a Philosophy of Human History* that the personality of German civilization could be established without undervaluing any other, was scarcely visible in the bitter invalid. This Herder was still lashing all imitation of Paris not only out of contempt for imitation as such, but also out of dislike for things French.[25]

It is to the credit of Goethe that, amid all the rancor, he found and modified for his own use certain positive aspects of Herder's philosophy, which their originator would succeed in freeing from snarling animosity only years later. Between the apparent alternatives offered to Germans of that day, Möser's localistic devotion to Osnabrück as a tiny "fatherland" and Winckelmann's sweeping, classical universalism, Herder was raising the ideal of the culture-nation. History was for him the story of such nations. And what was the greatest of a culture-nation's goods, the key to its creativity, the mirror of itself? Its language, of course, especially in two supreme forms, folk literature and the writings of those rare giants whose voices were those of whole peoples: Homer, the authors of the Old Testament, Shakespeare. Francophobia and admiration for Shakespeare could and did produce Anglophilia as a general attitude. Herder accepted "Ossian" as true British folk culture, read Fielding, Goldsmith, and Sterne aloud to Goethe and naturally encouraged the latter's already great enthusiasm for the Bard.

Immersed in his discussions with Herder, busily collecting Alsatian folk songs at his friend's behest,[26] conscious always of the cathedral he would shortly celebrate in the prose poem, *Von deutscher Baukunst,*[27] Goethe probably did, in the oft-quoted phrase, "feel his Germanness" in Strasbourg. As in other respects, however, his *Poetry and Truth* of forty years later should be read with caution when it describes the author's resistance to French culture, a resistance which is much less marked in letters he wrote at the time. In any event, he shared Herder's admiration for Rousseau and learned much from other French writers, notably Diderot and Voltaire.[28]

Goethe's most important and most lasting gain from his Strasbourg friendship with Herder was the basis for artistic creations quite different from any that German literature had previously known. Goethe and Herder had two powerful, impatient minds which sought a cultural synthesis that would avoid both the dry atomism of the Enlightenment, as it seemed to them, and the diffuse excesses of contemporary enthusiasm or *Schwärmerei*. From Herder, and especially from the notion of the richness of folk experience, Goethe obtained intellectual underpinning, so to speak, for what in his own case became a more personalized belief. It was a belief that both moral self-mastery and aesthetic creativity consisted in taking the sensations, passions, and inspirations of life as one lived it and transforming them into a coherent system of values. Mastery of self and of the world of experience were indistinguishable, he argued, since both lay in participation, comprehension, and organization.

Art could thus be viewed only as a "reproducing of the world around one through the world within," a recreation of reality through the ordering of its elements by one who felt them all. History, in turn, became not a source of bland optimism nor one of black pessimism; for the world had not become anything which could be judged as a product. Instead it was ceaselessly becoming something else. The young student's growing resistance to French legal studies, after his early interest, stemmed partly from revulsion at the attempt to codify the infinite possibilities of reality, when the real task was to make law "a science of life," based on a given community's past and modified with its changing needs.[29] The political implications of this view, for which Montesquieu might have claimed some credit, were in Goethe's case far less important than the aesthetic ones. For the recognition, the organization, and, to that extent, the control of an endlessly variegated world of experience represented ideals capable of inspiring a lifetime of artistic effort. They inspired a great deal immediately. Under the direct influence of Herder and the indirect impact of Shakespeare, Goethe conceived *Götz von Berlichingen,* whose emotive themes would find later echoes in *Egmont* as well. Furthermore, some of his earliest notions in the long progression toward *Faust* seem also to have dated from the Strasbourg period.[30]

A city does not write drama, and even an acquaintance like Herder leaves no simple, unmistakable traces in the literary products of a mind such as Goethe's. The complex milieu of the locality, however, and the questions raised by the harsh genius with a bandaged eye at least help to explain some of the ideas which went into *Götz* and eventually *Faust.*

The "Sesenheim idyl" shows us another Goethe, him of the love songs and the *Sorrows of Werther.* His romance with the village pastor's daughter is clearly marginal to Goethe's role in the cultural history of Strasbourg; but it is worth passing mention, if only for what it reveals of the place of the Alsatian countryside in the life of an eighteenth-century student at the university. It is also of some interest to observe how Goethe's idealization of the entire region could be personified in Friederike Brion.[31]

Friederike was not, as has sometimes been suggested, the original "Margarete," whatever the episode may have taught Goethe, in retrospect, about remorse. She was, however, the heroine of some of his best-known lyrics: "Kleine Blumen, kleine Blätter," "Mailied," "Es schlug mein Herz," "Das Heidenröslein," and several others. Furthermore, the memory of her led him to write what amounts to a romantic novella, which he set into *Poetry and Truth* as Books X and XI (and which Franz Léhar would one day turn into an operetta). The poet's own half-fictionalized version takes us from chance meeting and sudden love, through a springtime of blossoming or-

Prince Louis-Constantin,
Cardinal de Rohan 1697–1779

Marshal de Contades
1704–1793

Baroness d'Oberkirch
1754–1804

Baron Frédéric de Dietrich
1748–1793

EIGHTEENTH-CENTURY ARISTOCRATS

"La Belle Strasbourgeoise" by Largillière

chards, to renunciation of the country girl by the patrician's son from Frankfurt, and their sad parting on a summer day.

From his letters and from the dating of certain poems, we know he met Friederike one weekend in October 1770 when on a riding excursion into the country with Weyland, a friend of the Brions. He was a guest at the vicarage several more times during the ensuing six months, and apparently Friederike came once to Strasbourg with her mother, who had well-established relatives in the city. Then in May and June of 1771, as the girl's acknowledged fiancé, he stayed in Sesenheim for a protracted visit, which saw the culmination of the romance — and its end. His letters back to Salzmann in town reveal the young man's mounting uneasiness and sense of threatened confinement. Marriage would not have been impossible socially, for Sesenheim was a prosperous and fairly prestigious Lutheran pastorate; but Goethe was far from ready to surrender his freedom and his mobility. Though the final break was made only later, by mail, he left Friederike behind him once and for all when he rode back to Strasbourg that June.

Then, in July 1771, Goethe submitted his dissertation for the doctorate in jurisprudence. The subject, touching both religion and princely power, may not have seemed altogether prudent to the faculty. At the same time, it was not a work of care and devotion, and the dean's refusal to approve it for publication may have represented a sound qualitative judgment. In any event, the candidate was left, much to his father's chagrin, with only the chance to earn a *licence* by delivering a public disputation on a set of theses. This he did on August 6, departing for home almost immediately thereafter. That autumn, back in Frankfurt, he received from the Strasbourg law faculty an invitation to try again for the doctor's degree; but, as he wrote Salzmann, "having 'licentiated,' I've had enough." [32] The composition of *Götz* and the eulogy of Meister Erwin's cathedral left him no time to spare.

IV

Because of their subsequent fame, Goethe and Herder might easily dominate our whole impression of the *Sturm und Drang* at Strasbourg. Actually, however, a third figure was more specifically concerned than either of them with the city's linguistic and literary situation. Jakob Michael Reinhold Lenz was briefly, in the mid-1770's, second only to Goethe among German lyric poets. At the same time, he was as patriotic, in the cultural sense, as was Herder. Last but not least, his stay in Strasbourg was considerably longer than were those of his two great contemporaries.

Lenz was born in 1751 at Sesswegen, Livonia, the son of a successful Lutheran minister who in 1759 was named to a vacancy at Dorpat and eventually became General Superintendent of the province's entire church organization. Jacob Michael, though a Russian subject, was thus the product of a German community, however different it may have been from the Frankfurt of Goethe. In 1768 he entered the University of Königsberg in theology, and there encountered "Magister Kant," from whom he absorbed a series of critical views concerning eighteenth-century philosophical assumptions without, it must be said, adopting his teacher's orderly habits of mind. From Kant also, he learned of Rousseau and of Hamann, the "Magus of the North," center of his own mystical cult.[33]

It is worth recording that while still at Königsberg, Lenz first expressed resentment against French intellectual prestige and condescension. When Kant was inaugurated as a professor in August 1770, the youth wrote a congratulatory ode, which he presented on behalf of the Livonian-Courlandish students and which included the following:

> Ye sons of France! Scorn ye our Northland yet?
> Query if genius ever here is met:
> While Kant yet labors at his task
> That question shall ye dare no more to ask.[34]

For Lenz as for Herder resistance to French literature went hand in hand with admiration for English. Before coming to Strasbourg he had already translated Pope's *Essay on Man* and very probably by that date *Love's Labour's Lost* as well. Nevertheless, again like Herder, he was eager for some direct contact with the culture of France.

His chance came when two sons of a Courlandish Junker, Barons Friedrich and Ernst von Kleist, decided to enter French military service in Strasbourg and brought Lenz along as a companion. They arrived in the city in April 1771, barely soon enough for Jakob Michael to make the acquaintance of the departing Herder. More important, he soon met Goethe, Jung-Stilling, Lerse, and the rest of the Salzmann circle. Although he did not register formally at the university until much later, Lenz, with his mobile, almost childlike face and his intensity of interest and mood, quickly became a leading figure in the group around the dining table.

He stayed almost five years in Alsace,[35] until the autumn of 1774 maintaining his tie with the Kleists. Lenz observed their escapades and made Baron Friedrich's repudiation of a betrothal contract with Cleophe Fibich, daughter of a Strasbourg jeweler, the basis for his play, *Die Soldaten.*[36] In the summer of 1772 he followed one of the Kleist brothers to Fort Louis, near Sesenheim, and while there courted Friederike Brion, of whom he had heard from Goethe and for whom he wrote several lyrics to add to her remarkable collection.[37]

After two years back in Strasbourg, Lenz finally broke off all connection with the Kleists and on September 3, 1774, matriculated in theology at the university.[38] The ensuing eighteen months, though darkened by financial worries, constituted his one period of high productivity and relative happiness. To his Sesenheim lyrics, which are fully comparable to Goethe's, he added in rapid succession a series of published works — *Lustspiele nach dem Plautus, Der Hofmeister, Anmerkungen übers Theater, Der neue Menoza* — composed numerous articles for the weekly *Bürgerfreund,* and wrote *Die Soldaten,* which appeared in print at the end of 1776.

What makes Lenz especially significant in the intellectual history of Strasbourg, however, is not so much his formal writings while there, as his role in the local "German Society." This *Deutsche Gesellschaft zu Strassburg* had had its precursors. Back in the first years of the sixteenth century Jakob Wimpheling had been the founder of a literary club composed of consciously German humanists such as Sebastian Brant, Beatus Rhenanus, Gebweiler, Hedio, and Jakob Sturm.[39] Even more patriotic in its cultural ideals had been the "Sincere Society of the Fir Tree" (*Aufrichtige Tannengesellschaft*), also called the *Societas Philoteutonica Argentoratensis*, formed in 1633 by an Austrian, Rompler von Loewenhaupt, with the support of the anti-French Moscherosch.[40] There had been a discussion group, unrelated but also called the German Society, in the 1740's;[41] and in 1769, Conrad Pfeffel, who had many ties with Strasbourg, had formed at Colmar a reading club for the comparative study of French and German literature.[42] The immediate parent of Lenz' organization, however, was the "Society for Learned Exercises" which had existed under Actuary Salzmann's leadership since 1770, as an informal discussion group composed of the dining circle, with the addition of several other scholars and Protestant clergymen. Lerse and Jung-Stilling were early members; Goethe and apparently even Herder attended some meetings; but the most active, and after the departure of these others clearly the dominant, participant was Lenz.[43]

From the latter's correspondence, we get an idea of the hopes he had for this group, as well as his objections to its program under the sedate Salzmann. In the summer of 1775, for example, Lenz wrote to Goethe:

> I have much to overcome in the Society: on one side skepticism, disorder, vague snorings about belles-lettres, amounting to nothing but nettle blossoms; on the other, an ethical philosophy for gnats which creeps along its grandmotherly way.[44]

Furthermore, despite the efforts of some members to impose the exclusive use of German, most of the Strasbourgers in the circle showed a lamentable tendency to "lapse into bilingualism" and to cite French authorities.

Up in Hanover, at the very time when Lenz was airing these complaints to his friend, the two-year-old *Hainbund* of Göttingen students celebrated the poet Klopstock's birthday with a rally at which toasts were drunk to this idol of literary nationalists, as well as to Goethe and Herder, both by then renowned figures among educated youth. Simultaneously, the "voluptuous songster," Wieland, was burned in effigy, presumably for aping the French. As it happened, Frédéric-Rodolphe Salzmann, a cousin of the Actuary and tutor to Baron vom Stein while the future Prussian minister was studying at Göttingen, attended this demonstration just before starting home to Strasbourg. This younger Salzmann also stopped en route at Mannheim, where a "Deutsche Gesellschaft" had already been founded in Klopstock's presence and with his blessing. Thus it was that Strasbourg enthusiasts received direct reports on models for the sort of association Lenz had been hoping to create.

The local German Society, superseding the "Exercises Club," made its appearance in the fall of 1775. Actuary Salzmann declined to join but permitted the use of his home for its meetings; and most of the members of his old group entered the new association, whose register contains a list of thirty-two participants. Besides F.-R. Salzmann there were a number of native Strasbourgers: Professor Müller of the university; four Gymnasium teachers, one of whom was the future professor, Blessig; another man destined for a professorship, the young theologian, Isaac Haffner; the future Ammeister and deputy to the Estates General, Jean de Turckheim; Music Director Schoenfeld from the Temple-Neuf; plus assorted students. Among these last, two in law were to win some degree of literary fame — H.-L. Wagner and L.-J. Ramond, later known as Ramond de Carbonnières — while one in theology, Jean-Godefroi Röderer, was especially active in the society's publishing endeavors.[45] Among the non-Strasbourgers, aside from Lenz, the most active proved to be a Swede named Westmann, Christian Spener of the famous Berlin family of bookdealers, and finally, as a corresponding member, Goethe's brother-in-law, Schlosser, at Emmendingen across the Rhine.

The manuscript minutes[46] show that the society met thirty-four times between November 2, 1775, and January 9, 1777. Its history breaks rather naturally at the exact midpoint, in terms of meetings, which is to say after the seventeenth one, when Lenz left Strasbourg (March 1776). From that time on the sessions were less frequent and less concerned with the issue of German versus French. For it was Lenz who most insistently pressed for the cultivation of *Teutschheit*. At the very first meeting, having been named executive secretary, he immediately gave a talk on regional dialects as sources for the enrichment of High German. As long as Lenz was around, he completely dominated the proceedings. At the second meeting, he gave a paper on the superiority of German over French for scientific writing; at the fourth, he filled in for an absent speaker by reading one of his own imitations of Plautus; at the seventh, he gave a comedy sketch; at the eighth, he read from Dodsley's *Old English Ballads*; and so it went. Nevertheless, at other meetings a wide variety of essays were presented: Haffner on language (actually in opposition to Lenz), Blessig on Greek oratory, Leypold on Brant's *Ship of Fools,* Müller on Dutch history, Turckheim on the history of polygamy, while Ramond periodically read portions of his *Amours alsaciennes* in French.

Even after Lenz himself had departed for Germany, the society, with the younger Salzmann as acting secretary, continued to meet for another ten months at roughly bi-weekly intervals.[47] Though it disintegrated in the first days of 1777, it has left us in its minutes and its journal, *Der Bürgerfreund,* which among other things printed most of the essays delivered at successive meetings, an interesting picture of the intellectual emphases within this sizable group of young literati. These emphases were characteristic of the *Sturm und Drang* movement: the glorification of sentiment, especially as expressed in German writers, but also as found in Rousseau and in English literature, plus great reverence for folk culture as a source of dramatic themes and as a gold mine of language.

V

The literary movement we call the *Sturm und Drang,* as Goethe later explained, was a youthful revolt against previous models and authorities, especially against neo-classical drama, and against rigid formalism in poetic expression. Instead of symmetry, restraint, and precision, the new values were to be individualism, naturalism, and sentiment, set forth in language appropriate to a much increased emotional temperature. This inversion of standards found one source of inspiration in the religious outbursts of Wesleyanism in England and Pietism in Germany — Herder, Lenz, and Jung-Stilling, for example, had all been brought up in that atmosphere, while Goethe was only just breaking with Pietism when in Strasbourg. The movement may also have reflected an impatient striving for greater freedom on the part of the urban middle class, from which had sprung practically all the *Stürmer und Dränger* of Göttingen, Frankfurt, Mannheim, Strasbourg, and elsewhere. But it can best be explained, in literary terms, by the particular stage which German writing had reached by about 1770.[48]

The idol of the new generation, more than Hamann or Lavater, for all their emotionalism and espousal of the cult of genius, was Klopstock. His *Messias* (1751–1773) was read as the model for free expression, in defiance of Gottsched's desiccating rules of diction and Wieland's elegant adaptation of French standards. In actual fact, Lessing, whose *Miss Sara Sampson* was first played in 1755 and whose main critical writings appeared in the following decade, was at least as important as Klopstock in encouraging the development of a consciously German, bourgeois literature and in discrediting French neo-classicism. For Lessing, however, true classicism, the aesthetic of Greek antiquity, was still a marvel — what he objected to in modern "pseudo-classicism" was its failure to abide by the ancient discipline it claimed to honor. Hence, as different as were his plays from the formal productions which offended the young

rebels, Lessing remained too orderly, too restrained ever to challenge Klopstock's place in their affections.

What made this artistic revolt at least partly a national movement
was the position France had for so long occupied in the civilization
of the continent. If formalism was to be condemned, through
speeches and correspondence, periodical articles and printed pamphlets, then the French culture which paid so much attention to form
must be assaulted head-on. It is possible that prior dislike for
France, on general grounds, helped to make some young Germans
Stürmer und Dränger in literature, but the reverse seems to have
been true of more of them. Being foes of coldly rational canons of
artistic structure, they found it easy to identify France with such
canons and thus concentrate their fire on a satisfyingly tangible
enemy.

It is just this overlapping of aesthetics and patriotism which
makes Strasbourg in this period so significant for the movement.
Here the German and French languages existed side by side, while
for literate natives the attraction of cultural ideals from west of the
Vosges was for the first time since the sixteenth century being
seriously challenged by the appeal of great writers and thinkers
east of the Rhine. Here, furthermore, Germans arriving from the
Reich or even from Russian and Polish provinces came together
under circumstances calculated to give them a special feeling of
solidarity. In Frankfurt, Goethe would have been at home, and the
rest would have been "foreigners." In Westphalia, Jung-Stilling
would no doubt have felt separate from the outsiders, as would
Herder and Lenz in Riga or Königsberg. In Alsace, however, they
were all Germans sojourning within the political borders of the
nation whose artistic hegemony they were determined to upset.
They found Alsace a rich source of language and traditions previously strange to them but wonderfully, because archaically, Teutonic; and they were glad to cultivate native Alsatians who seemed
susceptible to this avowed Germanism.

This was not, be it noted, a political impulse. Strasbourg's own
Stürmer und Dränger showed no trace of disloyalty to their French

sovereign, and those from the Reich wasted little time lamenting Bourbon possession of the town. None of them, in fact, felt great allegiance to any German state — Herder, for example, despised Prussia, and Goethe already had only tolerant contempt for the Holy Roman Empire. What these men, especially easterners like Herder and Lenz, did feel was a great eagerness to win Alsace from the creeping Gallic corruption by restoring it to an appreciation of and place within Germanic culture.

The half-dozen years which began with the arrival of Goethe in 1770 and ended with the departure of Lenz in 1776 had witnessed the swift creation and equally swift dissolution of one of those collections of talent which can probably never be fully explained in causal terms. The question remains: why did Strasbourg's *Sturm und Drang* leave so few lasting traces in the city's own artistic and intellectual life? Why did the fascination of Paris, its thought and its affairs, continue to be so strong locally, despite all the ardent preachments of the 1770's?

One reason was that the rebels' case had from the first been weakened by their over-simplification of French-German cultural rivalry. Goethe praised the Strasbourg cathedral as a triumph of German architecture, which was what Gothic represented for him — since he had never seen Reims or Chartres or Amiens. Herder and Lenz dogmatically identified France with lifeless formalism, recognizing as the only exceptions Rousseau, whom they could explain away as a Swiss,[49] and Mercier, whose anti-classical *Essai sur l'art dramatique* they saw as the exceptional French work proving the rule.[50] But what about Diderot, or d'Alembert, or Voltaire? The young Germans owed much more to both the style and the insights of the *philosophes* than was admitted at the time. A campaign which sets up straw men and ignores nuances it ought to acknowledge is not apt to maintain its momentum for very long. By the early 1780's, Lenz was beyond the reach of orderly thought; but Goethe, Herder, and most of their former comrades already knew that the issues were more complicated than had seemed to be the case a decade earlier. They had all gone on to other preoccupations which made the crudely posed question of French versus German culture a matter of declining importance.

Even more significant in the present context is the subsequent record of native members of the German Society who remained in Strasbourg: Blessig, Turckheim, Haffner, Ott, F.-R. Salzmann. In the 1780's, without exception, these men were explicit in their political allegiance to France. All of them were to be enthusiastic participants in the first stages of the Revolution. Doubtless their experiences in the *Sturm und Drang* increased their appreciation of German and especially Alsatian folk culture; but they were not held for long by the specifically nationalistic aspects of those youthful discussions.

If Herder and Lenz and, for his brief period of agreement, Goethe had been right in arguing that France epitomized calcification, while Germany alone offered new vitality for the entire continent, then Strasbourg's own intellectual elite would surely have kept their eyes turned eastward, even after the gifted Germans had left. Instead, it rapidly became apparent that the France of Beaumarchais was no more dead than the France of Voltaire or that of Molière and Racine. Why should a thoughtful Strasbourger turn his back on Paris and look toward Weimar or Berlin or Königsberg? The boiling, critical energy of the new age, in every sphere of intellect and action, was strikingly apparent in France, about to become as never before the focus of interest for the entire European world.

VI

Just ten years after the departure of Goethe from Alsace, and five years after that of Lenz, Strasbourg's allegiance to the French monarchy was reaffirmed with unusual pomp. For Sunday, September 30, 1781, was the centenary of the city's capitulation.[51] On the preceding day the Magistrat and its guests assembled in the university auditorium to hear Professor Lorenz' long Latin panegyric of the monarchy, as well as a commemorative cantata written by a

Gymnasium instructor, Leipold, also in Latin, and set to music by Inspector Schoenfeld.[52] A full-length portrait of Louis XVI, his gift to the city, was presented at that session, which was followed by a public repetition of Leipold's cantata. Sunday morning was greeted with cannon salvos and special services at both the cathedral and the Temple-Neuf. Twenty young couples, ten Catholic and ten Lutheran, were married and endowed with funds voted by the city government. Later in the day there was free entertainment at the German Theater, as well as a banquet at each of the guilds for one of the newly married couples. With sundown, the city became a sea of lanterns; and at midnight began a costume ball at the Comédie for "persons of distinction and notable citizens," while in the streets the crowds surged from one wine fountain to another. Monday, October 1, saw the presentation at the Comédie of Rochon de Chabannes' play, *La Tribu.* Rochon knew nothing of Strasbourg; but from Paris he had sent his drama of an Alsatian mother who at first opposes her daughter's love for a French officer but finally relents and amid a torrent of patriotic speeches blesses the marriage of Strasbourg and France.

What did all this symbolize in terms of Alsatian "loyalism"? How far had Strasbourg come on the way from 1681 to 1871, when its spokesmen at Bordeaux would appeal tearfully against cession to Germany? The usual historical view has been that it was the new nationalism of 1789 and the shared struggles under the Revolutionary and Napoleonic regimes which made Alsatians "feel French." On the other hand, there were earlier signs of what Reuss has called "a predisposition of men's minds toward common aspirations and sympathies." [53] Both the importance of the old regime in this regard and the doubtless still greater importance of the Revolutionary era can be appreciated, if one uses the relevant concepts carefully and does not ask questions which would have been meaningless to people of the eighteenth century.

Without seeking to exaggerate the meaning of formal oratory and festive spirits in 1781, we can safely conclude that, over the hundred years then ending, the crown and the city had made great progress in their relations with one another.[54] Under Louis XIV, the most that could be said — as it was said by La Grange, Vauban, Chamilly, and others — was that the local inhabitants showed no inclination to revolt. In 1707 a Protestant divine, Bernard Wagner, newly elected President of the Convocation, delivered a long inaugural sermon without ever mentioning either the king or the royal armies, though both were badly in need of divine intercession at the time.[55] As Obrecht wrote to La Grange when the intendant was preparing the survey of 1697: "The government of the city of Strasbourg tends too strongly toward republicanism." [56] Even the cautious Ammeister Reisseissen, who had viewed resistance as hopeless in 1681 and had thereafter pinned his hopes on "a flowering of commerce instead of liberty," [57] lived almost thirty years after the capitulation without writing a single line which showed any warmth toward Louis XIV. The much-cited memorandum of 1709, passed around The Hague by the Prussian envoy, Schmettau, stating that "the inhabitants of Alsace are more French than the Parisians," was only a rather crude effort to focus attention on Franche-Comté as a more desirable acquisition for the Allies — and incidentally, one claimed by Prussia.[58]

After 1715 intendants like d'Angervilliers and Feydeau de Brou never missed a chance to assure the central government of the devotion felt by Strasbourg for the king's interests. It should be remembered, of course, that these men, like almost all other French agents concerned with Alsace, were convinced of the wisdom of restraint in dealing with local peculiarities and anxious to forestall any suspicions at Paris which might encourage experiments in arbitrary innovation. Even under Louis XV there were occasional charges that Strasbourgers, especially Lutheran ones, actually wished the king's enemies well; but such statements regularly came from angry ecclesiastics or homesick army officers, never it appears from any responsible administrative official. In general, the citizenry showed no enthusiasm for German-speaking enemies of France in the eighteenth-century wars, aside from some admiration for the Prussia of Frederick the Great — and that, after all, was no less fashionable in Paris.[59]

Military security was apparently a benefit to be accepted willingly from one's ruler, as indeed it had seemed as early as the 1690's.[60] Only with mid-1700's, however, and the growing sense of participation in French cultural life, does one begin to encounter evidences of a more positive, more enthusiastic attitude on the part of the city's articulate elements. The published works and the correspondence of Schoepflin are interesting in this connection, and fully typical. Born in Baden in 1694, professor at Strasbourg from 1720, *historiographe du roi* from 1740 until his death in 1771, he wrote flatly that "with the Treaty of Westphalia began the French period, the most recent and happiest for Alsace, restored, as a province of what had been Gaul, to its ancient fatherland." [61] In private letters, as one would expect, he felt freer to criticize. Thus, he wrote to Michaelis at Göttingen in 1763: "The so-called *beaux esprits* wish to rule France and are riding too high";[62] to Lamey at Mannheim in 1769: "Germany remains true to systematic learning, elsewhere it is mocked." [63] But most of the time he speaks proudly, as when he writes to the Margravine of Baden-Durlach in 1760: "We are on the threshold of great changes in our kingdom." [64] As for humbler men, though in the eighteenth century army service did not necessarily mean devotion to a cause, the twenty-thousand Alsatians who were in French uniform in 1788 could not help but feel somewhat differently toward the *fleur-de-lys* than their forefathers had.[65] All were volunteers.

The attitude expressed by Dr. Blessig in his centenary sermon of 1781 at the Temple-Neuf was in one sense a triumph for the royal policy of not upsetting Strasbourgers over non-essentials, of allowing them to retain a large measure of local identity:

Let us not efface the features which are characteristic of us; let us not become what we are not; but let us remain *ourselves,* while making use of these lessons [from the French]. . . . Thus we shall share, in the bosom of peace, with all the sons of France, the benefits of the powerful kingdom to which we belong. In the bosom of peace, we shall be, with our brothers, fortunate, contented, and happy.[66]

Full allowance made for rhetoric, these were words which one can scarcely imagine being spoken from that Protestant pulpit in the age of Louis XIV and Louvois.

Were Strasbourgers then already Frenchmen before 1789? Posed thus the question is unanswerable. For one thing, to speak of "Strasbourgers" in general would be to ignore all the variations in political influence and interests, in religious attitudes, in economic well-being, in social status which determine how different people in any community feel about the existing situation. Secondly, the term "Frenchmen" suggests either a completely inappropriate idea of nationality, given the period in question, or an ethnic group to which, in terms of language for instance, some residents of Strasbourg clearly belonged while others just as clearly did not.

What can and should be said is that by Louis XVI's time few Strasbourgers seem to have even considered being subjects of anyone but the King of France. Some of them had a greater stake than others in that relationship, more apparent cause to rejoice in it. Nevertheless, in any terms which make sense for the dynastic states of eighteenth-century Europe the people of Strasbourg were practically all "loyalists" well before the Revolution. If and when they thought about it at all, they doubtless preferred Louis XVI as a monarch; and those for whom a great cultural center had any meaning were proud to see theirs in Paris, especially since this implied no restriction on their continuing interest in things German. Before patriotism could represent anything more, there would have to be a new kind of *patrie* to which masses of people could feel committed in ways the old regime knew not.

CHAPTER TEN

Seventeen Eighty-Nine

I

One day in mid-summer 1789, the English agronomist, Arthur
Young, whose leisurely French travels kept crossing the path of
unexpected violence, made the following journal entry:

July 20th. To Strasbourg, through one of the richest scenes of soil and
cultivation to be met with in France, and rivalled only by Flanders,
which however, exceeds it. I arrived there at a critical moment, which
I thought would have broken my neck; a detachment of horse, with their
trumpets on one side; a party of infantry, with their drums on the
other, and a great mob hallooing, frightened my French mare; and I
could scarcely keep her from trampling on Messrs. the *tiers état*.[1]

Young frequently, if unintentionally, had newsman's luck; he had
dropped into the midst of Strasbourg's revolution at its first point
of open conflict. To understand how the conservative old city
reached this point, we shall have to take a brief look backward at
the early stages of the crescendo and a somewhat closer one at the
developments of that spring and summer.[2]

The first major break with the past, in an institutional sense, had
come two years before, with the adoption of Calonne's proposal for
the establishment of provincial assemblies. That of Alsace had convened in Strasbourg on August 18, 1787, at the call of Intendant La
Galaizière, and had proceeded to elect as its president Baron de
Flachslanden, Bailiff of the Order of Malta. The Assembly, which
met again the following November, was interesting because of certain reports submitted to it, but its real significance lay in the principles which had governed its very creation. The fact that it had

been called into being at all reflected the crown's anxiety over a deteriorating situation. Furthermore, while the king's selection of two dozen deputies, who in turn chose a like number to join them, was hardly revolutionary, the inclusion in the final forty-eight of twenty-four commoners, as against only twelve from each of the first two estates, and the latter's enforced acceptance of voting by head rather than by order foreshadowed great national issues of the immediate future. Finally, the half-dozen Secondary Districts into which Alsace was divided by Calonne's plan represented the first effort in history to subdivide the province according to a uniform, national system.

Though incapable of transacting much business in its plenary sessions, the Provincial Assembly did set up a five-man Intermediary Commission, which remained in existence until 1790, compiling a great deal of statistical data useful to administrators at the time, as well as to historians ever since.[3] But events were moving too fast for such cautious expedients. The bad harvest of 1787 was followed by one almost as bad in 1788, the *parlements* were in full revolt, and the crown's financial troubles grew steadily worse. By November 1788, when Louis XVI announced his intention to convoke the Estates General after a lapse of 175 years, all France was gripped by tense expectancy.

In Strasbourg, 1789 began on a misleadingly familiar note. Election day, January 8, saw no break in the customary procedure; and on Schwörtag, or Inauguration Day, the ruling Ammeister Zaepfel led the Senate-and-XXI in taking the ancient oath, little suspecting that it was for the last time. Shortly before the king's general call to the Estates General on January 24, Ammeister Poirot opined in the Council of Thirteen that there would not even be a separate place for the city, carrying with it separate responsibilities, in the forthcoming national gathering.[4] He was wrong. Louis XVI's letters patent of February 7, dealing specifically with Alsace, paired the six districts of 1787 and directed each pair to chose two deputies from the First and two from the Second Estate, or six Catholic clergymen and six noblemen in all. From the Third Estate, the district of

Colmar-Sélestat was to send three deputies; Belfort-Huningue, three; and Haguenau-Wissembourg, two. In addition, however, the ten cities of the Décapole were together to name two deputies, as was the city of Strasbourg by itself. The total of twelve commoners would thus produce the promised "doubling of the Third." [5]

II

News of the royal invitation to select delegates first reached Strasbourg in mid-February, through a letter to the Thirteen from Crolbois, the city's chargé d'affaires in Paris. The immediate reaction was joyous, but from the moment the Magistrat began to draw up rules for the election of these deputies, a sharp clash of political motives was revealed for all to see. Whereas the king's letter spoke of "election by the inhabitants," in Strasbourg only a fraction of the residents had ever been looked upon as enjoying the franchise. How would the new opportunity be reconciled with the ancient constitution?

The answer came on March 10, when the Senate-and-XXI approved and ordered published its special electoral plan.[6] Stating that the guild voting system would meet the royal prescription, the Magistrat invited each of the twenty corporations (including all non-tradesmen associated with them) to meet and choose electors, who would in turn vote for deputies to be sent to Versailles and would see to the drafting of a *cahier* or list of grievances. Each guild meeting was to choose two such electors for every one hundred members present, or fraction thereof, thus permitting individual corporations anywhere from two to twelve of these "representatives in the second degree." The protégés or *Schirmverwandten* were to meet as a body and choose one representative for every one hundred present. "Other [non-registered] inhabitants," the announcement added, "can only be looked upon as foreign to our civil organization." Finally, because the Catholic clergy had separate representation in the district meeting of the First Estate at Haguenau (as the *Constoffler* had in that of the Second), special town electors were accorded to the Lutheran bodies — one from the university, two each from the *Kirchenkonvent* and the Chapter of St. Thomas.

The primary meetings were held for the guilds on March 18, for the privileged Lutheran groups on March 20, and for the Schirmverwandten on March 21. Out of the several sessions came an electoral assembly of 126 representatives, of whom the Schirmverwandten had been permitted to name just ten, plus their hero, General Klinglin, grandson of the fallen praetor, as a special "honorary spokesman." [7] Two questions were inevitably posed by the guilds' domination of the newly formed body. Could it agree with the regular Magistrat, of whose members only a half-dozen had been chosen electors? [8] Could it, on the other hand, hold the support of hundreds of residents who had had only half a voice in its formation and thousands of others who had had no voice at all? Printed denunciations of the electoral procedure indicated that this issue was charged with threatening possibilities.[9]

On Tuesday, March 23, the 126 electors convened at the "Mirror," home of the merchants' guild, and proceeded at once to name a commission of thirty-two for the writing of the cahier of grievances. Then followed a wait of over a fortnight, full of excited arguments and conflicting public proposals, while the drafting committee did its work. On April 8 the eagerly awaited document was ready, and the electoral assembly reconvened at the "Mirror" in the presence of the full Senate-and-XXI.[10]

The meeting began with the reading of the cahier itself. It was a detailed list of demands, 135 articles in all; but its essential contents may be summarized under the five major headings adopted by the drafters.[11] Section one, relating to the kingdom as a whole, charged the city's two delegates with a number of aims to be pursued at Versailles: full representation for commoners through voting by head in the Estates-General; a constitutional charter for all of France; guarantees of civil liberty and freedom of the press; universal and proportional taxes; an end to excessive pensions; abolition of the General Tax Farm; creation of uniform provincial estates; application to the public debt of revenue from the royal domain; unrestricted admission of commoners to the higher military ranks; and several others of less general interest.

In section two, limited to provincial issues, the initial appeal to national solidarity received some hasty qualifications: all special rights enjoyed by Alsatians must be confirmed, and Alsace must remain, for customs purposes, "effectively foreign." [12] Under section three, on Strasbourg in relation to the kingdom, the familiar demands of particularism were set forth even more explicitly: confirmation of all privileges granted in 1681; retention of previous criminal and civil jurisdiction; recognition of municipal properties, taxes and tolls; exemption from militia service, anywhere in France, for citizens of Strasbourg.

All the foregoing was to be "carried to the foot of the throne," and at least section one accorded with the hopes of the Third Estate in the kingdom as a whole. It was decided at the April 8 meeting, however, that sections four and five, on local administration and guild matters, respectively, should be the subject of direct negotiations between the Magistrat and spokesmen for the citizenry. These sections contained some trivial, in the momentous context even ridiculous, appeals from interest groups as limited as the hatmakers (demanding an unenforceable monopoly of all head coverings sold in the city) and pointless resolutions such as that requesting the formal abandonment of Blondel's long-forgotten project for embellishing Strasbourg. They also contained their share of high explosive.

A request for new local elections had already been inserted under the rubric covering provincial affairs, and the drafters now made clear that their aim was to restore some of the popular controls lost over the course of centuries. The inert Assembly of Three Hundred, which had become nothing more than a faintly honorific body filled by coöptation, must be restored as a functioning institution responsible to the guilds. The Magistrat proper must be secretly elected by the Assembly. The prerogatives of the Secret Chambers must be subjected to thorough study. Municipal accounts must be made public and the tax system revised. Most of this could be called conservative, in that it demanded the elimination of obvious abuses, definable as such under constitutional principles supposedly revered by the entire community; but to an oligarchy which benefited from those very abuses, the choice by the electors of seven commissioners to deal with the Magistrat over reform proposals seemed a revolutionary departure.

First, however, another task lay before the meeting on April 8: the choice of deputies to the Estates General, now less than a month away. Under the surveillance of the three *scrutateurs* prescribed by the king's summons, the 126 electors dropped their ballots into an urn at the front of the hall. On the first poll, one deputy was chosen without difficulty — Ammeister Jean de Turckheim, Lutheran, thirty-nine years old, a veteran of both the Provincial Assembly of 1787 and its Intermediary Commission, a baron of the Holy Roman Empire, and recognized as such under French law, but authorized by royal *lettres de dérogeance* to assume common status for political purposes. So strong had the notion of the Alternative become, over the preceding hundred years, that scarcely an elector considered voting for other than a Catholic to sit beside Turckheim at Versailles. No candidate received an absolute majority on the second ballot; but on the third, the Syndic of the Directory of the Immediate Nobility, Joseph Schwendt, received 87 votes, winning easily over General Klinglin and Pierre Mayno, the tobacco king. In Schwendt, like Turckheim a former member of the Provincial Assembly and the Intermediary Commission, a commoner but professionally involved in the nobility's affairs, Strasbourg had a spokesman no more alarming to vested interests than was his colleague.

On April 19 the two deputies set out for Paris, where Crolbois was waiting to brief them on the coming Estates General. Behind them in Strasbourg, the local situation was about to enter a new phase. Ruling Ammeister Zaepfel had just appointed five members of the Magistrat, Stettmeister Chrétien d'Oberkirch, Ammeister Poirot, Thirteener Hennenberg, Fifteener Mogg, and Twenty-oner Berstett, to confer with the citizenry's seven commissioners, all of them lawyers or merchants, over the municipal matters touched upon in the cahier. From the time this joint committee began its negotiations on April 22, there was hope that pending issues might be resolved by a polite compromise among solid gentlemen. This, however, depended on whether or not the gentlemen remained polite, as well as whether or not they could keep matters in their own hands.

III

The Council of Thirteen, with its vestigial responsibility for external questions, was at first the principal agency for correspondence with Strasbourg's representatives at Versailles. Crolbois sent memoranda on such technical subjects as *per diem* pay and expenses for Turckheim and Schwendt.[13] On May 14 the Thirteeners heard an initial report from the two deputies themselves, dated the 9th and chiefly concerned with the disputes over honorific protocol which had surrounded the opening of the Estates-General four days earlier. Determined to prevent any erosion of Strasbourg's special position, even by ceremonial actions, the Council promptly sent a long reply detailing all the bases for the peculiar status of the city.[14] On June 7, however, the two delegates delivered to the emergent National Assembly, about to shed the restrictive organization by estates, a formal pledge of support on behalf of their constituency at home.

Meanwhile, said constituency was showing signs of internal stress which jarred noticeably with the display of solidarity among commoners at Versailles. In their meetings with the citizens' committee, Ammeister Poirot and his fellow spokesmen for the Magistrat spent over a month raising one objection after another to the reforms proposed by the cahier. On May 25, the joint meetings were suspended, ostensibly to provide time for further study of various demands, but actually to let both sides size up the distribution of power. Then, on June 2, the commissioners for the Magistrat issued a formal reply to the local articles of the cahier, citing all the practical difficulties which would allegedly interfere with any change in the regime.[15]

That same day, the death of Marshal de Stainville, military governor of the city, suddenly created a situation charged with considerable political importance. The offices of governor-general and provincial commandant had both been vacant since 1788, when the Duke d'Aiguillon had died and Marshal de Contades had retired. Hence Stainville's death left his deputy, the *lieutenant du roi,* who was supposed to be only fourth in the military hierarchy at Strasbourg, actual commander of all royal forces there until one or more of the vacancies above him should be filled. What made this circumstance peculiarly ominous for the old Magistrat was that the general in question was none other than Baron François-Joseph-Louis de Klinglin, darling of the voteless masses, a figure of unlimited personal ambition, and one whose family history gave him no cause to feel much affection for either the town fathers or the King of France.

The reappearance of Klinglin in a position of local power would alone have sufficed to emphasize the ironies inherent in any political crisis, when familiar names often turn up in strange places. Strasbourg, however, was about to witness an even more striking example. The fact that Praetor Gérard had been absent for some time had not seemed particularly worrisome so long as local affairs were following their normal course; but with unrest increasing daily, the central government decided on the appointment of a royal commissioner to discharge the duties of praetor, without bearing that title so long as Gérard lived. On June 28, Louis XVI issued the brevet creating this special commissionership and naming the forty-year-old Baron Frédéric de Dietrich to fill it. A great-great-grandson of the old Ammeister banished in 1685 by Louis XIV, Dietrich was the son of a wealthy mining magnate ennobled by Louis XV and elected honorary Stettmeister by Strasbourg some years before the Revolution. Frédéric de Dietrich was himself a specialist in metallurgy, as well as a successful industrialist, and since 1784 had served as Royal Commissioner of Mines. Now, in 1789, he returned from Paris to his native city in a key political role, being formally installed in office on July 6.[16]

The situation confronting Dietrich was one of acrimonious confusion. Disfranchised inhabitants cheered Klinglin, whose public bearing tended to suggest not so much a soldier as a paternalistic candidate for some as yet unspecified political office. Various interest groups were voicing their own demands (the Calvinists, for example, sent Turckheim and Schwendt a formal appeal for an end to all remaining disabilities),[17] and the Magistrat was being attacked in speeches and pamphlets for its resistance to local reform. The minutes of the Senate-and-XXI reveal a change in the whole tempo of regular deliberations that spring and summer, with shorter but more frequent and often very noisy sessions following one another in rapid succession. A meeting on June 25 actually broke up when interruptions by ordinary Senators prevented Advocate Metzler from completing a speech on problems of emergency administration, and the Thirteen, on his behalf, sent a formal protest to the Senate.[18]

Yet in early July these signs of trouble still did not amount to any concerted uproar. There was no apparent cause to worry about the discipline of the garrison, whatever the motives of its commander. Dissident Protestants seemed willing to wait for relief under the law. The joint committee to arbitrate the demands of the cahier had resumed its discussions on June 21, after a four-week recess, and was meeting regularly once more. The last full entry in the minutes of the Senate-and-XXI, covering the session of July 18, is concerned with such familiar topics as a dispute between the boatmens' and merchants' guilds over river shipping contracts and a discussion of means for reducing the competition of Kehl. The situation outside was already too tense to be called a lull before the storm, but a set of orderly changes still seemed the most likely prospect.

One reason for the generally optimistic atmosphere was a high degree of faith in the king and the Estates General, now the National Constituent Assembly, as pacesetters for nonviolent reform. An early expression of this attitude, whether consciously or unconsciously ironical, is the "French Confession of Faith" (in German) which has survived from the first phase of the Revolution:

I believe in Louis XVI, the almighty, father of his subjects, beloved in heaven and on earth.

And in Neker [sic], his loyal minister, our liberator, who was born to promote our welfare, suffered under Calonne, since he was banished and hence, through his absence, was dead to France, justified anew, resurrected and raised to the throne, sits beside the King, where he will judge great and small.

I believe in the Assembly of the Estates General, the recovery of France, the abolition of the Farm and of abuses, the remission of debts, the revival of trade and finances and a happy realm. Amen.[19]

The improvements expected of Versailles and those demanded of the town hall were inextricably linked, not only in men's minds but indeed in the facts of the situation. While the two currents flowed along parallel, the great debate far away, the local one near at hand, Strasbourg's populace watched and waited. Then, in mid-July, the national current broke from its course — and the populace would wait no longer.

IV

In 1789 the time required for news to travel between Paris and Strasbourg, or at least to have any general effect, allowing for the writing of a dispatch at one end and the dissemination of its contents at the other, was about four days. Thus it was that the king's dismissal of Necker on July 11 became known in Alsace during the afternoon of the 15th; and the consternation excited by this apparent royal coup gave way to wild elation only on the evening of the 18th, when the first reports concerning the fall of the Bastille arrived. By the time Turckheim's and Schwendt's official account reached Strasbourg on the 20th, happenings nearer at hand had combined with the word from Paris to produce the tumult which almost sent Arthur Young tumbling off his "French mare."

The preceding week had been a gloomy, menacing time, with suspicions growing that the National Assembly was about to be suppressed, and with the city's own Magistrat displaying renewed determination to stall demands for reform until the revolutionary enthusiasm spent itself. The citizens' committee and Commissioner Dietrich had both been arguing in vain that a show of intransigence

by the oligarchy would surely lead to an upheaval. The spokesmen
for the Senate-and-XXI merely smiled, apologized for the unavoid-
able delays, and brought up further objections.

All this began to change when the thunderclap from Paris came
rumbling across the Vosges; but it did not, perhaps it could not,
change quickly enough. On the 18th a new provincial commandant
at least arrived and took over his duties: the Count de Rochambeau,
aging hero of French participation in the American Revolution.[20]
Military orders from Versailles, however, were as confused as poor
Rochambeau was bewildered. Meanwhile, General Klinglin still
rode through the streets amid popular ovations. Ammeister Poirot
and his commissioners could only hope that a new display of gra-
ciousness toward the citizenry would not come too late. Hurried
meetings continued through Sunday, the 19th, with Dietrich alternately urging speed on the negotiators and issuing reassuring com-
muniqués to the populace. Nevertheless, a mob which besieged the
home of Ammeister Lemp during the evening, with the clear intention of hanging that particularly haughty oligarch, was dispersed
only by the advice of Klinglin — "Go home, my children, to where
your wives and mistresses await you!"

July 20, before it was over, appeared to have witnessed the peak of
the crisis and its successful resolution. All day crowds milled around
the town hall, where lines of cavalry stood by, as noted by Young,
and occasional groups of infantry filed past in rather aimless demonstrations of readiness. By the end of the afternoon enough stones
had been hurled through the windows of the Pfalz to send some
members of the Magistrat into flight and to convince those who
remained that there was no hope save in capitulation. At six o'clock,
therefore, Dietrich was able to announce the signing of an unqualified pledge that all abuses specified in the cahier would be speedily
corrected. Instantly, the threatening shouts became cheers of triumph. An exultant throng surged off to launch an all-night celebra-
tion, amid cries of "Long live Necker! Long live Klinglin! No more
taxes!"

The next day, Tuesday, the 21st, dawned hot and sultry. As the glaring sun rose in the sky, crowds began to form once more, still primarily cheerful but in a state of unstable excitement which offered little insurance against a sudden change of mood. About noon a rumor swept through the streets, obscure in origin but irresistible in its contagious force: "The Magistrat has canceled its agreement! We are betrayed!" This time there was no stopping the mass reaction.[21] A mob armed with hammers, hoes, axes — anything that could smash or chop — rushed toward the town hall. At this point the ubiquitous Arthur Young came wandering by again, having spent a quiet morning in the newspaper reading room. He promptly perched himself on the low roof of one of the market stalls across the little square from the Pfalz, whence he was able to observe and report the action of the rioters:

Perceiving that the troops would not attack them, except in words and menaces, they grew more violent, and furiously attempted to beat doors in pieces with iron crows; placing ladders to the windows. In about a quarter of an hour, which gave time for the assembled magistrates to escape by a back door, they burst all open, and entered like a torrent with a universal shout of the spectators. From that minute a shower of casements, sashes, shutters, chairs, tables, sofas, books, paper, pictures, etc., rained incessantly from all the windows of the house, which is 70 to 80 feet long, and which was then succeeded by tiles, skirting boards, bannisters, framework, and every part of the building that force could detach. . . . I was for two hours a spectator at different places of the scene, secure myself from the falling furniture, but near enough to see a fine lad of about fourteen crushed to death by something as he was handing plunder to a woman, I suppose his mother, from the horror which was pictured in her countenance. I remarked several common soldiers, with their white cockades, among the plunderers, and instigating the mob even in sight of officers of the detachment.[22]

Some of the documents thrown from the windows, but laboriously recovered afterward and returned to the Municipal Archives, have stained or crumpled pages which even now bring into the quiet reading room faint echoes of the din.[23] Down in the cellars of the Magistrat, the great storage casks were split open, and several drunken adventurers actually drowned, unable to rise after falling in the flood of wine.

The question of the troops was obviously crucial. It is clear that
many soldiers were in sympathy with the revolt, or at least glad to
join in pillaging, but the attitude of most of them was not yet one
of outright rebellion. Hence, all depended on the commanders. Of
these, Klinglin refused to order violence against "his people" (he
was belatedly transferred from Strasbourg the following winter and
eventually deserted to the Austrian army). It was the two colonels,
Prince Friedrich of the "Royal Hesse-Darmstadt" and Prince Max
of the "Royal Alsace," who during the evening of the 21st at last
cleared away the exhausted mob by ordering a bloodless advance of
their cavalry units. As for Rochambeau, who must have longed to
be back at Yorktown with Washington and De Grasse (or even
with Cornwallis), it was not until the next morning that he would
risk issuing five hundred halberds and twelve hundred sabers to
the hastily organized citizens' guard, designed to repress looting.
On the 23rd, young Christian Volkmar, arrested with coins apparently stolen from the town hall, and an ideal choice for stern
treatment since he came from Mainz, was solemnly hanged in the
Place d'Armes.

Despite these demonstrations of restored order, however, the situation of the old powers was still crumbling.[24] Specific groups were
angrily protesting to the public authorities — the Constoffler, for
instance, against the Third Estate's usurpation of power,[25] the
fishermen's guild against inequities in the guard duty roster,[26] and
so on. The Lutheran clergy had to be formally enlisted to preach
against sectarian demonstrations. Then, on the night of August 6,
mass violence flared again, this time in the form of a full-scale troop
mutiny.[27] The garrison, despite its ambiguous performance during
the sack of the town hall, had been voted a cash reward of twenty
sols per man by the perspiring Magistrat, but then — and here lay
the dangerous inconsistency — confined to barracks. Troops with
money to spend were not going to remain in their quarters. One
company or squadron after another burst out into the streets, pick-
ing up civilian allies, smashing shop windows, raiding cafés, finally
liberating all the prostitutes and numerous other prisoners confined

in the city jail. By the next morning, the 7th, most of the soldiers were back in their barracks, tired if not wholly repentant, but the prospects for maintaining the political status quo appeared worse than ever.

The culminating shock came two days later, with the news of the National Assembly's epic session of August 4, when the old regime's network of special rights and privileges had been sundered beyond repair. Once again the national revolution added impetus to Strasbourg's local one. On the morning of the 10th, the Council of Fifteen resigned en masse and was followed within a few hours by the rest of the Magistrat, Thirteeners, Twenty-oners, finally Senators as well. The next day the Assembly of Three Hundred, convoked by Dietrich, met long enough to dissolve itself in turn, after ordering the election of a new Three Hundred.

The reconstituted Assembly, chosen by forty-five electors from each guild on August 13, convened for the first time on the 17th, under the chairmanship of Ammeister Poirot.[28] It replaced not only the old Three Hundred but also the 126 representatives elected the previous March. It was, in fact, momentarily the only institution capable of reëstablishing local government on anything like a popular base, and it promptly set up a commission of forty members to recommend the best method for doing just that. The latter body reported back on August 20 and more fully on the 26th, presenting a plan for reform which still did not represent any violent break with tradition.

This new administration, installed on the 28th, was in fact strongly reminiscent of the old in many of its features and in more of its personnel. Ruling Ammeister Zaepfel was replaced by Ammeister Poirot; three of the four incumbent Stettmeisters were confirmed; and the new Common Council or *Gesamter Rat* of thirty members, ten nobles and twenty commoners, contained a clear majority of veterans from the Senate-and-XXI. Even the principle of permanent colleges was upheld, the former ones being replaced by three chambers, each of which was to contain about a third of the members of the Gesamter Rat, all elected by the Three Hundred for life. At the same time, these chambers, one for civil administration, the second for police business, and the third for finances, differed from the vanished Thirteen and Fifteen in having a somewhat clearer division of labor among themselves, but more than that, in having attached to them a total of twenty *Zumänner* or observers, chosen by the Assembly for two-year terms. Thus the Chamber of Finances, for example, besides three Constoffler from the old Magistrat and six familiar bourgeois figures, contained nine of these short-term representatives of the Three Hundred.

The first week of September saw the initial sessions of the modified regime and the beginning of what was to prove only a breathing spell before the advent of far more drastic changes. The Magistrat which had defied the cahier had been theoretically abolished. The control of affairs by permanent colleges of *Ratherren* was now tempered by surveillance on the part of the only organ which had retained its former name, the Assembly of Three Hundred, itself directly answerable once more to the guilds. Despite the partial carry-over of previous officials, this "regenerated Magistrat" might under other circumstances have appeared to be the product of fairly daring innovation. Instead, in 1789, it was only a belated adjustment to a situation already being left behind in the rush of events. The main question now was how soon a nation in flux would be ready to impose its own pattern on local government.

V

The prevailing mood in Strasbourg that autumn, as one might expect, was as uncertain as the memory of recent violence was strong. The new Common Council, after its first session on September 4, met on an average of three times per week;[29] and the Three Hundred, though not called together nearly that often, had more business than ever before in its history.[30] The important Chamber of Finances held regular meetings each Wednesday and Saturday morning, exerting itself especially to collect the tax moneys so badly needed by the central government.[31]

Strasbourg, even under its reformed administration, was officially unhappy over the speed with which national changes were being pushed. A long memorandum, already begun by the old Senate-and-XXI after the August 4 decrees at Versailles, was completed by the Common Council and sent off in late September.[32] This significant document, after a preamble pledging loyalty to the great crusade, runs through the usual historical explanation of the town's rights and exemptions. Strasbourg, it declares, is ready to accept a unified tax system but pleads for local control of assessment and collection; the municipal courts should be disturbed as little as possible; Lutheran rights should be confirmed; the town's economic privileges deserve to be respected and its separate voice in any future provincial assembly guaranteed; finally, the liquidation of French feudalism cannot be construed as altering the relationship of the city to its rural bailiwicks.

Unfortunately for these plaintive hopes, Louis XVI had already approved the anti-feudal and anti-particularistic legislation before the above petition was delivered to the National Assembly — just at a time, incidentally, when the latter, its more uncompromising wing strengthened by the riots of the "October days," was about to move into Paris. As a matter of fact, Turckheim had offered his resignation as a deputy in late September; and returning to Strasbourg a few weeks later, he published a *Rapport sur la situation de l'Assemblée nationale,* in defense of his unwillingness to participate in the destruction of so many ancient rights. The next year he was to emigrate to Baden, where he died in 1824, a holder of the Grand Cross of the Order of the Lion of Zähringen. His former colleague, Schwendt, stayed on in the Assembly, maintaining a prudent reserve.

Fear of "excesses" had begun to assail various Strasbourgers of widely differing persuasions and interests. Devout Catholics were shocked by proposals to confiscate church lands.[33] Lutherans too were worried about a possible nationalization of ecclesiastical assets, and in January Professor Koch would leave for Paris to defend the university and the prebends of St. Thomas.[34] Feudal landholders, meanwhile, were in a state of near panic.[35] Numerous merchants

raised queries about the frightening rumors of an impending standardization of the customs system for all of France. On November
24 Secretary Schérer of the Chamber of Finances submitted a blackly
pessimistic report on Strasbourg's economic prospects unless the
national mania for wiping out exceptions and irregularities were
curbed.[36]

What was happening that autumn in Strasbourg, as throughout
the nation, was a new polarization of opinion over issues which had
far outrun those of the previous spring. When the Estates General
had first convened, most of the local community had been in agreement on the need for a general reorganization of the national government; the debatable point had seemed to be whether the local
government too required overhauling. The upheavals of July and
August had made certain that the central administration of the
kingdom would in fact be basically altered and at the same time
had clinched the victory of at least moderate reform within Strasbourg. By the final third of that momentous year, new divisions had
emerged over questions newly posed. For the great problems were
no longer discussable solely in reformist terms. Men who had willingly debated ways in which to patch up the old kingdom were increasingly faced with the query: "What should the new France be?"
As the line between "aristocrats" and radicals grew sharper in the
Assembly at Paris, so the distinction became greater at Strasbourg
between those who hoped to save much of the royal free city's independence and those for whom the national revolution was a unifying, and not simply a liberating, force.

Among the former, besides Turckheim, Koch, Schérer, and others
fundamentally conservative from the start, were some who had at
first seemed more aggressive. Isaac Haffner, the "Zündelpatscher"
who in the spring had denounced the nobility and Catholic prelates
as "beasts of prey," was by the fall of 1789 pleading for restraint,
lest leveling zeal destroy all the advantages enjoyed by individual
towns and provinces. In December, F.-R. Salzmann (the former
comrade of Lenz, Turckheim, Haffner, and the others in the German Society) came out with a printed denunciation of secessionists

as traitors; yet his brochure concludes on a note of concern for private property, guild privileges, and all the other "old rights" of specific groups and individuals.[37] Just the preceding month, against a depressing background of record-breaking food prices, after the third bad harvest in a row,[38] Professor Oberlin had written to his friend, André Lamey, at Mannheim:

> We are on the eve of a great crisis. If the regeneration of France takes place and is carried out at all points, there is the prospect of our reaching the summit of good fortune, but if the thing goes wrong . . . the results are much to be feared. . . . One is only happy in tranquility. It is a blessing one scarcely finds any more.[39]

Against such councils, however, was rising an army of patriots in the newer sense, insisting that economic troubles could be solved and political security established only if Strasbourg willingly submerged itself in a unified state. The royal commissioner, Dietrich, was himself prepared to advance this position and did so in the stormy December debates of the Three Hundred, when local conservatives were in a fury over reports of the National Assembly's projected law on local government. The volume of political pamphlets had increased steadily through the year, and for every appeal to ancient rights there was an answering blast on behalf of new principles.[40] The latter were assured an even wider hearing when on December 6 the editorship of a regular newspaper, the *Patriotisches Wochenblatt* (founded the previous August), was taken over by Jean-Frédéric Simon, schoolmaster, future Jacobin, and translator of the "Declaration of the Rights of Man" into Alsatian German.[41] By the time the Society of Friends of the Constitution was formally established at the "Mirror" in mid-January, the ground had been so well prepared that this club, with its mild name and its stormy future, soon counted several hundred members.[42] One has only to compare the substance and the tone of political argumentation in the city at the end of 1789 with the discussions of the previous spring to realize how much of the old had already been destroyed, even if the pattern of the new was as yet hard to discern.

A Schwörtag in the 1780's

VI

Strasbourg's traditionalists, tardy in formulating their appeals to feudal custom after August 4, were equally behind the times in the fall and early winter, when they brandished their three-century-old constitution as an inviolable charter of local government. For the National Assembly had been pushing ahead rapidly with a Law of Municipalities, substantially completed by the vote of December 14. The full text, signed by the king and copied in final form, reached the city on the first day of 1790. The Common Council, under the royal commissioner's watchful eye, registered the law on January 2. On the 4th it was duly published in French and German. Despite all the clamor of the preceding weeks, there could be no serious thought of defiance to such explicit directions from the central power.

The administration to be elected under this law would include a mayor, a city attorney and his deputy, seventeen councilmen or *officiers de la municipalité,* and a consultative body of thirty-six *notables,* with the franchise extended to include all "active citizens," i.e., royal subjects paying an equivalent of at least three days' wages in direct taxes. The balloting for various posts extended over almost six weeks, beginning on February 3; but the decisive choice was made on the 5th, when Dietrich, Protestant and *constitutionel,* defeated Ammeister Poirot, Catholic and deeply conservative, for the office of mayor by 3,312 votes to 2,286.

As the elections for other positions went on, the initial scattering of support for literally hundreds of candidates gradually narrowed down, until by mid-March the full slate of officials was complete. The "regenerated Magistrat" of August 28 had included some new faces; and the *Municipalité* of 1790, not surprisingly, included more. Even so, the degree of continuity in personnel was greater than might have been expected from the early welter of candidacies. The city attorneys were former Advocates General Matthieu and Levrault. Among the seventeen councilmen were former Ammeister

Poirot, as well as Advocates General Fischer and Metzler, plus six veterans of the Gesamter Rat, of whom two (Brackenhoffer and Dorsner) had still earlier been Thirteeners and one (Ottmann), a Twenty-oner.

Nevertheless, this regime was very different from the old Magistrat, even in its modified form of the preceding six months. The franchise on which the new government was based was incomparably more extensive than any previously conceded; and the town leaders, of whom only two happened to be noblemen, were specifically accountable to the whole electorate. On the other hand, at least for the time being, "Herr Maire" Dietrich enjoyed a degree of personal power which no single Ammeister, Stettmeister, or even royal praetor could have claimed in the eighteenth century. The new structure was thus simpler than the old, more broadly based in some respects, but more monolithic in others.

March 18, 1790, exactly one year after the fateful progression had begun with the guild elections in 1789, saw the transfer of full authority to Dietrich and his colleagues. On the 17th, the Chamber of Finances met for the last time and closed its books for delivery to the nascent Municipality. Next morning, the Common Council assembled in the venerable Senate chamber, where Stettmeister Wurmser was to turn over the public seals to Dietrich, while outside the cathedral bells rang steadily and cheering crowds waited in the Place d'Armes to hear patriotic speeches. But first, there had to be other speeches in the meeting at the town hall, some congratulatory, some jubilant, some frankly nostalgic. It was hard for old men, about to retire from offices bearing names which would henceforth be used only in history books, not to linger over the meaning of 1482 and 1681. It was just as hard for new men, about to assume power in an onrushing age, not to dwell on the meaning of 1789 and 1790. Those members of the outgoing Common Council who had also been elected to the incoming Municipality doubtless experienced a mixture of sentiments.

Perhaps the most eloquent conclusion to the story of the Magistrat and hence, in a strictly political sense, to that of the old regime

in Strasbourg, was written by the Secretary of the *Gesamter Rat,*
the Common Council, in terminating the thick folio of that vanish-
ing assembly's minutes, still doggedly German in language and consistent in the use of ancient forms:

> When My Gracious Sirs had left their places [following adjournment],
> "Herr Maire" took a position between the two first-elected Officers of the
> Municipality, Herr Spielmann and Herr Hervé, just inside the door,
> where they remained until the Most Praiseworthy Magistrat, Herr Advo-
> cate General Mogg, the Secretary and the two Record Clerks had left
> the chamber. FINIS.[43]

VII

The most difficult single problem confronting anyone who watches
a particular locality in a period of great national crisis is that of
perspective. There is always a danger that he may forget the scale
of the situation, exaggerating the importance, for the world, of
developments which were vital to the community in question. The
opposite danger, however, is perhaps even more serious. We look
at specific issues admittedly trifling in themselves — butchers protesting a change of meat scales, hatmakers jockeying for retail protection, soldiers rioting largely because they have the money but not
the opportunity to buy wine — and we are tempted to dismiss the
Revolution at Strasbourg as only a side-show, a parody of the great
drama unfolding in the interior of France. That would be a mistake.
For the city's cahier of grievances was beyond any question a striking and informative document. The sack of the Hôtel de Ville was
certainly no joke. The triangular problem of tottering civil authority, popular rebellion, and unsure military action was nowhere
posed more clearly. In any case, it is impossible to appreciate the
full significance of the French Revolution as a whole unless one
perceives the differing levels of action and sources of resentment
which together produced and sustained it throughout the land.
It may well be that none of the provincial towns would have
known revolt in 1789, had not the defiant *parlements,* the hard-

pressed royal advisers, and the terrible crowds of Paris, in various ways, combined to fix the timing. In that sense, the downfall of Strasbourg's Magistrat was set in motion by distant agents having no special concern with Alsatian affairs. It is nonetheless true that in this, as in other outlying centers, there were pressures for change which, once released, quickly displayed the power to shape the local situation. They did more: they began almost at once to work back upon the course of events at the center of the stage. It is quite possible, indeed it is essential, to recognize the crucial role of the capital, without accepting the too easy notion that the rest of France patiently awaited, then unhesitatingly accepted, each decision taken at Paris.

Strasbourg's experience in 1789 illustrates this point. The royal call to the Estates General, by authorizing an unprecedented set of elections in March, supplied a crucial push from the outside. As soon as the local assembly of 126 "representatives in the second degree" had been constituted, however, there existed a body which not only could choose deputies to speak for it at the national level, but also could press numerous demands upon the town authorities. Thus in May and June a beleaguered oligarchy at home had to cover itself in part by giving loud support to the Third Estate of the kingdom, the beneficiary in this respect of regional situations all over France. By July it was the turn of the capital to supply a further impulse. In response to Parisian violence, the violence at Strasbourg did more than start the city's own Magistrat crumbling into extinction. Like other such blows struck in the provinces, it also strengthened the hand and increased the boldness of the National Assembly, particularly by exposing the indecision and even timidity of the military chiefs.

As a result, the Assembly once more pressed ahead of the local pace, enacting reforms in August which went well beyond the wishes of Strasbourg's temporary leadership, save for Dietrich, and going on to broach unifying projects which frankly terrified conservatives in Alsace. Only thus can be explained the city's official efforts to drag its feet that autumn. The momentum, however, both local and national, was irresistible. The December legislation at Paris, concerning municipal reorganization, was greeted at Strasbourg by individuals and groups impatient to put it into effect; and the elections of February and March 1790 carried the town into avowed agreement with a national government. Simultaneous reorganization of the province into the Departments of Haut-Rhin and Bas-Rhin only sharpened the break with the past.

Anyone who has followed Strasbourg through a century or more preceding 1789 can sense some implications of the crisis which might escape observers fresh upon the scene. He can recognize the traditional institutions around which resistance to change sought vainly to organize itself and the hallowed constitutional shibboleths uttered by all who had a stake in such resistance. He can also identify the sources of dissatisfaction, reformist zeal, and ultimately destructive fury which fed into the new situation from conditions imposed or tolerated by the old. The French Revolution was in part a national reaction against the hauteur of the nobility, against the blindness of a complacent church hierarchy, against the incompetence of the royal administration. It was also, however, in part a complex of assaults on restrictions and injustices specifically affecting local populations. In Strasbourg's case, the central target was the exclusiveness of an oligarchy whose shortcomings had been visible long before 1681 and whose ability to resist any pressure short of a general uprising had only been increased through capitulation to France. The anachronistic city state fell with the monarchy it had relied upon, in a cataclysm which was bewildering in its swiftness but which was truly a product of the ages.

Conclusion

The *Marseillaise*
(in Strasbourg German)

Iehr Männer uff, un unter d' Fahne
In d'heili Schlacht für's Vaterland!
Für zue rauwe dringe d' Tyrane
Zue es in mit blueticher Hand!
Zue es in mit blueticher Hand!
O höre doch wie iehri Schinder
Wild bruellen uff de Felder druss!
Sie stürme biss in euer Huss,
Un ermorde d' Wiwer un d' Kinder!
In d' Schlacht! iehr Bürjer! uff!
Schnell packen euer Flint!
Vorwärts! Vorwärts!
D' Furchte getränkt
Mit Bluet vun eure Find!
— *BNU Strasbourg, Ms. 1718.*

Not all of Strasbourg's past was liquidated at a stroke, of course, when the Magistrat gave way to the new Municipality in March 1790. Another year of debate and legislation at Paris was required to destroy the old guild system, nationalize feudal holdings in Alsace, and sweep away the customs regulations which had applied to "provinces effectively foreign." It was not until September 1793 that the Lutheran university, denounced in the Convention by Barère and Couturier as a stronghold of reaction and a "hydra of Germanism," was formally suppressed (to be revived only in 1872). Just three months later, while the triumphant Jacobins in Strasbourg considered tearing down the cathedral tower in the interests of equality, Frédéric de Dietrich, having been arrested in 1792 as a crypto-aristocrat, stripped of his office as mayor, and finally convicted of treason, was beheaded at Paris. With the fall of Robespierre the next summer, Strasbourg, like the rest of France, felt the waning of the Terror, of the craze to destroy which had sprung from determination to reform and purify. Thereafter, if Thermidor spelled relief for Alsace, the coming of Bonaparte spelled glory, as witness some of his generals named on the Arc de Triomphe: Kellermann, Schérer, Rapp, Kléber.

It would be easy at this point to be swept along into a detailed discussion of the revolutionary epoch, treating the events of 1789 and 1790 as a beginning. For the purposes of this study, however, they represent the end. The questions raised at the outset were all directed at the period from Westphalia, and more specifically from 1681, to the collapse of the old regime. Hence, any attempt to answer them must be made in terms of that era.

One of my initial problems, it may be recalled, was the arrangement of chapters. More was involved than just the tactics of presentation, for the very organization of a book about transition embodies a theory about how the transition proceeded. I did not know beforehand which kinds of change ought to be discussed first, and which could be treated only against the background thus established. However, when my research was finished, it seemed to me that there was a certain sequence in the metamorphosis of the city of Franziskus Reisseissen into that of the Baroness d'Oberkirch, and this sequence I have tried to follow in words.

The first, the very first, thing Louis XIV's government wanted to alter in Strasbourg was its military situation. What had until 1681 been an independent stronghold was therefore quickly converted into a bastion of French power, given new fortifications, defended by royal troops on the parapets, and by royal diplomats at the council table. Strasbourg's whole development in the ensuing century was conditioned by the fact that it was now a garrison town, the eastern outpost of a kingdom. From that starting point, the crown proceeded to make such modifications in the local government as were deemed essential to demonstrate Bourbon sovereignty and insure final control by Paris, without needlessly arousing local resistance. Before the end of the first decade of French rule, the supervisory echelon

of royal functionaries had been set up, although the full implications of their presence became apparent only over the period of two
more generations. Similarly, Louis XIV moved quickly to restore
the official position of the Catholic hierarchy, leaving to time, to
immigration, and to procreation the more fundamental task of creating a Catholic majority in the populace.

The years just after 1681, then, saw major changes in public
power: military, political, and religious. It is to the first half of
the eighteenth century that we must turn for the initial evidence of
new patterns in economic life, confessional allegiances, and ethnic
composition, as well as new styles in dress and art, all influenced by
France. Even such alterations as these are overshadowed, in turn, by
the much more rapid, more sweeping, and more intricately inter-
related social changes of the thirty to forty years just before the
Revolution. A local inhabitant who was born in the 1720's saw
Strasbourg become by the 1780's a city more than half Catholic, increasingly involved in French commercial life, essentially bilingual,
and dominated by French standards in everything from architecture
to entertainment. Yet in spite of all this, many German traditions
remained strong and popular; they became parts of a unique combination.

It is conceivable that one other phenomenon, the competition of
two great literatures, might under other circumstances have demanded notice early in my discussion, instead of near its end. In this
instance, however, the rivalry of French and German writing did
not become a real issue for the local intelligentsia, a subject of concern for German visitors in particular, until after Strasbourg's new
civic personality had become quite clear, that is, in the 1770's and
'80's. The reader who objects to resolutely sociologizing all intellectual and aesthetic tendencies may take some comfort from my
assurance that in this work the artists and scholars and poets do not
follow the soldiers and administrators because of any *a priori* conviction that this is the only place they can ever be fitted in. Here as
elsewhere, a roughly chronological progression seemed to emerge
from the data and virtually impose itself.

A second and altogether different question was posed at the start. It related neither to the organization nor to the process it must reflect, but to the suggestive possibilities of what we somewhat condescendingly call "mixed communities," using the term to indicate simply the juxtaposition of different national cultures. This is not a topic on which I feel tempted to issue a manifesto, for I doubt that one is needed. Almost everyone would agree that without some awareness of such communities, our picture of any civilization in any age would be wholly composed of crude patches of solid color, bereft of all finer shadings.

What I hope, of course, is that the reader has discovered in the preceding chapters some facets of early modern life which are additions to his knowledge or which, even if familiar in themselves, he was led to consider in a fresh light. He may have observed with interest the easy eclecticism with which Strasbourg architects superimposed German rococo embellishments on the elegant French Regency façade of the Hôtel de Klinglin, producing a result which is altogether indigenous, yet just as "European" as anything in Paris or Munich. He may have been struck by the advance of spoken French and the survival of German dialect, not on the basis of solemn educational decisions in thousands of Alsatian homes, but as the obvious response to a geographical and social situation which made bilingualism a practical advantage.

Where better than in Strasbourg can one survey the reading, touring, and letter-writing of a century which brought European culture to a new level of unity through publishing, travel, and epistolary zeal? Dom Ruinart, O.B., attending a Lutheran service, Professor Schoepflin at his writing desk, Arthur Young in the newspaper reading room assuredly do not represent the unity of medieval Latin studies; but they have in common the recognition of variation within a broadly shared value system and a common fascination with variety itself. Or where, to take another example, can one visualize more clearly than at Strasbourg the problems confronting government officials under the old regime, compelled to operate in a jumble of anachronistic forms and hastily contrived expedients? Yet some of these men, who had after all not created the maze and who had little authority to simplify it, nonetheless managed to demonstrate administrative intelligence of the highest order.

These are merely a few of many thoughts which come to mind when one looks through this particular window into the past. There remains one final question, however, which calls for a rather different kind of thinking, because it requires us to consider not only the distant view, but also the window through which we look and the intervening ground as well. Is there, to be quite explicit, anything in the relationship between the Strasbourg of the old regime and the Strasbourg of more recent times which can help us place our own era in historical perspective?

As the minimum basis for an answer, let us recall very briefly the principal milestones in the community's record of the past century and a half. The Napoleonic wars influenced that record in two ways, at once opposite and complementary. On the one hand, local enthusiasm for the Emperor, his victories, and his reliance on inland commerce called forth a degree of conscious patriotism, an emotional identification with France, which went far beyond any to be found under the old monarchy. On the other hand, the very conditions of the ultimate German uprising against French rule had by 1815 produced a new precision and vehemence in German demands for the return of all "Teutonic brethren" west of the Rhine. Strasbourg and its cathedral caught the imagination of French writers, actually for the first time, in the age of Michelet and Victor Hugo; but the next generation saw the whole situation upended by the power of Prussian guns. Shelled into military submission in 1870 and annexed over the protests of its elected spokesmen in 1871, Strasbourg entered the new German Empire as the capital of the *Reichsland Elsass-Lothringen*.

Such it remained for almost half a century, while the German government sought to win its allegiance and Frenchmen in Paris stared at black-draped statues representing the "lost provinces" of Alsace and Lorraine. Many Strasbourgers who grew up in this period turned away from France, even breaking with their families over the issue, but many others remained stubbornly hostile to the Kaiser. Whatever the balance of local sentiments, it was military victory which again, as in 1871, decided which flag should fly over the city — and in 1918 this flag was the tricolor. Even then, the worst still lay ahead, in the form of Nazi rule. Although Hitler repeatedly announced that the famous cathedral was not worth all the German blood which would be spilled in its recovery, there was reason to suspect that when other, larger aims had been achieved, the Third Reich would not forget this landmark. After the French collapse of 1940, therefore, it was no surprise to find the Führer stalking triumphantly across the Place Kléber, nor to behold Strasbourg adding a *Gauleiter* to its long roll of intendants, prefects, and Wilhelmian governors.

When at last the *Wehrmacht* fell back in defeat and peace was restored in 1945, it appeared briefly as though just one more stage had been passed in a struggle which could never be finally decided. Actually, however, a whole era had come to an end. Strasbourgers soon began to realize that what had seemed an interminable tug-of-war for possession of their city might prove to have been only a protracted episode in the life of nations. A few writers, it is true, hastened to resume the historic argument, but that argument, at least in the form in which it had raged since Napoleonic times, was over. One has only to contrast the aims and methods of the pre-war Institute for Alsace-Lorrainers at Frankfurt with those of present day research establishments in the Bonn republic to appreciate the change of tone in German scholarly discussions, always in the past an important concomitant of public policy. On the French side too, greater security in this area, as contrasted with many others, has produced a mood strikingly different from that of the 1920's and '30's regarding Strasbourg, today praised for the contributions of its double culture.

The city itself, seat of the Council of Europe since 1949, retains its special character. In a population of some 175,000 there is a massive Protestant, essentially Lutheran, minority and a smaller Jewish one, despite the clear numerical predominance of Catholics. Social

classes, occupational groups, even neighborhoods are still distinguishable partly by language. Upon leaving the French of the Opera
or a social evening at the fine university, one may be startled when
a passer-by, seeking the Avenue des Vosges, asks for the "Vogesen-
gass'." A brewing, tanning, printing, and tobacco center as in
earlier times, Strasbourg remains above all a river port, extremely
jealous of plans, such as that for the canalization of the Moselle,
which threaten its position. There are occasional flashes of its old
sensitivity — toward France in 1952, for example, during the Bordeaux trial of German and Alsatian SS men implicated in the
wartime massacre at Oradour, or toward Germany in the nervous
local reaction to the 1955 Saar plebiscite. But despite such tremors
of inherited emotion, the new Europe, suspended between gigantic
non-European powers, cannot afford to have the regional debates
of the past resume in their previous form.

For Strasbourg, after six or seven generations, the great pendulum
of history, though it knows no perfect recurrence, has swung back
in a striking fashion. In the eighteenth century this was a peculiarly
hybrid city, able to exist quite comfortably and to maintain its personality under the conditions of dynastic diplomacy and an international class culture. The emergence and growth of intolerant nationalism put an end to that state of affairs. The period from
Napoleon through Bismarck to Clemenceau and thence to Hitler
was one of violent reversals for the town, as well as conscious efforts
by successive rulers to revamp its very character in the idealized
image of either Germany or France. Such a city is what it is because
of accretion and assimilation from many outside sources. It was, I
submit, at its best in the cosmopolitan atmosphere of the 1700's,
after the wars of faith and before those of nationality. Surely it
suffered most as a shuttlecock for the violent German-French contest
of the past century and a half. Only now, with nationalism if not
softened by reason at least muted by economic and military necessity,
does Strasbourg appear once more the composite symbol of European
civilization it became under the old regime.

NOTES
GUIDE TO WORKS CITED
INDEX

Notes

NOTE ON ABBREVIATIONS

The following abbreviations have been used throughout to indicate the basic source collections:

AD Bas-Rhin	Archives Départementales du Bas-Rhin (Strasbourg)
AM Strasbourg	Archives Municipales de Strasbourg
BN Paris	Bibliothèque Nationale (Paris)
BNU Strasbourg	Bibliothèque Nationale et Universitaire de Strasbourg
BL Karlsruhe	Badische Landesbibliothek (Karlsruhe)
HHSA Vienna	Haus-, Hof- und Staatsarchiv (Vienna)

NF, inserted before a periodical volume number, indicates Neue Folge.

CHAPTER ONE

THE IMPERIAL FREE CITY

1. Winfried Katterfeld, "Die Vertretung Strassburgs auf dem westfälischen Friedenskongress," *Jahrbuch für Geschichte, Sprache und Literatur Elsass-Lothringens* (Strasbourg, 1912), 28:137–218.
2. *Strassburg im dreissigjährigen Kriege, Fragment aus der Chronik von J. J. Walter,* ed. Rodolphe Reuss (Strasbourg, 1879), 40–41.
3. Karl Theodor Eheberg, "Strassburgs Bevölkerungszahl seit dem Ende des 15. Jahrhunderts bis zur Gegenwart," *Jahrbücher für Nationalökonomie und Statistik* (Jena, 1883–1884), 41 (NF 7): 297–314 and 42 (NF 8): 413–430.
4. For an excellent survey of the city's past architecture, see *Strassburg und seine Bauten* (Strasbourg, 1894), published by the Architekten- und Ingenieur-Verein für Elsass-Lothringen.
5. Quoted by Carl Loeper, *Die Rheinschifffahrt Strassburgs in früherer Zeit und die Strassburger Schiffleut-Zunft* (Strasbourg, 1877), 23. This translation and all that follow, unless otherwise specified, are mine.
6. Among the general town histories, the two best are Rodolphe Reuss, *Histoire de Strasbourg* (Paris, 1922), and Emil von Borries, *Geschichte der Stadt Strassburg* (Strasbourg, 1909).
7. An interesting discussion of the name "Argentoratum" (later "Argentina")

by one of the city's most assiduous antiquarians will be found in Jean-Frédéric Hermann, *Notices historiques, statistiques et littéraires sur la ville de Strasbourg* (Strasbourg, 1817–1819), II, 64.

8. A monograph which treats the medieval political structure of the municipality in detail is Hermann G. Nagel, *Die Entstehung der Strassburger Stadtverfassung* (Strasbourg, 1916).

9. *Strassburg im dreissigjährigen Kriege.*

10. Willy Andreas, *Strassburg an der Wende vom Mittelalter zur Neuzeit* (Leipzig, 1940); also the published lecture by Gustav Schmoller, *Strassburg zur Zeit der Zunftkämpfe und die Reform seiner Verfassung und Verwaltung im XV. Jahrhundert* (Strasbourg, 1875).

11. Julius Rathgeber, *Strassburg im sechzehnten Jahrhundert, 1500–1598* (Stuttgart, 1871); H. Virck and O. Winckelmann, eds., *Politische Korrespondenz der Stadt Strassburg im Zeitalter der Reformation* (Strasbourg, 1882–1898).

12. Rodolphe Reuss, *Beiträge zur Geschichte des Elsasses im dreissigjährigen Kriege: Strassburg und die evangelische Union, 1618–1621* (Mulhouse, 1868); Karl Jakob, *Strassburger Politik vom Austritt aus der Union bis zum Bündnis mit Schweden, 1621–1632* (Strasbourg, 1899). The title of Jakob's book suggests more cordiality between the town government and Gustavus Adolphus than in fact existed. The Swedish "alliance" was no genuine resumption of Protestant solidarity, but rather a grudging concession necessitated by the presence of Swedish armies in Alsace.

13. *Topographia Alsatiae & c., des ist Beschreibung und eygentliche Abbildung der vornehmbsten Staett und Oerter im Obern und Untern Elsass* (Frankfurt am Main, 1644), with a supplement dated 1654. The quotation I have used is on page 49 of this later appendix. See also Ulrich Crämer, "Die Wehrmacht Strassburgs von der Reformationszeit bis zum Fall der Reichsstadt," *Zeitschrift für die Geschichte des Oberrheins* (Karlsruhe, 1931), 84 (NF 45): 46 ff.

14. HHSA Vienna, Kleinere Reichsstände: Strassburg, Fasz. 514 ff.

15. BNU Strasbourg, Ms. 605, provides clear evidence of the seventeenth-century Magistrat's determination to assert its independence of Vienna, including the legalistic collection of "privileges" or imperial concessions, dating from medieval times and carefully assembled in 1639.

16. F. W. Müller, *Die elsässischen Landstände* (Strasbourg, 1907).

17. The best representation of these scattered rural holdings is Map III at the back of Borries' *Geschichte der Stadt Strassburg.* See also the map in this book on page 9.

18. Strasbourg's Bibliothèque Nationale et Universitaire contains numerous manuscripts, dating from the seventeenth and eighteenth centuries, which supply important descriptions of the city's old political system. These documents, many of them stemming from the collection of the nineteenth-century antiquarian, Frédéric-Charles Heitz, include the various lists of

officeholders, e.g., Johann Christoph Meyer's "Tafeln deren Herren Am-meistern der Statt Strassburg vom Jahr 1332" (Ms. 640) and the much more comprehensive "Register der Aemter in Strasburg, 1332–1757" (Mss. 1513–1514). Mss. 1288 and 1299 contain the basic ordinances governing the Councils of Thirteen, Fifteen, and Twenty-One. Then there is the general description written by Johann Heckheler in the 1690's, "Der Statt Strass-burg Beschreibung in politischen Sachen" (Ms. 1293), as well as numerous other items easily identified by any student using the printed inventories of Barack, of Reuss, and of Wickersheimer. The official records of govern-mental operations, of course, are kept in the Archives Municipales. Among published works the most thorough monograph devoted to the constitu-tion of Strasbourg as an imperial free city is that of Ulrich Crämer, *Die Verfassung und Verwaltung Strassburgs von der Reformationszeit bis zum Fall der Stadt, 1521–1681* (Frankfurt am Main, 1931), which can be well used in conjunction with Reuss, *Histoire de Strasbourg.* The basic col-lections of printed sources bearing directly on this subject are the *Ur-kundenbuch der Stadt Strassburg,* published in seven volumes (Strasbourg, 1879–1900) under the direction of Wilhelm Wiegand and later editors, as Part One of the massive official series, *Urkunden und Akten der Stadt Strassburg;* and, the *Code historique et diplomatique de la ville de Stras-bourg* (Strasbourg, 1843–1848), one volume in two parts. It should be noted that the former of these two collections ends with the year 1400, while the latter comes only to 1500. For later developments still previous to 1681, Hermann's *Notices,* as old as the work is, remains invaluable.

19. Otto Winckelmann, "Zur Entstehungsgeschichte der Strassburger Einund-zwanzig und Dreizehn," *Zeitschrift für die Geschichte des Oberrheins* (Heidelberg, 1921), 75 (NF 36): 112–114.

20. *De duplici copia verborum ac rerum* (Strasbourg, 1514). The letter is appended to this edition.

21. *Les six livres de la république* (Paris, 1577), 720.

22. This quotation, reprinted by August Stoeber, *Curiosités de voyages en Alsace* (Colmar, 1874), 33, appeared first in the "Amsterdam" edition of Rohan's memoirs, published in 1644.

23. *Der Statt Strassburg Policey-Ordnung,* printed by Johann Carolus (Stras-bourg, 1628).

24. L. Metzger, "Essai sur l'histoire de la noblesse immédiate de la Basse-Alsace," *Annuaire administratif du département du Bas-Rhin* (Strasbourg, 1932), 5:5–14; Alfred Overmann, "Die Reichsritterschaft im Unterelsass bis zum Beginn des dreissigjährigen Krieges," *Zeitschrift für die Geschichte des Oberrheins* (Karlsruhe, 1896–1897), 50 (NF 11): 570–637 and 51 (NF 12): 41–82. An original and interesting analysis of this problem in its earlier stages is presented by Philippe Dollinger, "Patriciat noble et patriciat bourgeois à Strasbourg au XIVe Siècle," *Revue d'Alsace* (Stras-bourg, 1950), 90:52–82.

25. BNU Strasbourg, Ms. 1248, is the ordinance of 1661 on Jewish exclusion, confirming the old rules.
26. Camill Gerbert, *Geschichte der Strassburger Sectenbewegung zur Zeit der Reformation, 1524-1534* (Strasbourg, 1889); also Gustav Anrich, "Die Strassburger Reformation," in *Zwei Strassburger Reden zur Reformationsjubelfeier* (Leipzig, 1918), 43-70.
27. J. Schmidlin, *Die katholische Restauration im Elsass am Vorabend des 30jährigen Krieges* (Strasbourg, 1934); K. Rauch, "Reformation und katholische Restauration," in *Geschichte des Elsass,* ed. Luzian Sittler (Colmar, 1940), II, 75-122.
28. General descriptions will be found in Wilhelm Horning, *Handbuch der Geschichte der evangelisch-lutheranischen Kirche in Strassburg im XVII. Jahrhundert* (Strasbourg, 1903); and Johann Adam, *Evangelische Kirchengeschichte der Stadt Strassburg bis zur französischen Revolution* (Strasbourg, 1922).
29. Gerhard Meyer, *Die Entwicklung der Strassburger Universität aus dem Gymnasium und der Akademie des Johann Sturm* (Heidelberg, 1926); Rodolphe Reuss, *Les statuts de l'ancienne université de Strasbourg* (Mulhouse, 1873). For student rolls, see *Die alten Matrikeln der Universität Strassburg, 1621 bis 1793* (Strasbourg, 1897-1902), edited by Gustav C. Knod as Part Three of the *Urkunden und Akten der Stadt Strassburg.*
30. See especially L. Pariser, *Beitraege zu einer Biographie von Moscherosch* (Munich, 1891).
31. Julius Otto Opel, *Die Anfänge der deutschen Zeitungspresse, 1609-1650: Archiv für Geschichte des deutschen Buchhandels,* III (Leipzig, 1879), 44-64.
32. Elie Brackenhoffer, *Voyage en France de Strasbourg à Paris, 1643-1644,* ed. and tr. Henry Lehr (Paris, 1925), and *Voyages en Suisse 1643 et 1646,* also prepared for publication by Lehr (Paris, 1930); Walter, *Strassburg im dreissigjährigen Kriege,* especially the introduction by Reuss.
33. *Les colloques françois et allemands de Daniel Martin,* ed. Jacques Hatt (Strasbourg, 1929); *Parlement nouveau* (Strasbourg, 1637), edited by Charles Nerlinger (Paris, 1900) under the title, *Daniel Martin ou la vie à Strasbourg au commencement du XVIIᵉ siècle.*
34. Jacques Ungerer, *Le pont du Rhin à Strasbourg du XIVᵉ siècle à la Révolution* (Strasbourg-Paris, 1952).
35. In addition to the general characterization of the mid-seventeenth-century situation in Rodolphe Reuss, *L'Alsace au dix-septième siècle* (Paris, 1897-1898), important descriptions will be found in Eberhard Gothein, "Die oberrheinische Lande vor und nach dem dressigjährigen Kriege," *Zeitschrift für die Geschichte des Oberrheins* (Karlsruhe, 1886), 40 (NF 1): 1-45; in Louis Spach, *Histoire da la Basse-Alsace et de la ville de Strasbourg* (Strasbourg, 1858), 243 ff.; and in J. B. Ellerbach and August Scherlen, *Der dreissigjährige Krieg im Elsass* (Karspach-Brumath-Mulhouse, 1912-1928).

36. The basic general work on the guilds is Friedrich Carl Heitz, *Das Zunft-wesen in Strassburg* (Strasbourg, 1856). More specialized treatments of the local boatmen, weavers, tailors, printers, goldsmiths, and painters, respectively, are to be found in Loeper, *Rheinschifffahrt;* Gustav Schmoller, *Die Strassburger Tucher- und Weberzunft* (Strasbourg, 1879); F. A. Como, *Zunft und Gewerbe der Schneider im alten Strassburg* (Strasbourg, 1893); W. Stieda, *Zur Geschichte des Strassburger Buchdrucks und Buchhandels* (Leipzig, 1880); Hans Meyer, *Die Strassburger Goldschmiedezunft von ihrem Entstehen bis 1681* (Leipzig, 1881); and August Schricker, "Ordnungen der Strassburger Malerzunft," *Jahrbuch des Vogesen-Clubs* (Strasbourg, 1887), 3:99–105.

37. Jacques Hatt, *Quatre siècles de bourgeoisie strasbourgeoise* (Strasbourg, 1934), 27.

38. Reuss, *Histoire de Strasbourg,* 286.

39. Meyer, *Die Strassburger Goldschmiedezunft,* 213, 221–222.

40. Sittler, ed., *Geschichte des Elsass,* II, 30, 135–136.

41. Reuss, *Histoire de Strasbourg,* 222.

42. A clear discussion of the free city's income and usual expenses appears in Crämer, *Verfassungsgeschichte,* 128–142.

43. In the fourth quarter of 1656, for example, the city's expenditures were only 8,918 Strasbourg pounds, 3 shillings, 2½ pence, while the trimestral income came to 9,316 pounds, 11 shillings, 2½ pence. K. Th. Eheberg, *Verfassungs-, Verwaltungs- und Wirtschaftsgeschichte der Stadt Strassburg bis 1681* (Strasbourg, 1899), I, 734–740.

CHAPTER TWO

ANNEXATION

1. Bernhard Erdmannsdörffer, *Deutsche Geschichte vom westphälischen Frieden bis zum Regierungsantritt Friedrichs des Grossen, 1648–1740,* new edition (Leipzig, 1932), I, 37 ff. See also Xavier Mossmann, "La France en Alsace après les traités de Westphalie," *Revue historique* (Paris, 1893–1899), 51:26–43 and 224–249, 53:29–51 and 280–300, 70:241–281; as well as A. Overmann, *Die Abtretung des Elsass an Frankreich im westphälischen Frieden* (Karlsruhe, 1905).

2. Joseph Becker, "Die Verleihung und Verpfändung der Reichslandvogtei Elsass von 1408–1634," *Zeitschrift für die Geschichte des Oberrheins* (Karlsruhe, 1897), 51 (NF 12): 108–153. The last pre-French Oberlandvogt had been Archduke Leopold, brother of Ferdinand III. After Leopold's death in 1633, no replacement was named, because of the wartime confusion in Alsace.

3. The conflicting French and German views emerge most clearly in the contrast between Arsène Legrelle's interpretation of Westphalia in Chapter II of his *Louis XIV et Strasbourg* (Paris, 1884), 4th ed., on the one hand, and, on the other, Erich Marcks' review article on Legrelle in the *Göttingische gelehrte Anzeigen* (Göttingen, 1885), 114–142, expanded two years later into a Berlin lecture, "Ludwig XIV und Strassburg," to be found in Marcks' collected essays, *Männer und Zeiten* (Leipzig, 1922), 6th ed., 91–108.

4. For the sixteenth century, see Franziskus Petri, "Strassburgs Beziehungen zu Frankreich während der Reformationszeit," *Elsass-lothringisches Jahrbuch* (Frankfurt am Main, 1929 and 1931), 8:134–165, 10:123–192; Rüdiger Hachtmann, *Strassburgs Beziehungen zu Frankreich im 16. Jahrhundert* (Göttingen, 1931); and Alcuin Holländer's various monographs on the events of the 1570's.

5. Léonce Anquez, *Henri IV et l'Allemagne, d'après les mémoires et la correspondance de Jacques Bongars* (Paris, 1887); Léon G. Pélissier, *Henri IV, Bongars et Strasbourg* (Paris, 1888).

6. On Glaser's mission and its aftermath, see the two articles by Reuss in *Annales de l'Est* (Nancy, 1900–1901), 14:201–232 and 15:539–591.

7. See E. de Bouteiller and Eugène Hepp, eds., *Correspondance politique adressée au Magistrat de Strasbourg par ses agents à Metz, 1594–1683* (Paris, 1882).

8. From Reisseissen we have both a *Strassburgische Chronik von 1657–1677* (Strasbourg, 1880) and a *Strassburgische Chronik von 1667–1710, Memorial* (Strasbourg, 1877), both edited by Reuss. The former, Reisseissen's self-styled "schmahle büchlin," is a random set of rather gossipy personal notes, while the latter is a more formal political diary covering, it will be noted, a later and much longer period. This second work, an invaluable source, is referred to hereafter simply as the *Memorial*.

The selections from Walter's long chronicle relevant to this period should not be confused with his notes on the years before 1648, already cited in Chapter One. What we are here concerned with is the only other segment of the original to see print, in the form of a German text, with a French translation, edited by Reuss, *La Chronique strasbourgeoise du peintre Jean-Jacques Walter pour les années 1672–1676* (Paris, 1898).

9. Reisseissen, *Memorial*, 6 and 11.

10. BN Paris, Mss. fr. 4364 and 14373, and BNU Strasbourg, Ms. 1066, are a group of memoranda containing descriptions of and policy recommendations concerning Alsace, dating from the years 1656–1660. Although composed under Colbert de Croissy's direction, they were drafted, according to the eighteenth-century notes of Jean-Daniel Schoepflin, by one Rosselange, a native of Lorraine. Also in the BNU, Ms. 4294, is a memorandum of 1663, prepared and forwarded to Paris by Croissy's cousin and successor, also named Charles Colbert. Copies of this document exist in the BN Paris, Mss. fr. 4294 and 18677.

11. Paul Wentzcke, *Johann Frischmann, ein Publizist des 17. Jahrhunderts* (Strasbourg, 1904), 107.

12. Reisseissen, *Strassburgische Chronik, 1657–1677,* 50–51. A clear indication of how little the royal governor was concerned with Strasbourg in this period is the small number of references to the free city in Georges Livet's work, *Le duc Mazarin, gouverneur d'Alsace, 1661–1713* (Strasbourg-Paris, 1954).

13. BN Paris, Ms. fr. 4231. Other relevant memoranda include Mss. fr. 11474 and 20761. Still another, written by Robert Gravel in 1661, is found in printed form among the *Acta, memorabilia et declarationes,* BN Lk². 89. It is interesting to contrast the cautious tone of these official estimates with the wildly exaggerated expansionism of a published work like Antoine Aubery's *Des justes prétensions du Roy sur l'Empire* (Paris, 1667), which claims most of Europe west of the Elbe for Louis XIV, as heir to Charlemagne. Aubery, be it added, had gone too far for the royal government itself, which condemned his book and imprisoned him for several months.

14. B. Auerbach, "La question d'Alsace à la diète de Ratisbonne, 1663–1673," *Annales de l'Est* (Nancy, 1889), 3:309–336; Hermann Freiherr von Müllenheim-Rechberg, *Die Annexion des Elsass durch Frankreich* (Strasbourg, 1896), 2nd ed.

15. Sophie von Jakubowski, *Beziehungen zwischen Strassburg, Zürich und Bern im XVII. Jahrhundert* (Strasbourg, 1898), 78–80.

16. Wentzcke, *Johann Frischmann,* 91.

17. The official correspondence with the emperor concerning this crisis is to be found in the Haus-, Hof- und Staatsarchiv at Vienna, Kleinere Reichsstände: Strassburg, Fasz. 515. On the involved question of the bridge, and its misfortunes during the first months of the war, see Paul Wentzcke, "Der Strassburger Rheinpass im Holländischen Kriege (1672–73)" *Elsass-lothringisches Jahrbuch* (Frankfurt am Main, 1937), 16:126–180.

18. *Chronique strasbourgeoise,* 101–105.

19. *Memorial,* 57.

20. *Ibid.,* 30–32 and 50–51.

21. Jakubowski, *Beziehungen zwischen Strassburg, Zürich und Bern,* 88–89; Legrelle, *Louis XIV et Strasbourg,* 313–315.

22. Crämer, "Die Wehrmacht Strassburgs," 50.

23. Conrad Escher-Ziegler, "Eine schweizerische Garnison zur Beschützung der Neutralität der Reichsstadt Strassburg in den Jahren 1673–1679," *Neujahrsblatt der Feuerwerker Gesellschaft in Zürich* (Zürich, 1908).

24. Evidence of the conditions in Strasbourg during the Dutch War is to be found in the Minutes of the Council of Fifteen, though these have survived only down to 1674, with a lapse thereafter until 1686 (AM Strasbourg). Reisseissen's *Memorial,* 63 and *passim.,* and Walter's *Chronique strasbourgeoise,* 111 and *passim.,* can in this instance be supplemented by

Paul Conrad Balthasar Han's description, published in Nürnberg in 1676 under the title, *Das seelzagende Elsass* — "Heartbreaking Alsace."

25. Reisseissen, *Memorial,* 67; AM Strasbourg, Minutes of the Council of Thirteen, 1673–1678.
26. Crämer, "Die Wehrmacht Strassburgs," 78–79. AM Strasbourg, Minutes of the Senate-and-XXI, May 15, 1680, include the accounts presented by the Fortifications Masters, showing the heavy spending on the city's defenses at the end of the Dutch War.
27. AM Strasbourg, Minutes of the Council of Thirteen, January through August 1679. On April 3 the Council received and tabled the Duke of Lorraine's offer to provide a permanent imperial garrison.
28. This decision was taken by the Magistrat even before the formal proclamation of the peace. AM Strasbourg, Minutes of the Council of Thirteen, March 7, 1679.
29. Hermann Hackert, "Der Friede von Nimwegen und das deutsche Elsass," *Historische Zeitschrift* (Munich-Berlin, 1942), 165:472–509. This work is subject to the reservations that apply to most diplomatic history published under the Nazis.
30. AM Strasbourg, Minutes of the Council of Thirteen, September 24, 1680, and Minutes of the Senate-and-XXI, October 2, 1680. Both of these concern news of La Grange's "acceptance" of the oath of fealty from the city's bailiff at Wasselonne-Marlenheim. In addition, the municipal archives contain, Série VI, 36.1, a detailed report of the same ceremony at Obernai, affecting the bailiwick of Barr.
31. Reisseissen, *Memorial,* 101.
32. Fritz Dildey, "Beiträge zum Fall Strassburgs 1681," *Zeitschrift für die Geschichte des Oberrheins* (Karlsruhe, 1930), 83 (NF 44): 472–477; and Paul Wentzcke, "Wiener Beiträge zur Geschichte vom Fall Strassburgs (1680/81)," in *Gesamtdeutsche Vergangenheit: Festgabe für Heinrich Ritter von Srbik zum 60. Geburtstag* (Munich, 1938), 98–107.
33. AM Strasbourg, Minutes of the Council of Thirteen, August 2, 1680.
34. HHSA Vienna, Staatenabteilungen: Frankreich, Berichte, Vols. 39 and 41.
35. AM Strasbourg, Minutes of the Council of Thirteen, June 14, 1679, report Bremen's assurance that a letter of exchange for 240 Reichsgulden was on the way. For Nürnberg's remittance see these same minutes under date of April 14, 1680, and for Lindau's, May 8, 1680.
36. This figure is taken from a bill presented by the Magistrat to the imperial resident, Neveu, and forwarded by him to the emperor in a letter of November 4, 1680. HHSA Vienna, Kleinere Reichsstände: Strassburg, Fasz. 516.
37. Ferdinand Fehling, *Frankreich und Brandenburg in den Jahren 1679 bis 1684* (Leipzig, 1906), 35–133.
38. AM Strasbourg, Minutes of the Thirteen, October 20, 1680, contain the report of an interview between Advocate Frantz and the Imperial resident, Neveu, which brings out clearly the conflicting points of view. The minutes

of November 22, 1680, show that Advocate Binder in Regensburg was involved in similar debates with Dr. Stratmann.

39. Quoted by Reuss, *L'Alsace au dix-septième siècle*, I, 248.
40. Legrelle, *Louis XIV et Strasbourg*, 410.
41. Louis Maurer, *L'expédition de Strasbourg en septembre 1681* (Paris, 1923), Document No. XV.
42. *Ibid.*, No. XIII.
43. *Ibid.*, No. XIV.
44. *Ibid.*, No. XVI.
45. *Ibid.*, No. XVIII.
46. *Ibid.*, No. XIX.
47. *Ibid.*, No. XX.
48. *Ibid.*, No. XXVII.
49. HHSA Vienna, Staatenabteilungen: Frankreich, Berichte, Vol. 41.
50. Christian Pfister, "Les voyages de Louis XIV en Alsace," *Séances et travaux de l'Académie des sciences morales et politiques* (Paris, 1921), Pt. 1:397–408 and Pt. 2:28–44, for the royal journey of 1681.
51. Legrelle, *Louis XIV et Strasbourg*, 520–522.
52. HHSA Vienna, Kleinere Reichsstände: Strassburg, Fasz. 516, for the original.
53. The full text of the document has been published by Erich Marcks, from the original in the AM Strasbourg, as an appendix to his "Beiträge zur Geschichte von Strassburgs Fall im Jahre 1681," *Zeitschrift für die Geschichte des Oberrheins* (Freiburg im Breisgau, 1890), 44 (NF 5): 23–28.
54. Maurer, *L'expédition de Strasbourg*, Document No. LXVI.
55. The text and marginalia have been printed many times, e.g., in Reuss, *Histoire de Strasbourg*, 251–253.
56. Maurer, *L'expédition de Strasbourg*, Document No. LXXXV.
57. *De la correspondance de Fléchier avec Mme. Des Houlières et sa fille*, A. Fabre, ed. (Paris, 1871), 227–236.
60. A good example of these rancorous and uninformed commentaries, of which dozens were circulated, is C. F. Kranewitter's long diatribe, *Prodigium & Elogium Perfidae ac Ignavae Strasburgensis: Olim Civitatis Imperialis, Nunc Municipii Gallici* (Schwidnicii, n.d. [Schweidnitz, 1682]).
61. Wentzcke, *Johann Frischmann*, 107.
62. The correspondence of the imperial delegates at Frankfurt is found in two series at the HHSA Vienna. Letters to the Austrian Court Chancellor, primarily from Stratmann, show the anger, suspicion, and fear which beset the delegation in those October days of 1681. These are in the Oesterreichische Staatsregistratur, Repertorium N, Fasz. 26. The official reports sent almost daily to the emperor himself are among the Friedensakten, Fasz. 143b.
63. Legrelle, *Louis XIV et Strasbourg*, 598. He reproduces the full text of Louvois' letter.
64. The original of Wencker's chronicle was destroyed in the bombardment

of 1870, but not before Legrelle had obtained an extract of the section on Strasbourg's capitulation, which he reprinted in the fourth edition of *Louis XIV et Strasbourg*, 792–794. He also reproduces the text of the final message to the emperor, 554–555, for which I have earlier given the archival location in Vienna. But most striking of these accounts is the one written by Johann Joachim Frantz and sent over to Durlach, where his son-in-law, Baron von Beck, was a Baden official. Subsequently returned to Strasbourg, it is now in the BNU, Ms. 1094: "Kurtze, jedoch gründliche Erzehlung, wie und aus was Ursachen die Stadt Strassburg sich der Cron Frankreich Gewalt und Protection untergaben." As for Gottfried Stoesser's corroborative version, it was published at an unspecified place in 1696 under the title, *Send-Schreiben eines guten Freundes aus dem Elsass . . . Wie es bey Subjugation dess H. Reichs Stadt . . . Strassburg hergangen seye.*

CHAPTER THREE

FORTRESS OF FRANCE

1. Ms. fr. nouv. acq. 1548, "Mémoire sur la situation de Strasbourg, ses deffauts et avantages. . . ." Gaston Zeller comments on this memorandum, but does not reproduce it, in his brief article, "La forteresse de Strasbourg, jugée par Vauban," *Revue d'Alsace* (Strasbourg, 1948), 88:203–207.

2. BN Paris, Lk⁷. 9427, is a pamphlet printed in 1683, *Eigentlicher Bericht von Befestigung der so weit-beruehmten Stadt Strassburg,* which includes comments on the new fortifications, written from an anti-French point of view. Much more detailed is the *Extract eines Berichts von dem Fortifications-bau der Stadt Strassburg, so Anno 1683 ausgegangen, etc.* (s.l., 1724). See also Ungerer, *Le pont du Rhin,* 30; and Gaston Zeller, *L'organisation défensive des Frontières du Nord et de l'Est au XVIIᵉ siècle* (Paris, 1928), *passim.*

3. An analysis of the pre-Vauban fortifications is provided by F. von Apell, *Geschichte der Befestigung von Strassburg im Elsass . . . bis zum Jahre 1681* (Strasbourg, 1902).

4. Reisseissen, *Memorial,* 113–114.

5. Dildey, "Beiträge zum Fall Strassburgs," 477; Wentzcke, "Wiener Beiträge," 104 ff.; Legrelle, *Louis XIV et Strasbourg,* 611.

6. Wentzcke, "Wiener Beiträge," 98.

7. Legrelle, *Louis XIV et Strasbourg,* 600–601.

8. Friedrich Knöpp, "Hessen-Darmstadt und Hessen-Kassel in ihrer Stellung zur elsässichen Frage 1680/1682," *Elsass-lothringisches Jahrbuch* (Frankfurt am Main, 1932), 11:165–178.

9. See Legrelle, *Louis XIV et Strasbourg,* 595–652, for a full account.

10. Fehling, *Frankreich und Brandenburg,* 147–153. The full text of Rébenac's report of October 15, 1681, is given in the French original as an appendix to this work, 310–315.

11. Legrelle, *Louis XIV et Strasbourg,* 652–658.

12. *Ibid.,* 664–665.

13. Karl Hölscher, *Die öffentliche Meinung in Deutschland über den Fall Strassburgs während der Jahre 1681 bis 1684* (Munich, 1896); Hubert Gillot, *Le règne de Louis XIV et l'opinion publique en Allemagne* (Nancy, 1914); Hans von Zwiedineck-Südenhorst, *Die öffentliche Meinung in Deutschland im Zeitalter Ludwigs XIV* (Stuttgart, 1888). Of these three works, Hölscher's is obviously the most detailed and the most important for present purposes. Another monograph which, though it deals with a slightly earlier period, nonetheless supplies valuable background information, is that of Johann Haller, *Die deutsche Publizistik in den Jahren 1668–1674* (Heidelberg, 1892).

14. *Briefe der Herzogin Elisabeth Charlotte von Orléans,* ed. Wilhelm Ludwig Holland (Stuttgart, 1876), I, 20.

15. P. Paulus Volk, "Der Fall Strassburgs (1681) . . . in den Chroniken der Benediktinerklöster Gengenbach (Baden) und Münsterschwarzach (Unterfranken)," *Elsass-lothringisches Jahrbuch* (Frankfurt am Main, 1936), 15:208.

16. Erdmannsdörffer, *Deutsche Geschichte,* I, 632–633.

17. A. de Saint-Léger et al., *Louis XIV: La fin du règne, 1685–1715,* VIII[1] of Lavisse, ed., *Histoire de France depuis les origines jusqu'à la Révolution* (Paris, 1908), 12–13. Saint-Léger's chapters on international affairs in this volume are basic to the narrative at hand, as are Erdmannsdörffer's in his *Deutsche Geschichte, 1648–1740,* II, and Legrelle's *Louis XIV et Strasbourg.* See also Kurt Rheindorf, "Elsass, Lothringen und die Grossmächte im Zeitalter Ludwigs XIV," *Elsass-lothringisches Jahrbuch* (Berlin, 1924), 3:73–91.

18. For the imperial side, see especially Heinrich Ritter von Srbik, *Wien und Versailles, 1692–1697: Zur Geschichte von Strassburg, Elsass und Lothringen* (Munich, 1944); and for the French, A. Legrelle, *Notes et documents sur la paix de Ryswick* (Lille, 1894).

19. *Denkschrift von Kurfürst Friedrich III von Brandenburg an Kaiser Leopold I über die Nothwendigkeit der Wiedererwerbung Strassburgs, 1696* (Strasbourg, 1877).

20. Aloys Schulte, *Markgraf Ludwig Wilhelm von Baden und der Reichskrieg gegen Frankreich, 1693–1697* (Karlsruhe, 1892), II, 218–219.

21. Srbik, *Wien und Versailles,* Appendix I, 319–320.

22. *Ibid.,* 283.

23. *Ibid.,* Appendix II, 327.

24. *Ibid.,* 304 ff.

25. For the full text of the treaty, see J. C. Neuhaus, *Der Friede von Ryswick und die Abtretung Strassburgs an Frankreich, 1697* (Freiburg im Breisgau,

1873), 308–328. The critical commentary in this work has been completely superseded since its appearance.

26. BNU Strasbourg, Ms. 783, "Letzter Reichs-Abschied an die Statt Strassburg," is a handwritten copy of the piece. For the text in printed form, with an historical commentary, see Otto Ruppersberg, "Strassburg und die evangelischen Reichsstädte: Eine Frankfurter Flugschrift aus dem Jahre 1698," *Elsass-lothringisches Jahrbuch* (Frankfurt am Main, 1929), 8:230–264. In the Badische Landesbibliothek, Hss. des Klosters Ettenheim-Münster, 152, there are two copies of this poem, differing only slightly from one another but lacking the stanzas of criticism aimed at other Protestant cities in the Frankfurt printing. The presence of these manuscripts among the papers of a South German abbey suggests that the Dominican author of 1698 may have merely added topical comments to an older critique of Strasbourg already current for some years within the Reich.

27. The futile French efforts to woo "Türkenlouis" away from his imperial allegiance are discussed by Max Braubach, "Französische Bemühungen um den Markgrafen Ludwig Wilhelm von Baden vor Ausbruch des Spanischen Erbfolgekrieges," *Zeitschrift für die Geschichte des Oberrheins* (Karlsruhe, 1953), 101 (NF 62):413–435.

28. Max Braubach, "Um die 'Reichsbarriere' am Oberrhein," *Zeitschrift für die Geschichte des Oberrheins* (Karlsruhe, 1937), 89 (NF 50):481–530.

29. Emile Bourgeois, *Neuchâtel et la politique prussienne en Franche-Comté, 1702–1713* (Paris, 1887).

30. Braubach, "Um die 'Reichsbarriere,'" 488.

31. *Ibid.*, 493–494.

32. See A. Legrelle, *La diplomatie française et la succession d'Espagne* (Paris, 1888–1892), IV, 459 ff.

33. *Mémoires de M. de* **** *pour servir à l'histoire des négociations depuis le Traité de Ryswick jusqu'à la Paix d'Utrecht* (The Hague, 1756), I, 345 ff.

34. Werner Reese, *Das Ringen um Frieden und Sicherheit in den Entscheidungsjahren des Spanischen Erbfolgekrieges, 1708 bis 1709* (Munich, 1933), 247.

35. Saint-Léger in Lavisse, ed., *Histoire de France*, VIII^1, 119.

36. Quoted by Braubach, "Um die 'Reichsbarriere,'" 508.

37. Legrelle, *Louis XIV et Strasbourg*, 699, makes the *Pandours* of 1744 practically his concluding incident.

38. Léon Ehrhard, *La question d'Alsace-Lorraine et Frédéric le Grand* (Strasbourg, 1901); Aloys Schulte, *Frankreich und das linke Rheinufer* (Stuttgart-Berlin, 1918), 205; and more recently, Max Braubach, "Hat Friedrich der Grosse die Wiedervereinigung Elsass-Lothringens mit Deutschland verhindert?" *Elsass-lothringisches Jahrbuch* (Frankfurt am Main, 1935), 14:161–183.

39. Braubach, "Hat Friedrich der Grosse, etc.," 177.

40. *Ibid.*, 182.

41. *Ibid.*

42. BN Paris, Ms. fr. 8010, 1–208, is a "Mémoire sur la Localité des Places du département d'Alsace et des ressources qu'on y peut trouver pour le Service des vivres suivant l'Etat des choses au mois de Juillet 1754," one of the memoranda assembled by Marquet de Bourgade in 1755. It gives a full description of the integrated defenses of the province, with emphasis on the central importance of Strasbourg, on the eve of the Seven Years' War.

CHAPTER FOUR

THE KING'S RULE

1. AM Strasbourg, Série II, 103, contains correspondence from the years 1583–1584 on the initial refusal of the Thirteen to adopt the papal calendar reform. Louvois' role is shown in the minutes of the Thirteen, January 23 and February 11, 1682.

2. Legrelle, *Louis XIV et Strasbourg*, 586.

3. BNU Strasbourg, M.4681, is the printed *Copie de la Lettre de Monseigneur le Marquis de Barbesieux, Ministre d'Estat, escrite à Monsieur le Marquis d'Huxelles . . . En date de Marly du 25me Avril 1698,* which publicized the confirmation of privileges (also printed in German, M. 4682). The letters of Colbert de Torcy to Huxelles, BNU Strasbourg, Ms. 1530, reflect the royal government's interest in avoiding unrest in Alsace following 1697, a subject discussed by Louis Maurer in his "Strasbourg et le traité de Ryswijk," *Feuilles d'histoire du 17ᵉ au 20ᵉ siècle* (Paris, 1912), 7:289–294.

4. Karl Engel, *Strassburg als Garnisonstadt unter dem Ancien Régime* (Strasbourg, 1901), 14–42, gives a full analysis of the military command personnel from 1681 to 1789.

5. Bouteiller and Hepp, *Correspondance politique*, 344. For the syndic's importance just after the capitulation, see Rodolphe Reuss, ed., *Correspondances politiques et chroniques parisiennes adressées à Christophe Güntzer, syndic royal de la ville de Strasbourg, 1681–1685* (Paris, 1890).

6. AM Strasbourg, AA. 2523–2526, four bundles of documents from the royal praetor's files dealing with the office itself, constitute the basic source. Other references include BNU Strasbourg, Mss. 614 and 1702. On the question of emoluments, see E. Müller, *Le magistrat de la ville de Strasbourg* (Strasbourg, 1862), 19 ff. As old as Müller's work is, it is still indispensable.

7. AM Strasbourg, Minutes of the Thirteen, February 14 and 26, 1685, and Minutes of the Senate-and-XXI, April 30, 1685; Albert Metzenthin, *Ulrich Obrecht und die Anfänge der französischen Prätur in Strassburg, 1684–1701* (Strasbourg, 1914); Alfred Reh, "Brief des Stadtadvokaten Obrecht, in dem er dem Magistrat die bevorstehende Einführung als konigl. Prätor ankundigt," *Annuaire de la Société historique, littéraire et scientifique du Club Vosgien* (Strasbourg, 1934), NS 2:325–328; Jules Schwartz, "Un

manuscrit retrouvé d'Ulric Obrecht," *Revue d'Alsace* (Colmar-Thann, 1929), 76:109–119, 231–236, 376–384; and Fr. J. Wernert, "La conversion d'Ulric Obrecht, préteur royal de Strasbourg," *Revue catholique d'Alsace* (Strasbourg, 1920), 35:483–490.

8. In September 1685 Johann Georg Hecker, also a Catholic, was commissioned by the crown as "deputy royal praetor." In 1687, however, Hecker acceded to a regular place in the Magistrat, and the post was left vacant thereafter.

9. Georges Livet, *L'Intendance d'Alsace sous Louis XIV, 1648 à 1715* (Paris, 1956) provides over a thousand pages of meticulously documented narrative and analysis. See my notice in *The American Historical Review* for October 1957, 63:105–106.

10. Reisseissen, *Memorial,* 160–163, describes the local crisis involving venal offices in 1692. BNU Strasbourg, Ms. 1531, contains letters from Chamillart at court to Marshal d'Huxelles concerning another such cash payment, this time three hundred thousand livres, in 1699–1700.

11. BNU Strasbourg, Ms. 1702, on these officers.

12. For plentiful evidence of the hatred which existed between the first praetor and Güntzer, see *Correspondance intime entre Ulric Obrecht . . . et Jean-Baptiste Klinglin* (Strasbourg, 1899).

13. AM Strasbourg, AA. 2626–2628, are the praetor's papers on this affair.

14. BL Karlsruhe, Karlsruher Hs. 517, fol. 73–77, is a copy of Hatzel's "Memorandum of the Royal Syndic of the City of Strasbourg, Requesting a Definition of the Functions of the Royal Praetor of the Said City and Those of the Syndic." The effort to attract support from nearby German courts — Baden-Baden, Durlach, Mannheim, Karlsruhe, Stuttgart — was a regular feature of political disputes in eighteenth-century Strasbourg.

15. *Lettres écrites à la cour par M. d'Angervilliers, Intendant d'Alsace de 1716 à 1724,* Louis Spach, ed. (Strasbourg, 1878), 82–88.

16. BN Paris, Ms. fr. 8152, fol. 195, and Ms. fr. nouv. acq. 1932, fol. 4.

17. Livet avers that the office itself disappeared with Hatzel (*L'Intendance d'Alsace,* 746). However, Article 22 of the royal *règlement* of 1752 (see above, p. 85), explicitly reëstablished what it called the "suspended" title; and the Archives Municipales contain a good deal of correspondence about the *Syndicat,* especially about Spon in the 1760's.

18. *Lettres écrites à la cour par M. d'Angervilliers,* 38–42 and 159–161.

19. AD Bas-Rhin, Série C, comprises the official records of the intendants. BNU Strasbourg, Ms. 1702, gives a valuable summary of the intendancy, as organized in 1770. Georges Livet, "Les intendants d'Alsace et leur oeuvre, 1648–1789," in *Deux siècles d'Alsace française* (Strasbourg-Paris, 1948), 79–131, supplies a valuable short survey. Jean Benoist d'Anthenay, *Le premier administrateur de l'Alsace Française: Jacques de La Grange* (Strasbourg, 1930), has now been completely superseded by Livet's *L'Intendance d'Alsace,* as have all other studies of the pre-1715 period.

20. BN Paris, Ms. fr. 11383, contains letters from the successive intendants, Le

Pelletier de La Houssaye and d'Angervilliers to the Regent, 1715–1717, which give a clear idea of the frequency and transmission times of such correspondence.

21. Instead of seeking to list all the general reports by intendants to be found in collections at Paris and Strasbourg, I can here refer the reader to Christian Pfister's survey of this subject, in the first ten pages of his "Extrait d'un mémoire sur l'Alsace de l'année 1735," *Revue historique* (Paris, 1916), 123:54–88, adding to it only the memorandum of 1667, presumably by Charles Colbert, located subsequently by Charles Benoist and used by him in his otherwise not very valuable *Lois de la politique française et le gouvernement de l'Alsace sous Louis XIV* (Paris, 1929).

22. "Strasbourg est sans difficulté la capitale de la Basse Alsace et le pouvoit estre d'un royaume," wrote the Count de Boulainvilliers around 1700, in the manuscript for his *État de la France,* BN Paris, Ms. fr. 14337. A significant step in the consolidation of the intendant's power was the dispute between La Houssaye and the Court de Châtillon, named Grand Bailiff of Haguenau in 1714 by Louis XIV. Châtillon made an effort to assert his authority over the Décapole cities; but this office could no longer be made into anything more than a feudal distinction. In 1717, the Council of State settled the dispute in favor of the local prerogatives of the towns, under the general supervision not of the bailiff, but of the intendant. See Georges Livet, "La Préfecture de Haguenau et l'intendance d'Alsace à la fin du règne de Louis XIV," *Etudes haguenauiennes* (Haguenau, 1955), NS 1:127–138.

23. AD Bas-Rhin, C. 307, contains the exchange contract.

24. BL Karlsruhe, Karlsruher Hss. 517 and 522, contain two copies of a memorandum which Klinglin must have circulated widely in an effort to combat an attempt to expose him during the early 1740's. It is all a plot, this document explains, hatched by two Strasbourg noblemen, Bock and Wurmser, who are crypto-republicans, by the Marshal de Broglie, whose son is jealous of the praetor, and by Intendant de Brou, whose mistress is the wife of Bock and the daughter of Wurmser.

25. AM Strasbourg, Série VI, 94.12, is a file of corespondence to, from, and about the special commissioner.

26. BNU Strasbourg, Ms. 1310, supplies the full text. BL Karlsruhe, Karlsruher Hs. 517, fol. 128–131, is an interesting memorandum dated May 9, 1752, and devoted to exposing confusion in the administration of city finances by the Commissioners of the Treasury Tower. It is one of a number of such documents to be found at Karlsruhe in the Rochebrune collection on Strasbourg.

27. A good way to form an impression of this continuity is to follow the eighteenth-century political chronicle contained in Müller, *Le magistrat de la ville de Strasbourg.* The "Ammeister-Büchlein" from the 1780's, BNU Strasbourg, Ms. 1278, shows clearly how little change had occurred, even by that time, in the formal aspects of local government, as does Ms.

1279, a set of documents on administration from among the Heitz papers.

28. BNU Strasbourg, Ms. 640, Jean-Christophe Meyer's unpublished "Tafeln derer Herren Ammeistern der Statt Strassburg" (1786), and Jean-Martin Pastorius, *Kurze Abhandlung von den Ammeistern der Stadt Strassburg* (Strasbourg, 1761), may both be checked by the more detailed lists of officials in the annual printed almanac, *Strassburgs Regiments-Verfassung,* available for nearly every year from 1672 to 1789 in the BNU Strasbourg, M. 9529. The fullest printed lists in general circulation are those in Ernest Lehr, *L'Alsace noble* (Paris, 1870), III, 311–402, including bourgeois officers.

29. Reisseissen, *Memorial,* 145.

30. Engel, *Strassburg als Garnisonstadt,* 2–42.

31. AM Strasbourg, Minutes of the Thirteen, July 24, 1756.

32. BNU Strasbourg, Ms. 1295, "Lettres et arrêts concernant l'autorité judiciaire du Magistrat de Strasbourg." The municipal courts are discussed by all the standard authorities, of course, including Reuss, Hermann, Müller, and Crämer. Johannus Fridericus Lauth, *Conspectus Judiciorum Argentinensium* (Strasbourg, 1784), is a survey of the structure five years before the Revolution, presented as a doctoral thesis at the university.

33. The Lesser Senate (*Kleiner Rat*) has often been erroneously characterized as merely a subdivision of the Senate proper — the latter's "law lords," so to speak. Actually, it was composed of six noble and sixteen non-noble councilors, chosen by the Senators and thus launched on the normal route to later two-year terms in the Senate itself. It was presided over for three months out of the year by the "ruling" Ammeister *of the previous year* and during the other quarterly terms by three of the nobles among its own membership. It had no legislative authority of any kind, but by the eighteenth century it was the municipality's basic civil court.

34. BN Paris, Ms. fr. 8151, fol. 78, is Intendant La Grange's discussion of this Tribunal des monnaies in 1697.

35. François Wendel, *Le mariage à Strasbourg à l'époque de la réforme, 1520–1692* (Strasbourg, 1928), 89–90.

36. Of the many discussions of the Sovereign Council available in various contexts, the most important are: Gabriel Pillot and Ernest de Neyremand, *Histoire du Conseil Souverain d'Alsace* (Paris, 1860); Ernest Glasson, "La rôle politique du Conseil souverain d'Alsace," *Revue historique* (Paris, 1900), 72:1–45; and F. Dollinger, "Le Conseil souverain d'Alsace," *Bulletin de la Société des Sciences, Agriculture et Arts du Bas-Rhin* (Strasbourg, 1914), 48:14–40. The basic collection of its jurisprudence is President de Bourg's massive *Recueil des Edits, Déclarations, Lettres patentes et Arrêts du Conseil Souverain d'Alsace* (Colmar, 1775), supplementing and continuing the collection of Corberon, completed just fifty years earlier.

37. AM Strasbourg, AA. 2395–2402, deal with jurisdictional disputes between the Magistrat and various royal or episcopal tribunals in the city. AA. 2185–2186 contain similar documentation for such disputes between Strasbourg and the Sovereign Council.

38. BNU Strasbourg, Mss. 743, 1011, 1015, 1016, 1749, 1750, 1761, et al., are testaments and inventories, all of them executed in archaic German by notaries such as Winckler, Rohr, Oelinger, Schweighaeuser, and Stoeber between 1692 and 1769.

39. BN Paris, Ms. fr. 4285, fol. 30. For general comments on legal usages at Strasbourg, see Crämer, *Verfassungsgeschichte,* 58–61; and Hermann, *Notices,* II, 21–24.

40. Krug-Basse, *L'Alsace avant 1789,* 138–139.

41. BNU Strasbourg, Ms. 1278.

42. BNU Strasbourg, Ms. 1309.

43. AM Strasbourg contain a special series of minutes for the "Three Secret Chambers," extending from 1750 to 1789. Whether these refer to joint meetings of all Thirteeners, Fifteeners, and Twenty-oners, or, as seems more likely, to consultations of a joint commission is not clear from the participants mentioned; but it *is* clear that ordinary Senators were excluded.

44. AM Strasbourg, AA. 2212–2213.

45. Krug-Basse, *L'Alsace avant 1789,* 72.

46. BNU Strasbourg, Ms. 1427. AM Strasbourg, Minutes of the Senate-and-XXI, 1784–1789.

47. BNU Strasbourg, Ms. 1307, "Privilège de non evocando."

48. AM Strasbourg, AA. 2057, deals with the city's rural Ämter in the 1780's.

49. AM Strasbourg, AA. 2350. See also François Ritter, "La police de l'imprimerie et de la librairie à Strasbourg depuis les origines jusqu'à la Révolution française," *Revue des Bibliothèques* (Paris, 1922), 32:161–200.

50. *Lettres écrites à la cour par M. d'Angervilliers,* 129–131. The finally agreed list of exceptions is to be found in BNU Strasbourg, Ms. 1626, "Spécification des exempts de l'Ungueldt, oder Register der an dem Umbgeldt befreyten Persohnen, anno 1722."

51. *Histoire de la Basse-Alsace,* 265.

CHAPTER FIVE

CATHOLICS AND PROTESTANTS

1. *Voyage littéraire en Alsace,* ed. Jacques Matter (Strasbourg, 1864), 58.

2. Legrelle, *Louis XIV et Strasbourg,* 676, n. 1.

3. Christian Pfister, "L'Alsace et l'Edit de Nantes," *Revue historique* (Paris, 1929), 160:217–240; Rodolphe Reuss, *Louis XIV et l'église protestante de Strasbourg, au moment de la révocation de l'Edit de Nantes* (Paris, 1887).

4. Reuss, *Histoire de Strasbourg,* 252.

5. Friedrich Wilhelm Edel, *Die Neue-Kirche in Strassburg* (Strasbourg, 1825); L. Schnéegans, *Mémoire historique sur l'ancienne école paroissiale du Temple-Neuf* (Strasbourg, 1856); G. Kopp, *Rückblicke auf die Geschichte der Neuen Kirche in Strassburg* (Strasbourg, 1872).

6. Of the many monographs on individual Lutheran parishes, I have found especially useful Karl Theodor Gerold, *Geschichte der Kirche St. Niklaus* (Strasbourg, 1904); F. G. Heinemann, *Die Kirche Sanct-Aurelien* (Strasbourg, 1865); Wilhelm Horning, *Urkundliches über die Jung-St-Peterkirche und Gemeinde* (Strasbourg, 1888–1890), 2 vol.; Timotheus Wilhelm Röhrich, *Geschichte der Kirche St. Wilhelm in Strassburg* (Strasbourg, 1856); L. Schnéegans, *L'église de Saint-Thomas* (Strasbourg, 1842); Adam Walther Strobel, *Geschichte der Kirche zum alten St. Peter* (Strasbourg, 1824).

7. BNU Strasbourg, Ms. 1437, for personnel lists. Also Adam, *Evangelische Kirchengeschichte,* 448–472; and Wilhelm Horning, *Zur Strassburger Kirchengeschichte im XVIII. Jahrhundert* (Strasbourg, 1907), Pt. I.

8. G. Lepointe, "La Chambre ecclésiastique de Strasbourg," *Revue historique de droit français et étranger* (Paris, 1951), 4me Série, 29:522–557.

9. BN Paris, Ms. fr. 4285, fol. 9.

10. The Catholic parishes in Strasbourg have received less individual attention than have those of the Lutherans. Two such histories, however, deserve mention: X. Ohresser, *L'Eglise St-Etienne* (Strasbourg, 1935), and the collaborative volume, *St. Magdalena in Strassburg,* ed. Eugen Speich (Strasbourg, 1937). More important are several general works, including *Le vieux Strasbourg* (Strasbourg-Paris, 1890), by Modeste Schickelé; and Vols. III and IV, *Alsatia Sacra,* of the *Nouvelles oeuvres inédites* of Philippe-André Grandidier, published at Colmar, 1897, from the papers of that late eighteenth-century church scholar.

11. P. Archangelus von Altdorf, "Die Kapuziner in Strassburg 1681–1791," *Archiv für elsässische Kirchengeschichte* (Freiburg im Breisgau, 1927), 2:241–310.

12. Modeste Schickelé, *Etat de l'Eglise d'Alsace avant la Révolution* (Colmar-Strasbourg, 1877–1897), I, xxxviii-xli. C. A. F[rayhier], *Histoire du clergé catholique d'Alsace* (Colmar, 1876), 10–17.

13. A list of Jesuits in Alsace as of the effective date of their expulsion, 1765, shows a total of sixty-four in Strasbourg alone. AD Bas-Rhin, C. 343.

14. Joseph Gass, "Strassburgs Brüderschaften und Sodalitäten vor der Revolution," *Archiv für elsässische Kirchengeschichte* (Freiburg im Breisgau, 1927), 2:223–240; Joseph Brauner, "Der Dritte Orden des hl. Franziskus im Elsass im 18. Jahrhundert," in the same journal (1926), 1:277–294.

15. Joseph Gass, "Premières processions du Saint Sacrement à Strasbourg," *Revue catholique d'Alsace* (Strasbourg, 1929), 44:643–649.

16. BN Paris, Ms. fr. 4285, fol. 31, shows that the Magistrat was even permitted to deduct 2,544 livres from its annual fortifications payment to the crown after the cloister of St. Stephen was yielded to the Catholics in 1701, this having been the amount of the former Lutheran convent's contribution toward the salaries of clergymen.

17. Charles Schmidt, "Mémoire d'un R. P. Jésuite pour la conversion de la ville de Strasbourg," *Bulletin de la Société de l'histoire du protestantisme français* (Paris, 1855), 3:62–67.

18. AM Strasbourg, AA. 2573–2573a, contain such records as the praetor royal had in his files concerning conversions. Livet, *L'Intendance d'Alsace*, 462–467, offers some useful charts and statistics.

19. Fabre, ed., *De la correspondance de Fléchier*, 236. Another, later example of a highly publicized abjuration is to be found in the pamphlet printed at Vesoul and Avignon in 1715, under the title, *Discours prononcé dans l'église cathédrale de Strasbourg le 5 may 1715, par M. Jean Sigismond Nester, de Dresde en Saxe, cy-devant ministre luthérien, dans lequel sont exposés les motifs de son retour à l'Eglise catholique.*

20. For the full list, see J. Gass, *Studien zur elsässischen Kirchengeschichte* (Strasbourg, 1924–1926), I, 206.

21. Opel, *Die Anfänge der deutschen Zeitungspresse*, 64.

22. *Dr. Burnet's Travels, or Letters Containing an Account of What Seemed Most Remarkable in Switzerland, Italy, France, and Germany, &c.* (Amsterdam, 1687), Bk. III, 16.

23. BN Paris, Ms. fr. 8151, fol. 127.

24. AM Strasbourg, AA. 2056. This bundle and AA. 2056a–2057 together comprise the praetor's records concerning the *Alternative*.

25. *Memorial*, 156–157. The royal praetor's position in the dispute is touched upon in *Correspondance intime entre Ulric Obrecht . . . et Jean-Baptiste Klinglin*, 9–10.

26. AM Strasbourg, AA. 2646.

27. *Ibid.*, AA. 2517.

28. See above, p. 170.

29. AM Strasbourg, AA. 2517.

30. BNU Strasbourg, M. 40358, printed editions of the *état-civil*, showing births, marriages and deaths for 1697, 1729, and 1737 ff.

31. Schwartz in Sittler, ed., *Geschichte des Elsass*, II, 175. Using a low total, 45,000, he puts Catholics at 23,690 and Lutherans at 20,150.

32. Heitz, *Zunftwesen*, 80.

33. AM Strasbourg, AA. 2220.

34. AM Strasbourg, AA. 1659–1681, for the two Furstembergs, and AA. 1682–1689, for the four Rohans, help to emphasize this contrast — partly in the obvious quantitative decline in the bishops' political correspondence of interest to the royal praetor after 1704. The episcopal records themselves constitute Series G at the Archives Départementales. Published works of interest in this connection include A. Müntz, *Louis XIV et les Furstemberg en Alsace* (Colmar, 1886), and François Noël Le Roy de Sainte-Croix, *Les quatre cardinaux de Rohan* (Strasbourg, 1880).

35. AM Strasbourg, AA. 2473, for example, contains a file from the year 1718 concerned with the arrest on Du Bourg's orders of Christoph Güntzer, presumably a relative, though not a son, of the first royal syndic. Güntzer, having joined the Catholic church, had been unable to recover his children from his still Lutheran wife, despite the commandant's demand that they appear at once for religious training under the Jesuits. The defendant was finally released upon the recommendation of the diocesan authorities, who

decided further punishment would be useless and might have a bad effect on public opinion.

36. This situation is well brought out by Rodolphe Reuss, ed., *Documents relatifs à la situation légale des protestants d'Alsace au dix-huitième siècle* (Paris, 1888).

37. AM Strasbourg, AA. 2574.

38. *Ibid.*

39. As shown by the memorandum drawn up by Peloux, secretary to the intendant in 1735, BN Paris, Ms. fr. 8152, fol. 143.

40. Paul Grünberg, *Philipp Jakob Spener, sein Leben und Wirken* (Göttingen, 1893–1906), 3 vols.

41. Johann Joachim Zentgraff, *Dess Evangelischen Kirchen-Convents in Strassburg Abgenöthigter Historischer Bericht, von der jüngst daselbs entstandenen Pietistischen Brüderschafft u. Philadelphischen Gesellschafft* (Strasbourg, 1706).

42. AM Strasbourg, AA. 2573 (Chamillard to Klinglin, March 17, 1705).

43. Johann Friedrich Geller, *Aus der Geschichte der Brüdergemeinde in Strassburg* (Leipzig, 1899).

44. The tireless Rodolphe Reuss documented this situation fully in his *L'église luthérienne de Strasbourg au dix-huitième siècle* (Paris, 1892).

45. AM Strasbourg, Série VI, HH.VI. 22, for the Lutherans' share in administering the cathedral, as a building rather than as a Catholic church, of course.

46. This 1760 regulation is to be found both in AM Strasbourg, AA. 2056, and in BNU Strasbourg, Ms. 1302. Ms. 1663 in the latter collection is the memorandum prepared the year before by the Lutherans, for submission to the king.

47. Reuss, ed., *Documents relatifs,* 33–34.

48. Joseph Gass, "Les Rohan et la suppression des Jésuites," *Bulletin ecclésiastique du Diocèse de Strasbourg* (Strasbourg, 1924), 332–334.

49. BN Paris, Ms. fr. 8010, concerns Blien. The Cerf-Beer case turns up repeatedly in the records of the Magistrat. The Minutes of the Thirteen for February 1, 1787, for example, include a petition from him to the king, complaining of obstructionism by the Magistrat, and the latter's point-by-point reply, spelling out its bitter opposition to even the tiniest Jewish settlement.

50. AM Strasbourg, AA. 2575.

51. *Ibid.,* printed, with parallel texts in French and German.

52. AM Strasbourg, Série III, 49.3.

53. AD Bas-Rhin, C. 575 (102).

54. AM Strasbourg, Minutes of the Senate-and-XXI, September 20, 1788, contain the record of a debate over the royal permission extended to the Calvinists to move into town, which has appended to it the Magistrat's printed ordinance governing the status of the newly admitted worship.

55. Schickelé, *Etat de l'Eglise d'Alsace avant la Révolution,* opens with a

survey of Catholic parishes in Strasbourg in 1789. For the Lutherans, as of that date, see Johann Unselt, ed., *Die Verfassung der evangelischen Kirchen und niederen Schulen zu Strassburg* (Strasbourg, 1787), 4th ed.
56. AM Strasbourg, Série IV, 98.2, is an analysis of Lutheran worship, dated 1784.
57. Burdette C. Poland, *French Protestantism and the French Revolution* (Princeton, 1957), unfortunately does not include Alsace in the definition of his problem.

CHAPTER SIX

THE ECONOMICS OF AN ANOMALY

1. BN Paris, Ms. fr. 22807.
2. A good introduction to the local tariff situation appears in the first section of Robert Werner, *Le rattachement douanier de l'Alsace à la France, 1789–1791* (Strasbourg-Paris, 1950).
3. BN Paris, Ms. fr. 4285, fol. 33 f., contains information on the early history of royal minting at Strasbourg. Articles on the same general subject include Jean Weber, "Le dernier ducat d'or frappé par la monnaie de la ville libre de Strasbourg," *Cahiers d'archéologie et d'histoire d'Alsace* (Strasbourg, 1928–1929), 19–20:214–215; and F.-A. Schaeffer, "Les monnaies frappées à Strasbourg," *La vie en Alsace* (Strasbourg, 1927), No. 1, 13–18.
4. Both the livre tournois and Strasbourg's Pfund, like the British pound sterling, were originally subdivided according to Charlemagne's system: into twenty *sols* or Schilling, respectively, each of which contained twelve *deniers* in the one case, Pfennige in the other.
5. Johann Christian Nelckenbrecher, *Taschenbuch eines Banquiers und Kaufmanns,* 5th ed. (Berlin, 1781), 256. See also Auguste Hanauer, *Etudes économiques sur l'Alsace ancienne et moderne* (Paris, 1876–1878), I, 470 ff.; and Herman Ludwig [von Jan], *Strassburg vor hundert Jahren* (Stuttgart, 1888), 76–77.
6. Eheberg, "Strassburgs Bevölkerungszahl," 429. Birth figures are shown, as indicated in the preceding chapter, in the official état-civil for 1729 and 1737 ff., BNU Strasbourg, M. 40358. As late as 1771 a report on population submitted to the intendant shows a total of only 33,113; but this appears to refer only to citizens and registered protégés, with their families.
7. Heitz, *Zunftwesen,* 80.
8. BN Paris, Ms. fr. 8010.
9. *Strassburg als Garnisonstadt,* 141–143.
10. *Le magistrat de la ville de Strasbourg,* 103.
11. BN Paris, Ms. fr. 4285, fol. 31.
12. *Memorial,* 127.

13. Another outsider who noted the stepped-up commercial tempo was Franz Ruprecht von Ichtersheim, *Gantz neue elsässische Topographia* (Regensburg, 1710), 109 ff.

14. Reisseissen, *Memorial,* 126–128. The announcement of this auctioning of revenue farms, printed in both French and German and dated December 29, 1685, exists in the BNU Strasbourg, M. 39119, *Adjudication des droits & revenus de la Ville de Strasbourg, etc.*

15. BNU Strasbourg, M. 10383, *Tarifs des droicts qui se payent au bureau de l'Unguelt de la ville de Strasbourg* (1689, printed in French and German); M. 40944, *Tarif des droicts qui se payent au Zollkeller de la ville de Strasbourg* (1700, similarly printed).

16. Müller, *Le magistrat de la ville de Strasbourg,* 103–104; Krug-Basse, *L'Alsace avant 1789,* 69; Ernest Lehr, "Un budget de recettes de la ville de Strasbourg en 1685 et en 1750," in his *Mélanges de littérature et d'histoire alsatiques* (Strasbourg, 1870), 65–105 — from the papers of Intendant Mégret de Sérilly at the AD Bas-Rhin.

17. AM Strasbourg, AA. 2655.

18. Summarized in his Vol. II, 160–162.

19. Hanauer, *Etudes économiques,* II, 607. The *Wöchentliche Strassburger Frag- und Anzeigungs-Nachrichten* (the "Wochenblatt"), available from 1732 on in local collections, printed weekly summaries of wine, brandy, and butter prices, as well as some others on occasion.

20. Müller, *Le magistrat de la ville de Strasbourg,* 104. Engel, *Strassburg als Garnisonstadt,* 145–146, records a deficit of over 14 per cent, but he includes some expenditures not properly chargeable to the operating budget for 1789.

21. *Lettres écrites à la cour par M. d'Angervilliers,* 2–5.

22. The memorandum presented to Calonne and his Assembly of Notables in 1787 by the President of the Sovereign Council of Alsace reveals how important the German-Swiss trade still was to the province at that date. Adalbert Wahl, "Die wirtschaftlichen Beziehungen Elsass-Lothringens zu Frankreich und Deutschland vor der französischen Revolution," *Zeitschrift für die Geschichte des Oberrheins* (Heidelberg, 1902), 56 (NF 17): 531–538.

23. For tables showing the city's food imports and exports for 1784 and 1788, see Hermann, *Notices,* II, 158–159.

24. *Lettres écrites à la cour par M. d'Angervilliers,* 4.

25. Hoffmann, *L'Alsace au XVIIIᵉ siècle,* I, 655–656, quotes this document, which he found in the Bibliothèque de Haguenau.

26. AM Strasbourg, AA. 2421.

27. The basic historical study of Strasbourg's river shipping is that of Loeper, *Rheinschifffahrt,* already cited. See also G. Arnauld, *Le port de Strasbourg* (Paris, 1921); Roger Kronberg, *Le rôle économique du port de Strasbourg* (Paris, 1924); and Marc Lucius, *Le Rhin et le port de Strasbourg* (Paris, 1928), all of which contain some retrospective discussion. Much more

specialized is H. Lévy-Bruhl, "Strasbourg et la décadence de la navigation du Rhin au dix-huitième siècle," *La navigation du Rhin* (Strasbourg, 1932), 10:253–258. An important contemporary treatise is L. H. Nicolay, *Dissertatio de Argentinensium in Rheno navigatione* (Strasbourg, 1760). AD Bas-Rhin, C. 381, is the file of successive intendants on the French government's negotiations with Mainz, the Palatinate, and Baden.

28. BL Karlsruhe, Karlsruher Hs. 519, is a huge tome of 677 folios from the Rochebrune collection on Strasbourg. Bound in 1788, it is completely devoted to the Rhine shipping problem in the eighteenth century and contains numerous pieces showing how the situation was viewed from Baden, Speyer, Breisach, and elsewhere on the German side.

29. BNU Strasbourg, Ms. 1498.

30. BNU Strasbourg, Ms. 1667. The case of another merchant-banker who had important commercial dealings with Marseille, Bordeaux, and other French centers is revealed in the *Reissjournal und Glücks- und Unglücksfälle* of J. E. Zetzner, who died in 1735, edited by Rodolphe Reuss (Strasbourg, 1913).

31. The importance of French trade with Strasbourg in 1766 is discussed in the memorandum submitted to Choiseul by the Comte Du Muy, BN Paris, Ms. fr. 11410.

32. BNU Strasbourg, Ms. 1540.

33. AM Strasbourg, Série VI, HH.IV, is the basic local collection concerned with cartage and passenger coaches.

34. Quoted by Hoffmann, *L'Alsace au XVIIIe siècle,* I, 390.

35. AD Bas-Rhin, C. 456, 461, 475, 481–492, 505–506, 512, 692, 695, contain the bulky correspondence of the intendants concerning roads and bridges. See also Robert Werner, *Les ponts et chaussées d'Alsace au dix-huitième siècle* (Strasbourg, 1929).

36. "Zur Geschichte Strassburgs," *Zeitschrift für die Geschichte des Oberrheins* (Heidelberg, 1909), 63 (NF 24): 437–438. Kiener's generally negative view is supported by Ernest Lehr, "Le commerce et l'industrie en Alsace et spécialement à Strasbourg au milieu du XVIIIe siècle," in his *Mélanges de littérature et d'histoire alsatiques,* 37–64. Lehr's own data, however, drawn from several memoranda prepared between 1750 and 1753, give an impression of increasing activity, notably in tobacco, textiles, leather-goods, and metal products.

37. AM Strasbourg, AA. 2642, containing financial reports from all the guilds to the royal praetor in 1776, shows that fourteen of them had operating surpluses that year, while the other six had only small current deficits.

38. AM Strasbourg, AA. 2630–2637, contain a mass of documentation on the tobacco industry in eighteenth-century Strasbourg, drawn from the archives of the royal praetor. No other product occasioned so much conflict during this period, because of the many special regulations imposed by the crown and the changing official policies governing importation of raw tobacco.

39. Ferdinand Reiber, *Etudes gambrinales: Histoire et archéologie de la bière, et principalement de la bière de Strasbourg* (Paris, 1882).
40. Hatt, *Quatre siècles de bourgeoisie strasbourgeoise.*
41. Hans Haug, *Les faïences et porcelaines de Strasbourg* (Strasbourg, 1922); Emil Heuser, *Porzellan von Strassburg und Frankenthal im achtzehnten Jahrhundert* (Neustadt-an-der-Hardt, 1922).
42. AM Strasbourg, AA. 2421.
43. *Ibid.*
44. *Ibid.,* AA. 2654.
45. *Ibid.,* AA. 2423.
46. The collection of official documents in AM Strasbourg, AA. 2220, concerning royal efforts (1764–1785) to halt the emigration of French craftsmen to Prussia, Hungary, Russia, and other eastern states via Strasbourg, shows that "alien seduction" could and did work both ways.
47. AM Strasbourg, Série VI, 94.13.
48. *Ibid.,* AA. 2423.
49. *Ibid.,* Serie VI, HH.III and HH.VI, contain plentiful evidence of the economic conservatism of the Magistrat and the guilds, respectively. These files are full of protests against innovation and denunciations of parvenus.
50. BNU Strasbourg, Ms. 1651.
51. AM Strasbourg, AA. 2423.
52. *Ibid.*
53. BL Karlsruhe, Karlsruher Hs. 517, fol. 504 ff., is a copy of Paul Hannong's unsuccessful petition to the king in the early 1750's asking for exclusive rights to porcelain production in Alsace and freedom to sell it all over the realm.
54. AM Strasbourg, AA. 2423.
55. *Ibid.,* AA. 1689, contains data on this final stage in the Hannong débacle.
56. Quoted by Stoeber, *Curiosités de voyages en Alsace,* 169.
57. C.-E. Labrousse, *La crise de l'économie française à la fin de l'Ancien régime et au debut de la Révolution* (Paris, 1944), Vol. I.

CHAPTER SEVEN

SOCIAL CHANGES

1. Hermann, *Notices,* II, 279–282.
2. AD Bas-Rhin, C. 343.
3. For such descriptions see Charles de Mathei, Marquis de Valfons, *Souvenirs* (Paris, 1860), 45–68; Commandant Welschinger, "André Chénier sous-lieutenant à Strasbourg en 1782," *Revue des études historiques* (Paris, 1929), 95:263–274; and G. Pariset, "Le lieutenant Napoléon Bonaparte, étudiant à Strasbourg," *Revue historique* (Paris, 1917), 78–92. Pariset's claim that Napoleon was there in the spring of 1788 should be treated

with great caution. The three bits of evidence presented are interesting but certainly not conclusive; if the future emperor had been assigned to the garrison, the documentary traces ought to be much stronger. However, Pariset's description of a young officer's existence at that time is both sound and highly relevant to the present chapter.

4. Alfred Erichson, *Das Duell im alten Strassburg* (Strasbourg, 1897).

5. Karl Engel, "Strassburgs Garnison während des siebenjährigen Krieges," *Zeitschrift für die Geschichte des Oberrheins* (Heidelberg, 1902), 56 (NF 17): 142–161.

6. This is attested to by Müller, *Le Magistrat de Strasbourg,* 77, as well as by documents such as Chamilly's warning placard of 1681, reproduced in Legrelle, *Louis XIV et Strasbourg,* 796–798.

7. Lucien Klipffel, "La communauté de la citadelle de Strasbourg," *La vie en Alsace* (Strasbourg, 1938), 177–182.

8. Engel, *Strassburg als Garnisonstadt,* 101.

9. The merchant, J. E. Zetzner, has left us a full account of these festivities in his *Reissjournal,* ed. Reuss, 210–217.

10. François Le Roy de Sainte Croix, *L'Alsace en fête sous la domination des Louis de France, avec la réproduction des fêtes données par Strasbourg à Louis XV* (Strasbourg, 1880), for the remarkable engravings of J.-M. Weis, first published at Paris (1745?), *Représentation des fêtes données, etc.*

11. Jacques Hatt, "Marie-Antoinette à Strasbourg," *La vie en Alsace* (Strasbourg, 1923), Fascicule 11:1–8.

12. Valfons, *Souvenirs,* 50–55, give a good account of the young marquis' personal contacts with Frederick the Great at Strasbourg. A more detailed discussion, based on Broglie's report to the war minister and on Frederick's correspondence with Voltaire, is Jean de Boislisle, "L'équipée à Strasbourg de Frédéric le Grand," *Revue d'histoire diplomatique* (Paris, 1936), 50:158–181.

13. Valfons, *Souvenirs,* 111–112; Robert Mangin, "L'empereur Joseph II à Strasbourg," *Revue d'Alsace* (Colmar-Thann, 1930), 77:1–13.

14. *Mémoires de la baronne d'Oberkirch,* ed. Count de Montbrison (Paris, 1853), I, 397 and 406–412.

15. Georges Musset, "Les Rochelais à Strasbourg," *Comité des Travaux Historiques et Scientifiques: Bulletin de la section de géographie* (Paris, 1920), 35:191–206. An especially revealing example of German visitors' impressions is the work later attributed to T. F. Ehrmann, *Briefe eines reisenden Deutschen an seinem Bruder in H . . .* (Frankfurt-Leipzig, 1789). Letters 10 through 32, comprising 338 of the volume's 480 pages, are enthusiastically devoted to Strasbourg, in which the writer sees a point of contact with France accessible to his compatriots.

16. BNU Strasbourg, Ms. 786.

17. *Johann Daniel Schoepflins brieflicher Verkehr mit Gönnern, Freunden und Schülern,* ed. Richard Fester (Tübingen, 1906), 172.

18. *Boswell on the Grand Tour: Germany and Switzerland, 1764,* Frederick A. Pottle, ed. (New York, 1953), 187–191.

19. The basic monograph is Arthur Schulze, *Die örtliche und soziale Herkunft der Strassburger Studenten, 1621–1793* (Heidelberg, 1926). Other studies, more specialized but based, like Schulze's, on Knod's massive edition of *Die alten Matrikeln,* include K. A. Barack, "Württemberger auf der Strassburger Universität von 1612 bis 1793," *Württembergische Vierteljahrshefte für Landesgeschichte* (Stuttgart, 1879), 2:161–206; Werner Hossfeld, "Thüringer Landsleute auf der alten Strassburger Hochschule," *Das Thüringer Fahnlein* (Jena, 1936), 9:65–69 and 145–157; S. Hausmann, "Die Schweizer Studenten an der alten Universität Strassburg," *Zeitschrift für schweizerische Geschichte* (Zürich, 1928), 8:64–103. An important synthetic essay on this subject is Paul Wentzcke, "Die alte Universität Strassburg, 1621–1793," *Elsass-lothringisches Jahrbuch* (Frankfurt am Main, 1938), 17:37–112, summarized under the title, "Die alte Universität Strassburg und das Reich," *Historische Zeitschrift* (Munich-Berlin, 1938), 158:249–264. Aside from the valuable information he presents, however, Wentzcke characteristically builds up an extreme nationalist interpretation of German cultural claims on Alsace.

20. Schulze, *Die örtliche und soziale Herkunft,* 107.

21. D. Strémooukhoff, "Les Russes à Strasbourg au XVIIIᵉ siècle," *Revue d'Alsace* (Delle-Thann-Colmar, 1934), 81:3–21.

22. BL Karlsruhe, Karlsruher Hs. 517, fol. 118–119, contains a list of scholarships offered by local Strasbourg endowments in 1728. There were a total of twenty-three such *bourses,* of which the largest was six hundred livres per year, while the average was about three hundred.

23. Quoted by Strémooukhoff, "Les Russes à Strasbourg," 5.

24. A related example of cosmopolitan variety is revealed in the first two of a series of articles edited by Emile Longin, "Souveniers d'un étudiant de l'Université de Strasbourg, 1783–1793," *Revue catholique d'Alsace* (Strasbourg, 1921), 36:297–304 and 380–392. Longin had access to the journal of one Wilhelm Ludwig von Fergusson Tepper, son of a rich Warsaw banker descended from Scotch Calvinists. The young Pole, as a student from 1783 to 1789, was endlessly excited over being in France — for that is what Strasbourg meant to him.

25. "Aus dem Reise-Tagebuch des jungen Herzogs Karl August zu Sachsen-Meiningen, 1775," in Ludwig Bechstein, *Mitteilungen aus den Leben der Herzoge zu Sachsen-Meiningen* (Halle, 1856), 80–172.

26. *Nachgelassene Papiere,* ed. Prince Richard von Metternich (Vienna, 1880), I, 7 ff. See also H. Ritter von Srbik, *Metternich: Der Staatsmann und der Mensch* (Munich, 1925), I, 65–69, for this period in the Austrian statesman's life.

27. Johann Heinrich Jung, *Jung-Stillings Lebensgeschichte von ihm selbst erzählt,* ed. A. Dömel (Constance, 1929), 83–93.

28. C. Van Huffel, ed., *Documents inédits concernant l'histoire de France, et particulièrement l'Alsace et son gouvernement sous le règne de Louis XIV* (Paris, 1840), 135.

Social Changes 293

29. Reuss, *Histoire de Strasbourg,* 292–293, discusses this slow advance.
30. BNU Strasbourg, M. 9529, *Strassburgs Regiments-Verfassung* (annual).
31. AM Strasbourg, Série V, 52.84 and 52.92. It is interesting to note the high proportion of early French immigrants in Strasbourg engaged in retailing food and beverages. Later evidence shows that in 1748 the six *maîtres caffetiers* who petitioned the Magistrat concerning several tax questions were named Schropp, Chauvin, Dupont, Duclos, Falconnet, and Dürr. BL Karlsruhe, Karlsruher Hs. 517, fol. 444.
32. BNU Strasbourg, Ms. 1032, "Gerber Zunfft-Büchel."
33. Meyer, *Die Strassburger Goldschmiedezunft,* 214–224, reproduces the membership list from the guild's records.
34. BNU Strasbourg, Ms. 767.
35. Quoted by Loeper, *Rheinschifffahrt,* 44.
36. Figures from Georges Livet, "La monarchie absolue et la bourgeoisie alsacienne," in *La bourgeoisie alsacienne: Etudes d'histoire sociale,* Jean Schlumberger et al., eds. (Strasbourg-Paris, 1954), 137.
37. AM Strasbourg, Série VI, 94.19.
38. The inspiration for Johann Fischart's classic, *Das glückhafte Schiff von Zürich* (Strasbourg, 1577).
39. Hermann, *Notices,* I, 314–315.
40. AM Strasbourg, AA. 2445.
41. *Ibid.*
42. AD Bas-Rhin, G. 375.
43. Charles Gérard, *L'ancienne Alsace à table* (Colmar, 1862), *passim.*
44. "Le pâté de foie gras de Strasbourg, son histoire et ses inventeurs," *Almanach de l'Alsace et des Marches de l'Est* (Mulhouse, 1951), 87–89. The contributions of non-Alsatian Frenchmen to the development of Strasbourg's epicurean specialty are emphasized in this anonymous piece. Claude, called "Close" or "Clause" in Alsace, was a Lorrainer by origin. Nicolas-François Doyen, who during the Revolution completed the modern recipe by adding truffles to the pâté, was a Parisian who had come to Strasbourg after having been chef to the First President of the Parlement of Bordeaux.
45. Benoist d'Anthenay, *Le premier administrateur de l'Alsace française,* 45.
46. BN Paris, Ms. fr. 4285.
47. BNU Strasbourg, M. 40.358.
48. See above, pp. 124–125.
49. AD Bas-Rhin, C. 581, piece 92, *Arrêté du préteur Klinglin sur l'établissement d'une maison des enfants trouvés,* dated December 14, 1748, and printed in both French and German.
50. Jacques Hatt, "Intérieurs du vieux Strasbourg: I, L'hôtel Mueg en 1702," *Les Dernières Nouvelles du Dimanche, Supplément* (Strasbourg, February 11–18, 1923).
51. *L'Alsace au dix-septième siècle,* II, 36–42.
52. Quoted by Hoffmann, *L'Alsace au XVIIIᵉ siècle,* I, 8.

53. BN Paris, Ms. fr. 8151.
54. AM Strasbourg, Série IV, 102.
55. BNU Strasbourg, Ms. 1228, is a painstaking analysis of the forty-nine bona fide families of the Lower Alsatian *noblesse immédiate* in 1716. See also J. H. Wielandt, *Statuts et privilèges de la noblesse franche et immédiate de la Basse Alsace, accordés par les anciens empereurs, confirmés et augmentés par le Roy* (Strasbourg, 1713), also published in German.
56. For comments on French royal legislation touching noble status in Alsace, see Emil von Borries, "Das Geschlecht von Müllenheim, sein Aufsteigen, seine Entwicklung und Ausbreitung," *Zeitschrift für die Geschichte des Oberrheins* (Heidelberg, 1909), 63 (NF 24): 445–471.
57. AM Strasbourg, AA. 2188, contains the records of such a conflict over protocol among Constoffler, finally settled by the royal praetor.
58. BL Karlsruhe, Karlsruher Hss. 521–522, comprise a big collection of documents concerning Alsatian nobles' fiefs in Baden and Badeners' in Alsace, as well as numerous adjudications by the Directory of the Immediate Nobility in Strasbourg, showing how thoroughly interlocked feudal landholding remained, as between the left and right banks of the Rhine, until the Revolution.
59. AM Strasbourg, Série III, 52.23.
60. Johann Froitzheim, *Zu Strassburgs Sturm- und Drangperiode, 1770–1776* (Strasbourg, 1888), 60–87.

CHAPTER EIGHT

FRENCH INFLUENCES AND GERMAN RESIDUES

1. Henri Peyre, *La royauté et les langues provinciales* (Paris, 1933), concentrates on Alsace and Roussillon.
2. Letter to the Marquis d'Argens, dated March 3, 1754. Louis Moland, ed., *Oeuvres complètes de Voltaire* (Paris, 1880), XXXVIII, 182.
3. For the full text of this law, as well as an excellent discussion of costume as one of the areas of change during the first century of French rule, see Hans Haug, "Le style Louis XIV à Strasbourg: Essai sur la transition entre la 'manière allemande' et le 'goût français' (1681–1730)," *Archives alsaciennes d'histoire de l'art* (Strasbourg-Paris, 1924), 3:65–111.
4. AM Strasbourg, Série V, 54.3.
5. BN Paris, Ms. fr. 4285.
6. Ernst Polaczek, ed., "Das Strassburger Tagebuch des Johann Friedrich von Uffenbach aus Frankfurt (1712–1714)," *Elsass-lothringisches Jahrbuch* (Berlin, 1922), 1:70.
7. Paul Lévy, *Histoire linguistique d'Alsace et de Lorraine: Tome I, Des origines à la Révolution française* (Paris, 1929); Constantin This, *Die deutsch-französische Sprachgrenze im Elsass* (Strasbourg, 1888); Karl

Zwilling, "Die französische Sprache in Strassburg bis zu ihrer Aufnahme in den Lehrplan des protestantischen Gymnasiums," in *Festschrift zur Feier des 350 Jährigen Bestehens des Protestantischen Gymnasiums zu Strassburg* (Strasbourg, 1888), I, 255–304.

8. This exchange has been published by Edmond Arnould, "Document relatif à la conquête de l'Alsace," *Bulletin des Comités historiques. Histoire, sciences, lettres* (Paris, 1850), 2:157; and by Lévy, *Histoire linguistique,* I, 295–298.

9. BN Paris, Ms. fr. 8152.

10. AD Bas-Rhin, G. 375, contains the printed announcement of the *Wochenblatt's* double edition.

11. Hans Molz, *Die elsässische Presse im 18. Jahrhundert bis zum Ausbruch der Revolution* (Strasbourg, 1937), 62–65.

12. AM Strasbourg, Série VI, 94.13.

13. Concerning this change, see Jacques Hatt, "Le Gymnase en 1738," in *Quatrième centenaire du Gymnase Protestant de Strasbourg, 1538–1938* (Strasbourg, 1939), 299–324.

14. Lévy, *Histoire linguistique,* 329–338, devotes particular attention to language and social structure in Strasbourg.

15. Rodolphe Reuss, *Vieux noms et rues nouvelles de Strasbourg* (Strasbourg, 1883), 47–48.

16. See above, p. 22.

17. Such a tour, by Pastor Jean-Chrétien Oertel and the future professor, Lorenz, in 1768 is well described by the former, in a long letter printed by Ernest Hoepffner, *Der Pfarrer Georg Jakob Eissen, seine Freunde und seine Zeitgenossen* (Strasbourg, 1906), 122–127.

18. Orléans, for legal studies, had been especially popular.

19. Fritz Jaffé, *Elsässische Studenten an deutschen Hochschulen (1648 bis 1870) mit besonderer Berücksichtigung des 18. Jahrhunderts* (Frankfurt am Main, 1932).

20. This shift is clearly shown by Jaffé's tables. See also Maria Joseph Bopp, "Die elsässischen Studenten im Amicistenorden zu Jena, mit besonderer Berücksichtigung des Gründungsjahres 1770," *Elsass-lothringisches Jahrbuch* (Frankfurt am Main, 1943), 21:245–290.

21. A. Salomon, "Le pasteur alsacien C.-F. Baer, chapelain de l'ambassade de Suède à Paris (1719–1797). Appendice: Les Strasbourgeois à Paris au XVIIIᵉ siècle," *Bulletin de la Société de l'histoire du protestantisme français* (Paris, 1925), 74:448–452.

22. Fernand L'Huillier, "Remarques sur les journaux strasbourgeois de la première moitié du XVIIIᵉ siècle (1715–1760)," *Revue d'Alsace* (Delle-Thann-Colmar, 1936), 83:140.

23. Fester, ed., *Schoepflins brieflicher Verkehr.* Among the many other examples of scholarly correspondence, the following are of special interest: BNU Strasbourg, letters from Professor Lorenz to Academy Director André Lamey at Mannheim (Ms. 76 [1751–1785]), letters from Professor

J.-J. Oberlin to Lamey (Ms. 786 [1767–1797]), letters from Lorenz to Professor G. A. Francke at Halle (Ms. 1554 [1762–1770]); as well as Ernst Baumann, *Strassburg, Basel und Zürich in ihren geistigen und kulturellen Beziehungen im ausgehenden 18. Jahrhundert: Beiträge und Briefe aus dem Freundeskreise der Lavater, Pfeffel, Sarasin und Schweighaeuser, 1770–1810* (Gelnhausen, 1937).

24. AM Strasbourg, AA. 2647, contains Nicolay's letters to Praetor Baron d'Autigny.

25. AM Strasbourg, AA. 2298, a file of projects for the establishment of periodicals, sent to Praetor Gérard in the 1780's, shows how regular the appeal to the city's "middle-man" position had become by that time.

26. Molz, *Die elsässische Presse*, 65.

27. Despite Frédéric-Louis Ehrmann's respectable treatise, *Des ballons aerostatiques et de l'art de les faire* (Strasbourg, 1784), the Council of Thirteen tried in vain to prevent all ascensions, AM Strasbourg, Minutes for 1784, 295.

28. Jacques Matter, *Saint-Martin: Le philosophe inconnu,* 2nd ed. (Paris, 1864) 146–189.

29. C. Photiadès, *Les vies du comte de Cagliostro* (Paris, 1932), 192–245; Emile Edighoffen, "Cagliostro als Freimaurer in Strassburg," *Heimat* (Sélestat, 1922), 2:99–102; Heinrich Funck, "Cagliostro in Strassburg," *Archiv für Kultur-Geschichte* (Berlin, 1905), 3:223–234. The strange, diffuse work of Henri Béraldi, *Ramond de Carbonnières: Le cardinal de Rohan — Cagliostro* (Paris, 1919), manages to convey the weird atmosphere surrounding the whole episode, albeit sometimes by slipping into the fallacy of imitative form.

30. Ernst Wilhelm Martius, *Erinnerungen aus meinem neunzigjährigen Leben* (Leipzig, 1847), 74–76.

31. *Mémoires de la baronne d'Oberkirch,* I, 134–150, *passim.*

32. AM Strasbourg, AA. 2110, is the royal praetor's file on local opposition to Cagliostro.

33. It is impossible to list all of Haug's contributions to this general topic. Aside from his *Trois siècles d'art alsacien, 1648–1948* (Strasbourg, 1948), I should call attention to his articles on "Le style Louis XIV," already cited; "L'architecture régence à Strasbourg (1725–1760)," *Archives alsaciennes d'histoire de l'art* (Strasbourg-Paris, 1926), 5:133–197; "François-Rodolphe Mollinger et les services d'architecture strasbourgeois au XVIIIᵉ siècle," *ibid.*, 2:97–139 (1923); "Trois artistes méridionaux à Strasbourg," *ibid.*, 6:113–170 (1927); and *La ferronnerie strasbourgeoise au XVIIᵉ et au XVIIIᵉ siècle* (Paris-Strasbourg, 1933), a companion piece to his *Faïences et porcelaines de Strasbourg.*

34. Polaczek, ed., "Das Strassburger Tagebuch des Johann Friedrich von Uffenbach," 106–108.

35. Marcel Moeder, "Les *ex-libris* alsaciens du XVIᵉ siècle," *Archives alsaciennes d'histoire de l'art* (Strasbourg-Paris, 1922), 1:53–64; "Les *ex-libris*

alsaciens du XVIIᵉ siècle," *ibid.*, 3:55–64 (1924); "Les graveurs français et les *ex-libris* alsaciens du XVIIIᵉ siècle," *ibid.*, 5:199–209 (1926).

36. For a discussion of the catalogues of private galleries, see Hans Rott, "Strassburger Kunstkammern im 17. und 18. Jahrhundert," *Zeitschrift für die Geschichte des Oberrheins* (Karlsruhe, 1930), 83 (NF 44): 1–46.

37. Charles Schnéegans, "L'enseignement des arts en Alsace: Les écoles de dessin de Strasbourg au XVIIIᵉ siècle," *Archives alsaciennes d'histoire de l'art* (Strasbourg-Paris, 1927), 6:185–224.

38. A contemporary account of the obsequies and description of the monument appeared in the weekly, *Der Bürgerfreund,* as a supplement to its issue of August 22, 1777.

39. Ernst Polaczek, "Jacques-François Blondel und das Strassburger Münster," *Elsass-lothringisches Jahrbuch* (Frankfurt am Main, 1929), 8:265–270. An interesting discussion of how maintenance of the cathedral was organized in the eighteenth century, under exclusively "German" master-masons, will be found in François Pariset, "Etude sur l'atelier de la cathédrale de Strasbourg entre 1681 et 1789," *Archives alsaciennes d'histoire de l'art* (Strasbourg-Paris, 1929), 8:169–207.

40. Jeanne Lejeaux, "Jacques-François Blondel à Strasbourg," *La vie en Alsace* (Strasbourg, 1927), 32–39; Ernst Polaczek, "Der Strassburger Stadtregulierungsplan des Pariser Architekten Blondel (1765)," *Zeitschrift für die Geschichte des Oberrheins* (Heidelberg, 1915), 69 (NF 30): 410–426.

41. AM Strasbourg, St. Thomas 335, contains the notice of a small grant from the university to the Meistersänger as late as 1780. That same year, however, they gave their remaining assets to the municipal orphanage when they disbanded. Ernst Martin, *Die Meistersänger von Strassburg* (Strasbourg, 1882); and J. Lefftz, "Strassburger Meistersingertage im XVIII. Jahrhundert," *Elsassland, Lothringer Heimat* (Guebwiller, 1928), 8:260–264.

42. Ludwig, *Strassburg vor hundert Jahren,* 150–152.

43. Ernest Burglin, "La période strasbourgeoise de la vie de Mozart," *Saisons d'Alsace* (Strasbourg, 1954), 21:48.

44. *Ibid.*

CHAPTER NINE

TWO LITERATURES BUT ONE ALLEGIANCE

1. An excellent discussion of this problem is that by Ernest Hoepffner, "Les influences littéraires de la France sur les lettres en Alsace," *Bulletin de la Société des Amis de l'Université de Strasbourg* (Strasbourg, 1926), No. 12.

2. Voltaire, *Lettres d'Alsace à sa nièce Madame Denis,* G. Jean-Aubry, ed. (Paris, 1938), 199, dated April 12, 1754.

3. *Ibid.*, 217, dated May 12, 1754.

4. Maurice Mutterer, "Jean-Jacques Rousseau à Strasbourg," *Revue alsacienne illustrée* (Strasbourg, 1904), 6:63–67.

5. Fester, ed., *Schoepflins brieflicher Verkehr*, 187, to Lamey at Mannheim, November 13, 1765.

6. A letter to Thérèse Le Vasseur, written November 4, 1765, and unaccountably preserved among James Boswell's papers, reveals Rousseau's attitude as expressed to his mistress jut two days after reaching Strasbourg, in which he plans to rest and "from which I hope they will not chase me at this time of year and in my present state of health. . . . This city is large, beautiful and populous." *Boswell on the Grand Tour: Italy, Corsica, and France, 1765–1766,* Frank Brady and Frederick A. Pottle, eds. (New York, 1955), 318–320, including translation.

7. Georges Bergner, "Les comédiens allemands à Strasbourg au XVIIIe siècle," *Alsace française* (Strasbourg, 1926), 6:810–813.

8. *Ibid.*, 812.

9. Pantaléon Deck, *Histoire du Théatre français à Strasbourg, 1681–1830* (Strasbourg-Paris, 1948), 9–50.

10. Albrecht von Haller, *Tagebuch der Studienreise nach London, Paris, Strassburg und Basel, 1727 bis 1728,* E. Hintzsche, ed. (Bern, 1942), 39.

11. AM Strasbourg, AA. 2161. This payroll is for 1753–1754.

12. Stoeber, *Curiosités de voyages,* 187–188.

13. Anyone acquainted with the mass of available writing on Goethe will appreciate the impossibility of listing here, or in ensuing footnotes, all the works relevant to even this limited segment of his career. I am fortunate in being able to refer readers interested in such a catalogue to Reinhard Buchwald, ed., *Goethe, der Mensch, der Dichter, der Denker: Bücher von ihm und über ihn,* revised by Ruth Sierks (Hamburg, 1951). Goethe's own role as a source encompasses both his *Dichtung und Wahrheit,* most recently reprinted at Leipzig in 1952, Kurt Jahn, ed., translated by Minna Steele Smith, *Poetry and Truth* (London, 1908), and Max Morris, ed., *Der junge Goethe* (Leipzig, 1909), I. See also: Ernst Martin, *Goethe in Strassburg* (Berlin, 1871); Richard Weissenfels, *Goethe im Sturm und Drang* (Halle, 1894), I, 121–245; Ernst Traumann, *Goethe, der Strassburger Student* (Leipzig, 1923); Witkop, *Goethe in Strassburg,* already noted, and his *Goethe, Leben und Werk* (Stuttgart-Berlin, 1931), 45–73. On the French side, the following deserve special attention: Louis Spach, "La ville et l'université de Strasbourg en 1770," *Congrès scientifique de France, X^e session (1842):* I. *Procès-verbaux* (Strasbourg-Paris, 1843), I, 65–81; Jean de Pange, *Goethe en Alsace* (Paris, 1925); Edmond Vermeil, "Goethe à Strasbourg," in *Goethe: Etudes publiées pour le centenaire de sa mort* (Paris, 1932), 3–93; Albert Fuchs, *Goethe: Un homme face la vie: I. La jeunesse, 1749–1775* (Paris, 1946), 151–212.

14. Morris, ed., *Der junge Goethe,* II, 4–5.

15. Knod, ed., *Die alten Matrikeln,* I, 85.

16. Froitzheim, *Zu Strassburgs Sturm- und Drangperiode,* 12–18; August

Stöber, *Der Aktuar Salzmann, Goethe's Freund und Tischgenosse in Strassburg* (Frankfurt am Main, 1855); F. Dollinger, "Jean-Daniel Salzmann, ami de Goethe," *L'Alsace française* (Strasbourg, 1932), 23:241–249.

17. Dömel, ed., *Jung-Stillings Lebensgeschichte.*

18. "Goethe à Strasbourg," 43.

19. On this controversial figure, see Erich Schmidt, *Heinrich Leopold Wagner, Goethes Jugendgenosse* (Jena, 1879), 2nd ed.; A. Sauer, *Stürmer und Dränger: II, Lenz und Wagner* (Berlin-Stuttgart [1883]); and F. Wendel, "Les déboires de Henri-Léopold Wagner," *L'Alsace française* (Strasbourg, 1932), 23:250–256. Froitzheim devoted his *Goethe und Heinrich Leopold Wagner* (Strasbourg, 1889) to defending the latter against the former's unfavorable characterization in *Poetry and Truth.*

20. Morris, ed., *Der junge Goethe,* II, 13.

21. Knod, ed., *Die alten Matrikeln,* II, 632 (*Matricula Candidatorum Juris*).

22. The above-mentioned notes, which Goethe called his *Ephémérides,* were published at Heilbronn in 1883. They are scarcely more than jottings about reading done in 1770, mostly before coming to Strasbourg; but they do contain some indication of books he was interested in while there, as well as a few references to Alsatian manners and forms of speech. Reproduced by Morris, ed., *Der junge Goethe,* II, 26–50.

23. Eugen Kühnemann, *Herder* (Munich, 1927), 3rd ed., 101–121, gives a good account of the Nantes-to-Strasbourg period.

24. Hans Reisiger, ed., *Johann Gottfried Herder: Sein Leben in Selbstzeugnissen, Briefen und Berichten* (Berlin, 1942), 109.

25. Walther Goeken, *Herder als Deutscher* (Stuttgart, 1926), 46–49; Grete Eichler, *Der nationale Gedanke bei Herder* (Emsdetten, 1934). A discussion of Herder's nationalism stressing its later, modified form appears in Lucien Lévy-Bruhl, *L'Allemagne depuis Leibniz: Essai sur le développement de la conscience nationale en Allemagne, 1700–1848* (Paris, 1890), 151–188. The best discussions available in English are Robert R. Ergang, *Herder and the Foundations of German Nationalism* (New York, 1931); Robert Thomas Clark, *Herder: His Life and Thought* (Berkeley, 1955); and Alexander Gillies, *Herder* (Oxford, 1945).

26. Louis Pinck, ed., *Volkslieder von Goethe im Elsass gesammelt mit Melodien und Varianten aus Lothringen und dem Faksimiledruck der Strassburger Goethe-Handschrift* (Heidelberg-Metz, 1932); Max Freiherr von Waldberg, "Goethe und das Volkslied: Herders Einfluss auf den jungen Goethe," also "Einfluss und Anteil des Volksliedes auf Goethes Lyrik," *Vossische Zeitung, Sonntagsbeilage* (Berlin, 1889), Nos. 38 and 39.

27. In the collection, *Von deutscher Art und Kunst* (Hamburg, 1773), most recently printed at Frankfurt am Main in 1923 and at Berlin in 1940.

28. In addition to the essay by Henri Tronchon, "Goethe, Herder et Diderot," in *Goethe: Etudes publiées pour le centenaire de sa mort,* 113–126, see Geneviève Bianquis, "Goethe et Voltaire," in her *Etudes sur Goethe* (Paris, 1951), 91–98, for the influence on the poet of the old Frenchman's

style and "social impulse" as well. Hermann A. Korff, *Voltaire im litera-rischen Deutschland des XVIII. Jahrhunderts* (Heidelberg, 1918), devotes the concluding chapter, II, 751–769, specifically to Goethe's appreciation.

29. Vermeil, "Goethe à Strasbourg," 23.

30. *Ibid.* L. A. Willoughby's introduction to *Goethe's "Urfaust" and "Faust, ein Fragment"* (Oxford, 1943) stresses the importance of the period 1769–1771 in the development of Goethe's masterpiece.

31. Of the profuse literature concerning the Sesenheim idyl, I should here take space to cite only the following: Johann Froitzheim, *Friederike von Sesenheim* (Gotha, 1893); Adolf Metz, *Friederike Brion* (Munich, 1911); and Stephan Ley, *Goethe und Friederike: Versuch einer kritischen Schlussbetrachtung* (Bonn, 1947). Still of interest for its local color is the old work of Philipp Ferdinand Lucius, *Friederike Brion von Sesenheim* (Strasbourg, 1877).

32. Froitzheim, *Zu Strassburgs Sturm- und Drangperiode,* 11.

33. The fullest biography is that by M. N. Rosanow, *Jakob M. R. Lenz, der Dichter der Sturm- und Drangperiode* (Leipzig, 1909), tr. from the Russian by C. von Gütschow. See also Erich Schmidt, *Lenz und Klinger: Zwei Dichter der Geniezeit* (Berlin, 1878), 1–61.

34. Rosanow, *Lenz,* 54.

35. For relevant correspondence, see especially Karl Freye and Wolfgang Stammler, eds., *Briefe von und an J. M. R. Lenz* (Leipzig, 1918). Froitzheim's *Lenz und Goethe* (Stuttgart, 1891), though chiefly devoted to the later incidents at Weimar, also contributes to our knowledge of the Strasbourg period.

36. Froitzheim, *Lenz, Goethe und Cleophe Fibich von Strassburg* (Strasbourg, 1888); also L. Urlichs, "Etwas von Lenz," *Deutsche Rundschau* (Berlin, 1877), 11:254–292, for the text of the so-called "diary" which was actually the first outline of the plot for *Die Soldaten.*

37. Rosanow, *Lenz,* 99 ff.; August Stöber, *Der Dichter Lenz und Friederike von Sesenheim* (Basel, 1842).

38. Knod, ed., *Die alten Matrikeln,* I, 109 and 693 (the latter page referring to the *Matricula Studiosorum Facultatis Theologicae*).

39. Hermann, *Notices,* II, 368; Fritz Kiener, "L'humanisme alsacien," in *Publications de la Faculté des Lettres de l'Université de Strasbourg: Mélanges 1945* (Strasbourg, 1945), I, 93–110, stresses the importance of Wimpheling and his friends in the history of German national feeling, as does Joseph Knepper, at greater length but also with some anachronistic exaggeration, in his *Nationaler Gedanke und Kaiseridee bei den elsässischen Humanisten* (Freiburg im Breisgau, 1898).

40. Hermann, *Notices,* II, 369; Reuss, *L'Alsace au dix-septième siècle,* II, 223.

41. Sittler, ed., *Geschichte des Elsass,* II, 183.

42. Hoffmann, *L'Alsace au XVIII⁰ siècle,* I, 156–157.

43. Froitzheim, *Zu Strassburgs Sturm- und Drangperiode,* 24–32.

44. Rudolf Zoeppritz, ed., *Aus F. H. Jacobi's Nachlass* (Leipzig, 1869), II, 317–318.

45. August Stoeber, *Johann Gottfried Röderer von Strassburg und seine Freunde* (Colmar, 1874).

46. These twenty-two handwritten sheets form the basis for an important chapter in Froitzheim, *Zu Strassburgs Sturm- und Drangperiode,* 33–54.

47. In the *Leben* of Georg Zoëga, Friedrich Gottlieb Welcker, ed. (Stuttgart-Tübingen, 1819), I, 145, the Danish archaeologist and art historian tells of having attended a meeting of the group in April 1776, when he was passing through Strasbourg en route to Italy (cf. I, 29). Lenz was gone by then, but Blessig read a paper on logic, and F.-R. Salzmann recited from his own translation of *The Vicar of Wakefield.*

48. Besides the discussions of this situation to be found in the cited works of Rosanow, Froitzheim, Schmidt, Sauer, and, for that matter, Goethe himself, there are two major works by Hermann A. Korff, *Geist der Goethezeit* (Leipzig, 1923–1953), and *Die Dichtung von Sturm und Drang* (Leipzig, 1928).

49. An editorial in *Der Bürgerfreund* for July 4, 1777, remarks sadly that Rousseau now merely writes music and amuses people, but concludes: "Anyone who has done what Rousseau has, who has contributed so much to the enlightenment, to the improvement of mankind, borne so much and such harsh persecution and slander, who has had so much to overcome with respect to his health — and who has the heart left to write notes — him we shall absolve."

50. Oskar Zollinger, *Louis-Sébastien Mercier als Dramatiker und Dramaturg* (Strasbourg, 1899).

51. *Relation des réjouissances ordonnées et faites par la ville de Strasbourg dans les derniers jours du mois de septembre 1781, à l'occasion de l'époque séculaire de la soumission de cette ville à France en 1681* (Strasbourg, 1781).

52. BN Paris, 8° Lb^{37} .3748, is a printed French translation of this dreadful poem.

53. *L'Alsace au dix-septième siècle,* II, 599.

54. The most thorough effort to survey this development, from a French point of view, is that of Jacques Hatt, "Le loyalisme des Alsaciens depuis le traité de Ryswick jusqu'à la Révolution," *Revue historique* (Paris, 1930), 165:83–108, though Christian Pfister too, in his *Pages alsaciennes* (Strasbourg, 1927), 50–61, has devoted some perceptive paragraphs to the subject. Important background material appears in the chapter on Alsace and France which Georges Livet contributed to *Comment les Français voyaient la France au XVIIe siècle,* Roland Mousnier, ed. (Paris, 1955), 103–130, and in L. Batiffol, "Les difficultés de Louis XIV avec les Alsaciens," *Revue de Paris* (Paris, 1930), 37:564–593 and 843–871.

55. BNU Strasbourg, Ms. 1486.

56. BNU Strasbourg, Ms. 591.

57. *Memorial,* 103.

58. Bourgeois discusses this memorandum in his *Neuchâtel et la politique prussienne,* 126 ff. Various other historians have emphasized that this was

Notes to Chapter Nine

a propaganda piece; and Schulte, *Frankreich und das linke Rheinufer,* 210, even develops the theory that it was of Swiss origin, reflecting the Confederation's desire to see the French pushed out of Franche-Comté. There is no agreement on that point; but French and German scholars have joined in discounting the "Schmettau memorandum" as a possible source bearing on Alsatian attitudes.

59. For an example of violently anti-Hapsburg sentiment at the time of the War of the Austrian Succession, see Albert Burckhardt, ed., "Ein politisches Gedicht aus dem Elsass vom Jahre 1743," *Basler Jahrbuch* (Basel, 1883), 35–47.

60. Reisseissen in 1694, for example, was distinctly worried over the small size of the French garrison. *Memorial,* 177.

61. Christian Pfister, "Jean-Daniel Schoepflin," *Annales de l'Est* (Nancy, 1887–1888), 1:34–63, 184–220, 349–368; 2:176–223, amounts to a full analysis of his views.

62. Fester, ed., *Schoepflins brieflicher Verkehr,* 130.

63. *Ibid.,* 281.

64. *Ibid.,* 120.

65. Manfred Eimer, *Die politischen Verhältnisse und Bewegungen in Strassburg im Elsass im Jahre 1789* (Strasbourg, 1897), 2.

66. Quoted in Haug, "Le style Louis XIV," 108.

CHAPTER TEN

SEVENTEEN EIGHTY-NINE

1. *Travels in France during the Years 1787, 1788 & 1789,* Constantia Maxwell, ed. (Cambridge, 1929), 180.

2. The fullest rendering of the narrative is that by Manfred Eimer, *Die politischen Verhältnisse und Bewegungen in Strassburg . . . im Jahre 1789,* while Félix Ponteil, *Strasbourg en 1789* (Strasbourg, 1939), supplies a convenient summary in French. Both the early account by L. Hermann Engelhardt, in continuation of Adam Walther Strobel's *Vaterländische Geschichte des Elsasses* (Strasbourg, 1851), Vol. V, and that of Eugène Seinguerlet, *Strasbourg pendant la Révolution* (Paris, 1881), contain numerous small inaccuracies; but both recount interesting details not found in more compressed studies. A source collection of immense narrative importance is Rodolphe Reuss, ed., *L'Alsace pendant la Révolution française: I, Correspondance des députés de Strasbourg à l'Assemblé nationale, 1789* (Strasbourg, 1880).

3. Fritz Langenbeck, for example, based his article, "Die Politik der elsässischen Selbstverwaltung, 1787–1789," *Elsass-lothringisches Jahrbuch* (Frankfurt am Main, 1932), 11:179–229, on the minutes of the Provincial Assembly and the Intermediary Commission.

4. AM Strasbourg, Minutes of the Council of Thirteen, January 19, 1789.

5. This summons is inserted separately in AM Strasbourg, Minutes of the Senate-and-XXI for 1789. The only other cities accorded special representation in the Estates General were Paris, Metz, Valenciennes, and Arles.

6. BNU Strasbourg, M 40.527(2–3), copies of the Magistrat's printed announcement in French and German.

7. BNU Strasbourg, M 40.527(6), is a printed list of the 126 electors.

8. BNU Strasbourg, M 9504, for example, is a fifteen-page pamphlet, entitled *An meine Strasburgischen Mitbürger* and devoted to an attack on the Secret Chambers, particularly in connection with the administration of local taxes. The anonymous author, who speaks as a former Senator, believes the reckoning is at hand. M 40.527(5) is a similar statement, *Unmassgeblicher Vorschlag einiger Deputirten der Strasburgischen Zünfte zu einem Vereinigungspunkt ihrer Klagen, geschrieben Freitage Morgens den 20. März 1789.*

9. BNU Strasbourg, M 40.527(1), an eight-page pamphlet, *An die Bürger der Stadt Strassburg,* contrasts the election of deputies in other cities with the method imposed by the local Magistrat and demands a fuller voice for the citizenry in formulating appeals to the coming Estates General.

10. AM Strasbourg, Minutes of the Senate-and-XXI, April 8, 1789.

11. BNU Strasbourg, Ms. 1633, "Hefte der Wünsche der Bewohner des dritten Standes der Stadt Strassburg." This cahier is unaccountably missing from among the other Alsatian ones in the *Archives parlementaires de 1787 à 1860* (Paris, 1879), Vols. III and V, but may be found in Reuss, *L'Alsace pendant la Révolution,* I, 31–36.

12. Werner, *Le rattachement douanier de l'Alsace à la France,* 55–81, reproduces an interesting document which forms part of the background for this demand. It is a memorandum prepared by the Strasbourg merchants' guild, in opposition to any encroachment upon the region's customs privileges, and sent to the Intermediary Commission of the Provincial Assembly on February 19, 1789. One of the drafters who signed this statement, by the way, was the same Jean-Georges Schertz we saw earlier engaged in discoursing on tariff questions under the old regime (pp. 143–146, above).

13. The Senate-and-XXI had voted each of the deputies thirty livres per day subsistence and eight hundred livres for travel.

14. AM Strasbourg, Minutes of the Council of Thirteen, May 16, 1789.

15. BNU Strasbourg, M 40.527(7–8), *Rapport fait le 2 juin 1789, à MM. les représentants de la bourgeoisie, par les sept commissaires nommés pour conférer avec la députation du Magistrat* (Strasbourg, 1789), expresses the indignant reaction of the citizens' spokesmen to their opponents' manifesto of that day.

16. One of the best ways to follow Dietrich's official career is through the file of letters published by Rodolphe Reuss, in no fewer than thirty-three

instalments, "L'Alsace pendant la Révolution française: Correspondances adressées à Frédéric de Dietrich," *Revue d'Alsace* (Belfort-Colmar-Thann, 1921–1931). Gabriel Ramon's admiring biography, *Frédéric de Dietrich, premier maire de Strasbourg* (Nancy-Paris-Strasbourg, 1919), was sharply attacked by Albert Mathiez, "Un complice de Lafayette, Frédéric Dietrich," *Annales révolutionnaires* (Besançon, 1920), 12:389–408 and 471–499.

17. AD Bas-Rhin, C. 575(102), "Mémoire pour la communauté réformée de Strasbourg, etc."

18. AM Strasbourg, Minutes of the Council of Thirteen, July 1, 1789.

19. BNU Strasbourg, Ms. 875, fol. 17.

20. Jean-Baptiste-Donatien de Vimeur, Comte de Rochambeau, *Mémoires militaires, historiques et politiques*, C.-J. Luce de Lancival, ed. (Paris, 1809), I, 348–367, deals with the period of his service at Strasbourg, July to December 1789.

21. The most determined effort to solve the basically insoluble problem of individual roles in the causation of the riot is that by Rodolphe Reuss, "Le sac de l'hôtel de ville de Strasbourg," *Revue historique* (Paris, 1915), 120:26–55 and 289–322, an indictment of Klinglin in particular.

22. *Travels in France*, 183.

23. The surviving minutes of the Fifteen, for example, end on July 18 with a torn and apparently wine-soaked page.

24. An expression of the low esteem into which the Magistrat had fallen was the jeering poem, *Der Pöbelaufruhr zu Strassburg*, by Auguste Lamey (Dorlisheim, 1789).

25. BNU Strasbourg, Ms. 1159, fol. 6, dated August 3, 1789.

26. *Ibid.*, fol. 7, also dated August 3.

27. Adrien Blanchet, "Les journées de juillet et août 1789 à Strasbourg," *Revue historique* (Paris, 1921), 138:57–69, contains a valuable letter about this troop uprising, written by a veteran officer named Guiot to the secretary of the First President of the Parlement of Flanders, at Douai.

28. The first portion of Etienne Barth's long serialization of "Notes biographiques sur les hommes de la Révolution à Strasbourg," *Revue d'Alsace* (Colmar, 1877–1883), comprises data on all 269 men who actually made up this reformed "Three Hundred," 6:5–42, 145–176, 401–432, 504–548; 7:127–144.

29. AM Strasbourg, "Memoriale Eines Hochlöbl. Gesamten Raths."

30. AM Strasbourg, "Memoriale der algemeinen Schöffen-Versammlungen, 1789–1790," with "Acta" and "Rapiaria."

31. AM Strasbourg, Memorial der Finanzkamer, 1789–1790.

32. AM Strasbourg, Minutes of the Senate-and-XXI, in the volume of "Rapiaria, 1782–1789." The long *Mémoire de droit public sur la ville de Strasbourg et l'Alsace en général*, published anonymously by Jean de Turckheim in 1789 (with a simultaneous German edition, *Abhandlung*

das Staatsrecht der Stadt Strassburg . . . betreffend), was in effect only a development and defense of the city's official statement.

33. Among the printed denunciations of the August decrees by Catholic agencies were the pamphlet, *Pour le grand chapitre de la cathédrale de Strasbourg* (Strasbourg, 1789), a much longer *Mémoire et observations du prince-évêque de Strasbourg* (Versailles, 1789) and the *Promemoria der Clerisey des unteren Elsasses* (s.l., 1789). The last is summarized by F.-C. Heitz, *La contrerévolution en Alsace de 1789 à 1793* (Strasbourg, 1865), 3–4.

34. Jean Richerateau, *Le rôle politique du Professeur Koch* (Strasbourg, 1936), 29 ff.

35. BNU Strasbourg, M. 21.490, *Mémoire pour la noblesse immédiate de la basse Alsace,* printed in October 1789. On the reaction of the German *princes possessionnés* to the August decrees, see Theodor Ludwig, *Die deutschen Reichsstände im Elsass und der Ausbruch der Revolutionskriege* (Strasbourg, 1898), 123 ff.

36. Theodor Renaud, "Johann Benedict Scherer, ein Strassburger Autonomist in der Revolutionszeit," *Jahrbuch für Geschichte, Sprache und Literatur Elsass-Lothringens* (Strasbourg, 1910), 26:279.

37. BNU Strasbourg, M. 9532, *Drey Motionen in der Versammlung der Herren Schöffen zu Strassburg von einem Mitgliede derselben den 19. December 1789 vorgeschlagen und auf derselben Befehl gedrukt* (Strasbourg, [1789]).

38. Henry Brunschwig, *Les subsistances à Strasbourg pendant les premières années de la Révolution française* (Strasbourg, 1932), 15–47, shows how the food crisis of late 1789 contributed to the political tension and how its recession in 1790 helped to consolidate the new regime.

39. BNU Strasbourg, Ms. 786.

40. In late November, for example, F. J. J. Hoffmann, Bailiff of Benfeld south of Strasbourg, published an *Adresse à tous les bons citoyens de Strasbourg* (also printed in German), which attacked Turckheim's particularistic views and denounced the loudly proclaimed privileges of Alsace as so many chains in a free, national state. At about the same time, feudal claims were rebutted by the only Alsatian deputy to achieve fame at Paris, Reubel of Colmar, in a *Réponse d'un Français au mémoire de la noblesse immédiate d'Alsace.*

41. Theodor Renaud, "Johann Friedrich Simon, ein Strassburger Pädagog und Demagog," *Zeitschrift für die Geschichte des Oberrheins* (Heidelberg, 1908), 62 (NF 23): 449–500. The *Patriotisches Wochenblatt,* it should be noted, was only the best known of several newspapers to spring up in the late summer of 1789, when Strasbourg's local censorship collapsed. The two established weeklies also changed considerably that year. The old *"Wochenblatt"* added news stories, especially from Paris, to its advertisements and market reports. So did F.-R. Salzmann's *Privilegirte*

Zeitung, which with its issue of December 9 adopted the more ambitious title of *Strassburgische politische Zeitung.* The transition from a licensed to a revolutionary press would not be completed for another couple of years, but it was clearly underway.

42. Georges Roth, "Les 'Amis de la Constitution' de Strasbourg et la 'Revolution Society' de Londres," in *Comité des travaux historiques et scientifiques. Section d'histoire moderne (depuis 1715) et d'histoire contemporaine. Notices, inventaires et documents: VII, Etudes et documents divers* (Paris, 1922), 97–119.

43. AM Strasbourg, Minutes of the Common Council, March 18, 1790. A detailed account, *Procès verbal d'installation de la Municipalité de Strasbourg,* was published that year.

Guide to Works Cited

The simplified bibliographical index which follows does not attempt to list every work cited in the preceding notes, since many of the books and articles were mentioned only briefly, in passing. What the ensuing list does attempt to provide is a means for locating quickly the initial citation of any highly relevant work, including publication data. The first number following a given title identifies the page on which the full citation may be found, while the second, italicized number represents the specific note on that page.

Adam, *Evangelische Kirchengeschichte der Stadt Strassburg*, 270, *28*
Altdorf, "Die Kapuziner in Strassburg," 284, *11*
Andreas, *Strassburg an der Wende vom Mittelalter*, 268, *10*
Angervilliers, *Lettres écrites à la cour*, 280, *15*
Apell, *Geschichte der Befestigung von Strassburg*, 276, *3*
Architekten- und Ingenieur-Verein, *Strassburg und seine Bauten*, 267, *4*
Arnauld, *Le port de Strasbourg*, 288, *27*

Barth, "Notes biographiques sur les hommes de la Révolution à Strasbourg," 304, *28*
Batiffol, "Les difficultés de Louis XIV avec les Alsaciens," 301, *54*
Baumann, *Strassburg, Basel and Zürich*, 296, *23*
Benoist d'Anthenay, *Jacques de La Grange*, 280, *19*
Béraldi, *Ramond de Carbonnières*, 296, *29*
Bergner, "Les comédiens allemands à Strasbourg," 298, *7*
Bianquis, "Goethe et Voltaire," 299, *28*
Blanchet, "Les journées de juillet et août 1789," 304, *27*
Boislisle, "L'équipée à Strasbourg de Frédéric le Grand," 291, *12*
Borries, *Geschichte der Stadt Strassburg*, 267, *6*
Boswell on the Grand Tour, 291, *18*, and 298, *6*
Bouteiller and Hepp, *Correspondance politique adressée au Magistrat de Strasbourg par ses agents à Metz*, 272, *7*
Braubach, "Hat Friedrich der Grosse die Wiedervereinigung Elsass-Lothringens mit Deutschland verhindert?" 278, *38*
—— "Um die 'Reichsbarriere' am Oberrhein," 278, *28*
Brunschwig, *Les subsistances à Strasbourg pendant les premières années de la Révolution*, 305, *38*
Buchwald and Siercks, *Goethe: Bücher von ihm und über ihn*, 298, *13*
Burglin, "La période strasbourgeoise de la vie de Mozart," 297, *43*
Burnet, *Travels*, 285, *22*

Glasson, "La rôle politique du Conseil souverain d'Alsace," 282, *36*
Goeken, *Herder als Deutscher,* 299, *25*
Goethe, *Dichtung und Wahrheit,* 298, *13*
────── *Ephémérides,* 299, *22*
────── *Von deutscher Art und Kunst,* 299, *27*
Gothein, "Die oberrheinische Lande vor und nach dem dreissigjährigen Kriege," 270, *35*
Grandidier, *Alsatia Sacra,* 284, *10*

Haller, *Die deutsche Publizistik,* 277, *13*
Hanauer, *Etudes économiques,* 287, *5*
Hatt, "Le Gymnase en 1738," 295, *13*
────── "Le loyalisme des Alsaciens," 301, *54*
────── "Marie-Antoinette à Strasbourg," 291, *11*
────── *Quatre siècles de bourgeoisie strasbourgeoise,* 271, *37*
Haug, "L'architecture régence à Strasbourg," 296, *33*
────── *Les faïences et porcelaines de Strasbourg,* 290, *41*
────── *La ferronerie strasbourgeoise,* 296, *33*
────── "Le style Louis XIV à Strasbourg," 294, *3*
────── *Trois siècles d'art alsacien,* 296, *33*
Heitz, *Das Zunftwesen in Strassburg,* 271, *36*
Hermann, *Notices,* 268, *7*
Heuser, *Porzellan von Strassburg,* 290, *41*
Hölscher, *Die öffentliche Meinung in Deutschland über den Fall Strassburgs,* 277, *13*
Hoepffner, "Influences littéraires . . . en Alsace," 297, *1*
Hoffmann, *L'Alsace au XVIIIᵉ siècle,* 293, *52*
Horning, *Geschichte der evangelisch-lutheranischen Kirche in Strassburg,* 270, *28*
────── *Zur Strassburger Kirchengeschichte,* 284, *7*

Jaffé, *Elsässische Studenten an deutschen Hochschulen,* 295, *19*
Jakubowski, *Beziehungen zwischen Strassburg, Zürich und Bern,* 273, *15*
Jung[-Stilling], *Lebensgeschichte,* 292, *27*

Katterfeld, "Die Vertretung Strassburgs auf dem westfälischen Friedenskongress," 267, *1*
Kiener, "L'humanisme alsacien," 300, *39*
────── "Zur Geschichte Strassburgs," 289, *36*
Knepper, *Nationaler Gedanke . . . bei den elsässischen Humanisten,* 300, *39*
Knod, *Die alten Matrikeln der Universität Strassburg,* 270, *29*
Korff, *Die Dichtung von Sturm und Drang,* 301, *48*
────── *Geist der Goethezeit,* 301, *48*
────── *Voltaire im literarischen Deutschland,* 300, *28*

Uffenbach, "Strassburger Tagebuch," 294, 6
Ungerer, *Le pont du Rhin*, 270, 34

Valfons, *Souvenirs*, 290, 3
Van Huffel, *Documents inédits*, 292, 28
Vermeil, "Goethe à Strasbourg," 298, 13
Voltaire, *Lettres d'Alsace*, 297, 2
———— *Oeuvres complètes*, 294, 2

Wahl, "Die wirtschaftlichen Beziehungen Elsass-Lothringens zu Frankreich und Deutschland," 288, 22
Walter, *Chronique strasbourgeoise, 1672–1676*, 272, 8
———— *Strassburg im dreissigjährigen Kriege*, 267, 2
Weissenfels, *Goethe im Sturm und Drang*, 298, 13
Wendel, *Le mariage à Strasbourg*, 282, 35
Wentzcke, "Die alte Universität Strassburg," 292, 19
———— *Johann Frischmann*, 273, 11
———— "Der Strassburger Rheinpass im Holländischen Kriege," 273, 17
———— "Wiener Beiträge zur Geschichte vom Fall Strassburgs," 274, 32
Werner, *Les ponts et chaussées d'Alsace*, 289, 35
———— *Le rattachement douanier de l'Alsace à la France*, 287, 2
Wernert, "La conversion d'Ulric Obrecht," 280, 7
Willoughby, *Goethe's "Urfaust,"* 300, 30
Witkop, *Goethe in Strassburg*, 298, 13
———— *Goethe, Leben und Werk*, 298, 13

Young, *Travels in France*, 302, 1

Zeiller, *Topographia Alsatiae*, 268, 13
Zeller, *L'organisation défensive des Frontières*, 276, 2
Zentgraff, *Historischer Bericht*, 286, 41
Zetzner, *Reissjournal*, 289, 30
Zwiedineck-Südenhorst, *Die öffentliche Meinung in Deutschland*, 277, 13
Zwilling, "Die französische Sprache in Strassburg," 295, 7

Index